Changing Paradigms of Management Dynamics

Changing Paradigms of Management Dynamics

Tulika Saxena
Associate Professor
Science and Technology Entrepreneurs' Park
Harcourt Butler Technological Institute, Kanpur (UP), India

A.P.S. Bhadauria
Director
Five School of Business, Kanpur (UP), India

I.K. International Publishing House Pvt. Ltd.
NEW DELHI

Published by
I.K. International Publishing House Pvt. Ltd.
S-25, Green Park Extension
Uphaar Cinema Market
New Delhi–110 016 (India)
E-mail:info@ikinternational.com

ISBN 978-93-82332-97-8

Published by Krishan Makhijani for I.K. International Publishing House Pvt. Ltd., S-25, Green Park Extension, Uphaar Cinema Market, New Delhi–110 016 and Printed by Rekha Printers Pvt. Ltd., Okhla Industrial Area, Phase II, New Delhi–110 020.

Preface

The present scenario is characterized by the changing paradigms in management dynamics due to global competition, fierce quest for excellence, constant striving to break one's own performance records and establish new milestones. The liberalization, privatization, globalization and never lasting competition are forcing management to search for better alternatives for survival and success of the organizations. This will necessitate organizational change not once or twice but as many times as the business context shifts.

Changing Paradigms of Management Dynamics is a compilation of 35 chapters which includes articles, research and conceptual papers, cases from various academicians, corporate professionals, research scholars and students. The broad theme of the book is convincingly appropriate in the present scenario where organizational and individual values play a pivotal role in shaping the future.

The book is devoted to examining some key dimensions of management dynamics. It throws light on various aspects of business management like marketing, human resource management, information technology, international business, financial management, knowledge management, talent management, rural management, wealth management, etc. Management theory has also moved forward, and in some cases has become a well-established practice in the corporate world. The book offers this relevant view of management in a way that has a logical flow of content, succinct and clear in its writing style, rich in real-world examples, and remains focused on the role of managers.

We feel that the overall development encompassing social, economic, technological, innovation, values and ethics need a holistic approach in which management is an important ingredient. This book opens an enchanting window on how these changing paradigms affect dynamics of management. This intriguing work takes an original perspective on management issues, combining elements of present status, past and future avenues in overcoming management challenges ahead, particularly in India.

We extend our warm greetings to all the authors for their sincere efforts and endeavors. We owe a great deal of expertise and experience of everyone, whose support, interest and commitment has been instrumental in compilation of this book.

We believe that this book will be prove helpful in developing, serving and sustaining business houses, management students, researchers, entire corporate fraternity, institutes, policy makers and all concerned stakeholders of effective management dynamics.

Tulika Saxena
A.P.S. Bhadauria

Messages

I am happy to know that a book entitled "Changing Paradigms of Management

Dynamics" is coming up. I hope that the efforts of editors and chapter authors will prove helpful in developing and sustaining business houses and bringing prosperity in society. I also appreciate the contribution of IK International Publishing House Pvt. Ltd., New Delhi for supporting the academic endeavors.

My best wishes for the entire endeavor.

Jagat Vir Singh Dron
Mayor Kanpur (UP)

I am glad to learn that book entitled "Changing Paradigms of Management Dynamics" being brought by Dr. Tulika Saxena, Associate Professor STEP-HBTI,

Kanpur and Dr. A.P.S. Bhadauria, Associate Professor RIET, Kanpur. Innovative management practices are need of the hour. I hope the book will serve as reference guide to the students and faculty for comprehension of the challenges of management field in present scenario of liberalization and globalization. I appreciate the contribution of IK International Publishing House Pvt. Ltd. New Delhi for supporting the academic endeavors of the faculty of HBTI.

My best wishes to editors and to those who have contributed chapters in the book.

Prof. R. K. Khandal
Vice Chancellor
UPTU, Lucknow (UP)

I am glad to know that Dr. Tulika Saxena, Associate Professor STEP-HBTI, Kanpur and Dr. A.P.S. Bhadauria, Associate Professor RIET, Kanpur are coming up with a book entitled "Changing Paradigms of Management Dynamics". In the era of liberalization, privatization & globalization, I hope book would help in facing the issues and challenges of global competition. Academic activities are the base of any society. The efforts of editors and chapter authors are appreciable.

My best wishes to their all future endeavor.

Satish Kumar Nigam
MLA, Kalyanpur, Kanpur (UP)

I am glad to learn that one of our faculty members, Dr. A.P.S. Bhadauria, Associate Professor HOD-MBA coming up with coming up with book titled "Changing Paradigms of Management Dynamics" in coordination with Dr. Tulika Saxena, Associate Professor STEP-HBTI, Kanpur. I hope the book will prove a guide for the management scholars, and corporate fraternity in facing the challenges of the management field in the globalization era.

My best wishes to both the editors and chapter authors for their hard work.

Prof. (Dr.) B.K. Misra
Director
Rama Institute of Engg. & Tech., Kanpur

I am happy to learn that the book "Changing Paradigms of Management Dynamics" is an excellent attempt to bring some implausible & feasible measures to foster best practices of management in India. I am sure such efforts would go a long way in creating an environment for indispensible development in the interest of present & future generations in management sector. I hope this book is going to be a productive ground in this direction where corporate leaders as well as academicians has an opportunity to present solutions & recommendations for upgrading the most vital sector of the organizations and nations.

I wish all success for the endeavor!

Prof. (Dr.) R.K. Trivedi
Director STEP-HBTI, Kanpur

It is an agreed fact that there has been an exponential qualitative growth of good management practices in India in the post-independence era; still the aspect of quality and best practices for resource mobilization needs proper and focused address. I wish to congratulate Dr. Tulika Saxena and Dr. A.P.S. Bhadauria, the editors and authors of the book for selecting the relevant issue "Changing Paradigms of Management Dynamics" and extend my good wishes for the success of the book.

I am sure the book will be beneficial to the organizations, individuals and nations.

A.K. Mathur
Secretary
Lucknow Management Association

Acknowledgments

Concentration, dedication and application are necessary but not sufficient to achieve any goal. These must be aided by the guidance, cooperation and blessings to attain it. Feelings are short-lived but when put down in writing it gives larger life.

It is our privilege to acknowledge sincerely our gratefulness and personal regards to Shri Jagat Vir Singh Dron, Mayor Kanpur (UP); Shri Satish Kumar Nigam, MLA, Kalyanpur, Kanpur (UP); Prof. R. K. Khandal, Vice Chancellor – UPTU, Lucknow (UP); Prof. (Dr.) B.K. Misra, Director Rama Institute of Engg. & Tech., Kanpur; Prof. (Dr.) R.K. Trivedi, Director STEP-HBTI, Kanpur; and Mr A.K. Mathur, Secretary, Lucknow Management Association for appreciating our work and encouraging our endeavors.

We owe special gratitude to Prof. A.D.N. Bajpai, VC, Himachal Pradesh University, Shimla; Prof. J.V. Vaishampayan, VC, CSJM University, Kanpur; Prof. Munna Singh, VC, CSA University, Kanpur; Prof. Anirudh Pandey, Lucknow University; Prof. B.L. Bajpai, Amity University, Lucknow; and Prof. R. Prasad, Director Planning & Monitoring, CSA University, Kanpur for congratulating and charging us with the spirit and enthusiasm to produce this work with more vigor and perfection.

We extend our sincere thanks and regards to all contributors whose efforts and cooperation made this work possible.

Last but not the least, the word fails to express my indebtedness for the cooperation and generous support of our spouse and children who lost our attention for the entire period of work. In fact, they are our strength and will to work harder and harder. Special indebtedness to our parents who have been a source of inspiration and motivation for our all endeavors. We bow our heads to God who always gives us strength to move on in life on the right path.

Tulika Saxena
A.P.S. Bhadauria

Contributors

A.P.S. Bhadauria, Associate Professor, RIET, Kanpur
E-mail: apsb71@gmail.com

Ajaynath Dubey, Assistant Professor, Department of Management, Dr. VSICS, Kanpur
E-mail: dubey_ajay@rediffmail.com

Amima Shoeb, Assistant Professor, Faculty of Commerce & Management Studies, Rama University
E-mail: amimashoeb89@gmail.com

Anisur Rehman, Senior Lecturer, Department of Business Management, Faculty of Management and Research, Integral University, Lucknow
E-mail: anisur.rehman11@gmail.com

Ankita Agarwal, Assistant Professor, Banshi Group of Education, Kanpur
E-mail: ankita6390agarwal@gmail.com

Ankita Rajdev, Assistant Professor, Faculty of Management, JSSGIW, Bhopal
E-mail: Ankita.rajdevs@gmail.com

Ankita Sharma, Registrar, Dr. Virendra Swarup Education Foundation, Kanpur
E-mail: ankitasharma@vsef.org

Anshuman Kushwaha, MBA Final Year, STEP-HBTI, Kanpur
E-mail: anshumanmba2010@gmail.com

Archika Katiyar, Guest Faculty, UPTTI, Kanpur
E-mail: archikakatiyarmba@gmail.com

Arup Jyoti Bhattacharya, IOFS, Indian Ordnance Factory, Kanpur
E-mail: arup-jt@rediffmail.com

Ashish Kumar Shukla, Assistant Professor, Bareilly University
E-mail: ashish59.2009@rediffmail.com

Charu Modi, Assistant Professor, Faculty of Management, JSSGIW, Bhopal
E-mail: jain04.charu@gmail.com

Deepali Gupta, Research Scholar, RIET, Kanpur
E-mail: deepaliguptadg@gmail.com

Garima Jain, Faculty Trainee, Institute of Bank Personnel Selection, Mumbai
E-mail: clicktogarima@gmail.com

Ghazala Shoeb, Scholar, Shobhit University
E-mail: gazala.shoeb@gmail.com

Indu Shukla, Assistant Professor, Department of Management, RIET, Kanpur
E-mail: ap.indushukla@gmail.com

Javerya Fatima, Executive HFS Builders, Houston, USA
E-mail: javerya_fatima@hotmail.com

José G. Vargas-Hernández, MBA, PhD, Salvador Ortiz Sánchez, University Center for Economic and Managerial Sciences, University of Guadalajara
E-mail: jvargas2006@gmail.com, josevargas@cucea.udg.mx

Jyotsna Sinha, Lecturer, Department of Humanities & Social Sciences, MNIT, Allahabad

Keshav Shyam, Assistant Professor, Dept. of Commerce, University of Allahabad
E-mail: keshavshyamsax@yahoo.com

K.P. Singh, Assistant Professor, Department of Management, RIET, Kanpur
E-mail: kps907@gmail.com

Krishna Gopal Chaubey, Associate Professor, NCET, Kanpur
E-mail: chaubeykrishna@yahoo.co.in

Krishna Murari Mishra, Assistant Professor, LDC Institute of Technical Studies, Allahabad
E-mail: krishnauim@gmail.com

Mahak Shrivastava, Assistant Professor, Faculty of Management, JSSGIW, Bhopal
E-mail: s.mahak26@gmail.com

Manoj Kumar Srivastava, Research Scholar, Faculty of Management Studies, Banaras Hindu University, Varanasi. (UP)
E-mail: manojsrifms@gmail.com

Manoj Trivedi, HNB (PG) College, Allahabad

Meenal Yadav, Associate Professor, LBSIMDS, Lucknow
E-mail: meenal.yadav@gmail.com

Minali Mehra, Associate Professor, Global Institute of Management & Emerging Technology, Amritsar
E-mail: minali.mehra@gmail.com

Neetu Singh, Assistant Professor, Faculty of Management, Naraina Group of Institutions, Kanpur
E-mail: neetu_mba@yahoo.com

Pratik Dwivedi, Research Scholar, Singhania University, Rajasthan
E-mail: dwivedi.pratik@gmail.com

Preeti Srivastava, Assistant Professor, Department of Business Management, Sherwood College of Engineering Research & Technology, Barabanki,
E-mail: srivastava.preeti369@gmail.com

Raman Kumar, Assistant Professor, Department of Business Management, Sherwood College of Engineering Research & Technology, Barabanki
E-mail: raman.kr24@gmail.com

Rashi Saxena, Lecturer, A.I.T.H. Kanpur
E-mail: rash_saxena@rediffmail.com

Rashmi Singh, Assistant Professor, Department of Management, RIET, Kanpur
E-mail: rashmi.hrexpert@gmail.com

Reeta Singh Rathore, Principal, BJSGP PG College, Unnao
E-mail: rathore.ritasingh@rediffmail.com

Richa Mishra, Assistant Professor, STEP- HBTI, Kanpur
E-mail: 15.richamishra@gmail.com

Rohit Dron, System Engineer, Power Grid Corporation London (U.K.)
E-mail: rohitdron@gmail.com

Sadaf, Faculty, School of Languages, Dubai
E-mail: sadaf_khan@gmail.com

Sadhika Katiyar, MBA Final Year, IBM, C.S.J.M. University, Kanpur
E-mail:mesadhikakatiyar@gmail.com

Sapna Tripathi, Assistant Professor, Dept. of Management, Axis Group of Institutions
E-mail: sapna.tripathi192@gmail.com

Satish Chandra Ojha, Assistant Professor, STEP-HBTI, Kanpur
E-mail: satish2011@gmail.com

Shivani Kapoor, DAMS, Kanpur
E-mail: kapoor.shivani_dams@rediffmail.com

Shweta Guwalani, Assistant Professor, JSSGIW, Bhopal, MP
E-mail: Address: shwetaguwalani09@gmail.com

Smita Dron, Assistant Professor, STEP-HBTI, Kanpur
E-mail: dsmitadron@yahoo.com

Suchita Shukla, Assistant Professor, STEP-HBTI, Kanpur
E-mail: suchi_vs@yahoo.com

Sunil Shukla, Associate professor, GHS-IMR, Kanpur
E-mail: drsunilghs@yahoo.co.in

Tazyn Rahman, Dean, Jaipuria Institute, Ghaziabad (U. P.)
E-mail: tazyn08@gmail.com

Tripti Barthwal, Professor, LBSIMDS Lucknow
E-mail: drtbarthwal@gmail.com

Tulika Saxena, Associate Professor, Dept. of Management, STEP- HBTI, Kanpur
E-mail: tulika_28@yahoo.com

Vijeta Gautam, Research Scholar, Department of Humanities & Social Sciences, MNIT, Allahabad
E-mail: vijetagautam81@gmail.com

Yasir Arafat Elahi, Assistant Professor (Business Administration), Oman College of Management and Technology, P.O. Box 680, P.C. 320, Barka, Sultanate of Oman
E-mail: dr.yaelahi@gmail.com

Contents

1

A Workshop Study on Implementation of Corporate Governance Standard Practices on Small and Medium Enterprises in India: Road Map to Success

Javerya Fatima
Executive HFS Builders, Houston, USA
Sadaf
Faculty, School of Languages, Dubai
E-mail: javerya_fatima@hotmail.com

ABSTRACT

Small and medium enterprises (SMEs) are crucial for developing countries because of their role in economic growth, employment generation, poverty alleviation and overall progress of the country. As companies globally face issues relating to transparency, accountability and timely disclosure of material information, the concept of corporate governance and business ethics has gained significant importance. This paper is an attempt in the direction of highlighting standard practices to be executed to overcome challenges faced by SMEs, viz., access to finance both domestically and internationally and developing international trade linkages, etc. The main limiting factor to their growth is lack of adequate adherence to corporate governance structure. There is generally lack of awareness among these enterprises regarding significance of corporate governance and if there is any awareness, they abstain themselves from adopting these practices because of the high cost of implementation. This paper proposes certain systems and guidelines for encouraging SMEs to adopt good governance practices. The paper emphatically discusses the framework through a code for SMEs and suggests mechanism to develop it. The main objective of this paper is to provide business owners and entrepreneurs with a useful instructional tool for introducing their organizations to general principles of corporate governance with a view to improving their competitiveness, reducing operational risk factors, overcoming barriers to trade, successfully meeting the challenges of globalization, accessing lower-cost sources of financing and reconciling business practices with commitments incurred under agreements entered into with the World Trade Organization.

INTRODUCTION

The paper addresses some of the underlying factors that promote efficient corporate governance, and examines some of the strengths, weaknesses, and economic implications associated with various corporate governance systems. Small and medium enterprises (SMEs) are engines of growth in prosperous and growing economy and play an important role in creating economic growth. SMEs contribute to economic development by creating employment for rural and urban population, providing flexibility and innovation through entrepreneurship and increase international trade by diversifying economic activity. The relationship between corporate governance and economic performance has become one of the most controversial issues faced by policy makers today. Each country has through time developed a wide variety of mechanisms to overcome the agency problems that arise from the separation of ownership and control. While some systems are characterized by wide dispersed ownership (outsider systems), others tend to be characterized by concentrated ownership or control (insider systems). In outsider systems of corporate governance the basic conflict of interest is between strong managers and widely dispersed weak shareholders. In insider systems, on the other hand, the basic conflict is between controlling shareholders and weak minority shareholders. Therefore, one of the most striking differences between countries' corporate governance systems is in the ownership and control of firms, and the identity of controlling shareholders. In the developed countries SMEs are major contributors to GDP and private sector employment contributing as much as 60% to workforce. In developing countries, they employ more than 70% of labor force. The abundance of labor and the shortages of capital which are characteristics of developing countries are comparable with the SMEs labor intensive character.

STATEMENT OF THE PROBLEM

The advent of globalization and opening up of Indian economy to outside world has taken up a big leap. Competition among industries have become stiff, industries also have to strive continuously to remain in frontline. Execution of standard practices of corporate governance is the need of the hour. This will have great bearing on the corporate image of the firms across the country. These objectives can only be achieved by bridging the gap between what is said and what is in actual, in terms of governance of corporate. As any other ambitious society, India also started placing great importance on commercial activities as a catalyst to socio-economic development.

OBJECTIVES OF THE RESEARCH

1. To make an audit regarding status of implementation and effect of corporate governance practices in terms of sustainability and excellence, with special reference to SMEs operating in eastern region of U.P. through workshop.
2. To recommend and suggest action plans for acquiring excellence, growth and success to the sample under study.

DATA AND RESEARCH METHODOLOGY

The present study is an evaluative and diagnostic study based on secondary and primary sources of data and information. The data has been compiled from various surveys, reports (on trends) and progress of SMEs in eastern region of U.P. in India. For preparation of present study various journals, magazines and newspaper have also been used. The period covered under the study is 2013-14.

The Workshop

Profile Report of Respondents: In all, twelve (12) SMEs representatives (owners/proprietors/officials), served as participants. There were 3 females and 9 male members as participants. They ranged in age between 32 and 54 years. In regard to education, all were literate and educated, the educational qualification ranged from graduate to postgraduate in academics and professional disciplines. Their experience ranged from 10 to 36 years.

Research Design: A one-day workshop, was conducted, comprised of two sessions. The program was conducted by a team of researchers and professionals.

The first session was devoted to micro-lab and interactive session on conceptual framework of implementing corporate governance. The session was devoted to acquaint the participants with the objectives of the program and its relevance for their role. The participants were asked to reveal their expectations from the role and were also given to know the expectations of the role from them.

In the second session unstructured data collection tools were administered on the subjects in a classroom setting in psychologically approved manner and as explained by the author. It was followed by interview sessions, observation analysis in an open forum discussion, formal talks, and interaction.

After they confirmed of having responded to their satisfaction, the third session was started. In this session, subjects were asked to self-evaluate their responses and then it was reevaluated by the team of experts.

DISCUSSIONS AND RECOMMENDATION

The analysis of the data throws up some pertinent issues. The responses were analyzed to suggest action plans.

General Principles

The underlying principles of the framework code are transparency, accountability, fair treatment of partners/shareholders and the responsibility of small- and medium-size enterprises vis-à-vis their respective interest groups.

1. **The Rights of Partners/Shareholders in SMEs Entitle them to:**
   - **a.** Be notified of, take part in and vote at meetings of the company's top governing body;

b. Share in company dividends and profits;
c. Have a say in the appointment and dismissal of administrators and evaluate their performance;
d. Have full, timely access to company information;
e. Enter into mutual agreements for the exercise of their rights;
f. Refer matters to the Board of Directors for discussion. In cases where the Board objectively determines such matters to be immaterial as far as the company is concerned, the partners/shareholders are to be informed of its determination and of the grounds for its decision;
g. Be compensated for services rendered as company employees or executives;
h. Be informed of the company's comprehensive management plan;
i. Record business transacted at meetings of the company's top governing body, and the information is to be used only for legitimate purposes;
j. Know exactly who controls the company and any other firms they may control.

2. **The Obligations of Partners/Shareholders in SMEs are as follows:**
   a. Evaluate and approve amendments to company bylaws or partnership agreements including, but not limited to, business reorganization processes such as mergers, breakups, restructuring, etc.;
   b. Examine, approve or reject year-end financial statements and balance sheets;
   c. Declare dividends and ensure that company bylaws or partnership agreements include clear policies for the protection of minority or noncontrolling partners/shareholders;
   d. Appoint and dismiss members of the Board of Directors and establish fair compensation systems for Board members;
   e. Appoint a statutory auditor where required by law and set his fee. In cases of companies not legally required to have a statutory auditor, the partners/shareholders are to appoint an outside auditor and set his fee;
   f. Discuss reports and actions by the Board of Directors;
   g. Establish fair compensation systems for partners/shareholders and their family members working as company employees or executives;
   h. Set statutory ceilings on the authority of administrators to engage in and approve business transactions;
   i. Approve business transactions exceeding the statutory ceiling imposed on the Board of Directors;
   j. Prohibit payments of any household or personal expenses of partners/shareholders with company funds;
   k. Establish rules for granting of loans by the company to its partners/shareholders and vice versa.

- **l.** Refrain from using company information for illegitimate purposes;
- **m.** Establish principles of business ethics.

3. Partners'/Shareholders' Agreements

- **a.** Two or more partners/shareholders other than company administrators may enter into agreements for the protection of their mutual interests under which they may promise to vote in the same or a specific way at Partners' or General Shareholders' Meetings.
- **b.** Any partners'/shareholders' agreement involving company assets or the appointment or dismissal of company administrators must be disclosed to the other partners/shareholders prior to carrying out the decisions established thereunder.
- **c.** Partners/shareholders are to be encouraged to freely adhere to pre-existing agreements by a particular group.
- **d.** Companies are to encourage such agreements to ensure that their partners/shareholders have a representative with a deciding vote on their Board of Directors.

4. Fair Treatment of Partners/Shareholders

Firms are to ensure fair treatment to their minority and foreign partners/shareholders through the following types of mechanisms:

- **a.** Minority partners/shareholders holding at least 10% of the partnership or share capital may request that the Office of the Superintendent of Corporations convene a meeting of the top governing body;
- **b.** Absent or dissenting partners/shareholders may exercise their right of withdrawal in cases of a decision by the Partners' or General Shareholders' Meeting to restructure, merge or break up the company increasing their liability or undermining their ownership rights;
- **c.** Companies are to establish necessary mechanisms for furnishing all partners/shareholders with matcrial information.

5. Regular or Special Meetings of the Top Governing Body

The bylaws or partnership agreements of business enterprises are to include provisions for mechanisms designed to ensure the rights and fair treatment of partners/shareholders at regular or special meetings of their top governing body. At a minimum, company bylaws or partnership agreements are to address the following specific issues:

- **a. Notices of Meetings:** Legal requirements notwithstanding, notices of meetings of the top governing body may be given as follows:
  - (i) Notices of Partners' or General Shareholders' Meetings for the approval of financial statements, business reorganization processes and major business transactions are to include attachments referring to the matters to be addressed;
  - (ii) Companies may notify their partners/shareholders by electronic media, fax, and registered mail and, in general, by any appropriate

means of communication ensuring that they are duly informed of the meeting in question.

b. Agenda: All partners/shareholders must be furnished with a copy of the agenda prior to the scheduled date of the meeting of the company's top governing body. Firms are to make every effort to ensure that the agenda does not include an item labeled simply as "other business" to make certain that their partners/shareholders are in a position to make informed decisions.

c. Representation and Voting Mechanisms: All companies are to establish mechanisms allowing their partners/shareholders to vote through proxies, hold teleconferences and vote in absentia. It is prohibited for partners/shareholders to be represented at meetings by members of management, except for purposes of their legal representation.

d. Disclosure of Information: Partners/shareholders may raise any questions considered relevant by the statutory auditor, the accountant and the Board of Directors at meetings of the company's top governing body.

e. Qualified Majorities: Company bylaws or partnership agreements are to include provisions requiring qualified majorities representing at least 70% of the partnership or share capital for the approval of business reorganization processes (mergers, breakups, restructuring).

ADMINISTRATORS

The members of the Board of Directors and the chief executive officer are company administrators, who are to act in good faith, with the loyalty and due diligence of good businessmen. They are to act in the company's best interests, bearing in mind the interests of its partners/shareholders. In carrying out their duties, company administrators are to:

a. Make every effort to duly and properly achieve the company objective;
b. Ensure strict compliance with legal or statutory provisions;
c. Ensure the due and proper performance of statutory auditing functions;
d. Look after and protect the company's goodwill;
e. Refrain from using any inside information for illegitimate purposes;
f. Treat all partners/shareholders fairly and respect their wishes to exercise their inspection rights;
g. Refrain from engaging in any activities competing with the company's own operations or in any acts liable to engender conflicts of interest, either personally or through an intermediary, in their own personal interest or on behalf of a third party, except where expressly authorized to do so by the company's top governing body, and furnish the appropriate body with all necessary information for making an informed decision on such matter;

- **h.** Respect and enforce the rules of corporate governance adopted by the company's top governing body;
- **i.** Keep investors informed in the manner and with the regularity required by the Code of Good Corporate Governance.

Board of Directors

Organizational Structure of the Board of Directors

The Boards of Directors of firms should be structured in such a way as to ensure that they have the proper capabilities and experience and independent decision-making authority, as outlined below:

- **a. Number of Members:** The Board of Directors should have an odd number of members ranging from a minimum of three (3) up to a maximum of nine (9), according to the needs of the firm in question.
- **b. Make-up of the Board of Directors:** The Board of Directors should include at least one outside and/or independent director.
  - ***(i) Outside Directors:*** Outside directors are Board members other than partners/shareholders who do not work for the firm in question.
  - ***(ii) Independent Directors:*** Independent directors are Board members who: (i) do not represent controlling partners or majority shareholders; (ii) have not worked for the firm for the last three years; (iii) do not supply the firm with goods and/or services; (iv) are not employed by the firm; and (vii) [sic] are not related to any of the parties referred to above by ties of kinship up to the second degree, by marriage or by civil union.
  - ***(iii) Qualifications of Outside or Independent Board Members:*** The members of the Board of Directors must have mutually complementary, interdisciplinary skills and attributes such as: (i) experience in business management and/or economics, administration, law or related fields; (ii) a good name and reputation for professional competence and integrity; and (iii) they may not simultaneously sit on more than five Boards of Directors.

Role of the Board of Directors

The Board of Directors is the top authority responsible for producing reasonably good earnings for partners/shareholders and for overseeing the work of key company executives. It is also responsible for preventing disputes and reconciling the interests of different groups. The responsibilities of the members of the Board of Directors are to be spelled out in the company bylaws and should include, without being limited to, the following:

- **a.** Ensure that the company's performance is in line with market conditions;
- **b.** Ensure the effectiveness of its information disclosure mechanisms;

c. Devote sufficient time to the performance of their duties as Board members;

d. Ensure implementation of the good corporate governance policies adopted by the company;

e. Meet at least once in a month;

f. Brief new Board members on decisions taken prior to the date of their appointment, on the company's financial standing and on rules and standards of corporate governance;

g. Work with key executives in the framing of a business strategy, approve the strategy and monitor and oversee its implementation, which strategy is to include the following elements: (i) the company's mission and vision; (ii) management objectives and indicators; (iii) a financial plan; (iv) a risk management plan; (v) a plan for protecting the company's image; (vi) a marketing plan; (vii) labor policies; (viii) policies for handling conflicts of interest; (ix) policies for settling internal and outside disputes; (x) business shutdown policies; (xi) a training plan for reassigning some of the duties of the CEO;

h. Establish policies for the selection, appointment, performance evaluation and dismissal of key company executives;

i. Establish compensation systems for key executives. The Board of Directors is to establish fair fixed or variable compensation systems in line with company needs. Likewise, it is to make provisions for unique circumstances under which key executives may receive special bonuses;

j. The Board of Directors will establish criteria for defining and distinguishing business and non-business expenses;

k. Request reports from key executives on the company's standing as deemed necessary. The Board of Directors and/or Board committees on auditing, corporate governance and/or compensation and hiring are to solicit any and all necessary information from key company executives to enable them to discharge their duties;

l. Confirm that accounting procedures meet legal requirements and reflect the company's true financial position;

m. Ensure the soundness of statutory or other audits;

n. Refer what they consider to be necessary amendments to the company's Code of Good Corporate Governance to its top governing body;

o. Authorize the company to engage in business transactions with partners/shareholders and/or related parties;

p. In the case of family businesses, in order to ensure the firm's continuity, the Board of Directors should: (i) advocate the adoption of a Family Business Protocol or Agreement including a succession plan; (ii) encourage family members involved in the business to undergo professional training; (iii) help prevent and settle family disputes by forming and holding family councils.

Board Committees

It is recommended that the Board of Directors form committees to advise it on specific matters such as auditing, corporate governance, hiring and compensation. These Board committees are to be made up of members of the Board of Directors and, wherever possible, independent Board members. They may also include outside experts in their specific sphere of work.

Compensation Systems for Members of the Board of Directors

Companies are to set up compensation systems for members of their Board of Directors. The compensation plan must be approved by their top governing body and be in keeping with the level of effort of Board members, their work on Board committees, where applicable, and the company's financial standing.

Chief Executive Officer

The chief executive officer or CEO is in charge of implementing the guidelines and business strategies approved by the Board of Directors or the Partners' or Shareholders' Meeting.

Selection

All companies must have an explicit statement of necessary qualifications for the position of chief executive officer as the basis for the hiring process. Among the factors to be taken into account are experience, professional training, knowledge and skills.

Appointment

The chief executive officer is to be appointed by the Board of Directors or top governing body, as the case may be.

Responsibilities

The chief executive officer, as the company's top manager and legal representative, in addition to the normal responsibilities of company administrators, the chief executive officer will:

- **a.** Implement the business strategy devised by the Board of Directors;
- **b.** Appoint and dismiss company officials according to policies set by the Board of Directors or the top governing body;
- **c.** Submit periodic and management reports at the request of the Board of Directors or as required by the top governing body;
- **d.** Duly furnish the Board of Directors with necessary information for discharging its functions, which information must be timely and complete;
- **e.** Issue notices of meetings of the top governing body and Board of Directors, attaching any and all necessary information for the transaction of business at such meetings in keeping with the guidelines established by this code with respect to notices of meetings.

CONFLICTS OF INTEREST

A conflict of interest is any situation or event in which the direct or indirect personal interests of any partners/shareholders, administrators or officials are incompatible with those of the company interfere with the performance of their assigned duties or give them cause to act otherwise than in a manner befitting the due and proper fulfillment of their responsibilities. Companies are to establish effective mechanisms to help prevent and to facilitate the handling and disclosure of any eventual conflicts of interest between partners/shareholders, executives, interest groups and members of the Board of Directors. Suggested mechanisms include:

- **a.** The submission by candidates for appointment to the Board of Directors or for executive positions with the company of bios and information on their business career and activities;
- **b.** The requesting of express authorization from the top governing body or Board of Directors to proceed in the case of a conflict of interest;
- **c.** Families controlling one or more businesses should establish a separate fund completely independent from the business for handling family emergencies or for making necessary loans to family members. Members of family businesses could earmark a percentage of their earnings from the business for this fund;
- **d.** The establishment of procedures for ensuring that company procurements of goods and services are in keeping with principles of efficiency and transparency.

Prescribed Practices

Company executives, members of the Board of Directors and employees are to be barred from engaging in any of the following practices:

- **a.** Taking or offering bribes or any other type of compensation in species or in kind liable to influence official decisions;
- **b.** Under no circumstances may company executives grant any special compensation to members of the Board of Directors;
- **c.** Unlawfully use inside or privileged information to their own advantage or to protect their personal interests or those of any third parties;
- **d.** Use their standing, position or relationship with the company to engage in politicking;
- **e.** Bring family members into the company without regard for their qualifications or for established policies.

Disclosure

Company employees, executives, partners/shareholders and members of the Board of Directors and its committees are to disclose any conflicts of interest they may be experiencing and to refrain from voting either for or against the matters in question.

STAKEHOLDERS

Companies are to recognize the rights of stakeholders and help strengthen synergies with a view to fostering the creation of wealth and jobs and improving their competitiveness. Each company will identify its corresponding interest groups according to its particular line of business and the location of its facilities, which groups may include but are not limited to:

a. **Partners/Shareholders:** Companies will strive to create wealth for corresponding investors and ensure that their requests and requirements are treated fairly, with respect and with due diligence.
b. **Customers:** Companies will establish mechanisms for allowing their customers to make inquiries, suggestions and claims.
c. **Suppliers:** Companies will establish fair and impartial procurement procedures for goods and services based on considerations of quality, pricing and performance.
d. **Creditors:** Companies are liable to their creditors for debts incurred according to the terms and conditions of corresponding agreements.
e. **Government Regulatory and Oversight Agencies:** Companies are to establish mechanisms for monitoring compliance with laws and regulations governing their line of business and furnish regulatory and oversight agencies with adequate, timely, complete information for such purpose.
f. **Competitors:** Companies are to establish mechanisms designed to prevent their engaging in unfair competition or unfair practices stifling free competition and to take appropriate measures to comply with labor policies.
g. **Employees:** In addition to complying with labor legislation, companies are to institute mechanisms designed to ensure the fair treatment of their employees, foster their comprehensive development and merit-based promotion, prevent brain drain and espouse values promoting good business ethics and establish incentive policies for employees.
h. **The Local Community:** Companies are to establish mechanisms for passing benefits along to the surrounding community and for creating growth and employment opportunities, according to the company's financial resources and the needs of each particular community.
i. **The Family:** Family businesses will need to establish mechanisms for distinguishing between business and family relationships and property and for reconciling corresponding interests such as family councils, a family business protocol or agreements between family members.

SOCIAL RESPONSIBILITY

Businesses should inspire confidence among the members of the local community and set goals serving the common good, without neglecting their objective of maximizing financial returns for their partners/shareholders. Business firms are to establish mechanisms designed to help them meet the requirements of the globalization process, commerce policies and international agreements with a view to strengthening their competitiveness and promoting foreign investment. Companies are to establish the following as well as other types of policies:

Environmental Policy

Each company will need to develop strategies for preventing and minimizing environmental and human impacts and risks, protecting the environment in their local area through the efficient and effective use of natural resources, raw materials and energy, prevent and minimize pollution, wastes and environmental impacts and introduce the use of clean technologies and continuous improvement practices through the promotion of cleaner production processes and of business environmental self-regulation and self-management procedures. Enterprises, including industrial as well as other enterprises, will promote sound environmental management and help control the environmental impact of their operations, products and services based on the following guidelines:

1. ***Planning.*** Companies will need to familiarize themselves with applicable environmental legislation and regulations, to expand their strategic plans or planning processes to include environmental assessment and enhancement programs to comply with legal requirements and to mount projects going beyond minimum statutory requirements in cases where corresponding costs are deemed reasonable in the light of expected benefits.
2. ***Prevention.*** Companies are to establish pollution prevention policies grounded in the use of clean technologies and due and proper industrial waste management.
3. ***Clean Technologies.*** Companies are to develop environmental management systems as part of their routine production processes and promote the use of clean technologies in different stages of their production processes with the active involvement of employees, suppliers and other outside parties.
4. ***Industrial Wastes.*** Companies are to develop safe, efficient collection, disposal, storage and recycling systems for industrial wastes.
5. ***Efficient Use of Resources.*** Companies must consider the efficient use of energy and other inputs, the sustainable use of renewable resources and the minimization of adverse environmental effects in the development, design and operation of their facilities, as well as in their business operations and corresponding products and services.

6. ***Education and Promotion.*** Companies are to establish mechanisms for promoting environmental management, proper industrial waste management, sustainable development and the use of clean technologies and for educating their employees, suppliers, contractors and the general public in their local community with respect to these concepts.

Protection of Intellectual Property Rights

Companies must ensure compliance with domestic legislation and international agreements with respect to copyrights and industrial and intellectual property rights protecting third-party innovations by establishing the following types of mechanisms:

1. ***Internal Regulations*** governing the use, replication, distribution and other related actions with respect to their own internal and other products protected by intellectual property rights (such as software, background music, photocopies, trademarks, patents, etc.) designed to prevent employees or the company per se from deliberately or unintentionally infringing on any such rights.
2. ***International Agreements*** recognizing the protection accorded to different elements of intellectual property in other countries to ensure their international protection, where appropriate, regardless of the provisions of domestic legislation.
3. ***Contractual Provisions*** inserting special clauses for the protection of intellectual property into contracts with employees, suppliers and other outside parties dealing with the company clearly establishing corresponding right holders and defining the due and proper use of such property to prevent any future misinterpretations.
4. ***Promotional Activities*** for educating, training and motivating employees with respect to the importance and legal ramifications of intellectual property protection.
5. ***Contraband.*** Companies are to help promote the protection of intellectual property rights by their suppliers and contractors by discouraging the purchasing of any contraband or unlicensed products.
6. ***Valuation of Intellectual Property.*** Firms are to consider their innovations precious assets, to be valued according to established accounting practices.

Anti-Graft and Anti-Corruption Policies

It is recommended that businesses institute the following types of mechanisms designed to preclude and prevent internal graft and corruption:

1. Embrace ethical principles, preferably developed as part of an internal, collective effort from within the company.

2. Publicize standards of ethics and issue warnings with respect to the company's steadfast determination to enforce such standards as part of its day-to-day operations.
3. Have prospective bidders in competitive bidding and prequalification processes sign pledges of truthfulness and transparency as a tool for addressing structural problems in government procurement processes by publicly discussing corresponding bids, evaluating bids on bases emphasizing the spirit of the law rather than matters of form and promoting company monitoring.
4. Develop clear, equitable, viable, transparent internal procedures.
5. Report any irregularities observed within the company or in any other enterprise.
6. Train company personnel in civic and social responsibility as part of the business strategy.
7. Form ethics committees within the company to examine and settle any disputes between its members.

Social Investment Policies

Business enterprises are to develop programs designed to improve the quality of life in their local communities and to promote and encourage their members to get involved in public projects.

Information Policy, E-governance

Companies making use of information technologies are to establish mecanisms designed to ensure that any and all electronically transmitted data meets the highest standards of confidentiality, truthfulness and integrity.

Law Enforcement Policy

Companies will need to establish mechanisms for ensuring compliance with constitutional provisions, legislation and regulations with respect to labor and tax issues and free competition.

TRANSPARENCY, FREE FLOW AND TRUTHFULNESS OF INFORMATION

Businesses are to strive to establish mechanisms for ensuring the accurate, regular and timely reporting of company information. Such information disclosure mechanisms should not place an unduly heavy administrative or financial burden on corresponding firms. Businesses are responsible for disclosing only material facts and not any information liable to endanger their competitive position and are to maintain books of account conforming to current accounting standards.

Disclosure of Financial Information

1. ***Recipients of Financial Information*** This information is to be disclosed to the company's partners/shareholders, Board members and statutory and other auditors, as well as to any interest groups for which such information is deemed relevant in light of their relationship with the company.

2. ***Balance Sheets and Financial Statements*** (i) At a minimum, company financial statements are to include a general balance sheet, an income statement, a cash flow statement, a statement of changes in financial position and notes to the financial statements. (ii) Balance sheets and income statements are to be accompanied by a descriptive report by the company's chief executive officer. (iii) Business groups or controlled and controlling corporations are to present consolidated annual financial statements.

3. ***Compensation Systems for Company Administrators*** Companies must disclose the compensation systems established by their Boards of Directors for key executives, as well as the compensation systems established by their top governing body for members of their Boards of Directors.

Disclosure of Nonfinancial Information

At a minimum, SMEs are to disclose the following types of information:

a. Information on the company's mission, vision and objectives;
b. Their Code of Good Corporate Governance;
c. Information on voting rights and procedures;
d. Reports on the implementation of good corporate governance practices;
e. Information on the make-up, qualifications and performance evaluations of company executives and members of their Board of Directors.

1. ***Types of Nonfinancial Incidental Information*** (i) information on appointments and dismissals of key executives; (ii) information on business reorganization processes; (iii) information on changes in the company's image; (iv) information on nonfinancial risks; (v) information on changes in the business strategy; (vi) information on high-impact labor disputes.

2. ***Information Disclosure Mechanisms*** Companies are to establish appropriate, accessible information mechanisms. It is recommended that businesses host web-sites and use electronic media (fax transmissions or e-mail) for this purpose.

3. ***Auditing Systems*** Businesses will permit their partners/shareholders to establish an outside auditing mechanism, whose cost is to be borne by the requesting party.

4. *Statutory Audits* Statutory audits are designed to protect the rights of partners/ shareholders and other investors and, as such, are to be conducted in good faith, with no interference from key executives, members of the Board of Directors or partners/shareholders.

DISPUTE RESOLUTIONS

SMEs are to establish dispute management and settlement systems as a means of promoting foreign investment, trade and harmonious relations between partners/ shareholders, interest groups and management. Colombian businesses will establish dispute management and settlement systems for the following types of cases:

Disputes with Outside Parties

Companies are to establish mechanisms designed to expeditiously, economically and skillfully settle disputes stemming from company relations with administrators and interest groups or stakeholders. To this end, they are to establish direct negotiation programs, mediation mechanisms and specialized arbitration procedures tailored to their specific needs and characteristics.

Internal Dispute Settlement Mechanisms

SMEs are to establish internal procedures for the prevention, handling and settlement of disputes between the company per se, its key executives and company employees. Such mechanisms are designed to promote harmonious relations between labor and management.

Family Businesses

It is recommended that the Family Business Protocol includes provisions for alternative dispute settlement mechanisms such as direct settlements and family councils.

CONCLUSION

The objective of this Framework Code of Good Governance is to furnish closely held SMEs of Kanpur region with a tool for ensuring the sustainability and competitiveness of businesses in today's globalized economy. This Framework Code of Good Governance may help as a guide for the independent SMEs, to adapt corporate governance best practices on an individual basis. The standards established in this paper are general guidelines with respect to the Corporate Governance model that shall be adapted by each firm to its own organizational structure, line of business and sources of financing.

References

1. www.SSSRN_id214890.pdf
2. www.w111.pdf
3. Fernando A.C. "Corporate Governance: Principles, Policies and Practices". Pearson Publications (2012)
4. Paul Davies, Klaus Hopt, Richard "Corporate Boards in Law and Practice: A Comparative Analysis in Europe" Nowak, Gerard van Solinge Published: November 2013 by Oxford University Press (2013)
5. Reinier Kraakman, John Armour, Paul Davies, Luca Enriques, Henry Hansmann, Gerard Hertig, Klaus Hopt, Hideki Kanda, Edward B. Rock "The Anatomy of Corporate Law, A Comparative and Functional Approach" (2nd Revised edition) Oxford University Press (2009)

2

Fuelling the Indian MSMEs: The Engines of Economic Growth

Tripti Barthwal
Professor, LBSIMDS, Lucknow
E-mail: drtbarthwal@gmail.com

ABSTRACT

The micro, small and medium enterprises (MSMEs) sector occupies a strategically important place in Indian economy in view of its considerable contribution to employment, production and exports. These enterprises existed in India for a long time in various sectors and contributed significantly in bringing down regional imbalance; generating employment opportunities, output, and exports; reducing poverty; fostering entrepreneurship and accelerating economic development. MSMEs are complementary to large industries as ancillary units and this sector contributes enormously to the socioeconomic development of the country. The primary responsibility of promotion and development of MSMEs is of the State Governments. However, the Government of India, supplements the efforts of the State Governments through various initiatives. Over the years, the small scale sector in India has progressed from the production of simple consumer goods to the manufacture of many sophisticated and precision products like electronics control systems, microwave components, electromedical equipment, etc. The process of economic liberalization and market reforms has further exposed these enterprises to increasing levels of domestic and global competition. This paper examines the growth and performance of MSMEs in India. It discusses the major challenges faced by the MSME sector in India. The paper concludes with recommendations to ensure sustainable growth and performance of MSMEs in India.

INTRODUCTION

Micro, small and medium enterprises (MSMEs) was Mahatma Gandhi's dream. He supported the growth of micro, small and medium enterprises in India, because these enterprises are not capital based, but the talent and effort based business. With its less capital intensive and high labour absorption nature, MSME sector has made significant contribution to employment generation and also to rural industrialization.

The MSME sector has three tiers which are differentiated on the basis of the upper limit on investment as under:

Table 1 Investment Limit for Micro, Small & Medium Enterprises

Classification	*Manufacturing Enterprises**	*Service Enterprises***
Micro	25 Lakhs	10 Lakhs
Small	5 Crores	2 Crores
Medium	10 Crores	5 Crores

* Investment limit in plant & machinery

** Investment limit in equipment

Source: Annual Report 2011-12, Ministry of Micro, Small and Medium Enterprises, Government of India.

Significance of the MSME Sector

Worldwide, MSMEs have been regarded as the engines of economic growth and for promoting equitable development. The MSMEs constitute over 90% of total enterprises in most of the economies and are credited with generating the highest rates of employment growth and account for a major share of industrial production and exports. The micro, small and medium enterprise sector also played very important role in developed countries of the world. Its contribution to gross domestic product (GDP) in 1999 was 48% in USA, 57.20% in Canada, 51.45% in United Kingdom and 42.50% in Germany. It has also played a major role in the economic growth in the OECD area. In these countries small medium enterprises constitute over 95 percent of the enterprises which account for 60 to 70 percent of employment and the weight of micro, small and medium enterprises in the economy is increasing.

In India too, the MSMEs play a pivotal role in the overall industrial economy of the country. It is estimated that in terms of value, the sector accounts for about 39% of the manufacturing output and around 40% of the total exports of the country. It is the second largest employer of human resources after agriculture, providing employment to people in the rural and urban areas of the country. Their significance in terms of fostering new entrepreneurship is well-recognized. This is because, most entrepreneurs start their business from a small unit which provides them an opportunity to harness their skills and talents, to experiment, to innovate and transform their ideas into goods and services and finally nurture it into a larger unit. Further, in recent years the MSME sector has consistently registered higher growth rate compared to the overall industrial sector. The major advantage of the sector is its employment potential at low capital cost. As per available statistics, the labor intensity in the MSME sector is estimated to be almost 4 times higher than the large enterprises.

Table 2 showcases the performance of MSME sector in India from 2000-01 to 2011-2012 in terms of number of units, employment, market value of fixed assets and gross output.

Table 2 MSMEs Performance: Units, Employment, Investments, Production & Exports

Sl. No.	*Year*	*Total Working MSMEs (in Lakhs)*	*Employment (in Lakhs)*	*Market Value of Fixed Assets (In Crore)*	*Gross Output (In Crore)*
1.	2001–02	105.21	249.33	154349.00	282270.0
2.	2002–03	109.49	260.21	162317.00	314850.00
3.	2003–04	113.95	271.42	170219.00	364547.00
4.	2004–05	118.59	282.57	178699.00	429796.00
5.	2005–06	123.42	294.91	188113.00	497842.00
6.	2006–07	361.76†	805.23†	868543.79*	1351383.45*
7.	2007–08	377.37	842.23	917437.46	1435179.26
8.	2008–09	393.70	881.14	971407.49	1524234.83
9.	2009–10	410.82	922.19	1029331.46	1619355.53
10.	2010–11	428.77	965.69	1094893.42	1721553.42
11.	2011–12	447.73	1012.59	1176939.36	1834332.05

† Including activities of wholesale/retail trade, legal, education & social services, hotel & restaurants, transports and storage & warehousing (except cold storage) for which data were extracted, Economic Census 2005, Central Statistics Office, M/o SPI.

* Estimated on the basis of per enterprise's value obtained from sample survey of unregistered sector for activities wholesale/retail trade, legal, education & social services, hotel & restaurants, transports and storage & warehousing (except cold storage) which were excluded from Fourth All India Census of MSME, unregistered sector.

Source: Annual Report 2012–13, Ministry of Micro, Small and Medium Enterprises, Government of India).

Major Challenges before MSME Sector

During the first 4 years of XI Plan, MSME sector exhibited a growth rate of 13% on an average, an impressive performance compared to most of the other sectors. However, the sector is suffering from quite a few impediments, which need to be addressed immediately to make Indian MSMEs a global hub of entrepreneurship and global supplier of competitive and innovative products of highest quality.

Operation Costs: Rising global cost of commodities continues to haunt local manufacturers. In addition to rising inflation, the MSME sector has, in many ways become a 'talent pool' from which skilled labour and professionals are often fished to fill higher paying jobs in large domestic and international companies. As a result, MSMEs face higher recruitment and training costs while dealing with high employee attrition rates.

Risk Capital: As the MSME sector emerges to become the nation's economic growth engine, raising finance to power that growth remains an impediment to sustained expansion. Venture Capital firms are generally wary of investing in relatively young or unproven technologies. Banks too are unable to provide debt financing. In addition, there is no formal mechanism for MSMEs to raise investment from capital markets. As a result, MSMEs either raise money through informal means, or scale back on their product and service offering.

Complacency: Many MSME entrepreneurs have started reaching the point of satisfaction. Asset price inflation has increased their wealth manifold in the last decade. Inflation in real estate and stock in trade (bought most of the time on leverage) has unexpectedly raised their net worth beyond their expectations.

This unexpected rise in wealth has dampened MSME entrepreneurs' hunger for growth. The challenges of taking business to the next level in terms of investment, manpower and professionalising the organisation, among others, are too much of a risk to take for the satisfied entrepreneur. Some SMEs are being run in neutral gear rather than in top gear.

Disinterest in Second Generation: Many second-generation MSME entrepreneurs do not want to step into their parents' shoes. Some of them are settled abroad. Some of them are educated enough to pursue well-paying jobs. Some of them do not want to run the factory or business as the efforts of running the business are not rewarded through adequate profitability. For example, grocery stores in Mumbai are finding it difficult to get their next generation in the same business. Some of them don't have the entrepreneurial zeal of their parents to work at the non-air-conditioned shop floor level. In the absence of the next generation's commitment, further investment to take the MSME business to the next level is not being done. Neutral gear versus top gear comes into play due to the non-commitment of the next generation.

Absence of Joint Family Support: Break-down in the joint family system is limiting, to some extent, SME entrepreneurs' ability to start a new business. In the absence of support from a joint family system, an entrepreneur has to do multiple roles resulting into long gestation period or higher cost, eventually leading to higher mortality. The vacuum left by joint family system is not filled completely by friends as the emotional bonding of friendship sometimes doesn't stand the test of commercial considerations. Absence of ecosystem to nurture and support at different stages of growth of a MSME is a growing concern.

Other Constraints: The MSME sector is facing continuous demand on productivity and efficiency gains from their large counterparts. These demands require investments in business on a regular basis. Reward for making such investment is not proportionate to the capital and efforts that are put in. This, in turn, is affecting investments by MSMEs. Upcoming entrepreneurs are constrained by the high cost of setting up business, availability of finance and increasing complexity of doing business. Technology start-ups are obviously an exception to this due to the low capital requirement. MSME exchange is a good beginning to provide equity to this sector. Encashment of MSME business value has not yet picked up as the merger and acquisition opportunities are limited due to emotional attachment to the business (till it is too late to detach) and the difference in the perception of value.

Sustaining the MSME Growth in India

Keeping in view the importance of MSME sector in fostering growth and promoting employment, the Government of India enacted the Micro, Small and Medium Enterprises Development Act, 2006. Public Policy in India has accorded high priority to this sector in order to achieve balanced, sustainable, more equitable and inclusive growth in the country. Some of the important measures that have been taken by Government of India and Reserve Bank of India and that can be taken up to address them have been set out below.

Financing Facilities: *Access to timely and adequate credit* is critical for MSME growth and development in India. To ensure enhanced credit flow to the sector, and more so to the micro units, banks have been advised to achieve a 20% year-on-year growth in credit to micro and small enterprises. Advances extended to the MSME sector are treated as priority sector advances and as per the extant Reserve Bank guidelines, banks are required to extend at least 60% of their advances to the MSME sector to micro enterprises by 2012-13 and achieve a 10% annual growth in number of micro enterprise accounts. The Reserve Bank is closely monitoring the achievement of targets by banks on a quarterly basis and banks have been advised to device strategies to step up their lending to micro units. However, the MSME sector needs to be competitive and should not expect subsidized interest rates as this may not help them much as the cost of credit forms a relatively small proportion of their overall cost.

Flow of Capital: Apart from bank credit, there is a growing need for *venture /risk capital* for financing high-growth-potential and start-up MSMEs. The Government of India, in the Union Budget 2012-13 proposed to set up a Rs. 5000 crore India Opportunities Venture Fund with SIDBI in order to enhance availability of equity to the MSME sector. *Access to Equity capital* is another genuine problem. At present, there is almost negligible flow of equity capital into this sector. SEBI has permitted BSE and NSE to set up an Exchange for MSMEs, which would help Indian MSMEs to raise funds from capital markets.

Skilled Manpower: The SME sector often feels the constraint of *non-availability of skilled labour*. It is indeed ironic that in a nation of more than a billion individuals, skilled labour is cited as scarce. India needs to capitalize on its unique demographic dividend (it has a very large and young workforce). The Government of India and various State governments have been implementing a number of schemes and programs over the years. The Rural Self Employment Training Institutes (RSETIs) are also working in this direction. In line with the overall target set by the Prime Minister's National Council on Skill Development, the Ministry of MSME and the agencies under targeted conducting skill development programmes for 4.78 lakh persons during 2011-12. Further, the Ministry aimed to train 5.72 lakh persons in the year 2012-13 through its various programmes for development of self-employment opportunities as well as wage employment opportunities in the country. In addition to the initiatives taken by Government agencies, the industry, through a process of training and handholding, has to contribute to building up a large base of appropriately skilled workforce available for employment in MSMEs.

Infrastructure Development To ensure competitiveness of the MSMEs, it is essential that the *availability of infrastructure is* in tune with the global trends. The state of infrastructure, including power, water, roads, etc. in areas where SMEs are located is inadequate and unreliable. There is a need for common infrastructure projects for MSMEs. MSMEs, through coming together and sharing the costs of infrastructure, which are otherwise prohibitive for individual MSMEs, could benefit from economies of scale, synergy and collective bargaining by collaborating with each other particularly on aspects of common infrastructure, common facilities, raw material procurement, marketing & transportation of finished goods, testing laboratory, common tooling/machining, research & development, etc.

Marketing The competitiveness of any economy depends on how efficiently all the resources in the process of production are utilised and how efficiently these are marketed, hence the entire chain of production has to be efficient. This means that the process of production has to be cost efficient and meets quality needs of the consumers. To withstand the onslaught of competition from large enterprises within and outside, MSMEs need to respond promptly to the evolving marketing needs and innovations. The sector needs to be provided better market access facilities in order to sustain and further enhance its contribution towards output, employment generation and exports. The Ministry has taken several initiatives to facilitate MSMEs to enhance their market access both within and outside the country. Various organizations under the Ministry of MSME organize exhibitions/ fairs and buyer-seller meets across the country, providing MSMEs with an opportunity to display their products and capabilities. The Ministry of MSME could also enlarge its existing schemes relating to product designing, packaging, and setting up of marketing hubs, etc. in order to expand their reach and coverage of larger number of MSME units

Technological Upgradation: The MSME sector in India, with some exceptions, is characterized by low technology levels, which acts as a handicap in the emerging global market. Though India has a vast pool of technical talent with a well developed intellectual infrastructure, the country still scores low in the matter of developing and adapting new technologies in the MSME sector. The MSME sector today needs an effective information system to support and deliver information to different users. Such information systems will be used to provide effective interface between users and computer technology and will also provide information for managers on day-to-day operations of the enterprises. The lack of access to new and better technology has prevented Indian MSMEs from growing at a rate that's equivalent to their potential. This improvement can come through the use of latest technology. It can be additionally pointed out that since the majority of India's MSMEs, especially the small businesses, generate a large proportion of their revenue from the local market; they still rely on traditional media like telephone directories and newspapers to reach their customer base. Therefore, there arises a need for the sector to build capacities to develop ICT and other tools in order to cater to the growing marketing needs.

Cluster Approach: The government has adopted the **cluster approach** as a key strategy for enhancing the productivity and competitiveness as well as capacity building of MSEs in the country. During the year 2011-12 (up to 31 January 2012), 8 new clusters were taken up for diagnostic study, 5 for soft interventions, and 4 for setting up of common facility centres (CFCs). With this, a total of 477 clusters have been taken up for diagnostic study, soft interventions, and hard interventions. Apart from these clusters, 134 infrastructure development projects have also been undertaken.

Factoring Services Apart from the above-mentioned factors, efforts are on to promote *factoring services* to tackle delayed realization of receivables, which adversely affects the recycling of funds and business operations of MSME units. To facilitate factoring services, the Parliament has recently passed the Factoring Regulation Bill that would address delays in payment and liquidity problems of micro and small enterprises. The Factoring Bill creates the legislative environment for factoring and makes the process easier.

CONCLUSION

Micro, small and medium enterprises (MSMEs) contribute to economic development in various ways such as creating employment opportunities for rural and urban population, providing goods & services at affordable costs by offering innovative solutions and sustainable development to the economy as a whole. In order to transform India into a major manufacturing hub like China, the Indian MSMEs must embrace change so that they can survive and find a place for themselves in the global competitive environment. The most important change needed is in the attitude of the stakeholders and in the mindset of the institutions which are engaged in the task of small enterprise development. Efforts should be made to take full advantage of opportunities made available by globalization. This is possible only through enhancing efficiency and competitiveness of the enterprises through continuous technological innovations, quality improvement, better access to finance, diversification into new geographies and markets, modernization, adoption of better risk management and corporate governance practices, better human resource management, better infrastructure, investment climate reform, etc. All stakeholders in the development of MSMEs, viz., government, RBI, banks and other agencies like MSME associations/ chambers and large industry associations should gear up to provide an enabling environment to the MSMEs for taking them to a higher and sustained growth trajectory. MSMEs, on their part, should strive hard to take advantage of the available opportunities while staying clear of the potential pitfalls that confront them in their natural progression into large corporations or even into multinational corporations of the future.

References

1. Annual Report, 2011-12, Ministry of Micro, Medium and Small Enterprises, Government of India.
2. Banerjee Parthasarathi (2005), *Corporate Governance and Competence in SME's in India*, CACCI Journal, Vol. 1
3. Berry Albert (2007), *The Importance of SMEs in the Economy*, ITD Global Conference on Taxation of Small and Medium Enterprises.
4. Blakely, E. J. and Bradshaw, T. K. (2002), *Planning Local Economic Development: Theory and Practice*, Sage Publications.
5. Chakrabarty Dr. K C (2012), *Empowering MSMEs for Financial Inclusion and Growth- Role of Banks and Industry Associations*, address at the SME Banking Conclave 2012.
6. Economic Survey, Government of India, 2011-12
7. G20 Seoul Summit (October 2010), Scaling-Up SME Access to Financial Services in the Developing World.
8. Global Partnership for Financial Inclusion (GPFI) website, Sub-Group on SME Finance, G20.
9. Malecki, E. J. (1997), *Technology and Economic Development: the Dynamics of Local, Regional and National Competitiveness,* Longman, London.
10. Markku Virtanen, "*Modernising and Diversifying Existing SMEs*", OECD Paper.
11. Meyer-Stamer, J., (1995), "Micro-Level Innovations and Competitiveness", World Development, Vol. 23, pp. 143–148.

12. "Promoting Entrepreneurship and Innovative SMEs in a Global Economy: Towards a More Responsible and Inclusive Globalisation", Istanbul, Turkey 3-5 June 2004, 2nd OECD Conference of Ministers Responsible for Small and Medium-sized Enterprises (SMEs)
13. Report of the PM's Task Force on MSMEs, January 2010 (Chairman: Shri T.K.A.Nair) Website http://msme.gov.in/msme_ars.htm

3

Entrepreneurship for Benchmarking

Manoj Trivedi
HNB (PG) College Allahabad
Shivani Kapoor
DAMS, Kanpur
E-mail: kapoor.shivani_dams@rediffmail.com

ABSTRACT

Sustainable economic growth is enabled by the production of wealth, i.e., development of entrepreneurship. Opportunities for its development, and so the sources of the country's economic wealth, may be found today not only in the proper level of macroeconomic indicators (labor cost, interest rates' level, currency exchange rate, etc.), but also in regional (effective and efficient use of locally diverse opportunities, development predisposition, and cooperation between organizations) and microeconomic conditions (differences in management styles).

Innovation has become the base of the growth and competitiveness in the global economy. Every enterprise, endeavouring to survive and keep the necessary flexibility in a complicated economic latter-day situation has to be creative and innovative. Benchmarking can be taken as an expedient tool for the implementation of innovative and tried processes or methods in an organization. Unfortunately, this tool doesn't come up with expectations, if it is employed by the ill-prepared organization, which is stick to conservatism, formalism and avoidance of risk. In other words, a special culture, stimulating changes, proactivenes is necessary for the successful results of the benchmarking use. Entrepreneurial enterprises distinguish themselves for their ability to tolerate risk and ambiguity, promote creativity, improvement and innovativeness. So, entrepreneurship can be described as the basic element for success in the process of the creation of innovations using benchmarking.

The objective of the article is entrepreneurship as the basic element for successful employment of benchmarking and business innovations. The purpose of this article is to stress the link between entrepreneurship and benchmarking by detecting entirely entrepreneurial abilities, which help to use benchmarking successfully in the activity of business innovations. The following methods were applied in this article: systematic and comparative analysis of scientific literature, which allowed to study entrepreneurship, innovations, benchmarking and their interrelationship; logical deduction method was useful and expedient trying to explain the main features, linking together entrepreneurship and benchmarking as the activities of innovations creation; inference generation. Applying the mentioned methods, the links among entrepreneurial management of the enterprise and benchmarking are reduced. Primarily, big attention is paid to the entrepreneurship influence on the creation of innovations. This influence is analysing standing on the concise research of concepts, formulated by different authors. The similarity of innovative enterprise to entrepreneurial enterprise is examined too. After the consideration of entrepreneurship as the base of innovations' creation the benchmarking's possibilities to change, improve and innovate the enterprise are explored. Lastly, entrepreneurship as the enabler or successes factor of the benchmarking is presented. In the conclusion it can be noticed that the connection between the entrepreneurship and benchmarking is tight enough. Benchmarking can be analysed as entrepreneurial tool, because it enables to transform organizational processes, bring changes in the obsolete work's order and to create innovations. But it should be stressed that benchmarking's successful termination depends on the possibilities to invoke entrepreneurial thinking, because carrying the purpose practice is not the simple process of copying. Obviously, that the substantial discernible and latent differences, existing among enterprises, demand creativity and flair to use attainments of others for their own organization's improvement and innovations.

INTRODUCTION

Today's economic situation induces and enforces business to conform to the difficult conditions of activity and to stand the considerable challenges. The new methods of work and the different attitude to own moves and to the working of the other units of economy system must be invoked in order to escape deciding setback and failure.

However, looking on the bright side, the global economic crisis is the best time to find the overlooked or newly emerged possibilities. Entrepreneurship is the phenomenon, which enables to create innovations using the unconventionality and opportunities, which are unnoticed by the other members of traditional business. Commonly, entrepreneurship and innovation are adduced as very associated concepts. All the main features which are typical for innovative enterprise, for example, orientation to changes, decentralization, tolerance of risk, promotion of personal initiative, can be applicable for the entrepreneurial organization too. Entrepreneurs have abilities to create innovations embodying courageous ideas and unusual decisions. Sometimes the progressive methods of the organization's work can be detected in the practice of successful, but very different and dissimilar enterprises. In that case the innovative system of the activity can be transferred to the organization, which is ready to read up on the new working model, using benchmarking.

The Research Problem

Benchmarking can be a very effective tool trying to improve business and create innovations. It helps to avoid the waste of time creating the improvements, which have already been made up by other enterprises. In other words the organization doesn't need to "reinvent the wheel". Besides it can walk away from the difficulties, upspring evaluating the benefit of the new model, because this benefit is tested in the practice of a deviser. However, the advantages of the benchmarking can be achieved not by all enterprises, because the special features are necessary in this process. The organization, which endeavours to apply benchmarking, has to be very perceptive, flexible, venturesome and creative. In other words in the process of creating innovations in an organization using benchmarking, entrepreneurial contemplation is necessary. Entrepreneurship can be construing as the enabler or success factor for benchmarking, because it helps to create organizational culture, which allows avoiding the main reasons of enterprises failure in being innovative. Negative organizational culture barriers, such as behavioural inertia, conservatism, lack of commitment and are not normal in the entrepreneurial enterprise; contrarily, the proactive activity and originality are in great demand. The entrepreneurial sight of internal and external processes helps to descry the possibilities for improving performance and innovating ordinary course throughout the achievements of other enterprises.

Literature Review

The relation between entrepreneurship and innovation has been analysed by many researchers (McDaniel, 2002; Zhao, 2005 [66]; Drucker, 2007; Morris, Kuratko, et al., 2007). But the entrepreneurship as the success factor of the benchmarking's process hasn't been investigated properly and the studies, proposing the entrepreneurial internal culture of an organization as the best environment for the use of benchmarking method, has not been detected. However, the entrepreneurship should be analyzed as the enabler of benchmarking, as it precludes the existence of barriers ruinous for the best practice's implementing. The object of the article is entrepreneurship as the basic element for successful employment of the benchmarking and business innovations. The purpose of the article is to stress the link between entrepreneurship and benchmarking by detecting the entirely entrepreneurial abilities, which help to use the benchmarking successfully in the activity of business innovations. The methods of scientific investigations: systematic and comparative analysis of scientific literature, logical deduction method, inference generation. The role of entrepreneurship for the innovation creation. Innovations are one of the most important factors of the country's economy or the successful development of an enterprise. The development and activation of the innovative activity ensure the possibility to modernize miscellaneously the supply structures of the manufacture and services, to create the new products and improve producible articles or usable technologies herewith enlarging their international competitive ability, which is one of the most important factors of the country's economic expansion. Innovation and orientation to changes and the usage of the newest knowledge enterprises are the substructure of economic growth and the source of productivity (Jakubavicius et al., 2008). The development of the activity of innovations implementation permits to deal with the problems of the enlargement of competitive ability and enables organizations to exclude the dependence on the discrepancy of products' cycles (Levanas, Ramanauskiene, 2008). Consequently, the European Union endeavours to promote entrepreneurship as "a true backbone of the European economy, being primarily responsible for wealth and economic growth, next to their key role in innovation" (Fact and figures about the EU′s Small and Medium Enterprise (SME), (2010 Internet source). There is no doubt that the development of any economic and social system is based, to a large extent, on the development of entrepreneurship (Startiene, Remeikiene, 2008), because small business plays a rather high role in ensuring the country's economic and social welfare (Mickaitis et al., 2009). Low demand of capital, quick reaction to the market changes and flexibility while adapting to them, new markets or filling of niches, creating competition for state enterprises, servicing big enterprises, creating new and frequently higher quality products, services, manufacturing processes – these are the main advantages of small or medium size enterprises revealing their effectiveness and importance (Tamosiunas, Lukosius, 2009). Entrepreneurship enhances competitiveness (Krisciunas, Greblikaite, 2007; Foltean, Feder, 2009; Vorley, 2010; Colwell, Narayanan, 2010) as it stimulates innovations, which are highlighted how the fundamental factor of the competitive ability by many authors (Banyte, Salickaite, 2008; Grundey, et al., 2008; Melnikas, 2008; Adekola, et al., 2008; Ghazinoory, Ghazinouri, 2009). To distinguish between a small business owner and entrepreneur, Carland, et al. propose that a small business owner establishes and manages a business for the purpose of personal goals and as a source of income and as such the business is bounded with family needs. An entrepreneur establishes and manages business for the purpose of profit and growth and is characterized by innovative behaviour (Hansemark, 1998).

As a result, entrepreneurial firms with favourable prospects for growth do not simply contribute to job creation and social cohesion. They are also important because of their impact in terms of innovative and competitive power, in particular when they possess the right human capital endowment and an educated workforce able to implement new technologies (Santarelli, 2006). Accordingly, entrepreneurship is associated with innovations by many authors (Schumpeter, 1982; Zhao, 2005; Jatuliaviciene, et al., 2007, Jucevicius, 2008, Holbrook J. A. 2010). Entrepreneurs seek opportunities (Cheng, 2009; Short, et al., 2010) and innovations often provide the instrument for them to succeed (Zhao 2005 [65]; Jatuliaviciene, et al., 2007; Kriaucioniene, 2008). In other words, innovation is a specific tool of entrepreneuship by which entrepreneurs exploit changes as an opportunity for a different business or service (Zhao, 2005). J. A. Schumpeter claimed innovation as the sole domain of the entrepreneur (McDaniel, 2002). Entrepreneurship has been recognized as a micro-driver of innovation and economic growth (Nooteboom & Stam, 2008). An entrepreneur's main feature is to foster innovations in various levels.

Entrepreneur destroys status quo or equilibrium by innovations. The essence of entrepreneurship is realized by implementing new combinations. These combinations could be: the development of new products, new ways of production, the discovery of new markets, new resources, the creation of new business units, the implementation of new management concepts within the organization. Schumpeter describes entrepreneurship as an economic process of "creative destruction" (Stripeikis, 2008). The importance of the entrepreneur as a destroyer of the 'established rules of the game' and a creator of the new ones indicates that human intervention lies at the very core of any innovative activity (Jucevicius, 2008). Introducing the concept of entrepreneurship or construing the definition of entrepreneurs many researchers mention innovation as an inseparable part of the entire phenomenon of entrepreneurship:

- Entrepreneurship encompasses acts of organizational creation, renewal, or innovation that occurs within or outside an existing organization (Sharma, Chrisman, 2007).
- Entrepreneurship is a unique combination of desicions, striving for innovations and risk, encouraging business and it efficiency (Vijeikis, Makstutis, 2009).
- Entrepreneurs tend to be individuals with high motivation, risk-taking and proactive behaviour, who seek to create value for themselves and their customers by exploiting innovations, opportunities and perhaps by creating new ventures (Brown, Ulijn, 2004).
- Entrepreneur is a person who habitually creates and innovates to build something of recognized value around perceived opportunities (Bolton, Thompson, 2004).

Drucker explained the relationship between innovation and entrepreneurship, stating that "Innovation is the specific function of entrepreneurship it is the means by which entrepreneur either creates new wealth-producing resources or endows existing resources with enhanced potential for creating wealth (Terziovski, 2008).

Russel and Russel found a strong correlation between an organizational culture that supports innovation and successful entrepreneurial strategies. Covin and Slevin argued that an organization's entrepreneurial orientation was the summation of top management proclivity to take business-related risks, in order to bring about change and innovation resulting in a competitive advantage for their firm to compete aggressively with other firms. Zhao found that entrepreneurship and innovation are positively related to each other and are complementary in nature (Flamholtz, Kannan-Narasimhan, 2007). The tie between entrepreneurship and innovations can be identified trying to analyse the similarity of an innovative enterprise to entrepreneurial enterprise. In other words, entrepreneurs are the "catalysts of change" (Kuratko, 2008; Robertson, 2009), who not only act with the persistent drive, but have abilities to activate other people and create value. Such orientation to progress is one of the most important traits of an innovative enterprise. Additionally, the inquisitiveness of entrepreneurs, which stimulates to widen the horizon, conduces to find the ways of effective information's search processes. The entrepreneurial networks are the evidence that entrepreneurial enterprises sustain constant information channels, which are the second feature of innovative enterprise. One trait that seems to be necessary for an entrepreneur (but not sufficient), however, is leadership (Rekhi et al., 2003). Entrepreneurial leadership is not just about giving people jobs to do; it is also about offering them the support they need in order to do those jobs (Wickham, 2006). So, entrepreneurial leadership can be defined as the entrepreneur's ability to anticipate, envision, maintain flexibility, think strategically, and work with others to initiate changes that will create a viable future for the organization (Kuratko, 2008). Therefore, entrepreneurs are the persons, who recognize the value of good team work and efforts and who have the necessary features for the assembling, inspiring and managing of such teams. Consequently, the requirement for innovative enterprise to maintain the team work is verified in the case of entrepreneurial management. The next features of an innovative enterprise are decentralization of the organizational structure, risk tolerance, defiance of formalism and promotion of personal initiative. Obviously, entrepreneurial organizations promote the autonomy and empowerment of employees. They stimulate personal initiative, responsibility and risk taking including high tolerance of risk, too. Such proactiveness, that is typical for entrepreneurs and other employees of an entrepreneurial enterprise, finally, shows that an entrepreneurial organization reasonably can be ranked as the innovative enterprise. Such tough tie is useful trying to understand why "innovation and entrepreneurship are often regarded as overlapping concepts" (Nooteboom, Stam, 2008).

As entrepreneurship is often connected with innovations, its impact on benchmarking, which analogically is used like the tool for organizational improvements and novelties, conversely, is not suitably researched. Entrepreneurship influences benchmarking from the start, the benchmarking concept seemed to lend itself most readily to manufacturing or administrative functions – anything easily definably and quantifiable. In operations such as human resources in general, and training, and development in particular, measurement and replication have always appeared to be more difficult and nebulous.

Yet benchmarking offers exactly what trainers and other HR practitioners need – a means of objectively defining and improving their work, its outcomes, and its strategic role within an organization (Cheney, 1998). It enables to change the less effective business performance to the advanced ways of activity. Every organization changes. The changes may be driven from external forces such as competition or shifts in market or customer requirements, or they may be driven internally through leadership, culture or other factors. Companies that embrace change have found that the identification and transfer of "best practices" is key to successful change or improvement initiatives. They know that designing new processes using successfully demonstrated practices, ideas, and insights from others not only reduces costs and cycle time but also ultimately provides a competitive advantage in the marketplace (Coers et al., 2002). So, the experience of many companies such as Xerox (Jacobson, Hillkirk, 1986 Lester et al., 1992; Zairi, 1996), Hewlett-Packard (Codling, 1995), Statoil (Andersen, Pettersen, 1996) which are studied by different researches; can be evident that benchmarking can infuse the improvements, positive shifts and useful changes into organization's life.

Certainly, the possibility to innovate, exchange come down to the nature of benchmarking. Benchmarking is not only a tool for comparison, a learning mechanism, and an improvement means, but it is also a catalyst causing a change in our attitude and behaviour, when benchmarking is positioned properly, in an organization (Andersen, Pettersen, 1996). Benchmarking reinforces change because it involves key stakeholders and process owners who can initiate change based on what benchmarking teaches them; surfaces performance gaps; identifies key improvement opportunities through process analysis; uncovers other processes and practices that can serve as models for improvement; reduces barriers through demonstrated success; and fosters excellence through the adaptation of the best practices (Coers et al., 2002). Benchmarking is primarily used to identify better ways of doing things; in short, to identify "best practices". Throughout the exercise, gaps between how things are currently being done, and how they are done better elsewhere, are identified (Organization for Economic Cooperation and Development, 2002). So, measurement is the key of benchmarking (Ahmad, Benson, 1999). It helps to accomplish comparison and improve activity. Consequently, measurement, comparison and improvement are the main focal points, which are used by researchers defining the concept of benchmarking:

- Benchmarking is an improvement process used to discover and incorporate best practices in operation. Benchmarking is the preferred process used to identify and understand the elements (causes) of superior of world-class performance in a particular work process (Damelio, 1995).
- Benchmarking is the process of comparing and measuring organization against others, anywhere in the world, to gain information or philosophies, practices, and measures that will help your organization take action to improve its performance (Coers, et al., 2002).
- Benchmarking is a structured and analytical process of continuously identifying, comparing, deploying and reviewing best practices worldwide to gain and maintain competitive advantage (Anton, Gustin, 2000).
- Benchmarking is an ongoing process of measuring and improving business practices against the companies that can be identified as the best worldwide (Wireman, 2004).

- Benchmarking is the process of measuring an organization's business processes against leaders in any industry to gain insights to improve performance (Saul, 2004).

Best-practice benchmarking is called innovation benchmarking by Davenport as the target processes are often born out of innovative thinking and bold managerial implementation (Betts, 1999). So, obviously, benchmarking is very closely related with innovation. But it is necessary to understand, that conception of innovation doesn't essentially mean the great invention (Petuskiene, Druica, 2009). Innovation in a modern business context is therefore about organizations' ability to provide the extra dimension of quality that will differentiate a product or service, through newness and originality. Most importantly, innovation in a modern business context is related to everything that impacts on customer satisfaction/ delight and is therefore only related to aspects of value-added contributions to the end customer (Zairi, 1998).

Camp argues that the innovative nature of benchmarking is in the implementation of the best-practice process where there is usually an opportunity to adjust the operation of the source company (Betts, 1999). The implementation of benchmarking can be difficult and many successful companies have encountered problems in their early attempts to implement benchmarking practices. All such facts prove that benchmarking has to be adopted in enterprises in a creative way. The ability to envisage the possibilities of the own enterprise looking in the practice of rivals or other market shares, which are very different and sometimes works under unlike conditions is very important (Petuskiene, Druica, 2009). So, benchmarking is not the copier machine that copies processes from one organization into another (Anderssen, Pettersen, 1996). Lack of understanding of corporate-wide innovating activity is often partly why companies do not achieve high competitive standards and fail to exploit market opportunities. Cultures which promote innovation activity by placing emphasis on products and services only, while regarding certain functional areas as "superstars" are unlikely to be leaders in the marketplace (Zairi, 1998). Entrepreneurship can be taken as the basic element for success in the process of benchmarking and business innovation, because entrepreneurial organizational culture stimulates changes, improvements and innovations.

Analysing the organizational culture of the enterprises which employ benchmarking can be educed the main reasons for an organization failing to innovate: behavioural inertia; organization conservatism; lack of strategic direction; lack of capability; lack of commitment and will (Zairi, 1998). So, using the Amabile opinion, it can be emphasized, that successful innovation may depend on organizational cultural norms that groups develop and the extent to which the group's cultural orientation aligns with, and is supported by, the organization's overall orientation (Poskiene, 2006). It is evident that entrepreneurial organizations are venture organizations (Dvir et al., 2009; Zhang, et al., 2009; Baum, Bird, 2010; Ruvio, et al., 2010). They behave proactive and influence changes even in the external environment. So, behavioural passivity, inertness, organization conservatism are unrepresentative features for them. Capability, strong commitment and purpose enable entrepreneurial enterprises to gain noticeable achievements. Therefore, entrepreneurship embraces leading enablers of benchmarking. Enablers are a broad set of activities or conditions that help to enhance the implementation of the best business practice. An essential part of a true benchmarking approach is the analysis of management skills and attitudes that combine to allow a company to achieve best business practices. This hidden narrative is as important during the benchmarking exercise as are the visible statistical factors and the hard processes. The enablers, then, are behind-the-scene or hidden factors. They allow the development or continuation of the best practices. Examples include leadership, motivated workforces, management vision, and an organizational focus. Although these factors are rarely mentioned by specific statistics, they have a direct impact on the company's exceptional performance. They lead to company's exceptional performance (Wireman, 2004). As it was mentioned, the final results of benchmarking depend very much on the conditions under which it is implemented. The entrepreneurial enterprise is the place where favourable conditions really exist. In other words, such organization leaders have the ability to see opportunities of improvement looking at the internal activities or watching the work results of other completely different organizations. So, entrepreneurs contrive how to adapt the experience of other enterprises in their own organization. If the best practice cannot be narrowly adjusted, entrepreneurial thinking helps to remake it creatively. It is evident that an exactly mentioned way can safeguard better results than trying to copy the best practice of unlike market share using thorough imitation. The attempt to become the second enterprise, which has the same best practice being different by many other characteristics and signs, can influence the failure of the application of benchmarking. So, the entrepreneurial environment of an organization can positively affect benchmarking consequents and final results in summary can be emphasized that the benchmarking can be a very effective tool for changes, innovations and improvements when it is used by the enterprise, which is capable to absorb the new contemplations and standpoints, herewith, keeping its singularity ingeniously adopting of the discrepant methods and experience. The entrepreneurial culture is exactly such success factor or enabler making the benchmarking's decisions meaningful and high-scoring.

CONCLUSION

Entrepreneurship, as the act of organizational renewal and innovation creation, is the base engine of economy and development. Innovation can be presented as the essential element of entrepreneurial efforts. In other words, entrepreneurship and innovation go hand to hand in many contexts. The innovation in the entrepreneurial business is the specific tool for the progress and availing of opportunities. Entrepreneurs have enough courage to take the risk implementing the venturesome decisions, which frightens other enterprisers or seem senseless, on the surface. This ability to accept changes naturally and openness to new ideas, as the source of organization's vitality, signify that entrepreneurial companies can be revealed as the innovative companies.

Benchmarking is a continual process of measuring and comparing best practices endeavouring to improve own performance through the experience and developed success clue of other enterprises. It allows to use the achievements of other organizations saving time and work. Benchmarking involves stakeholders in learning processes, which changes attitudes and fosters elimination of performance gaps, it can be named as a catalyst of change. So, benchmarking is very relative to entrepreneurship, as it enables to bring necessary changes, update the organizational processes and generate innovations. In consideration of the difficulties, which arise trying to educe, transfer and adopt the best practices in organization, entrepreneurial thinking is very topical for advantageous benchmarking termination. The work methods, rejiged processes created by the leaders of industry cannot be simply copied to the different and unlike environment of the improver. The originality of progressive devise, made by the creator of the best practice has to be kept, in company, with the novel adoptive enterprise's decisions, designed for the successful implementation. So, insight, creativity, flexibility are necessary for the application of benchmarking. Only entrepreneurial culture, characterized as open for the changes and innovations, can properly and effectively adjust the best practice. Due to this cause the entrepreneurship can be extracted as the basic element for the success in the process of benchmarking.

References

1. Adekola, A., Korsakiene, R., & Tvaronaviciene, M. (2008). Approach to Innovative Activities by Lithuanian Companies in the Current Conditions of Development. Technological and Economic Development of Economy, 14(4), 595–611.
2. Ahmad, M., & Benson, R. (1999). Benchmarking in the process industries. Warwickshire: IChemE, 155. Andersen, B., & Pettersen, P. G. (1996). The benchmarking handbook – step-by-step instructions. London: Chapman & Hall, 192.
3. Anton, J., & Gustin, D. (2000). Call center benchmarking – how good is "good enough". USA: Purdue University Press, 84.
4. Banyte, J., Salickaite R. (2008). Successful Diffusion and Adoption of Innovation as a Means to Increase Competitiveness of Enterprises. Inzinerine Ekonomika-Engineering Economics, (1), 48–56.
5. Baum, J. R., & Bird B. J. (2010). The Successful Intelligence of High-Growth Entrepreneurs: Links to New Venture Growth. Organization Science, (21), 397–412.

6. Betts, M. (1999). Strategic management of IT in construction. Oxford: Wiley-Blackwell, 406.
7. Bhagavatula, S., Elfring, T., Van Tilburg, A., & Van de Bunt, G. G. (2010). How social and human capital influence opportunity recognition and resource mobilization in India's handloom industry. Journal of Business Venturing, (25), 245–260.
8. Bolton, B. K., & Thompson, J. (2004). Entrepreneurs – talent, temperament, technique. Oxford, 415.
9. Brown, T. E., & Ulijn, J. (2004). Innovation, entrepreneurship and culture – the interaction between technology, progress and economic growth. Massachusetts, 255.
10. Carsrud, A. L., & Brannback M. E. (2007). Entrepreneurship, Westport, 182.
11. Cheney, S. (1998). Benchmarking. Alexandria: American Society for Training and Development, 16.
12. Cheng, Z. H. (2009). An Investigation into the Entrepreneurial Opportunity Discovery Process: The Role of Information. Proceedings of 2009 International Conference on Growth of Firm and Management innovation, 385–392.
13. Codling, S. (1995) Best practice benchmarking – a management guide, Hampshire: Gower Publishing, Ltd., 156.
14. Coers, M., Gardner, C., Higgins, L., & Raybourn, C. (2002). Benchmarking – A Guide for Your Journey to Best Practice Processes. Houston: American Productivity and Quality Center, 86.
15. Colwell, K., & Narayanan, V. K. (2010). Foresight in economic development policy: Shaping the institutional context for entrepreneurial innovation. Futures, (42), 295–303.
16. Damelio, R. (1995). The Basics of Benchmarking. Portland: Productivity Press, 80.
17. Drucker, P. F. (2007). Innovation and entrepreneurship – practice and principles. Oxford: Elsevier, 253.
18. Dvir, D., Sadeh, A., Pines, A. M., & Shenhar, A. J. (2009). Key Entrepreneurial Traits and Their Relationship to Venture Uncertainty and Venture Success. Proceedings of Picmet 09 - Technology Management in the Age of Fundamental Change, Vols. 1-5, 1769–1775.
19. Fact and figures about the EU's Small and Medium Enterprise (SME) (2010). Internet source:
20. http://ec.europa.eu/enterprise/policies/sme/facts-figures-analysis/index_en.htm Flamholtz, E. G., & Kannan-Narasimhan, R. (2007). The role of effective organizational culture in fostering innovation and entrepreneurship. The creative enterprise: managing the innovative organizations and people. London, (2), 123–154.

21. Foltean, F., & Feder, E. S. (2009). Market Orientation and International Entrepreneurship. Transformations in Business & Economics, 8(3), 23–43.
22. Ghazinoory, S., & Ghazinouri, R. (2009). Nanotechnology and Sociopolitical Modernity in Developing Countries; Case Study of Iran. Technological and Economic Development of Economy, 15(3), 395–417.
23. Grundey, D., Toluba, B., Pifinkus, D., & Verbauskiene, L. (2008). The role of institutional policy in developing innovative entrepreneurship in Lithuania. Transformations in Business & Economics, 7(2), 86–101.
24. Hansemark, O. C. (1998). The effects of an entrepreneurship programme on Need for Achievement and Locus of Control of reinforcement. Inte Jnl of Entrepreneurial Behaviour & Research, 4(1), 28–50.
25. Holbrook, J. A. (2010). Innovation in Public Sector Services: Entrepreneurship, Creativity, and Management. Science and Public Policy, (37), 161–162.
26. Jacobson, G., & Hillkirk, J. (1986). Xerox, American Samurai. Macmillan, 338.
27. Jakubavicius, A., Jucevicius, R., Jucevicius, G., Kriaucioniene, M., Kersys, M. (2008). Inovacijos versle: procesai, parama, tinklaveika. Vilnius, 180.
28. Jatuliaviciene, G., Kucinskiene, M., & Garuckas, R. (2007). Environmental Challenges for Entrepreneurship and Innovations Development. Vadyba, Vilnius, (3-4), 16–17.
29. Jucevicius, G. (2008). Social Dimensions of Technological innovations: Culturial and Institutional Perspectives. Socialiniai mokslai–Social Sciences (1), 29–41.
30. Kriaucioniene, M. (2008).The Dynamics of Technological Innovations in National Innovation System: the Perspective of Transformation Countries. Socialiniai mokslai–Social Sciences (1), 7–20.
31. Krisciunas, K., & Greblikaite, J. (2007). Entrepreneurship in Sustainable Development: SMEs Innovativeness in Lithuania. Inzinerine Ekonomika-Engineering Economics (4), 20–26.
32. Kuratko, D. F. (2008). Entrepreneurship – Theory, Process, and Practice. Eighth edition, Mason, 544.
33. Lester, R. H., Enrick, N. L., & Mottley, H. E. (1992). Quality control for profit – gaining the competitive edge, New York: CRC Press, 569.
34. Levanas, G., & Ramanauskiene, J. (2008). Naujoviu diegimo problema konkurencijos salygomis. Vadybos mokslas ir studijos – kaimo verslu ir ju infrastrukturos pletrai 13(2), 100–106.
35. McDaniel, B. A. (2002). Entrepreneurship and innovation – an economic approach, New York, 269.
36. Melnikas, B. (2008). The Knowledge-Based Economy in the European Union.

37. Transformation Strategies. Transformations in Business & Economics, 7(3), 170–192.
38. Mickaitis, A., Bartkus, E. V., & Zascizinskiene, G. (2009). Empirical Research of Outsourcing in Lithuanian Small
39. Business Segment. Inzinerine Ekonomika-Engineering Economics (5), 91–100.
40. Morris, M. H., Kuratko, D. F., & Covin, J. G. (2007). Corporate entrepreneurship and innovation – entrepreneurial development within organizations. Thomson/South-Western College Pub. 423.
41. Nazem, F. (2007). The compilation of math patter for quality of staff's working life based on higher education managers' entrepreneurship in Islamic Azad university. Proceedings of the 2nd European Conference on Entrepreneurship and Innovation, Dublin, 131–140.
42. Nooteboom, B., & Stam, E. (2008). Micro-Foundations for Innovation Policy, Amsterdam, 385.
43. Organisation for Economic Co-operation and Development (2002). Benchmarking Intermodal Freight Transport. OECD Publishing, 146.
44. Petuskiene, E., & Druica, E. (2009). Benchmarking as entrepreneurial tool for business improvement and innovations.
45. Changes in social and business environment. Proceedings of the 3rd international conference, Kaunas: Technologija, 306–312.
46. Poskiene, A. (2006). Organizational Culture and Innovations. Inzinerine Ekonomika-Engineering Economics (1), 45–50.
47. Rekhi, K., Prahalad, C.K., Kleiner, E., Murthy, N., & Senge, P. (2003). The entrepreneurial spirit. Essentials of entrepreneurship – what it takes to create successful enterprises. New Jersey, 1–16.
48. Robertson, L. (2009). Deliberate Pause – Entrepreneurship and Its Moment in Human Progress, New York, 372. Inzinerine Ekonomika-Engineering Economics, 2011, 22(1), 69-77.
49. Ruvio, A., Rosenblatt, Z., & Hertz-Lazarowitz, R. (2010). Entrepreneurial leadership vision in nonprofit vs. for-profit organizations. Leadership Quarterly, (21), 144–158.
50. Santarelli, E. (2006). Entrepreneurship, growth, and innovation – the dynamics of firms and industrines, New York, 285.
51. Saul, J. (2004). Benchmarking for nonprofits– how to measure, manage, and improve performance, Saint Paul: Fieldstone Alliance, 96.
52. Schumpeter, J. A. (1982). The Theory of Economic Development – an inquiry into profits, capital, credit, interest, and the business cycle. Cambridge Mass: Harvard, 255.
53. Sharma, P., & Chrisman, S. J. J. (2007). Toward reconcilation of the definition issues in the feald of corporate entrepreneurship. Entrepreneurship - concepts, theory and perspective. New York, 83–105.

54. Short, J. C., Ketchen, D. J., Shook, C. L., & Ireland, R. D. (2010). The Concept of "Opportunity" in Entrepreneurship Research: Past Accomplishments and Future Challenges. Journal of Management, (36), 40–65.
55. Startiene, G., & Remeikiene, R. (2008). Gender Gap in Entrepreneurship. Inzinerine Ekonomika-Engineering Economics, (5), 95–103.
56. Stripeikis, O. (2008). Entrepreneurship formation in Lithuanian small and medium - sized firms. Summary of Doctoral Dissertation. Kaunas, 36.
57. Tamosiunas, T., & Lukosius, S. (2009). Possibilities for Business Enterprise Support. Inzinerine ekonomikaEngineering Economics(1), 58–64.
58. Terziovski, M. (2008). Entrepreneurship and innovation management. Energizing management through innovation and entrepreneurship – European Research and Practice, London and New York, 1–5.
59. Vijeikis, J., & Makstutis, A. (2009). Small and medium-sized business competitiveness in Lithuania. Ekonomika ir vadyba: aktualijos ir perspektyvos (2): 328–338.
60. Vorley, T. (2010). Making Poor Nations Rich: Entrepreneurship and the Process of Economic Development. Journal of International Development, (22), 538–539.
61. West, III G. P. (2003). Connecting levels of analysis in entrepreneurship research: a focus on information processing, asymmetric knowledge and networks. New movements in entrepreneurship. Cornwall, 51–70.
62. Wickham, P. A. (2006). Strategic entrepreneurship. London, 613.
63. Wireman, T. (2004). Benchmarking best practices in maintenance management. New York: Industrial Press Inc., 212.
64. Zairi, M. (1996). Effective benchmarking– learning from the best. London: Chapman & Hall, 379.
65. Zairi, M. (1998). Benchmarking for best practice – continuous learning through sustainable innovation. Oxford: Butterworth-Heinemann, 496.
66. Zhang, J., Ren, R. W., & Fan, W. (2009). An Empirical Study on Corporate Entrepreneurship and Corporate Performance under Dynamic Environmental Affection. Proceedings of Academy of Innovaton and Entrepreneurship 2009, 270–277.
67. Zhao, F. (2005). Maximize Business Profits Through E-Partnerships. Hershey, London, Melburne, Singpore. 252.
68. Zhao, F. (2005). Exploring the Synergy between Entrepreneurship and Innovation. International Journal of Entrepreneurial Behaviour & Research. 11. Internet access: http://www. emeraldinsight.com/10.1108/135 52550510580825

4

Film Based Merchandising: Promotions, Revenues and More

Manoj Kumar Srivastava
Research Scholar
Faculty of Management Studies
Banaras Hindu University, Varanasi

ABSTRACT

This paper examines the notion of movie merchandising and briefly talks about its emergence and current arena in the US film industry. But the focal point is its status in the Indian film industry. Moreover, the problems allied with movie merchandising in India have been examined along with its future scenario in the country.

INTRODUCTION

"Marketers in the US have successfully understood the science of reading consumers' minds and creating properties with great longevity. On the other hand, the value of celebrities is diffused in India by the sundry products they endorse and this has a bearing on creating strong affiliations."

Nanette D'sa
Senior VP (Licensing and Merchandising)
STAR India

"Merchandising in India is event-based and the interest dips post-event unlike in the West where properties have been created to sustain consumer interest over a long period of time. Marketers here are doing precious little to sustain the post-event sales momentum."

Harish Bijoor
Brand Consultant

'Harry Potter' a hero in the world of entertainment. He comes from a bestselling novel, popular not only among the kids but many adults are also addicted to him. Talk about the earnings and Harry Potter has broken all the records. The first movie of Harry Potter series "Harry Potter & The Sorcerer's Stone" has earned approx. US $ 1 billion from the worldwide sale/licensing of Harry Potter merchandise only—figurines, food tie-ups, posters, accessories, comic strips, stationery to magic kits and home furnishings featuring Harry and friends from the Hogwarts school. According to a reliable source it has banged the market with a whopping 12 billion dollars in the beginning only.

Not only Potter, another superhero has a complete shop offering different merchandise like toys, posters, costumes, action figures, games, etc., solely based upon movie 'Spiderman'.

Movie merchandising is a well-versed phenomenon in Hollywood where it offers $ 16 bn annually to the retailers and manufacturers collectively. But when it comes to Bollywood, film based merchandise is still in a nascent stage. This paper is an attempt to understand the concept of film-based merchandise, its present status in Indian film industry and future trends that are likely to evolve with the growth of the industry.

HISTORICAL BACKGROUND

Merchandising can be traced back to early 1920s where Walt Disney discovered that extra earnings from merchandising based activities could provide them much needed financial backup. However, credit for giving way to movie merchandising in Hollywood goes to 'Star Wars', a major blockbuster of 1977.

The current phenomenon known as entertainment licensing is a result of merchandising successes of Star Wars (1977) and E.T.–the Extra-Terrestrial (1982), Action based films of the 1990s (for instance, Batman [1989] and Spider-Man [2002]), as well as the successful franchise films in the early twenty-first century (such as The Lord of the Rings [2001–2003] and Harry Potter [beginning in 2001]) gave it further boost.

Hitherto, merchandising has been a success in Hollywood. The $9 billion earned by Director George Lucas from merchandising and sequel rights of "Star Wars" is one of the most successful deals ever. 'Harry Potter' series have so far fetched $11.8 billion from different contracts to its producers. Ace filmmaker Steven Spielberg earned over $1 billion from the "E.T." merchandise.

CONCEPT OF MOVIE MERCHANDISING

Filmmakers have always been in search of novel and innovative ideas to promote and popularize movies in all sections of society. Ideas that can help them to connect with the viewers as well as increase the earnings. Film based merchandising is just another expansion of films and their enchantment.

In general, merchandising can be understood as a collection of display, stocking, and sales promotion techniques that ultimately results in increasing the market share of a product in retail outlets. Merchandising may include clothing, toys, food products, or music and often extends well beyond the core business of the producer of the original product. Merchandising based on a specific movie may significantly add to its total revenues through appropriate licensing opportunities.

Selling articles that are specifically linked to a movie or its characters can be termed movie merchandising. These articles can range from toys, posters, accessories, clothes, games, ringtones, stationery and various other gift items. Basically, movie merchandising is just another way of making the whole experience of watching movie a memorable one. It is a tool that aids the viewers in taking the movie to their homes.

BOLLYWOOD & MOVIE MERCHANDISING: A LONG WAY TO GO

Before we start penetrating the scope of movie merchandising in the Indian film industry, consider these:

- According to "Film industry in India: New Horizons", latest study by EY and LA India Film Council, the Indian film industry is projected to grow from US$3.2 billion in 2010 to US$5 billion by 2014 at a CAGR (Compound Annual Growth Rate) of 14.1% and is further expected to benefit from an increased collaboration with Hollywood.
- According to the estimates of Assocham, revenues from Indian film industry, valued at about Rs 8,190 crore in 2010, are expected to grow by 56% to Rs 12,800 crore by 2015, due to increasing digitalization of the sector.
- Deloitte & Assocham, in their report titled 'Media & Entertainment in India: Digital Road Ahead' (2011), suggested that film segment revenues in India comprise ticket collection at the box office (both domestic and overseas), home video (CDs and DVDs sale and on rent) and ancillary revenues that includes broadcast syndication rights, mobile VAS and other film related sales through new media. The report informs that film industry stood at nearly US$2.0 billion in 2007. It grew by 12% to reach US$2.2 billion in 2008 but has been registering negative growth over the last two consecutive years and stood at around US$ 1.8 billion in 2010. The falling revenues of the film industry in 2009 and 2010 can be attributed to average performance of most films at the box office and closing down of single-screen theatres. The industry is expected to grow by 9% p.a. till 2015 and reach nearly US$2.8 billion. This is expected to be fuelled by the multiplex chains' renewed focus on expansion, increase in average ticket prices and expected higher quality content.

Despite such an impressive growth projections, Bollywood could not utilize film based merchandising in an organized manner. The reason is simple; till recently Indian film industry was not working as an organized sector, only few years back big corporate like Future Group, Adlabs, Studio18 and UTV entered the entertainment industry. These corporate houses not only bring core corporate culture with them but they also intend to change the dynamics of film-making and its marketing.

You would be surprised to learn that movie merchandising in India has its traces back in 1973 when "Bobby", a super hit from R.K. Films was released. The wonderful accessories (clips, hairpins, etc.) worn by the lead actress were a craze amongst the young girls. Coming to a more recent example, the gorgeous series and whole styling of another leading lady of Bollywood in her milestone movie "Hum Aapke Hain Kaun" created a buzz in the market. Tailors were piled up with the orders where they have to just design the outfits in the same fashion. However, production houses did not consider the whole thing a significant opportunity of enriching the film experience holding a lot of potential for huge profits then.

Movies and cricket – national obsessions, as they are often called, are still to be cashed into their fullest extent. With strong branding and merchandising efforts cricket and Bollywood can be promoted as national tools of entertainment. Barring the Rs 300 crore market for cartoon characters-based merchandising, sports and film merchandising hasn't fetched anything significant here. Indians invest a lot of time and money to films and sports and that too with full devotion and energy. Unlike Hollywood, where 15-35 per cent of a film's revenues come from merchandising (accessories, clothing), Bollywood merchandising contributes barely 2 per cent of a film's income. With IPL, cricket merchandising has found its way in the Indian market. As far as film based merchandising is concerned, experts consider it a risky venture.

The main problems that can be held accountable for such limited growth of merchandising in B'wood are:

- Piracy—Rajjat A. Barjatya, managing director of Rajshri Media, said that Rajshri Films had brought out a limited range merchandise of their superhit movie "Hum Aapke Hain Kaun", but pirated copies arrived in the market soon, affecting the sale of the original products.
- Box-office performance and its aftermath – the sale of licensed products of a movie is directly related to its box-office performance. We can take example of 'Dhan Dhana Dhan Goal'; Reebok entered into a tie-up with UTV Motion Pictures to release merchandise based on the film, but the demand dipped when the movie could not create buzz at the box office.
- Absence of a lead-time before the movie releases—"If enough time is spent, then one can produce merchandising of good quality," says Navin Shah, CEO, P9. Integrated P9, franchisee of animation based movie 'Hanuman' had seen sales of Rs 60 lakh in the first three months after the release of Hanuman Part 1 in 2005, with merchandising still clocking in Rs 2 lakh every month!

However, production houses are fastly catching up with the trend of movie merchandising with Hrithik Roshan-starrer 'Krrish', animated movie 'Hanuman', 'Om Shanti Om' and 'Saawariya' being the initiators. At least some of the recent merchandising activities suggest so.

- Saawariya signed a deal with the Future Group, worth Rs 10 crore, for merchandising products like apparel, bed and bath linen, and beauty products.
- The Om Shanti Om team tied up with "Shoppers Stop" for Rs 6-7 crore for the clothing line right from the film itself and also with brands like Sia Jewellery and Nokia.
- Zapak, the online gaming website owned by Reliance Big Entertainment, has won the distribution rights of the Drona movie merchandise.
- Tata's jewellery brand Tanishq was associated with Ashutosh Gowarikar's 'Jodhaa Akbar' right from the movie's conceptual stage. Tanishq, over a two-year time frame on Jodhaa Akbar had invested close to Rs 5 crore.
- The Aamir Khan starrer "3 Idiots" entered into a tie-up with Pantaloons.
- Provogue launched a stylish T-Shirts collection inspired by the movie "Wake Up Sid" as a result of tie-up between the company and the producers.

ROAD AHEAD

Production houses in India have certainly noticed movie merchandising as another off-screen deal loaded with enormous revenues. At the same time, it is perceived as a concrete way of connecting with the customers. They have already taken it up as a separate promotion activity to be carried out in an organized fashion and that too carefully.

The entertainment, media and communications company Percept has entered into a tie-up with Future Group to form Bollywood Retail. This tie-up will result into certain specific sort of businesses like a chain of Bollywood Cafes, walkthroughs, and theme parks to be set up within the Future group's retail network. Bollywood merchandising is just the first of many things that this joint venture is likely to take up. This initiative will start from 8 cities including Hyderabad, Kolkata, Bangalore and Delhi. The joint venture will invest Rs. 500 million initially to sell Bollywood merchandise. The international market is familiar to the concept of merchandising and is much more mature. "The domestic market is still nascent, but I am sure that in due course, the consumers will lap up the concept in a big way," says a confident Shailendra Singh, joint MD, Percept Ltd.

With the advent of organized retail and its various formats, movie merchandise finds a new platform to be displayed well, which was lacking earlier. According to a research note from analytics firm CRISIL, growth of the overall organized retail segment, which accounts for seven per cent of the Rs 25 lakh-crore Indian retail market, slowed to 10 per cent in FY2013, compared with 20 per cent seen in 2011-12. Still, the Indian retail sector accounts for over 20% of the country's gross domestic product (GDP) and contributes 8% to total employment. The current estimated value of the Indian retail sector is about 500 billion USD and is pegged to reach 1.3 trillion USD by 2020. The grand potential of organized retail give vigorous signs of simultaneous growth of movie merchandising also. Big brands can leverage on their retail presence to create a productive environment for their merchandising deals.

V. Govindraj, VP, Retail & Marketing, Tanishq says "It's a question of putting it in the right setting. Formats enable us to showcase the same piece which consumers see in the movie and create an ambience, which complements the visual imagery."

CONCLUSION

The whole concept of movie-based merchandising has a lot of potential that is yet to be exploited. Brands such as Shopper's Stop, Pantaloons, Reebok and Tanishq have garnered impressive revenues from associations with the respective movies right from beginning. With a keen focus on merchandising as a way to popularize and effectively market entertainment, very soon India will be seen as a serious player in the merchandising space.

References

1. http://www.screenindia.com/old/fullstory.php?content_id=5877
2. http://www.ey.com/IN/en/Newsroom/News-releases/Press-Release_Indian-film-industry-to-drive-growth-with-Hollywood-collaboration
3. www.expressindia.com
4. http://www.deloitte.com/assets/dcom-india/local%20assets/documents/me%20-%20whitepaper%20for%20assocham.pdf
5. http://dictionary.bnet.com/definition/merchandising.html
6. www.mproft.org
7. www.bollywoodhungama.com
8. http://mutiny.in/2008/10/06/bollywood-and-movie-merchandising-still-a-long-way-to-go/
9. www.thehindubusinessline.com
10. http://retail.franchiseindia.com/articles/Retail-Practice/New-Trends/Movie-makers-take-the-merchandising-way-148/
11. The Economic Times (29th March, 2008, 31st May, 2008)
12. http://rajeshthambala.blogspot.in/2013/02/indian-retail-industry-2012-2013.html

5

New Challenges for Priority Sector Lending in India

Minali Mehra & Pratik Dwivedi
minali.mehra@gmail.com,
dwivedi.pratik@gmail.com

ABSTRACT

Priority Sector Lending is an important role given by the Reserve Bank of India (RBI) to the banks for providing a specified portion of the bank lending to few specific sectors like agriculture or small-scale industries. This is essentially meant for an all-round development of the economy. Private sector lending in India is concerned with the development of financing to the weaker sections of the society. This paper is all about the role and development of public sector and private sector banks in priority sector lending. For the purpose of study secondary data has been collected from Statistical Tables Relating to Banks in India, and Report on Trend and Progress of Banking in India. The scope of study covers the data of public sector banks and private sector banks in India. There is no doubt that priority sector advances and agricultural advances of both the types of banks public and private sector banks. Their performance had improved manifold over the study period. But, they were still lacking behind to achieve the targets set for them by RBI in agriculture sector. It was observed that the performance of private sector banks in respect of all the parameters was better than that of public sector banks. The need of time is to increase the withdraw attention of both the public and private sector banks on the priority sector of the economy.

INTRODUCTION

The priority sector comprises a vast section of the population in sectors such as agriculture, micro and small enterprises (MSEs), education and housing. Bank is such institution which provides financial assistance to the public at the time when they are in the need of money. Creation of Bank is meant for the same purpose. Banks exist for providing financial assistance to the customers. Banks are life blood of an economy which ensure its borrowers they will help them anywhere anytime. It is the only mean which assures its customers that their needs will be fulfilled anyhow. Customers without having any kind of doubt in their mind can easily approach to the nearby bank branch. Banks are the core of the financial system of a country. Banks includes financial institutions, public sector banks, private sector banks, commercial banks, cooperative societies, etc. Amongst all these institutions commercial banks are the oldest institutions having a wide network of branches, commanding utmost public confidence and having the lion's share in total banking system.

Commercial banks play a pivotal role in the economic development of a country. Economic development involves investment in the various sectors of economy. The banks collect savings from the people and mobilize it for investment in industrial projects. They are simple business or commercial concerns which provide various types of services to customers in return for payment in one form or another. They have been in existence in India for the past several decades. At the beginning of the new millennium, 260 million people in the country did not have incomes to access a consumption basket which defines the poverty line. Of these, 75 per cent were in the rural areas. India is home to 22 per cent of the world's poor. Such a high incidence of poverty is a matter of concern in view of the fact that poverty eradication has been one of the major objectives of the development planning process. Indeed, poverty is a global issue. Its eradication is considered integral to humanity's quest for sustainable development. The loan for agriculture purpose is not received by farmers in an easy way.

IMPORTANT POINTS RELATED TO PRIVATE LENDING

I. At a meeting of the National Credit Council held in July 1968, it was emphasized that commercial banks should increase their involvement in the financing of priority sectors, viz., agriculture and small-scale industries.

II. On the basis of facts and figures provided by NCC (National Credit Council), the Reserve Bank prescribed a modified return for reporting priority sector advances and certain guidelines were issued in this connection indicating the scope of the items to be included under the various categories of priority sector.

III. Although initially there was no specific target fixed in respect of priority sector lending, in November 1974 the banks were advised to raise the share of these sectors in their aggregate advances to the level of $33\frac{1}{3}$ per cent by March 1979.

IV. At a meeting of the Union Finance Minister with the Chief Executive Officers of public sector banks held in March 1980, it was agreed that banks should aim at raising the proportion of their advances to priority sector to 40 per cent by March 1985.

V. On the basis of the recommendations of the Working Group on the Modalities of Implementation of Priority Sector Lending and the Twenty Point Economic Programme by Banks all commercial banks were advised to achieve the target of priority sector lending at 40 per cent of aggregate bank advances by 1985.

VI. Sub-targets were also specified for lending to agriculture and the weaker sections within the priority sector. Since then, there have been several changes in the scope of priority sector lending and the targets and sub-targets applicable to various bank groups.

VII. The guidelines were last revised in the year 2007 based on the recommendations made in September 2005.

VIII. Accordingly, Reserve Bank of India in August 2011 set up a committee to re-examine the existing classification and suggest revised guidelines with regard to priority sector lending classification and related issues.

IX. The revised guidelines are operational with effect from July 20, 2012. The priority sector loans sanctioned under the guidelines issued prior to this date will continue to be classified under priority sector till maturity/renewal.

I. CATEGORIES UNDER PRIORITY SECTOR

(i) Agriculture
(ii) Micro and Small Enterprises
(iii) Education
(iv) Housing
(v) Export Credit
(vi) Others

II. TARGETS/SUB-TARGETS FOR PRIORITY SECTOR

(i) **Table 1**

The targets and sub-targets set under priority sector lending for domestic and foreign banks operating in India are furnished below: Categories	Domestic commercial banks/ Foreign banks with 20 and above branches	Foreign banks with less than 20 branches
Total Priority Sector	40 per cent of Adjusted Net Bank Credit [ANBC defined in sub-paragraph (iii) below] or credit equivalent amount of Off-Balance Sheet Exposure, whichever is higher.	32 per cent of ANBC or credit equivalent amount of Off-Balance Sheet Exposure, whichever is higher.
Total agriculture	18 per cent of ANBC or credit equivalent amount of Off-Balance Sheet Exposure, whichever is higher.	No specific target. Forms part of total priority sector target.

Of this, indirect lending in excess of 4.5% of ANBC or credit equivalent amount of Off-Balance Sheet Exposure, whichever is higher, will not be reckoned for computing achievement under 18 per cent target. However, all agricultural loans under the categories 'direct' and 'indirect' will be reckoned in computing achievement under the overall priority sector target of 40 per cent of ANBC or credit equivalent amount of Off-Balance Sheet Exposure, whichever is higher.		
Micro and Small Enterprises (MSE)	(i) Advances to micro and small enterprises sector will be reckoned in computing achievement under the overall priority sector target of 40 percent of ANBC or credit equivalent amount of Off-Balance Sheet Exposure, whichever is higher. (ii) 40 per cent of total advances to micro and small enterprises sector should go to Micro (manufacturing) enterprises having investment in plant and machinery up to Rs.10 lakh and micro (service) enterprises having investment in equipment up to Rs. 4 lakh; (iii) 20 per cent of total advances to micro and small enterprises sector should go to micro (manufacturing) enterprises with investment in plant and machinery above Rs.10 lakh and up to Rs.25 lakh, and micro (service) enterprises with investment in equipment above Rs.4 lakh and up to Rs.10 lakh	No specific target. Forms part of total priority sector target.
Export Credit	Export credit is not a separate category. Export credit to eligible activities under agriculture and MSE will be reckoned for priority sector lending under respective categories.	No specific target. Forms part of total priority sector target.
Advances to Weaker Sections	10 per cent of ANBC or credit equivalent amount of Off-Balance Sheet Exposure, whichever is higher.	No specific target in the total priority sector target.

(ii) For foreign banks with 20 and above branches, priority sector targets and sub-targets have to be achieved within a maximum period of five years starting from April 1, 2013 and ending on March 31, 2018 as per the action plans submitted by them as approved by RBI.

(iii) The current year's targets for priority sectors and sub-targets will be computed based on Adjusted Net Bank Credit (ANBC) or credit equivalent of Off-Balance Sheet Exposures of preceeding March 31st. The outstanding priority sector loans as on March $31^{st}$of the current year will be reckoned for achievement of priority sector targets and sub-targets.

(iv) For the purpose of priority sector lending, ANBC denotes the outstanding Bank Credit in India [(as prescribed in item No.VI of Form 'A' (Special Return as on March 31st under Section 42 (2) of the RBI Act, 1934] minus bills rediscounted with RBI and other approved financial institutions plus permitted non SLR bonds/debentures in Held to Maturity (HTM) category plus other investments eligible to be treated as part of priority sector lending (e.g., investments in securitized assets).

1. Computation of Adjusted Net Bank Credit

Table 2

Bank Credit in India (As prescribed in item No.VI of Form 'A' (Special Return as on March 31) under Section 42 (2) of the RBI Act, 1934.	I
Bills Rediscounted with RBI and other approved Financial Institutions	II
Net Bank Credit (NBC)*	III (I-II)
Bonds/debentures in Non-SLR categories under HTM category + other investments eligible to be treated as priority sector.	IV
ANBC	III+IV

2. Micro and Small Enterprises

Table 3

The limits for investment in plant and machinery/equipment for manufacturing/service enterprise, as notified by Ministry of Micro Small and Medium Enterprises, vide, S.O.1642(E) dated September 9, 2006 are as under: Manufacturing sector	
Enterprises	Investment in plant and machinery
Micro Enterprises	Do not exceed twenty five lakh rupees
Small Enterprises	More than twenty five lakh rupees but does not exceed five crore rupees
Service Sector	
Enterprises	Investment in equipment
Micro Enterprises	Does not exceed ten lakh rupees
Small Enterprises	More than ten lakh rupees but does not exceed two crore rupees

The Reserve Bank of India released on its website revised guidelines on Priority Sector Lending—Targets and Classification.

The priority sectors are broadly taken as those sectors of the economy which, if not designated as priority sectors, may not get timely and adequate credit. Typically, these are small value loans to farmers for agriculture and allied activities, micro and small enterprises, poor people for housing, students for education and other low income groups and weaker sections.

The revised guidelines aim at implementing the essence of recommendations of Nair Committee without dismantling the established and accepted structure of priority sector lending. The overall target under priority sector is retained at 40 percent as suggested by the Nair Committee. The targets under both direct and indirect agriculture are retained at 13.5 per cent and 4.5 per cent respectively while refocusing the direct agricultural lending to individuals, Self-Help Groups (SHGs) and Joint Liability Groups (JLGs) directly by banks. The focus of the revised guidelines is also on direct lending by banks and not through intermediaries like Non Banking Financial Companies (NBFCs) and Housing Finance Companies (HFCs).

Highlights of the revised priority sector guidelines

- Overall target under priority sector is retained at 40 per cent as suggested by Nair Committee.
- The targets for both direct and indirect agricultural lending are kept unchanged at 13.5 per cent and 4.5 per cent of Adjusted Net Bank Credit, respectively.

The following important activities, among others, form part of priority sector lending as per the revised guidelines:

- Loans to Micro and Small Service enterprises up-to ₹1 crore and all loans to Micro and Small manufacturing enterprises
- Loans up to ₹25 lakh for housing in metropolitan centres of population above 10 lakh and ₹15 lakh at other centres.
- Loans to Food and Agro processing units.
- Loans to individuals for educational purposes including for vocational courses upto 10 lakh in India and 20 lakh abroad.
- Loans for housing projects exclusively for economically weaker sections and low income groups, provided the cost does not exceed ₹5 lakh per dwelling unit.
- Loans to distressed farmers indebted to non-institutional lenders.
- Overdrafts up to ₹50000/- in No-Frills account.
- Loans to State Sponsored Organizations for scheduled castes and scheduled tribes.
- Loans to individuals for setting up of off-grid solar and other off-grid renewable energy solutions for households.
- Loans to individuals other than farmers up to ₹50000/- to prepay their debt to non- institutional lenders.

- Foreign banks having 20 or more branches in the country will be brought on par with domestic banks for priority sector targets in a phased manner over a maximum period of 5 years starting April 1, 2013. They will be required to submit an action plan for achieving the targets over a specific time-frame to be approved by RBI.
- The foreign banks with less than 20 branches will have no sub-targets within the overall priority sector lending target of 32 per cent. This is expected to allow them to lend as per their core competence to any priority sector category.
- Bank loans to Primary Agricultural Credit Societies (PACS), Farmers' Service Societies (FSS) and Large Adivasi Multi-Purpose Co-operative Societies (LAMPS) ceded to or managed/controlled by such banks for on-lending to farmers for agricultural and allied activities are included under direct agriculture.
- Investments by banks in scrutinised assets, outright purchases of loans and assignments to be eligible for classification under priority sector provided the underlying assets qualify for priority sector treatment and the interest rate charged to the ultimate borrower by the originating entity does not exceed base rate of such bank plus 8 per cent per annum.

OBJECTIVES OF THE STUDY

The objectives of the study are:

1. To study the contribution of private sector and public sector banks in financing priority sector lending.
2. To evaluate the performance of the banks in priority sector lending.

RESEARCH METHODLOGY

For the purpose of study secondary data has been collected from statistical tables relating to banks in India, reports on trends and banking in India. The scope of study covers data of public and private sector banks. Various statistical tables have used for the purpose of the study.

REVIEW LITERATURE

Sahu and Rajasekhar (2005), in their research paper analyzed the trends in credit flow to agriculture by scheduled commercial banks during 1980-81 to 1999-2000. They observed that the share of credit to agriculture in total bank credit for all the bank groups declined significantly, especially after banking sector reforms in spite of many efforts. They analyzed that scheduled commercial banks provided large quantum of funds to better-off farmers and to the activities earning high interest income only. They established the negative relationship between agriculture credit and investment in government security, credit subsidy and proportion of credit provided by the co-operative. They recognized that increasing lending rate reduced the credit disbursed to agriculture by scheduled commercial banks and affected the average quality of their loan portfolio so they suggested not to increase the interest rate to offset losses from defaults or to meet the lending cost, but to strengthen the quality of credit delivery system and ensure prompt repayment of loans for supporting the agriculture sector.

Mohan (2006), in his research paper examined the role of agricultural credit in supporting agricultural production in India and reviewed the performance of agricultural credit in India during the period 1950-51 to 2003-04. He found that there was rapid increase in total number of rural branches, resulting into the growth of rural credit. The share of commercial banks in total rural credit of the banking system increased rapidly during the study period. He found a wide disparity in disbursement of agricultural credit by commercial banks. Southern states had higher share of agricultural credit to net state domestic product, followed by the northern and central regions. He observed that the proportion of NPAs for commercial banks were higher for agriculture sector than that of non-priority sector.

He revealed that although the overall flow of institutional credit increased over the years but there existed several gaps in the system like inadequate provision of credit to small and marginal farmers, paucity of medium and long-term lending, and limited deposit mobilization. He recommended reviewing the agriculture policy and adoption of package approach in different segments of agriculture and agro industry for developing the status of agriculture sector.

Rao (2006), in his article, demonstrated the importance and progress of priority sector for economy during the period 1994-95 to 2003-04. He highlighted in his study that priority sector credit including farm credit of scheduled commercial banks declined during the said period indicating the preference of banks for bigger borrowers with higher credit limits instead of large number of small borrowers. He observed the decline in indirect credit to agriculture and small-scale industries sector but relatively better position in credit to other priority sectors during the study period. He referred the observations of RBI committee to stress much on direct agriculture lending, small-scale industrial lending, lending to small road and water transport operators (owning more than five vehicles), retail trade and small business under priority sector.

In his study, he highlighted various problems of rural credit and suggested to improve input delivery system, water management system, power supply, irrigation facilities, market information and general rural infrastructure, educational and medical facilities, reforming RRBs, state and central co-operatives and scheduled commercial banks for extending rural credit in rural areas.

Uppal (2009), in his research paper, evaluated the performance of public, private and foreign banks in India and analyzed the target achievement by them during 2006-07. He found that priority sector advances of public and private sector banks were higher than foreign banks. He observed that public sector banks were unable to achieve the target of priority sector, while private sector banks have achieved the target. Private sector banks could not achieve the target for weaker sections.

Foreign banks could achieve the targets for priority sector, small-scale industries sector and export sector. He further, found that NPAs of public sector banks was highest followed by private sector banks and foreign banks. Main reason for more NPAs in public and private sector banks was found to be more NPAs in agriculture sector. He examined various issues related to priority sector like, low profitability, more NPAs, Government interference, high transaction cost, etc. He also suggested various strategies to overcome these issues.

RECENT TRENDS

Inter Bank Participation Certificates Bought by Banks

Inter Bank Participation Certificates (IBPCs) bought by banks, on a risk sharing basis, shall be eligible for classification under respective categories of priority sector, provided the underlying assets are eligible to be categorized under the respective categories of priority sector and the banks fulfil the Reserve Bank guidelines on IBPCs.

Bank loans to Micro Finance Institutions (MFIs) for on-lending

(a) Bank credit to MFIs extended on, or after, April 1, 2011 for on-lending to individuals and also to members of Self-Help Groups (SHGs)/Joint Liability Groups (JLGs) will be eligible for categorization as priority sector advance under respective categories, viz., agriculture, micro and small enterprise, and 'others', as indirect finance, provided not less than 85% of total assets of MFI (other than cash, balances with banks and financial institutions, government securities and money market instruments) are in the nature of "qualifying assets". In addition, aggregate amount of loan, extended for income generating activity, is not less than 70% of the total loans given by MFIs.

(b) A "qualifying asset" shall mean a loan disbursed by MFI, which satisfies the following criteria:

- The loan is to be extended to a borrower whose household annual income in rural areas does not exceed 60,000/- while for non-rural areas it should not exceed 1,20,000/-.
- Loan does not exceed 35,000/- in the first cycle and 50,000/- in the subsequent cycles.
- Total indebtedness of the borrower does not exceed 50,000/-. Tenure of loan is not less than 24 months when loan amount exceeds 15,000/- with right to borrower of prepayment without penalty.
- The loan is without collateral.
- Loan is repayable by weekly, fortnightly or monthly instalments at the choice of the borrower.

COMMON GUIDELINES FOR PRIORITY SECTOR LOANS

Banks should comply with the following common guidelines for all categories of advances under the priority sector.

1. Rate of interest

The rates of interest on various categories of priority sector loans will be as per DBOD directives issued from time to time.

2. Service charges

No loan related and adhoc service charges/inspection charges should be levied on priority sector loans up to 25,000.

3. Receipt, Sanction/Rejection/Disbursement Register

A register/electronic record should be maintained by the bank, wherein the date of receipt, sanction/rejection/disbursement with reasons thereof, etc., should be recorded. The register/electronic record should be made available to all inspecting agencies.

4. Issue of Acknowledgement of Loan Applications

Banks should provide acknowledgement for loan applications received under priority sector loans. Bank Boards should prescribe a time limit within which the bank communicates its decision in writing to the applicants.

NON-ACHIEVEMENT OF PRIORITY SECTOR TARGETS

All scheduled commercial banks having shortfall in lending to priority sector target/sub shall be allocated amounts for contribution to the Rural Infrastructure Development Fund (RIDF) established with NABARD and other Funds with NABARD/NHB/SIDBI/other financial institutions, as decided by the Reserve Bank from time to time.

For the purpose of allocation of RIDF and other Funds, as decided by Reserve Bank from time to time, the achievement levels of priority sector lending as on the March 31st will be taken into account. The deposits under the various Funds will be called upon by NABARD or such other Financial Institutions as per the terms and conditions of the scheme.

The interest rates on banks' contribution to RIDF or any other Funds, periods of deposits, etc. shall be fixed by Reserve Bank of India from time to time and will be communicated to the concerned banks every year by the Reserve Bank at the time of allocation of funds.

The misclassifications reported by the Reserve Bank's Department of Banking Supervision would be adjusted/reduced from the achievement of that year, to which the amount of declassification/misclassification pertains, for allocation to various funds in subsequent years.

Non-achievement of priority sector targets and sub-targets will be taken into account while granting regulatory clearances/approvals for various purposes.

CURRENT INFORMATION

As many as 28 banks, including 16 from the public sector, have failed to achieve the 40 per cent target of overall priority sector lending which includes loans to MSMEs and agriculture, as on March 31, 2013. "As on March 31, 2013 domestic banks (both public and private) were below the target of priority sector lending," according to the Reserve Bank of India.

As on the last reporting Friday of March 2012 and March 31, 2013, the target set for priority sector advances was 40 per cent of the Adjusted Net Bank Credit (ANBC) or credit equivalent of off-balance sheet exposure (OBE), whichever is higher, as on March 31 of the preceding year for domestic banks and 32 per cent for foreign banks.

"During this period, 16 of the 26 public sector banks, 10 of the 20 private sector banks and 2 of the 41 foreign banks could not achieve the target of overall priority sector lending," the RBI annual report said.

According to the RBI data, as on the last reporting Friday of March 2013, public sector banks had lend Rs. 12,822.12 billion which is 36.2 per cent, the private sector banks lent Rs. 3,274.06 billion which is 37.5 per cent while the foreign banks lent Rs. 848.54 billion which is 35.1 per cent.

The scheduled commercial banks, both domestic and foreign, that failed to achieve the priority sector targets/sub-targets will be required to deposit the shortfall to the extent of corpus of funds announced by the Government in the Rural Infrastructure Development Fund (RIDF) set up with the National Bank for Agriculture and Rural Development (NABARD) and other funds set up with the Small Industries Development Bank of India (SIDBI) and the National Housing Bank (NHB).

During the year 2013-14, RIDF XIX, with a corpus of Rs 200 billion, has been set up with NABARD. In addition, the MSME (Refinance) Fund with a corpus of Rs 100 billion with SIDBI, the Warehouse Infrastructure Fund with a corpus of Rs 50 billion, the Short Term Co-operative Rural Credit (STCRC) (Refinance) Fund with a corpus of Rs 300 billion, the Short Term RRB Credit Re-Finance Fund with a corpus of Rs 200 billion with NABARD and the Rural Housing Fund with a corpus of 60 billion with NHB, have been set up during 2013-14. Another fund, viz., the Urban Housing Fund with a corpus of Rs 20 billion has been set up this year with NHB. However, credit to the MSE sector by SCBs has registered a growth of 29.8 per cent in 2012-13 over the previous year. To speed up the process of identifying a unit as sick and detecting incipient sickness and to lay down procedures for banks to adopt before declaring unit unviable, revised guidelines for the rehabilitation of sick units in the MSE sector were issued on November 1, 2012.

SUGGESTIONS

- Public sector banks should speed up their performance regarding priority sector lending. As their performance in terms of priority sector, agricultural, small scale industrial and other priority sector advances was slower than that of private sector banks.
- Besides giving impetus to other priority sector advances, banks should lay stress on agricultural and small scale industries advances also, as their performance is deteriorating in this regard.
- Considering the importance of priority sector advances in the country like India where agriculture is the major occupation, it is suggested that both public and private sector banks should make committed efforts to achieve the national targets for agriculture sector.
- Banks should make committed efforts to achieve the national targets for agriculture sector so that the major proportion of beneficiaries may be benefited.
- The banks with the co-operation of Government should take steps to generate new sources of income for the agriculture sector beneficiaries.
- The recovery procedure of the banks should be strengthened by organizing recovery camps with the co-operation of local government, creating awareness among beneficiaries about the importance of prompt repayment, fixing recovery targets, regular visits to the borrowers, sending notices to them, taking strict actions against them in case of default and setting up separate cell for recovery of priority sector loans as NPAs are highest in this sector.
- Banks should be given some incentives to achieve the targets set for priority sector.
- Proper awareness should be given to public regarding the schemes of priority sector by RBI.

References

Books & Journals

1. Chawla, A.S. (1987). "*Nationalization and Growth of Indian Banking*", Deep and Deep Publications, New Delhi, p. 216.
2. Mohan, R. (2006). "*Agricultural Credit in India: Status, Issues and Future Agenda*", Economics and Political Weekly, March (18-24), Vol. XLI No. 11, pp. 1013–1040.
3. Patel, K.V.; and Shete, N.B. (1984). "*Priority Sector Lending by Commercial Banks in India*", Prajnan, Vol. XIII, No.1 (Jan-March), p. 151.
4. Rao N. K. (2006). "*Bank Credit: Redefining Priorities*", Professional Bankers, ICFAI University Press, Hyderabad, pp. 11–14.

5. Reserve Bank of India (1969). Report of the Gadgil Study Group on the Organisational Framework for the Implementation of Social Objectives, Mumbai, pp. 5–6.
6. Reserve Bank of India (2005), Draft Technical Paper on Review of Priority Sector Lending, Mumbai, pp. 16–17.
7. Reserve Bank of India, Report on Trend and Progress of Banking in India, Mumbai, various issues.
8. Sahu, G.B.; and Rajasekhar, D. (2005), "*Banking Sector Reforms and Credit Flow to Indian Agriculture*", Economic and Political Weekly, Vol. XL, No. 53, pp. 5550–5559.
9. Uppal, R.K. (2009), "Priority Sector Advances: Trends, issues and strategies", Journal of Accounting and Taxation, Vol. 1 (5), December 2009, pp. 79–80.

Websites

1. http://rbi.org.in/scripts/AnnualPublications.aspx?head=Trend%20and%20Progress%20of%20Banking%20in%20India, accessed on 25/10/2013.
2. http://rbi.org.in/scripts/Publicationsview.aspx?id=4310, accessed on 12/10/2013

6

Customer Perception on Banking Services: With Special Reference to Indian Private Banks in Allahabad Region

Krishna Murari Mishra
Assistant Professor
LDC Institute of Technical Studies, Allahabad.
Email:krishnauim@gmail.com

Keshav Shyam
Assistant Professor
Dept. of Commerce
University of Allahabad
Email: keshavshyamsax@yahoo.com

ABSTRACT

Banking industry in India has undergone radical changes due to the liberalization and globalization measures undertaken since 1991. During 1969 and 1980 banking companies were nationalized based on the thrust aim of supplementary banking, i.e., rapid spreading out of banking activities. Whereas now the industry is operated on the concept of customer centric banking, i.e., changed from "More Banking to Better Banking" in order to face the market challenges. Before manual systems of banking were operated. After start adopting liberalization, banking industry went for technological improvement. As a result of this now industry is customer centric banking industry. Today, Indian Banking industry is one of the largest in world. There has been a great surge in efficient customer services. A highly satisfied and delighted customer is a very vital non-financial asset for the banks. Based on this background an attempt has been made to draw the answer for the question whether the banking industry is giving importance to the customers and customers are satisfied about the banking services. To enhance reputation and gain customer loyalty, a study of the performance of the banks is done to see if the perception of service quality has an effect on the banks. It has been observed that in the banking sector, it is the HDFC bank which is perceived to be offering better quality of services followed by the other private banks. With the increasing competition amongst banks, the findings can act as a strategic tool to achieve competitive advantage and customer satisfaction. It is also an eye-opener for the banks to see the gap between customer expectation and perception regarding the quality of services rendered which should further act as a motivation which results, increases reputation and to achieve customer loyalty. The present study is an attempt in the direction, where quality perceptions of the four leading banks have been compared to reach at logical conclusion.

INTRODUCTION

Banking system occupies an important place in a nation's economy. A banking institution is indispensable in a modern society. It plays a pivotal role in the economic development of a country and forms the core of the money market in an advanced country. The phenomenon of globalization brought about significant changes in terms of products and services that are being offered to Indian customers and consequently the complexion of the banking sector in India too underwent a noteworthy change in the last decades. The emergence of new private sector and foreign banks is one of the major challenges before the public sector commercial banks in India and this prompted the Indian banking industry to reckon with the challenges posed by the competition while rendering services to the customers.

Private banks dealing in retail banking industry is consequently put into lot of pressures due to increase in global competition. Various strategies are formulated to retain the customer and the key of it is to increase the service quality level. Typically, customers perceive very little difference in the banking products offered by private banks dealing in services as any new offering is quickly matched by competitors. Parasuraman et al. (1985) and Zeithaml et al. (1990) noted that the key strategy for the success and survival of any business institution is the deliverance of quality services to customers. The quality of services offered will determine customer satisfaction and attitudinal loyalty.

Initially, all the banks in India were private banks, which were founded in the pre-independence era to cater to the banking needs of the people. In 1921, three major banks, i.e., Banks of Bengal, Bank of Bombay, and Bank of Madras, merged to form Imperial Bank of India (IBI). In 1935, the Reserve Bank of India (RBI) was established and it took over the central banking responsibilities from the Imperial Bank of India, transferring commercial banking functions completely to IBI. In 1955, after the declaration of first-five year plan, Imperial Bank of India was subsequently transformed into State Bank of India (SBI). In 1994, the Reserve Bank of India issued a policy of liberalization to license limited number of private banks, which came to be known as New Generation tech-savvy banks. Global Trust Bank was, thus, the first private bank after liberalization, it was later amalgamated with Oriental Bank of Commerce (OBC). At present, Private Banks in India includes leading banks like ICICI Banks, ING Vysya Bank, Yes Bank, Karnataka Bank, Kotak Mahindra Bank, HDFC BANK, etc. Undoubtedly, being tech-savvy and full of expertise, private banks have played a major role in the development of Indian banking industry.

OBJECTIVES OF THE STUDY

The main objectives of study are:

- To study different services provided by the bank to the customers.
- To identify the areas which need improvement, so that the services of these banks are enhanced.
- To learn and understand the customer perception regarding service quality.
- To analyze the banking service of private banks.

For the purpose of data collection, questionnaires were administered to the customers of four banks in Allahabad. Among them we selected four banks, namely, ICICI Bank, HDFC Bank, Kotak Bank and Indusind Bank.

HYPOTHESIS OF THE STUDY

The responses were collected on five dimensions of service quality, namely, assurance, tangibility, reliability, responsiveness, and empathy for all the banks under study. The responses of the respondents were tabulated and subjected to the validity tests. Subsequently, the validated data was compressed in the form of different tables which succeed the discussion on the same. The discussion on the data focuses upon the prime purpose of meeting the objectives outlined and drawing the conclusion and inferences for suggesting suitable remedies for the banks. The hypothesis of the study is **'The customers' perception is in favour of private banking service providers'**.

RESEARCH METHODOLOGY

The service quality model developed by Zeithamal, Parsuraman and Berry (1988) has been used in the present study. The main assumption of the model is that service quality is a multidimensional concept. These dimensions contribute to the assessment of the service quality in any setting. The data was analyzed to reach a conclusion regarding the customer's perceptions of service quality.

Data Collection

The data for the study was collected through secondary as well as primary source. Primary data was collected using questionnaire. The statements in the construct are one-dimensional and performance based. The statements have been grouped under five dimensions, i.e., assurance tangibility, reliability, responsiveness, and empathy. In order to ascertain the perceptions of service quality, Likert's 5-point scale has been used for its suitability to estimate the range and variations in the perceptions. The scale 1 – 5 represents '5' as mostly agree and '1' as mostly disagree. Secondary data were collected from books, journals, magazines and websites.

Sampling

A pilot study was conducted to ascertain the suitability of the construct in the Indian bank setting. After ascertaining of the suitability, the questionnaire was administered to the customer's sample size of 100 respondents.

DATA ANALYSIS & INTERPRETATION

The data analysis is done on the following dimension.

Assurance Dimension

On assurance dimension of service quality deals with trust, safety and support. It is also an important dimension of service quality, which has been represented in Table 1. As depicted in the table, it is clearly indicated that assurance has the highest score of 4.28.

Table 1 Dimension in Assurance Banks

Banks	*Assurance Factor*	*Ranks*
ICICI BANK	4.20	2
HDFC BANK	4.28	1
KOTAK BANK	3.75	3
INDUSIND BANK	3.20	4
MEAN	3.86	

Tangibility Dimension

The comparison between the average score of tangibility factor and individual scores, it can be concluded that all the banks have an overall positive perception. However, the HDFC has the score more than the average score. This can be interpreted as the bank has a potential to lead in terms of tangibility.

Table 2 Tangibility of Banks

Banks	*Tangibility Factor*	*Ranks*
ICICI BANK	4.18	2
HDFC BANK	4.25	1
KOTAK BANK	3.40	3
INDUSIND BANK	3.10	4
MEAN	3.73	

Empathy Dimension

The comparison between the individual bank scores and average scores also indicates that the calculated mean value is 3.73, which is less than the HDFC Bank and ICICI Bank. Empathy dimension of service quality deals with the approach towards the customers and understanding their needs effectively. The analysis of the responses of the customers towards empathy (see Table 3) indicates that the HDFC Bank has scored the highest value of 4.25. It is followed by ICICI Bank with a score of 4.18, KOTAK follows them with an empathy value of 3.40 and last among all is INDUSIND Bank with a score of 3.10.

Table 3 Empathy Dimension in Banks

Banks	*Empathy Factor*	*Ranks*
ICICI BANK	4.18	2
HDFC BANK	4.25	1
KOTAK BANK	3.40	3
INDUSIND BANK	3.10	4
MEAN	3.73	

Responsiveness Dimension

The analysis of the dimension of service quality, i.e., responsiveness indicates that the dimension has a lot of significance in the service quality, HDFC has scored a very high value among three of the four banks under study. It is only the Indusind bank, for which the score has been the lowest. Among the other banks, it is again the HDFC Bank, which has the highest value of 4.66, followed by ICICI Bank at 4.53. Kotak is at the third place with a score of 4.29. The average mean score for responsiveness has been worked at 4.26. On comparing the individual values with the average mean, it can be concluded that again all the three banks except Indusind bank have higher than average scores.

Table 4 Responsiveness Dimension in Banks

Bank	*Responsiveness*	*Rank*
ICICI BANK	4.53	2
HDFC BANK	4.66	1
KOTAK BANK	4.29	3
INDUSIND BANK	3.57	4
MEAN	4.26	

Reliability Dimension

Reliability dimension of service quality deals with the approach towards the customers trust. The analysis of the reliability of the customers indicates that the HDFC Bank has scored the highest value of 4.64. It is followed by KOTAK Bank with a score of 4.42. ICICI Bank follows them with a value of 4.28 and last among all is Indusind Bank with a score of 3.67. The analysis of the scores clearly depicts that the three banks in the sample, viz., ICICI Bank, HDFC Bank and Kotak have the scores higher than '4', which represents more than satisfactory perception of consumers towards reliability.

Table 5 Reliability Dimension in Banks

Bank	*Reliability Factor*	*Rank*
ICICI BANK	4.28	3
HDFC BANK	4.64	1
KOTAK BANK	4.42	2
INDUSIND BANK	3.67	4
MEAN	4.25	

Private Sector Banks Score (Sample banks)

The analysis reveals that among the private sector banks all the dimensions of service quality are equally important. However, the scores have been different for these banks. While comparing the dimensions, the scores for HDFC has been higher in comparison to other banks.

Table 6 Private Sector Banks

Factor	*Private Sector Banks*
Reliability	4.25
Responsiveness	4.26
Assurance	3.86
Empathy	3.73
Tangibility	3.79
Mean	3.97

CONCLUSION AND SUGGESTIONS

The study included five dimensions of service quality perceptions, which are tangibility, reliability, responsiveness, assurance and empathy. The analysis of these dimensions identified that, among the four banks in Allahabad under study, it is the HDFC Bank, which has the highest reliability in terms of the employees, physical evidence and ambience. Although, the bank has only one branch in the Allahabad, but it has been able to instill a higher reliability value among its customers. As compared to it, the other private sector bank, Indusind Bank has the lowest reliability value.

The analysis of the other dimension, responsiveness represents the HDFC again as the front-runner among the four banks followed by ICICI Bank, Kotak Bank and Indusind Bank, respectively. This can be interpreted as the employees' capability to respond to the customers. This fact is well represented in the voluminous increase in the retail trade of these banks. The analysis reveals that Indusind Bank has the lowest service quality perception value, whereas the HDFC Bank has the highest perception. This is also correlated to the factors of reliability, as reliability leads to trust, support, etc.

The banks shall have to reorient themselves in terms of the customer service parameters to instill the concept of quality service in the mind of the customer and therefore the growth. Strategically speaking, the banks in the private sector should focus more on improving the infrastructure. The infrastructure not only involves the information technology input in the branches but also the physical evidence, internal environment and layout. This is due to the fact that recently like in other services, in banking also the internal ambience of the organization has a positive impact on the customers.

The growing needs of the customers are evident from the wide array of services being offered by the banks like insurance, mutual funds, depository services, etc. According to Reserve Bank of India, the voluminous increase of 14,85,643 crore in the retail financing schemes of the various banks indicates the varied needs of the customers, in which the private sector banks have emerged as the significant players. This in turn points towards the degree of readiness, which these banks are demonstrating towards the customers and their needs. Besides this, these banks should follow the strategy of differentiation of service offers from one another.

The customer base of the public sector banks is very big as compared to the private sector banks. It becomes imperative for the private sector banks to train their employees to treat the customers with empathy. This can give the required leading edge and finally the competitive advantage over the public sector banks.

The study indicates that the responsiveness is a most critical factor. The private sector banks like HDFC & ICICI Bank have emerged as the leading bankers. It is more so due to the fact that they have proven to be more responsive to the customers' needs. However, in order to be more successful in the market, the private sector banks shall have to be more innovative in terms of the product offered to the customers and compete aggressively in the market. The other aspect however, which needs to be strategized is the reliability. As indicated by the study, the private sector HDFC Bank leads in reliability when compared to the other private sector banks. Therefore, these banks should make relevant strategies for gaining reliability.

They should promote their recent achievements so that the customers are aware of these and rely more on the banks. Those banks, which have long established parent organizations like HDFC Bank (HDFC Corporation), should promote their linkage to the parent institutions. This would not only increase the reliability of these banks in the minds of the customers but also the assurance. The private sector banks should also take steps to enhance the human resource element by training their employees to serve the customers effectively and thereby enhance the customers' quality perceptions.

References

1. Brown, Tom J., Churchill Jr, Gilbert A. and Peter, J. Paul (1993) 'Improving the Measurement of Service Quality'; Journal of Retailing, 69:1, 127–139.
2. Business Today, 2011, 'India's Best Banks, BT-KPMG Survey', 12:24, Nov. 24-Dec 7, Delhi, 66–71.
3. Cooper, Robert G. and Edgett, Scott J. (1996) 'Factors for New Financial Services', Marketing Management, 5:3, 37.
4. Brady, Michael, K. and Cronin, Joseph, J. Jr. (2001),'Some New Thoughts on Conceptualizing Perceived Service Quality: A hierarchical Approach', Journal of Marketing, 65:3, 34–49.
5. Gronroos, Christian (1984) 'A Service Quality Model and its Implications', European Journal of Marketing, 18:4, 36–44.
6. Narasimham, M. (1991) Report on Financial Sector Reforms-1991, New Delhi, Committee of Financial Sector, Ministry of Finance, Government of India.
7. Parsuraman A., Zeithaml, Valerie A. and Berry, Leonard L. (1985) 'A Conceptual Model of Service Quality & Its Implications for Future Research', Journal of Marketing 49: Fall, 41–50.
8. Parsuraman A., Zeithaml, Valerie A. and Berry, Leonard L. (1991) 'Refinement & Reassessment of SERVQUAL scale'; Journal of Retailing, 67:4, 420–450.
9. Parsuraman A., Zeithaml, Valerie A. and Berry, Leonard L. (1994) 'Reassessment of Expectations as a Comparison Standard in Measuring Service Quality: Implications for Future Research', Journal of Marketing, 58: February, 201–230.
10. Rust, Roland T. and Oliver, Richard L. (1994) 'Service Quality: Insights and Implications from the Frontier Service Quality, in Rust, Roland T. & Oliver, Richard L. (Eds). New Directions in Theory and Practice, Thousand Oaks CA, Sage Publications, pp. 1–19.
11. Brown, Stephen W. and Teresa A. Swartz (1989) 'A Gap Analysis of Professional Service Quality'; Journal of Marketing, 53: April 92–98.
12. Cronin J., Joseph Jr. and Taylor, Taylor, Stephen A. (1992) 'Measuring Service Quality: A Reexamination and Extension', Journal of Marketing, 56, 55–68.
13. Debasish, Satyhya Swaroop (2003) 'Service Quality in Commercial Banks: A Comparative Analysis of Selected Banks in Delhi', Indian Journal of Marketing, 33:3, 3–9.

7

Changing Face of Microfinance in India with Special Reference to Reliance Capital

Ankita Rajdev
Assistant Professor, Faculty of Management, JSSGIW, Bhopal
Email: Ankita.rajdevs@gmail.com

ABSTRACT

Microfinance is a refined model of microcredit delivery. Microfinance is any activity that includes the provision of financial services for entrepreneurs and small businesses of low income level and those lacking access to banking and related services. It is an activity that includes the provision of financial services such as credit, savings, and insurance to low income individuals which fall just above the nationally defined poverty line, and poor individuals which fall below that poverty line, with the goal of creating social value. In India, the microfinance aimed at cost-effective mechanism that helps in reaching finance to poor like the 'Self-Help-Groups (SHGs) – Banks Linkage Program'. Microfinance is not just about giving micro credit to the poor rather it is an economic development tool whose objective is to assist poor to work their way out of poverty. It covers a wide range of services like credit, savings, insurance, remittance and also non-financial services like training, counselling, etc

This paper analyzed the evolution of microfinance concepts in India and initiatives taken by the banks. It also explores the importance of microfinance. This is an informative study to the existing branch of knowledge and studies in banking industry and is useful for other researchers, banks and government agencies. The study concentrated on Reliance Microfinance. There is a negligible awareness of microfinance among customers. Along with the increase in business, the Reliance group can take initiatives to enhance their activities towards being microfinance which will help in their brand building and can serve the community and earth.

INTRODUCTION

Microfinance is any activity that includes the provision of financial services for entrepreneurs and small businesses of low income level and those lacking access to banking and related services.

The two main mechanisms for the delivery of financial services to such clients in India are:

1. Relationship-based banking for individual entrepreneurs and small businesses.
2. Group-based models.

where several entrepreneurs come together to apply for loans and other services as a group. Microfinance is the provision of financial services such as loans, savings, insurance, and training to people living in poverty. Microfinance is not just about giving micro-credit to the poor rather it is an economic development tool whose objective is to assist the poor to work their way out of poverty. It covers a wide range of services like credit, savings, insurance, remittance and also non-financial services like training, counselling, etc.

Microfinance refers to small-scale financial services for both credits and deposits—that are provided to people who farm or fish or herd; operate small or micro enterprise where goods are produced, recycled, repaired, or traded; provide services; work for wages or commissions; gain income from renting out small amounts of land, vehicles, draft animals, or machinery and tools; and to other individuals and local groups in developing countries in both rural and urban areas' (Marguerite S. Robinson).

Microfinance Background

Microfinance in India can trace its origins back to the early 1970s when the Self Employed Women's Association (SEWA) of the state of Gujarat formed an urban cooperative bank, called the Shri Mahila SEWA Sahakari Bank, with the objective of providing banking services to poor women employed in the unorganized sector in Ahmedabad, Gujarat. The microfinance sector went on to evolve in the 1980s around the concept of SHGs, informal bodies that would provide their clients with much needed savings and credit services. From humble beginnings, the sector has grown significantly over the years to become a multibillion dollar industry, with bodies such as the Small Industries Development Bank of India and the National Bank for Agriculture and Rural Development devoting significant financial resources to microfinance. Today, the top five private sector MFIs reach more than 20 million clients in nearly every state in India and many Indian MFIs have been recognized as global leaders in the industry.

Some of the major MFIs of India are

1. SKS Microfinance Secunderabad, Pvt. Ltd.
2. Spandana Sphoorty Hyderabad, Public Ltd.
3. Share Microfin Limited (SML) Hyderabad, Public Ltd.
4. Asmitha Microfin Ltd. (AML), Hyderabad, Public Ltd.
5. Shri Kshetra Dharmasthala.
6. Bhartiya Samruddhi Hyderabad, Public Ltd.
7. Bandhan Kolkata,

8. Cashpor Micro Credit (CMC) Varanasi
9. Grama Vidiyal Micro Tiruchirappalli, Pvt. Ltd.
10. Grameen Financial Bangalore, Pvt. Ltd.

Need of the Study

The need of microfinance arises because the rural India requires sources of finance for poverty alleviation, procurement of agricultural and farms input.

So the researchers are interested to find out the scopes of microfinance in rural India. This research paper is highlighting a picture of presence of microfinance in retail by Reliance.

RESEARCH METHODOLOGY

Objectives of the Study

The main objectives of the research work are:

1. To study the concept of 'Microfinance'.
2. To study the Reliance Microfinance.

Methodology of Study

Secondary data has been collected from the various Books, Journals, Research articles and Internet websites.

Research Design Used

This is a descriptive research paper based on secondary data.

Reliance Microfinance: Background

Reliance Capital, the financial services company of the Reliance Anil Dhirubhai Ambani Group, launched its microfinance initiative in partnership with Microfinance institutions (MFIs) in March, 2008. The company announced its tie-up with two MFIs—MAS Financial Services and Gujarat-based Vardan Trust—as a part of the initiative that was launched by Tina Ambani. This initiative is in line with the group's commitment to play a serious role in bringing value to the lives of the underprivileged and the aged in India. Reliance capital plans to fund MFIs in Gujarat and Maharashtra in the first phase, and subsequently have a national presence. The initiative envisages lending to MFIs, who would then be on-lending finances to self help groups, individuals and joint liability groups as per their norms. MFIs often find raising capital a difficult proposition. This partnership will help Reliance and MFIs in optimally utilizing the expertise in distribution of credit to tiny and small enterprises for income generation activities, consumption and emergency needs. This tie-up according to Reliance is to help them in spreading their network further and meeting the growing need for finance by micro-entrepreneurs such as agriculture labourers, farmers, small shop owners, artisans, unskilled labourers and small enterprise workers.

Reliance Philosophy

The Reliance philosophy has always been to make everyone believe that if they dream it, they can do it. The tagline for the entire service is "**Tailor your way towards your big aspirations with tailor-made Reliance Microfinance".** Reliance seamlessly tailored microfinance solutions make it possible for everybody to take the first step towards bigger things. With Reliance perfectly sewed microfinance solutions, you get higher loan eligibility at minimal documentation, and competitive interest rates. Reliance Microfinance vision is to provide access to finance right at the grassroots level, by partnering with MFIs serving rural and semi-urban areas. Reliance customer centric microfinance initiative is in-line with the group's commitment to bringing value and empowerment to every Indian.

Features of Reliance Microfinance

- Convenient EMIs
- Higher loan eligibility
- Flexibility of loan tenure
- Easy repayment option by way of simple EMIs

Reliance Micro Loans

Reliance micro loans can be availed when you have a registered microfinance institutions (MFIs are registered as societies as per Societies Registration Act 1860 or state legislation and as Trusts as per Public Trust Act 1920 or Indian Trust Act 1882. Section 25 companies are registered as per the Companies Act (1956) with permission from Central Government.) and NBFC (other legal forms including NBFCs registered as Section 25 companies, for profit NBFCs, Cooperative Banks and Local Area Banks are regulated by the Reserve Bank of India (RBI). Cooperatives are registered as per the State, National and MACS Acts and governed by the State Registrar of Cooperatives. The loans can be avail ranging from Rs 30,00,000/-to Rs 20,00,00,000/-depending on persons eligibility, income and repayment capacity.

New Initiative in Microfinance

Reliance Retail, joined hands with Wal-Mart, for the micro-credit space as they look to establish rural supply chain linkages to service their mega retail forays. The move could significantly pep up the currently under-serviced microfinance sector. Micro-lending to the economically active poor, both urban and rural, is pegged at around Rs 7000 crore, as reflected in bank outstanding. As against this, back-of-the-envelope calculations put the demand at around Rs 2 lakh crore.

According to sources, Reliance Retail is likely to move the RBI seeking permission to set up an NBFC arm that will operate as a microfinance institution

(MFI). It may also look at partnering existing MFIs as part of its ambitious supply chain with rural and semi-urban markets for which the company is said to have earmarked Rs 8,000-10,000 crore.

CONCLUSION

However, the changing face of microfinance in India appears to be positive the major constraints to microfinance in India are: lack of funding, lack of poverty impact indicators, and lack of an enabling policy environment. India's microfinance movement, including the government-sponsored self-help group-bank linkage programme and MFIs backed by new generation private banks. Many mid size MFI will have to face challenge in terms of recourses and capital funding. The study concludes that in spite of a lot of opportunity in microfinance; Indian banks, companies, etc. are far behind in the implementation of microfinance. Companies, banks and other financial institute must literate their customers and their employees about microfinance and adopt all strategies to implement it.

References

1. Armendariz de Aghion and Jonathan Morduch. The Economics of Microfinance. The MIT Press. 2005.
2. Anis Chowdhury, Microfinance as a Poverty Reduction Tool—A Critical Assessment, DESA Working Paper No. 89ST/ESA/2009/DWP/89, 2009
3. D. Padmavathi (2011). Sustainable Development of Rural Women Entrepreneurs. International Conference on Business, Economics and Tourism Management. Vol. 24, pp. 67-70
4. Ghate, Prabhu. Microfinance in India – A State of the Sector Report, 2006. Microfinance India. New Delhi. 2006.
5. Mahajan, Vijay, Bharati Gupta Ramola and Mathew Titus, 2000, Dhakka Starting Microfinance in India in K. Basu and K.Jindal (eds.), Microfinance: Emerging Challenges, Tata McGraw-Hill, New Delhi.
6. Management and Research. Centre for Microfinance. 2007
7. M-CRIL. India Microfinance Review 2007
8. Meenu Goyal, Jai Parkash (2011). Women entrepreneurship in India—problems and prospects. International Journal of Multidisciplinary Research Vol. 1, No. 5, pp. 198-202
9. Michael Strong. Empowering Women Entrepreneurs Alleviating Poverty & Promoting Peace through Enterprise Development, FLOW
10. Microfinance Institutions Affects Incumbent Lenders. The Economic Journal. Vol. 115; No. 506, pp. 987-1004. 2005.

11. Patil, Ganesh, Govind, P.S. and Bhamare, Priyanka D. (2008) Microfinance. A Combat against Poverty., The Indian Journal of Commerce, Vol. 61, No. 4, p. 169.
12. Singh, Lakshmeshwar Pd. (2008). Microfinance. The Emerging Horizons for Poor and weaker section. The Indian Journal of Commerce, Vol. 61, No. 4, p. 173.
13. Sriram MS (2002): Information Asymmetry and Trust: A Framework for Studying Microfinance in India. WP No. 2002-09-02. Ahmedabad: Indian Institute of Management. (Mimeo).
14. Rutherford, Stuart (2000): The Poor and Their Money. New Delhi: Oxford University Press.
15. http://www.reliancecommercialfinance.com
16. http://crisil.com/pdf/ratings/CRISIL-ratings_india-top-50-mfis.pdf
17. http://www.iitk.ac.in/ime/MBA_IITK

8

Role and Impact of Information Technology in Indian Banking Services After Liberalization: Trends, Issues and Challenges

Krishna Gopal Chaubey
Associate Professor
NCET, Kanpur
E-mail:chaubeykrishna@yahoo.co.in

ABSTRACT

After liberalization Indian banking is passing through drastic changes. Technology has a definitive role in facilitating transactions in the banking sector and the impact of technology implementation has resulted in the introduction of new products and services by various banks in India. For the last ten years, technology has been the driving force in the banking industry. As foreign and private banks poured huge sums of money to counter the branch advantage of public sector banks, they discovered that technology gives them a large competitive advantage. Some are investing in it to drive the business growth, while others are having no option but to invest, to stay in business. Everyone today is convinced that the technology is going to hold the key to future of banking. The achievements in the banking today would not have make possible without IT revolution. In this backdrop, the paper attempts to trace the latest trends and the role of IT in the banking services, its implications, issues and challenges.

INTRODUCTION

The changes, after the liberalization and globalization processes initiated since 1991, have had a significant impact on the financial sector, particularly on the banking industry. The fast pace of the changes have radically and perceptibility transformed the operational environment of the banking sector. The IT revolution is entirely changing the way banking business is done, and has considerably widened the range of products and increased the expected demands of the customers. The world is becoming a global market, characterized by economic interdependence. National boundaries have become less significant with the interlinked effect of technology, information flows and foreign investment mobility. In the era of liberalization and globalization, the leading banks, therefore, quickly shifted their focus to provide prompt and efficient customer service, offering a variety of hi-tech banking products/services (Vashisht, 2004, p. 2). Economic reforms in the real sectors of an economy will fail to realize their full potential without a parallel reform in the financial sector.

Indian banking today is witnessing sea changes. The liberalization of the financial sector and banking sector reforms have exposed the Indian banks to a new economic environment that is characterized by increased competition and new regulatory requirements. As a result, there is a transformation in every sphere of activities of the banks in India, especially in governance, nature of business, style of functioning and delivery mechanisms.

The new generation banks brought the necessary competition into the industry and spearheaded changes towards higher utilization of technology, improved customer service and innovative products. In spite of their strong and larger network, public sector banks proved to be surprisingly quick and flexible to meet the emerging needs of customers.

CHANGING PATTERN IN THE BANKING INDUSTRY

The changes in the political, economical, social, cultural and environmental perspective can be seen in business environment too. Above all, the business scenario is highly influenced by the changes in the needs and aspirations of the people. The human factors such as, the mindset of the people, ethics and values, social system, lifestyle, work culture, etc., greatly induce the different sections of the people for changing their day-to-day requirements. But today, the degree of such changes is so fast and more frequently experienced by them. Therefore, the consumer status is changed from; isolated to connected, unaware to well-informed, passive to active.

Consumers now seek to exercise their influence in every walk of the business system, interact with firms and co-create value. As the outreach is enlarged in the industry with the increased number of banks and wider network, the customer demands convenience, comfort, speed, cost-effective and quality services in the banking operations. In the recent years the Indian banking industry saw a host of new faces called new generation banks entering with their innovative strategies. All these bankers are generally slim in structure but heavily using the technology and multi-channel facilities to reach out to a large section of the customers.

INFORMATION TECHNOLOGY AND BANKING SERVICES: THE TREND

In this context, Information Technology and Enabled Services (ITES) have emerged as the integrator; assisting banks in managing transformation that takes place continuously. RBI has taken several initiatives with the broad objective of providing systems which impact beneficially on efficient housekeeping in banks, better customer service and overall systemic efficiency. The Reserve Bank has assigned priority to the upgradation of technological infrastructure in the Indian financial system. The RBI's role in the transformational of IT deployment in banking has been commendable. RBI established in 1996 with a vision and foresight, the Institute for Research and Development in Banking Technology (IDRBT). In order to establish an efficient, cost-effective and dependable communication backbone, the Indian Financial Network (INFINET) has been set up. About 150 banks, primary dealers and mutual funds have become members.

Technology has a definitive role in facilitating transactions in the banking sector and the impact of technology implementation has resulted in the introduction of new products and services by various banks in India. During the last decade, payment services offered by banks to the common persons as well as the corporate bodies have improved substantially. It is partly due to increased use of technology in service delivery and partly due to procedural changes necessitated in the wake of competition amongst the banks.

With the introduction of electronic banking, banks are moving their focus of payments from the physical presence of money to the use of electronic money. Electronic banking refers to the use of technology which allows customers to access banking services electronically whether it is to pay bills, transfer funds, view accounts or to obtain information and advices. It refers to the electronic services that are made available to the customers through phone, personal computer, television and the Internet. Customers can perform banking transactions such as balance enquiries, bill payments, transaction histories, and transfer of money between accounts, obtain quotes and submit equity option and mutual fund offers without having to step into the office of the branch. Payments can be made in India in the form of cash, cheque, demand drafts, credit cards, debit cards and also by means of giving electronic instructions to the banker who will make such a payment on behalf of his customers.

DEVELOPMENTAL ROLE OF THE RBI

The Reserve Bank of India (RBI) as the central bank of the country has been playing the said developmental role and has taken several initiatives for a safe, secure, sound and efficient payment system under electronic banking. Payment systems are used by individuals, banks, companies, governments, etc., to make payments to one another. In other words, anybody who has to make a payment to anyone else can use one or the other form of payment system to make such a payment for which IT enabled channels create a platform.

INNOVATION IN BANKING SERVICES

The new private sector banks have the technology to access customer data housed in their central warehouses. They are beginning to use it for generating new business leads. Public sector banks are making a beeline for core banking solutions (CBS)

– the technology that enables them to integrate all customer channels seamlessly. Branches are becoming delivery channels and employees salesmen. Banks are going beyond conventional banking and offering a lot more than vanilla deposits and loans. Following are the innovative services offered by the industry in the recent past.

1. Electronic Payment Services – E Cheques

Nowadays we are hearing about e-governance, e-mail, e-commerce, e-tail, etc. In the same manner, a new technology is being developed in US for introduction of e-cheque, which will eventually replace the conventional paper cheque. India, as harbinger to the introduction of e-cheque, the Negotiable Instruments Act has already been amended to include; Truncated cheque and E-cheque instruments. Electronic payments can also be made in the form of electronic funds transfer (EFT), electronic clearing service (ECS) and through real time gross settlement (RTGS). Many banks in India have begun to offer certain banking services through the Internet that facilitate transfer of funds electronically.

2. Real Time Gross Settlement (RTGS)

Real time gross settlement (RTGS) system, introduced in India since March 2004, is a system through which electronic instructions can be given by banks to transfer funds from their account to the account of another bank. The RTGS system is maintained and operated by the RBI and provides a means of efficient and faster funds transfer among banks facilitating their financial operations. As the name suggests, funds transfer between banks takes place on a 'real time' basis. Therefore, money can reach the beneficiary instantaneously and the beneficiary's bank has the responsibility to credit the beneficiary's account within two hours.

3. Electronic Funds Transfer (EFT)

Electronic funds transfer (EFT) is a system whereby anyone who wants to make payment to another person/company, etc., can approach his bank and make cash payment or give instructions/authorization to transfer funds directly from his own account to the bank account of the receiver/beneficiary. Complete details such as the receiver's name, bank account number, account type (savings or current account), bank name, city, branch name, etc., should be furnished to the bank at the time of requesting for such transfers so that the amount reaches the beneficiarie's account correctly and faster. RBI is the service provider for EFT.

4. Electronic Clearing Service (ECS)

Electronic clearing service (ECS) is a retail payment system that can be used to make bulk payments/receipts of a similar nature especially where each individual payment is of a repetitive nature and of relatively smaller amount. This facility is meant for companies and government departments to make/receive large volumes of payments rather than for funds transfers by individuals.

5. Automatic Teller Machine (ATM)

Automatic teller machine (ATM) is the most popular device in India, which enables the customers to withdraw their money 24 hours a day and 7 days a week. It is a device that allows customer who has an ATM card to perform routine banking transactions without interacting with a human teller. In addition to cash withdrawal, ATMs can be used for payment of utility bills, funds transfer between accounts, deposit of cheques and cash into accounts, balance enquiry, etc.

6. Credit/Debit cards

Credit/debit cards are being widely used in the country as they provide a convenient form of making payments for goods and services without the use of cheques and cash. Banks issue credit/debit cards to their customers. The merchant establishment who accepts credit/debit card payments will claim the amount from the customer's bank through his own bank. For a customer the question may arise; *how is a debit card different from credit card?* Debit card is a direct account access card. (Amount transacted gets debited immediately.) The amount permitted to be transacted in debit card will be to the extent of the amount standing to the credit of the card user's account. On the other hand, a credit card involves provision of credit to the card user, which is paid by the card user on receipt of the bill either in full or partially in installments.

7. Point of Sale Terminal

Point of sale terminal is a computer terminal that is linked online to the computerized customer information files in a bank and magnetically encoded plastic transaction card that identifies the customer to the computer. During a transaction, the customer's account is debited and the retailer's account is credited by the computer for the amount of purchase.

8. Tele Banking

Tele banking facilitates the customer to do entire non-cash related banking on telephone. Under this device automatic voice recorder is used for simpler queries and transactions. For complicated queries and transactions, manned phone terminals are used.

9. Corporate Banking Terminal

Corporate banking terminal enables the large corporate customers to log into the banks database and have access to their accounts/ transactions from their business houses.

10. Electronic Data Interchange

Electronic data interchange is the electronic exchange of business documents like purchase order, invoices, shipping notices, receiving advices, etc., in a standard, computer processed, universally accepted format between trading partners. EDI can also be used to transmit financial information and payments in electronic form. EDI has resulted in huge savings in costs of exchanging trading information.

IMPLICATIONS

The banks quickly responded to the changes in the industry; especially the new generation banks. The continuance of the trend has redefined and re-engineered the banking operations as whole with more customization through leveraging technology. As technology makes banking convenient, customers can access banking services and do banking transactions any time and from anywhere. The importance of physical branches is going down. Thus, the changes have the following implications:

- Anywhere anytime any place banking
- Timeless and placeless banking
- Banking at convenience
- Dismantling of physical structure
- Goodbye to traditional instruments and invitation to new instruments
- Disappearance of conventional risk and arrival of new risks
- Leading to currency-less monetary system

REGULATION AND SUPERVISION

The board for regulation and supervision of payment and settlement systems (BPSS) is a sub-committee of the Central Board of the RBI and is the highest policy making body on payment system. The Board is assisted by a technical committee called National Payments Council (NPC) with eminent experts in the field as members. The Board as well as the council is assisted by a newly created department of payment and settlement systems (DPSS).

The Board has been entrusted with the responsibility to authorize, prescribe policies and set standards for all existing and future payment systems in the country. The Board also has the powers to determine membership criteria to these systems and related policies. The customer may approach the bank concerned to redress the complaint. In case of lack of response/satisfactory redressal by the bank, the customer may approach the grievance redressal cell in the local RBI office, if any. The customer may also approach the office of the banking ombudsman for redressal of his complaint.

Most people today convinced that the Information Technology is going to hold the key of future banking. These developments changed the course of banking in India as it altered the basic platform of the Indian banking. This would not have made possible without the IT revolution. However, technology driven banking can be traced in; hyper competition, shrinking margins and need to reduce cost, meeting the changing customer expectations, offer better and improved products and services, simplify the process and procedures for better management, reduce or alter the risk, resource constraints such as physical and/or financial, pressure from regulators or the conglomeration of few of the above or all.

ISSUES AND CHALLENGES

For the last 10-20 years, technology has been the driving force in the banking industry. As foreign and private banks poured huge sums of money to counter the branch advantage of public sector banks.They discovered that technology gives them a large competitive advantage. Technology is helping the banks to reduce transaction cost and improve efficiency. ITES becomes unique selling proposition (USP) of the many players in the industry as it facilitates the innovations in all functional management activities—accounting and finance, production and designing, marketing and customer management, research and development activities, and so on. In the last decade banks have invested heavily in the technology such as e-commerce, data warehousing and data mining, customer relationship management solution software, knowledge management systems, etc.

Some are investing in it to drive the business growth, while others are having no option but to invest to stay in business. The choice of right channel, justification of IT investment on ROI, e-governance, customer relationship management, security concerns, technological obsolescence, mergers and acquisitions, penetration of IT in rural areas, and outsourcing of IT operations are the major challenges and issues in the use of IT in banking operations. The main challenge, however, remains to motivate the customers to increasingly make use of IT while transacting with banks. For small banks, heavy investment requirement is the compressing need in addition to their capital requirements. The coming years will see even more investment in banking technology, but reaping ROI will call for more strategic thinking.

Everyone today is convinced that technology is going to hold the key to future of banking. The achievements in the banking today would not have possible without IT revolution. Therefore, the key point is while changing to the current environment the banks have to understand properly the trigger for change and accordingly find out the suitable departure point for the change.

CONCLUSION

Banking today is re-defined and re-engineered with the use of Information Technology and it is sure that the future of banking will offer more sophisticated services to the customers with the continuous product and process innovations. Thus, there is a paradigm shift from the seller's market to buyer's market in the industry and finally it affected at the bankers level to change their approach from "conventional banking to convenience banking" and "mass banking to class banking". The shift has also increased the degree of accessibility of a common man to bank for his variety of needs and requirements.

References

1. Arvind Sharma (2007), IT in Banking – Promise of More Benefits, The Hindu Survey of Indian Industry-2007, pp. 54–58.
2. Banerjee, A., and Singh, S. K. (2000). Banking Sector Reforms in India. Deep and Deep Publications Pvt. Ltd., New Delhi.
3. Chauhan, M. (2006). Banking Industry in India: The Developing trends. Monthly Commentary on Indian Economic Condition, May, 57(10), 28–32
4. ICFAI University Press, 33–37.
5. Mittal R.K, and Dhingra Sanjay (2007), Technology in Banking Sector: Issues and Challenges, Vinimaya, Vol.XXVII, No. 4, Jan-March, 2007, pp 14–22.
6. Mohan Chandran.K (2003), Electronic Cheque - The Emerging Payment System, IBA Bulletin, Vol XXV, No.7, July 2003, pp. 6–18.
7. Narayan Tarun (2004), Banking on Technology, Indian Management, Vol. 43, Issue 8, August, 2004, pp. 18–28.
8. Sathish.D and BalaBharathi. Y (2007), Indian Banking Industry:Challenging Times Ahead, Chartered Financial Analyst, February 2007, pp. 68–70.
9. Services: A Study on Indian Private Sector Banks. Indian Management Studies Journal, 11,1–14.
10. Silva, A. FC. Da. (2007). Social Banking - The Need of the Hour. Professional Bankers.
11. Singh, A. K., and Tripathi, S. K. (2007). Perceptual Difference of Quality in Banking.

9

Microfinance: An Instrument to Develop Rural India

Shweta Guwalani
Assistant Professor, JSSGIW, Bhopal, MP
Email: shwetaguwalani09@gmail.com

ABSTRACT

Microfinance is budding as a powerful tool for poverty improvement in the new economy. A majority of the microfinance programs has come up with the clear purpose of dropping poverty and empowering women. Microfinance programs like the Self Help Bank Linkage Program in India have been with time promoting for their positive economic impact and the belief that they empower women. The SHG Program has come up with a new system of saving and lending as a way of delivering microfinance to its predominantly female members. In 1980s, microfinance programs have improved upon original methodologies and extended beyond conventional thinking.

Microfinance is not just about giving micro credit to the poor rather it is an economic development tool whose objective is to assist poor to work their way out of poverty. It covers a wide range of services like credit, savings, insurance, remittance and also non-financial services like training, counseling, etc.

Microfinance is usually understood to bring about the condition of financial services to micro-entrepreneurs and small businesses, which has less access to banking and related services due to the high transaction costs linked with assigning these client categories. It is provided with very small loans to very poor families with the purpose to help them employ in fruitful activities or care for their very small businesses. In addition, an increasing number of microfinance institutions prefer women members as they believe that they are more responsible and trustworthy.

INTRODUCTION

Microfinance is usually understood to entail the provision of financial services to micro-entrepreneurs and small businesses that lack access to banking and related services due to the high transaction costs associated with serving these client categories.

The two main mechanisms for the delivery of financial services to such clients are (1) relationship-based banking for individual entrepreneurs and small businesses; and (2) group-based models, where several entrepreneurs come together to apply for loans and other services as a group.

In some regions, microfinance is used to describe the supply of financial services to low-income employees, which is closer to the retail finance model prevalent in mainstream banking. For some, microfinance is a movement whose object is "a world in which as many poor and near-poor households as possible have permanent access to an appropriate range of high quality financial services, including not just credit but also savings, insurance, and fund transfers." Many of those who promote microfinance generally believe that such access will help poor people out of poverty. For others, microfinance is a way to promote economic development, employment and growth through the support of micro-entrepreneurs and small businesses. It also aims at the following:

- To provide small loans to the rural poor for the working capital requirements.
- Nominal assessment of borrowers and investments as compared to commercial banks.
- These institutions require compulsory savings and group guarantees but no collateral security is being demanded.

Literature Review

Microfinance is a new and dynamic approach which has aided in global poverty eradication and empowerment of women and society by making them financially self-reliant. Professor Yunus, Managing Director of Grameen Bank, promoted it in 1974 in Jobra, a village in Chittagong of Bangladesh, and it has spread all over the world. It is a program that extends small loans and other financial and business services to very poor people for self-employment projects that generate income, thereby enabling them to take care of themselves and their families.

Microfinance is a broad category of services, which includes microcredit. Micro credit is provision of credit services to poor clients. Microcredit is one of the aspects of microfinance and the two are often confused. Critics may attack microcredit while referring to it indiscriminately as either 'microcredit' or 'microfinance'. Microfinance is not just about giving micro credit to the poor rather it is an economic development tool whose objective is to assist poor to work their way out of poverty. It covers a wide range of services like credit, savings, insurance, remittance and also non-financial services like training, counseling, etc.

Salient Features of Microfinance

- Borrowers are from the low income group
- Loans are of small amount – micro loans
- Short duration loans
- Loans are offered without collaterals
- High frequency of repayment
- Loans are generally taken for income generation purpose

Gaps in Financial System and Need for Microfinance

Microfinance plays as a major contributor to financial inclusion and has helped out remarkably in eradicating poverty. Reports show that people who have taken microfinance have been able to increase their income and hence the standard of living. About half of the Indian population still doesn't have a savings bank account and they are deprived of all banking services. Poor also need financial services to fulfill their needs like consumption, building of assets and protection against risk. Microfinance institutions serve as a supplement to banks and in some sense a better one too. These institutions not only offer micro credit but they also provide other financial services like savings, insurance, remittance and non-financial services like individual counseling, training and support to start own business and the most importantly in a convenient way. The borrower receives all these services at her/his door step and in most cases with a repayment schedule of borrower's convenience.

Channels of Microfinance

In India, microfinance operates through two channels:

1. SHG-Bank Linkage Programme (SBLP)
2. Micro Finance Institutions (MFIs)

SHG-Bank Linkage Programme: This is the bank-led microfinance channel which was initiated by NABARD in 1992. Under the SHG model the members, usually women in villages are encouraged to form groups of around 10-15. The members contribute their savings in the group periodically and from these savings small loans are provided to the members. In the later period these SHGs are provided with bank loans generally for income generation purpose. The group's members meet periodically when the new savings come in, recovery of past loans are made from the members and also new loans are disbursed. This model has been very much successful in the past and with time it is becoming more popular. The SHGs are self-sustaining and once the group becomes stable it starts working on its own with some support from NGOs also.

Micro Finance Institutions: Those institutions which have microfinance as their main operation are known as microfinance institutions. A number of organizations with varied size and legal forms offer microfinance service. These institutions lend through the concept of Joint Liability Group (JLG). A JLG is an informal group comprising 5 to 10 individual members who come together for the purpose of availing bank loans either individually or through the group mechanism against a mutual guarantee. The reason for existence of separate institutions, i.e., MFIs for offering microfinance are as follows:

- High transaction cost – generally micro credits fall below the break-even point of providing loans by banks.
- Absence of collaterals – the poor usually are not in a state to offer collaterals to secure the credit.
- Loans are generally taken for very short durations.
- Higher frequency of repayment of installments and higher rate of default.

Objectives of the Study

- To study the role of microfinance in empowering women and society.
- To study the problems and recommendations in the sphere of microfinance.

Methodology of Study

Secondary data has been collected from the various

- Books,
- Journals,
- Research articles
- Internet website.

Research Design Descriptive research design is used in this research paper.

Limitations of the Study

- The study contains only secondary data collected from various sources.
- More information about microfinance can be explored further.

Role of Microfinance in Women Empowerment and Society

Microfinance is a powerful tool to assist the stumbling economies to recover and strengthen, thereby making the lives of millions of poor people more self-respecting and dignified. Microfinance helps in integrating the financial needs of poor people into a country's mainstream financial system. It has been acknowledged that the development of a healthy national financial system is an important goal and catalyst for the broader goal of national economic development, which microfinance serves very well. Microcredit has made women and society more productive by providing them opportunity to be self-dependent in terms of their finance, helping them earn, making them aware of their rights and making them independent which in turn has empowered them. Women are now included into socio-economic activities of the country, they are contributing to family income and are a part of decision-making process in the family and they are able to exercise more control over their reproductive rights. Microfinance helps the poor, including women in not just obtaining loans but also inculcating in them habits of savings, investing in insurance policies and money transfer services. It helps them to raise income, be self-dependent, build up assets and have a better life and better standard of living.

Rural India represents a vast opportunity with its largely unmet demand for financial services. ICICI Bank seeks to tap the significant rural commercial opportunity as well as create a social impact on the rural poor. The primary function of RMAG is to provide financial solutions to the vast rural hinterland. The group is thus responsible for all of ICICI Bank's rural, micro-banking and agri-business initiatives. Poor people, with access to savings, credit, insurance, and other financial services, are more resilient and better able to cope with the everyday crises they face. Even the most rigorous econometric studies have proven that microfinance can smooth consumption levels and significantly reduce the need to sell assets to meet basic needs. With access to micro insurance, poor people can cope with sudden increased expenses associated with death, serious illness, and loss of assets.

Access to credit allows poor people to take advantage of economic opportunities. While increased earnings are by no means automatic, clients have overwhelmingly demonstrated that reliable sources of credit provide a fundamental basis for planning and expanding business activities. Many studies show that clients who join and stay in programs have better economic conditions than non-clients, suggesting that programs contribute to these improvements. A few studies have also shown that over a long period of time many clients do actually graduate out of poverty.

By reducing vulnerability and increasing earnings and savings, financial services allow poor households to make the transformation from "everyday survival" to "planning for the future." Households are able to send more children to school for longer periods and to make greater investments in their children's education. Increased earnings from financial services lead to better nutrition and better living conditions, which translates into a lower incidence of illness. Increased earnings also mean that clients may seek out and pay for health-care services when needed, rather than go without or wait until their health seriously deteriorates.

In our country also, micro finance can be a tool for making women self-reliant. These women can provide their children, including girls, with education which in turn can empower them, thereby setting a new trend of independent women, enjoying their full potential. One of the powerful approaches to woman empowerment is the movement of SHGs, which can transform woman from being alive to live with dignity. The empowerment of women and improvement of their status and economic role needs to be integrated into economic development programs, as the development of any country is inseparably linked with the status and development of women.

Problems and Recommendations

Microfinance also faces various discrepancies and hurdles in the implementation of the services provided by various financial institutes. The following are listed below:

1. Financial Illiteracy: One of the major hindrances in the growth of the microfinance sector is the financial illiteracy of the people. This makes it difficult in creating awareness of microfinance and even more difficult to serve them as microfinance clients. Though most of the microfinance institutions claim to have educational trainings and programs for the benefit of the people, according to some of the experts the first thing these SHG and JLG members are taught is to do their own signature.

2. Inability of Institutions: Inability of MFIs to raise sufficient fund remains one of the important concern in the microfinance sector. In absence of adequate funding from the equity market, the major source of funds for MFIs are the bank loans, which is the reason for high Debt to Equity ratio of most MFIs. MFIs receive debt from banks against their equity and in order to increase their portfolio size they need to increase their debts for which they further need to increase their equity. It very difficult to get bank loans because of their small portfolio size and so they have to look for other costlier sources of fund.

3. Dropouts and Migration of Group Members: Majority of the microfinance loans are disbursed on group lending concept and a past record of the group plays an important role in getting new loans either through SHG-Bank linkage or through MFIs. The two major problems with the group concept are dropouts (when one or more members leave the group) and migration (when one or more members move to another group). Most MFIs lend on the basis of the past record of the group, i.e., SHG or JLG and also on the individuals repayment performance.

4. Transparent Pricing: Though the concern about the transparent pricing in the microfinance sector has been an older one, it is gaining significance with the growing size and the increasing competition in the sector. Non-transparent pricing by MFIs confines the bargaining power of the borrowers and their ability to compare different loan products, because they don't know the actual price. In absence of the proper understanding of the pricing, clients end up borrowing more than their ability to payback which results in over-indebtedness of the borrower.

5. Multiple Lending and Over Indebtedness: Both of these are outcome of the competition among the MFIs. MFIs are ending up giving multiple loans to same borrowers which in some cases is leading to over-indebtedness (a situation where the borrower has taken loans more than her/his repaying capacity) of the borrower. MFIs are getting affected because borrowers are failing to make payments and hence their recovery rates are falling, while over-indebtedness is making the borrower go to depression and in some cases forcing them to commit suicide.

Recommendations

1. Proper Regulation: The regulation was not a major concern when the microfinance was in its nascent stage and individual institutions were free to bring in innovative operational models. However, as the sector completes almost two decades of age with a high growth trajectory, an enabling regulatory environment that protects interest of stakeholders as well as promotes growth, is needed.

2. Field Supervision: In addition to proper regulation of the microfinance sector, field visits can be adopted as a medium for monitoring the conditions on ground and initiating corrective action if needed. This will keep a check on the performance of ground staff of various MFIs and their recovery practices. This will also encourage MFIs to abide by proper code of conduct and work more efficiently. However, the problem of feasibility and cost involved in physical monitoring of this vast sector remains an issue in this regard.

3. Encourage Rural Penetration: It has been seen that in lieu of reducing the initial cost, MFIs are opening their branches in places which already have a few MFIs operating. Encouraging MFIs for opening new branches in areas of low microfinance penetration by providing financial assistance will increase the outreach of the microfinance in the state and check multiple lending. This will also increase rural penetration of microfinance in the state.

4. Complete range of Products: MFIs should provide complete range of products including credit, savings, remittance, financial advice and also non-financial services like training and support. As MFIs are acting as a substitute to banks in areas where people don't have access to banks, providing a complete range of products will enable the poor to avail all services.

5. Transparency of Interest Rates: As it has been observed that, MFIs are employing different patterns of charging interest rates and a few are also charging additional charges and interest-free deposits (a part of the loan amount is kept as deposit on which no interest is paid). All this makes the pricing very confusing and hence the borrower feels incompetent in terms of bargaining power. So a common practice for charging interest should be followed by all MFIs so that it makes the sector more competitive and the beneficiary gets the freedom to compare different financial products before buying.

6. Technology to Reduce Operating Cost: MFIs should use new technologies and IT tools and applications to reduce their operating costs. Though most NBFCs are adopting such cost cutting measures, which is clearly evident from the low cost per unit money lent (9%-10%) of such institutions. NGOs and Section 25 companies are having a very high value of cost per unit money lent, i.e., 15-35 percent and hence such institutions should be encouraged to adopt cost-cutting measures to reduce their operating costs. Also initiatives like development of common MIS and other software for all MFIs can be taken to make the operation more transparent and efficient.

Suggestions

- MFIs should include various constraints, like the share of women clients in the loan and savings portfolio, into client watch and evaluation methods.
- Non-financial services with different conditions to credit access, like well designed women literacy and business training programs to poor people, can help women's access to better jobs and income-generating opportunities and possibly the most effective means of promoting women entrepreneurship.
- Special training programs for entrepreneurship should be organized by government and different non-governmental organizations.
- Government should organize trade fairs to promote the work of entrepreneurs in the rural areas.
- Government should provide separate financial funds for women's entrepreneur and poor people with special benefits, subsidy, and lower interest rate on loans.

CONCLUSION

In today's context we are in an enhanced position where entrepreneurship is increasing at a noteworthy rate. Efforts are being taken at the economy for laws which has guaranteed equal rights of contribution in political process and equal chances and rights in education and employment for every section of the society. In spite of this there are few lacking parameters which needs to be addressed soon. Short-term assistance programs should be focussed which aims at increasing the productivity of women's labor and small enterprises by providing credit, technology, and skill training. Microfinance programs should offer women with detailed tailored products through suitable methods, which can propose competitiveness to their business and their families.

References

1. Microfinance in India edited by K.G. Karmarkar (2008) article SHG Bank Linkage Programme: progress and prospects by Sukhbir Singh.
2. The article by Vighneswara Swamy P.M. an evaluation of transaction costs in SHG BANK LINKAGE Models, Bank Quest The Journal of Indian Institute of Banking and Finance April – June 2007.
3. Reddy CS, APMAS CEO, Sandeep Manak, APMAS Intern, Mahila Abhivruddhi (October 2005) Self-Help Groups: A Keystone of Microfinance in India—Women empowerment & social security.

4. International Review of Business and Finance ISSN 0976-5891 Vol. 2 No. 1 (2010), pp. 29–35 © Research India Publications.
5. Microfinance as an Anti Poverty Vaccine for Rural India Manish Kumar, Narendra Singh Bohra and Amar Johari.
6. Hess, Ulrich and Klapper, Leora F. (2003). "The Use of New Products, Processes and Technology for the Delivery of Rural and Microfinance Loans in India". Background paper prepared for the World Bank. World Bank, Washington DC.
7. Women's Empowerment in Bangladesh," World Development 24 (4): 635–653.
8. Hickson, Robert (1999). Reaching extreme poverty: financial services for the very poor.
9. Nairobi, Kenya: MicroSave-Africa.

10

Integrated Farming System: A Path for Rural Development

A.P.S. Bhadauria
Associate Professor
RIET, Kanpur
*E-mail: apsb71@gmail.*com

ABSTRACT

India is a country of villages. About 70 per cent population of India still lives in the rural area/villages. As per census 2011, 83.3 crore (total population - 121 crore) people of India resides in rural area. Government has taken enormous steps in order to develop the rural area. Integrated farming system (IFS) is one such initiative. It constitutes different enterprises such as food grain production, olericulture, floriculture, mushroom cultivation, fruit cultivation, multistoried cropping, pisciculture, dairy, goat and sheep rearing, bee-keeping, broiler farming (chicken and duck) units, biogas plant and agro-forestry. Integrated farming system is particularly suited to small and marginal famers, which constitute 80 per cent of the total Indian population, presently 121 crore (Census 2011). It helps farmers to meet his domestic requirements and provides employment opportunity to his family/village members for complete year. Being a multi-enterprise system, it also acts as an insurance against failure of any single enterprise due to unforeseen reasons.Government is supporting farmers through its various schemes financial and guidance activities.

While undertaking rural development there is need of little caution. The developmental efforts in the urban area have many draw backs. Today, it is almost impossible to get contamination free air, water and food in the urban area. The level of air pollution is matter of concern as there are many consequences of it like global warming, respiratory diseases, etc. Keeping in view such experiences, there is need to go for natural farming in the interest of all, human as well as nature. Extensive research & development (R&D) activities are required to be taken-up in order to facilitate natural farming. Sincere efforts of all stakeholders will lead to sustainable development as envisaged.

INTRODUCTION

India is a country of villages. About 70 per cent population of India still lives in the rural area/villages. As per Census 2011, 83.3 crore (total population - 121 crore) people of India reside in rural area. Government has taken enormous steps in order to develop the rural area particularly, so that employment opportunities can be provided in such areas. This was also an effort of the government to control migration of rural youths towards towns. Rural development generally refers to the process of improving the quality of life and economic well-being of people living in rural area. Integrated farming system (IFS) which constitutes the different enterprises such as food grain production, olericulture, floriculture, mushroom cultivation, fruit cultivation, multistoried cropping, pisciculture, dairy, goat and sheep rearing, broiler farming (chicken and duck) units, biogas plant, agro-forestry, etc. is/could proving/prove a better venture for rural development. It provides regular employment to village people. Integrated Farming System also takes care of future uncertainties which usually farmers face. In case of failure of one enterprise the other makeovers the loss. Thus, ensure regular income to the farmers. The endeavours of Integrated Farming System, if coupled with natural process, will lead to sustainable development. Sustainability is a challenge which human beings are facing in all area of developments. IFS is boon for the farmers and rural development. Financial institutions under the guidelines of Reserve Bank of India are playing an important role in rural development.

DEVELOPMENT OF RURAL AREAS: A WIND ON CHANGE

Integrated Farming System

Integrated farming system (IFS) is constitution of different enterprises such as food grain production, olericulture, floriculture, mushroom cultivation, fruit cultivation, multistoried cropping, pisciculture, dairy, goat and sheep rearing, bee keeping, broiler farming (chicken and duck) units, biogas plant and agro-forestry.

Integrated farming system is particularly suited to small and marginal famers, which constitute 80 per cent of the total Indian population, presently 121 crore (Census 2011). It helps farmers to meet his domestic requirements and provides employment opportunity to his family/village members for complete year. Being a multi-enterprise system, it also acts as an insurance against failure of any single enterprise due to unforeseen reasons (Sharma, 2013).

ENTERPRISES OF INTEGRATED FARMING SYSTEM

Integrated Farming System (IFS) is a multi-enterprise system. Brief discussion on IFS is put in succeeding paragraphs.

FoodGrain Production Unit: Different cereals such as wheat, rice, maize, etc. are taken in this unit along with pulses and oilseeds. The slurry obtained from biogas plant is used as manure in the fields. Vermiculture units provide enriched vermicompost (1.2-1.6% N, 1.8-2.0% P and 0.50-0.75% plant elements).

Olericulture (Cultivation of Vegetables): Under olericulture, farmers produce variety of vegetables around the year. This is good source of income for the famers throughout the year. Timing of production play a important role in it. Proper care of crops fetches good result in it.

Fruit Cultivation: Guava, banana, papaya, mango, coconut, etc. are such fruits which are grown in this unit. The cost of production is low. Thus, leads to better profit to the farmers. They also help in in checking soil erosion.

Pisciculture: Fish farming is profitable in pond based farming system. Rohu, Catla and prawn, etc., are reared in the pond. A channel is connected from biogas plant to the pond, so that the slurry reached the pond directly and help in development of zooplankton (food for fish).

Dairy Unit: It is one of the most promising businesses at present. It provides milk to the family members and dung for biogas plant. The excess milk is being sold. The wastes of the crops become feed for the cattle. The farmer need not to pay extra for it. The presence of major dairy companies in rural area encouraging farmers to take up this business.

Broiler Farming: In it the house for broiler birds is constructed on the pond and above the water surface. So the dropping of the birds directly fall into the pond water and create zooplankton for fish. The house of the ducks is constructed on the bund of the pond and they act as sanitary agent by cleaning the water.

Biogas Plant: Biogas plant provides cooking gas and light for households, manure for farms and food for fish. It is one of the sustainable ways to meet the energy requirement in rural area.

Any combination of the above can be adopted by the farmers as per situation of farm, climate, total land holding, capital available, labour available and market demand of that particular area.

Apiculture: It is bee keeping. At least six boxes are kept in one hectare area of land. The honey collects bee from mustard, sunflower, and many other flowering trees, herbs and shrubs. The honey obtained is used by households and excess honey is sold.

Floriculture Unit: In order to improve the sanitary conditions and to create scenic beauty, different seasoned and perennial ornamental plants are planted around the farmhouse and on the field bunds or on complete field. Flowers become source for bee in honey production. Flowers give return nowadays.

Agro-forestry: Forests give us: food, oxygen, rains, environment protection, and timber. This enterprise provides fuel for the farm family and feed for livestock. Wood from trees is used for construction of agricultural implements. Green leaves are used as green manure. Trees help in reducing soil erosion. In fact, trees provide life to us and other species on the earth.

FINANCIAL ASSISTANCE TO FARMERS

Government of India has several steps for rural development. The steps are taken with a view to check the migration of rural population to urban area. Under the RBI guidance, banks are providing financial assistance to the farmers at very low rate of interest. As a sample schemes of Bank of Maharashtra are taken in this study. Bank of Maharashtra provides short agriculture loans to farmer at 7 per cent interest out of which governement gives subsidy of 3 per cent. Agriculture loan scheme of Bank of Maharashtra as government initiative to support rural population in rural developmentis given below.

MAHABANK—AGRICULTURE LOAN SCHEMES

Agriculture

Direct Finance to Farmers for Agricultural Purposes

Short-term loans for raising crops, i.e., for crop loans. In addition, advances upto Rs. 10 lakh to farmers against pledge/hypothecation of agricultural produce (including warehouse receipts) for a period not exceeding 12 months, where the farmers were given crop loans for raising the produce, provided the borrowers draw credit from one bank.

Medium and long-term loans (provided directly to farmers for financing production and development needs).

(i) **Purchase of agricultural implements and machinery**

- (a) **Purchase of agricultural implements:** Iron ploughs, harrows, hose, land-levellers, bund-formers, hand tools, sprayers, dusters, hay-press, sugarcane crushers, thresher machines, etc.
- (b) **Purchase of farm machinery:** Tractors, trailers, power tillers, tractor accessories, viz., disc ploughs, etc.
- (c) Purchase of trucks, mini-trucks, jeeps, pick-up vans, bullock carts and other transport equipment, etc., to assist the transport of agricultural inputs and farm products.
- (d) Transport of agricultural inputs and farm products.
- (e) Purchase of plough animals.

(ii) **Development of irrigation potential through**

- (a) Construction of shallow and deep tube wells, tanks, etc., and purchase of drilling units.

(b) Constructing, deepening clearing of surface wells, boring of wells, electrification of wells, purchase of oil engines and installation of electric motor and pumps.

(c) Purchase and installation of turbine pumps, construction of field channels (open as well as underground), etc.

(d) Construction of lift irrigation project.

(e) Installation of sprinkler irrigation system.

(f) Purchase of generator sets for energization of pump sets used for agricultural purposes.

(iii) **Reclamation and land development schemes**

Bunding of farm lands, levelling of land, terracing, conversion of dry paddy lands into wet irrigable paddy lands, wasteland development, development of farm drainage, reclamation of soil lands and prevention of salinization, reclamation of ravine lands, purchase of bulldozers, etc.

(iv) **Construction of farm buildings and structures, etc.**

Bullock sheds, implement sheds, tractor and truck sheds, farm stores, etc.

(v) **Construction and running of storage facilities**

Construction and running of warehouses, godowns, silos and loans granted to farmer for establishing cold storages used for storing own produce.

Production and processing of hybrid seeds for crops.

(vi) **Payment of irrigation charges, etc.**

Charges for hired water from wells and tube wells, canal water charges, maintenance and upkeep of oil engines and electric motors, payment of labour charges, electricity charges, marketing charges, service charges to Customs Service Units, payment of development cess, etc.

Other Types of Direct Finance to Farmers

(a) Short-term loans

1. To traditional/non-traditional plantations and horticulture.
2. For allied activities such as dairy, fishery, piggery, poultry, bee-keeping, etc.

(b) Medium and long-term loans

1. Development loans for all plantations, horticulture, forestry and wasteland.
2. Development loans for allied activities
3. Development of dairying and animal husbandry in all its aspects.
4. Development of fisheries in all its aspects from fish catching to stage of export, financing of equipment necessary for deep sea fishing, rehabilitation of tanks (freshwater fishing), fish breeding, etc.

5. Development of poultry piggery, etc., in all its aspects including erection of poultry houses, pig houses, bee-keeping, etc.
6. Development and maintenance of stud farms, sericulture including grainages, etc. However, breeding of race horses cannot be classified here.
7. Biogas plants.
8. Financing of small and marginal farmers for purchase of land for agricultural purposes.
9. Financing for setting up Agriclinics and Agribusiness Centres by agriculture graduates.

INDIRECT FINANCE TO AGRICULTURE

(i) Credit for financing the distribution of fertilizers, pesticides, seeds, etc.

(ii) Loans upto Rs. 40 lakh granted for financing distribution of inputs for the allied activities such as, cattle feed, poultry feed, etc.

(iii) Loans to Electricity Boards for reimbursing the expenditure already incurred by them for providing low tension connection from step-down point to individual farmers for energising their wells.

(iv) Loans to SEBs for Systems Improvement Scheme under Special Project Agriculture (SI-SPA).

   (a) Loans to farmers through PACS, FSS and LAMPS.

   (b) Deposits held by the banks in Rural Infrastructure Development Fund (RIDF) maintained with NABARD.

   (c) Subscription to bonds issued by Rural Electrification Corporation (REC) exclusively for financing pump set energization programme in rural and semi-urban areas and alsofor financing System Improvement Programme (SI-SPA).

   (d) Subscriptions to bonds issued by NABARD with the objective of financing exclusively agriculture/allied activities.

Other Types of Indirect Finance Such as:

(i) Finance for hire-purchase schemes for distribution of agricultural machinery and implements.

(ii) Loans for constructions and running of storage facilities (warehouse, market yards, godowns, silos and cold storages) in the producing areas.

Loans to cold storage units which are mainly used for hiring, provided:

   (a) the cold storage unit is in the rural areas,

   (b) the unit is used for storing mainly agricultural produce, and

(c) the unit is not registered as a small-scale industrial unit. If the cold storage unit is registered as SSI unit, the loans granted to such units may be classified under advances to SSI, provided the investment in plant and machinery is within the stipulated ceiling.

Source: Hand Book—Bank of Maharastra 2014-15.

TECHNICAL ASSISTANCE TO FARMERS

Besides the soft loans provided from various nationalized banks and cooperatives through different programmes, the technical know-how is being provided to the farmers by the Directorate of Farming Systems Research (ICAR) Meerut (UP), agriculture scientists of Kissan Vikas Kendra (KVKs) and State Agricultural Universities (SAUs) through research-extension network. Apart from that the Agricultural Department of the State has appointed officers (agricultural extension officers, agricultural officers, horticultural officers) to supply the technical know-how to the farmers without any fee. Some agricultural universities also set up agro-clinics to help the farmers. The Government of India has provided the facilities to farmers for question-answer-KCC (Kissan Call Centre) Toll free No. 1800-180-1551.

E-choupalan initiative which use series of village Internet kiosks run by an agricultural conglomerate (ITC Limited) to provide more than four million farmers with real-time and customized market information while offering a platform to them to negotiate sales of their produce to ITC. This helps ensure they receive fairer prices for their crops. (Vikas Pawariya and Sarita Jakhar, 2014)

RURAL DEVELOPMENT WITH A WORD OF CAUTION

The developmental efforts in the urban area have many drawbacks. Today, it is almost impossible to get contamination-free air, water and food in the urban area. There is scarcity of potable water. The level of air pollution is a matter of concern as there are many consequences of it like global warming, respiratory diseases, etc. The side effects of development are badly affecting the health of people. Keeping in view the above, the following is suggested.

Natural Farming: The harmful effects of fertilizers, pesticides and insecticides (Bhatinda Farmer's case of cancer) are now apparent. Hence, there is need to go for natural farming in the interest of all, human as well as nature.

Research and Development (R & D) Activities: There is need to take up extensive research & development activities in order to facilitate natural farming.

Inclusion of Local Farmers in R & D Activities: In the research and development activities the main stakeholder, i.e., farmers may be included. Their involvement will facilitate in taking care of local concerns and practical problems faced by them while innovating any thing for themselves.

Personal Relation of Specialist Officers with Farmers: The agricultural extension officers, agricultural officers, and horticultural officers may maintain personal relations with farmers. Their appointments and activities should not limit to the official formalities only. The farmers and they should be like part of family who are working together for a common cause.

Sincere Execution of Schemes: During interaction with Gram Pradhans and farmers, it has been learnt that they are not aware of many schemes of government. They also reportedly do not get cooperation and support from the specialist officers. Many activities remain in papers as formalities only. Thus, sincere execution of schemes and whole-hearted cooperation and support is desirable for development as envisaged.

CONCLUSION

India is the country of villages. Eighty per cent of the total Indian population, presently 121 crore (Census 2011) is still dependent on farming. Food grain production, olericulture, floriculture, mushroom cultivation, fruit cultivation, multistoried cropping, pisciculture, dairy, goat and sheep rearing, bee-keeping, broiler farming (chicken and duck) units, biogas plant and agro-forestry can be taken up by them. Combination of any of the above can be adopted by the farmers as per situation of farm, climate, total land holding, capital available, labour available and market demand of that particular area. This will ensure them a regular income to them to meet their life requirements.

Integrated Farming System together with financial institutions and other government initiatives will go a long way in developing rural areas. In fact, they are a path for rural development. Management skills can contribute a lot in it. They have proved boon for the development of organizations with greater pace than expected. They are more focused in industrial/urban areas. Now the change is apparent for rural development also. It seems that management skills are more required for rural development as country's two-thirds population resides in rural areas. Development of rural areas will be true development of the country.

References

1. Hand Book—Bank of Maharashtra 2014-15.
2. Sharma Adita, 2013: Integarated Farming Systems in Agriculture: Boon for Farmers, Pratiyogita Darpan Issue 88, November 2013, pp. 878-879.

3. Vikas Pawariya, Sarita Jakhar (2014): Food Security and Other Development Challenges, Pratiyogita Darpan Issue 42, March 2014, p. 80.
4. Definition of Rural Development is extracted from http://en.wikipedia.org/wiki/ Rural_developmentat 07:30am on 14 April 2014.
5. Rural population has been taken from http://censusindia.gov.in/2011-prov-results/paper2/ data_files/india/Rural_Urban_2011.pdf at 07:35am on 14 April 2014.

11

The Role of Information Technology in Developing Rural India

Richa Mishra
Assistant Professor
STEP- HBTI, Kanpur

ABSTRACT

The role of Information Technology to develop agricultural research, education and extension to improve quality of life in rural area is well established. IT can help an average Indian farmer to get relevant information regarding agro-inputs, crop production technologies, agro-processing, market support, agro-finance and management of farm agri-business. The agricultural extension mechanism is becoming dependent on IT to provide appropriate and location specific-technologies for the farmers to furnish timely and proficient advice to the farmers. IT can be a best mean not only to develop agricultural extension but also to expand agriculture research and education system. The excellent scopes of the Internet are waiting to develop agricultural education management through smart exposure of agricultural teachers and educational planners, classrooms, virtual class as well as dropout agricultural learners. For agricultural extension management, role of IT can be encouraged for future resource documentation, as methods of extension and linkage between research and extension.

INTRODUCTION

There are many examples about the role of IT in strengthening rural livelihoods, providing market information and lowering transaction costs of poor farmers and traders. One of them is the Grameen Bank. Grameen Bank, best known as a micro-credit institution, has also pioneered in IT related activities with the poor. As poor people are often unaware of their rights, entitlements and the availability of various government schemes and extension services, IT can also improve their access to the information they need. Through info kiosks or with the help of mobile phones farmers can access information on market prices or on extension services. Timing is often crucial when it comes to the sale of produce. Workers can also get information on available jobs and minimum wages.

The population of India has already crossed 103 billion mark and is still increasing alarmingly putting a great pressure on the food grain production of India. On a rough reckoning it is an acceptable fact that India achieved a marvellous success in food grain production from a bare 51 million tons in 1951-52 to 212 million tons in 2003 but India is still hungry. What would happen if India needs to produce an additional 50 million tons in the near future to feed its increased population? This poses a major challenge not only for the policy makers but also more directly to the agricultural educationist, scientists and extension workers.

IT in agricultural research management for textual and non-textual documentations and deciding prioritization of research areas needs to be reinforced. The crop forecasting, input management, command area management, watershed management, land and water resources development, drinking water potential mapping precision management, natural disaster management, fishery management, hill area development and post-harvest management are the key areas, where Information Technology can play its imperative impact.

The report of the 'Task Force on India as Knowledge Superpower' (GOI, 2001) emphasized the necessity of developing the capacity to generate, absorb, disseminate and protect knowledge and exploit it as a powerful tool to derive societal transformation. Information and Communication Technology (ICT) is seen as an important means of achieving such a transformation. When used as a broad tool for providing local farming communities with scientific knowledge, IT heralds the formation of knowledge societies in the rural areas of the developing world. However, this can only be realized when knowledge and information are effectively harvested for overall agricultural and rural development. IT has a significant role to perform in evolving such a paradigm, as was evident from the "Interdisciplinary Dialogue on IT: Reaching the Unreached" (Swaminathan, 1993).

IT IN AGRICULTURAL EDUCATION MANAGEMENT

Today with over 3,00,000 teachers, the Indian higher education system is the second largest in the world. Considering this scenario of agricultural education the enrolment of students in agriculture remained only 1.5% in agriculture and allied fields. However, the percentage of students studying for professional degrees is extremely low. In Japan more than 30% students are studying for engineering degrees, whereas in India, it is hardly 5%. Everyday where one college is being opened in India, only 6 % of Indian population in the age groups of 18 to 23 years is getting the benefit of higher education. With this background in view, we can be able to understand, how difficult it is to face the challenges of higher education in 21st century which is being dominated by the Information Technology. This clearly indicates that all out efforts need to be made in higher education especially in the field of science and technology to harness the youth potential of rural India.

IT for Research Documentations: Textual and non-textual documents – To present information in the form of written text, e.g., books, periodicals, catalogues, statistical compendia, trade publications, patents, etc., and non-textual documents, e.g. maps, plans, graphs, diagrams, posters, paintings, photographs, slides, sound tapes, films, videotapes, artistic monuments and magnetic documents for computer processing IT can be the best mean in agricultural research management.

IT in Prioritization of Research: The changing scenario under Indian and global context affects the entire process of agricultural research, especially the identification of thrust areas of research. The skill to distinguish between what is urgent and what is important will hold key to the success in deciding priorities. Such skill can be acquired by IT.

IT in Research Communication: The benefits of the Internet connectivity can be utilized for better collaboration amongst scientists for exchange of their views.

IT IN AGRO-BASED RURAL DEVELOPMENT

It is assumed that 60 to 85% of household consumption belongs to agricultural products. So agriculture plays an important role in industrial development, it provides raw materials to industries like cotton textiles, jute, sugar, tobacco, edible and non-edible oils, leather, plantation industries, etc. The food processing industries is also dependent on agriculture. Lots of agro based materials are exported in European and Gulf countries by India. In all such agro-based industries, role of IT needs to be improved. IT tools are very useful in creating effective linkages in agro-based industry activities. These linkages are concerning dissemination of useful information. Linkages of the producers can be with State Federations and National Federation and Boards, Finance Corporation. Advertisement is best way to add value of products. This market again can be very well established with available database of product wise information on products with comprising data of competing nations of the world. IT can help in this direction.

IT IN AGRICULTURAL PRODUCTION

The IT Approach for commercial crops, horticultural crops or floriculture have to focus on Integrated System may be for plant nutrition or plant protection. The well established Integrated Plant Nutrition Approach and Management and Integrated Pest Management (IPM) need to be strengthened with the help of IT tools. The Post Production Technology (PPT) needs to be utilized properly. The end user, beneficiaries and all concerned especially with export of agricultural produce need to be trained to access the Internet facilities available as one of the most useful IT tools of the computer era.

IT AS GEOGRAPHICAL INFORMATION SYSTEM (GIS) IN AGRICULTURE

The use of IT through GIS is very encouraging in India. The important areas like Crop forecasting (procurement policy, crop insurance, relief measure), cropping System (input management: fertilizer, crop diversification, intensification, degradation measures, sustainability measures), Command Area Management, Watershed Management, Land and Water Resources Development, Drinking Water Potential Mapping Precision, Natural Disaster Management (flood, drought),

Fishery (inland, marine), Hill Area Agriculture Development Management, Post-Harvest Management and Precision Farming can be reinforced with the help of Information Technology in India. Few websites are active in India in this field.

Indian Agricultural Websites

- www.ycmou.com/agri
- www.khetiwadi.com
- www.kisan.net
- www.krishiworld.com
- www.nic.in/agrico
- www.pravara.com
- www.agrinto.com
- www.nabard.org
- www.agriwatch.com
- www.ciks.org/agri.html
- www.agri.mah.nic.in

IT INITIATIVES FOR AGRICULTURAL DEVELOPMENT IN INDIA

There have been some initiatives in India, using ICT for agricultural development. In most of these projects, agriculture is only a small component. Indian experiences with IT projects are:

- Gyandoot project (Madhya Pradesh);
- Warana Wired Village project (Maharashtra);
- Information Village project of the M S Swaminathan Research Foundation (MSSRF) (Pondicherry);
- iKisan projcct of the Nagarjuna Group of Companies (Andhra Pradesh);
- Automated Milk Collection Centres of Amul Dairy Cooperatives (Gujarat);
- Land Record Computerization (Bhoomi) (Karnataka);
- Computer-Aidcd Online Registration Department (Andhra Pradesh);
- Online Marketing and CAD in Northern Karnataka (Karnataka);
- Knowledge Network for Grass Root Innovations –Society for Research and Initiatives (SRISTI) (Gujarat);
- Application of Satellite Communication for Training Field Extension Workers in Rural Areas (Indian Space Research Organization); In addition to the above, a few non-governmental organizations (NGOs) have initiated ICT projects such as:
- Tarahaat.com by Development Alternatives (Uttar Pradesh and Punjab);
- Mahitiz-samuha (Karnataka);

- VOICES – Madhyam Communications (Karnataka);
- Centre for Alternative Agriculture Media (CAAM).

Some exclusive agricultural portals are also available, such as:

- Haritgyan.com
- Krishiworld.net
- TOEHOLDINDIA.com
- Agriwatch.com
- ITC's Soyachoupal.com
- Acquachoupal.com
- Plantersnet.com, etc.

Despite the huge potential to harness IT for agricultural development, only a few isolated projects have been initiated in India and a few in other parts of the world. Interestingly, many of these projects were started by NGOs, private organizations, cooperative bodies and governmental organizations other than agricultural departments. This shows the apathy of agricultural development departments towards incorporating IT into their day-to-day activities.

CONCLUSION

Quick dissemination of technological information from the agriculture research system to the farmers in the field and reporting from farmers' feedback to the research system is one of the critical inputs in transfer of agriculture technology. To reach over 110 million farmers, spread over 500 districts and over 6000 blocks is an uphill task. The diversity of agro-ecological situations adds to this challenge further. Farmers' needs are much more diversified and the knowledge required to address them is beyond the capacity of the grass roots level extension functionaries. Today, it is possible to find a solution to this situation by using the potential of satellite based the Internet based technologies to meet the location specific informational needs of the farmers. Information and communication networks are expanding very fast.

The IT based agricultural information on the Internet is building up slowly but surely. There is still a lot of work to be done by policy makers to understand and act on this issue because the satellite-based extension through the use of the Internet facility still has a long way to go to be "user-friendly" for rural people. People who work in the field of satellite based extension should have proper understanding that extension through satellite based communication in rural areas is not impossible but it requires unique administrative, participatory and organizational efforts. Many organizations are supporting a number of SAUs to digitize their technical information on the web. At the same time research and training organizations, both in public and voluntary sectors are being supported in building their capacity to digitize the rural and agricultural information and make it available on the www.

References

1. Bhatnagar, Subhash and Robert Schware (2000). *Information and Communication Technology in Development: Cases from India*, New Delhi: Sage Publications.
2. Chauhan Narendrasinh B., *Information Technology for Agricultural Development in India*, Varanasi: Ganga-Kaveri Publishing House.
3. GOI (2001) 'Report of Prime Minister's Task Force on India as Knowledge Superpower'. Planning Commission, Government of India, New Delhi.
4. Kaushik P. D., and Nirvikar Singh (2004). Information Technology and Broad-Based Development: Preliminary Lessons from North India, forthcoming, *World Development.*
5. Meer Shaik. N, Jhamtani Anita, and Rao D.U.M. (2004). *Information and Communication Technology in Agricultural Development: A Comparative Analysis of Three Projects from India,* Agricultural Research & Extension Network.
6. Richardson, D. (1996). The Internet and rural development: recommendations for strategy and activity – final report. Rome : Sustainable Development Department of the Food and Agriculture Organization of the United Nations. http://www.fao.org/sd-dimensions.
7. Interdisciplinary Dialogue on IT: Reaching the Unreached (Swaminathan, 1993) has been retrieved from http://www.mssrf.org/mssrfdoc/ar/AR1993-1994.pd at 09:00 on 19 March 14.

12

A New Paradigm of Self-Help Group: An Empirical Study on Social Responsibility Initiatives by CEMEX

Charu Modi
Assistant Professor, Faculty of Management, JSSGIW, Bhopal
E-mail: jain04.charu@gmail.com

ABSTRACT

The Corporate Social Responsibility program seeks out to study and progress the efficacy of corporate social responsibility. It is a multidisciplinary and multi-stakeholder effort. Corporate social responsibility covers not only what companies do with their profits, but also how they make them. It goes ahead of patronage and fulfilment and addresses how companies manage their economic, social, and environmental impacts, as well as their relationships in all key spheres of influence: the workplace, the marketplace, the supply chain, the community, and the public policy realm. At its best, a social responsibility policy builds lasting and meaningful relationships with customers, employees and the public. Taking the broader centre of population needs into account is often valuable to a business's financial well-being. Creating long-term partnerships with the community, and avoiding environmentally and socially detrimental short-term solutions, secures enduring economic stability. There are many approaches to social responsibility defined by an organization's size and resources, but working with community-based initiatives, growing philanthropic efforts and developing business plans that are creating shared value are three of the most recognized are Community, Philanthropy and Shared Value. In this paper an attempt is made to discuss about the approach which CEMEX has followed through self-help group model for sustainable growth of their employee and community as a whole.

INTRODUCTION

Defining Corporate Social Responsibility

Corporate Social Responsibility (CSR) is becoming a gradually more important activity to businesses nationally and internationally. As globalization gathers speed and large corporations serve as universal providers, these corporations have increasingly documented the benefits of providing CSR programs in their various locations. CSR activities are now being undertaken all the way through the globe.

The rationale for CSR has been uttered in a number of ways. In essence it is about building sustainable businesses, which need healthy economies, markets and communities.

The key drivers for CSR are:

1. Enlightened self-interest
2. Social investment
3. Transparency and trust
4. Increased public expectations of business

The role of corporate by and large has been understood in terms of a commercial business paradigm of thinking that focuses purely on economic parameters of success.

Where should big corporations be spending their CSR resources?

Value	Purpose	Impact	Benefits
CSR as value creation ☆☆☆☆☆	Innovative and promotes sustainable business model	Fundamental strategic and operational impact	• Shared value (business – institutions and communities) • Promote competitiveness and innovation • Promote a sustainable business model • Integrates business into the community • Develops Human Capital (key in developing countries) • Incorporated into the Business Strategy
CSR as risk management ☆☆☆	Compliance	Medium to high strategic and operational	• Mitigates operational impact • Mitigates operational risks • Supports external relationships
CSR as corporate philanthropy ☆☆	Providing funding and skills	Little strategic and operational impact	• Corporate philanthropy and sponsorships • Short-term benefits/not always sustainable • Limited funds available • Impact diluted because limited budget is allocated to many charities • Corporate competencies and other business assets not fully utilized • Misalignment between business and social responsibility strategies and functions • Result in minimal social and business impact of social programs

Source: http://www.citehr.com/427873-csr.html#1934444

LITERATURE REVIEW

Philosophers like Kautilya from India and pre-Christian era philosophers in the West moralized and encouraged ethical principles while doing business. The concept of helping the poor and deprived was quoted in much of the ancient literature. The idea was also supported by numerous religions where it has been entwined with religious laws. "Zakaat", followed by Muslims, is donation from one's earnings which is purposely given to the poor and deprived. Similarly, Hindus follow the principle of "Dhramada" and Sikhs the "Daashaant". (KPMG, 2008).

In the universal background, the recent history goes back to the seventeenth century when in 1790s, England experienced the first large-scale consumer boycott over the issue of slave harvested sugar which finally forced importer to have free-labour sourcing. In India, in the pre-independence era, the businesses which pioneered industrialisation along with fighting for independence also followed the idea. They put the idea into action by setting up charitable foundations, educational and health-care institutions, and trusts for community development. (KPMG, 2008).

This can be corroborated by the fact that while in 1977 less than half of the Fortune 500 firms even mentioned CSR in their annual reports, by the end of 1990, approximately 90 percent Fortune 500 firms embraced CSR as an essential element in their organizational goals, and actively promoted their CSR activities in annual reports (Boli and Hartsuiker, 2001).

Research Methodology

1. Objectives of the Study

- To study the corporate social responsibility and sustainable development.
- To study the self-help group model adopted in different approach by CEMEX.
- To study how CEMEX blazes the Social Innovation Trail.

2. Research Design: For this study the descriptive research design is used.

3. Data Collection: For this study the data has been collected from the secondary sources like websites, published and unpublished research articles, white papers, working papers and newspapers.

Self-Help Group Approach

Self-help group is a method of organising the poor people and the marginalized to come together to solve their individual problem. The SHG method is used by the government, NGOs and others worldwide. Take the example of the Grameen Bank of Bangladesh, it is a people bank formed by the poor to provide easy loans for themselves. The poor collect their savings and save it in their own banks. In return they receive easy access to loans with a small rate of interest to start their micro unit enterprise. Thousands of the poor and the marginalized population in Bangladesh are building their lives, their families and their society through self-help groups.

1. Socio-economic Changes through SHGs: Villages are faced with problems related to poverty illiteracy, lack of skills, health care, etc. These are problems that cannot be tackled individually but can be better solved through group efforts. Today these groups known as self-help groups have become the vehicle of change for the poor and marginalized. The same concept of SHGs has been used in different perspective by the Mexican corporation named CEMEX, and that program name is "Patrimonio Hoy."

Case Study

Name: CEMEX Corporation of Mexico
Thematic Areas: Community building
Case Study: Patrimonio Hoy

The Mexican construction materials giant company named CEMEX, with $15 billion in revenues and over 50,000 employees, is the world's third-largest seller of cement and—if it's other products are added in, such as readymade cement—the world's biggest supplier of building material. CEMEX leverages its core business strengths—institutional knowledge and experience, employees' talent and time, and capital—to support the social and economic development of communities in ways that foster self-reliance and empowerment.

The case gives an overview of the major social responsibility initiatives including environmental conservation and community welfare undertaken by Mexico based Cemex; one of the largest cement companies in the world. In more than 30 countries in which the company operated, Cemex had taken several steps to improve the quality of living of the people residing in the local communities. The case describes in detail, the Cemex's 'Patrimonio Hoy' program introduced in Mexico, which aimed at fulfilling the housing needs of low income group in Mexico. Under the program, Cemex developed and delivered affordable building products and services to the poor people living in Mexican cities to construct their own houses.

Enabling the Poor to Build Housing

CEMEX Combines Profit & Social Development

The CEMEX Corporation of Mexico has launched an innovative experiment that enables 20,000 very poor families to purchase building materials and upgrade their homes without receiving any subsidies. Rather, this program provides new profit-making opportunities for CEMEX.

Patrimonio Hoy

Introduction of the Program: In 1998 an innovative experiment was undertaken by CEMEX as Patrimonio Hoy with the purpose of providing a market-based solution to tackle the housing needs of low-income families and thereby to make them powerful to progress the quality of their lives.

Objective of the Program: Patrimonio Hoy provides low-income families living in urban and semi-urban areas with right to use the building materials such as cement, concrete blocks, and steel. Patrimonio Hoy provides these products at average market prices as well as microfinancing, technical advice, and logistical support to aid participants in building their own homes. The program accomplishes this through a collaborative network of local CEMEX distributors (new form of SHGs concept); community-based promoters, mainly women trained and empowered through the program that build faith and make safe participation of community members; and the families themselves.

Contribution: In addition to housing, Patrimonio Hoy contributes to the improvement of local public school infrastructure, including classrooms, bathrooms, and sports facilities, with the active participation of the program participants.

Benefits of the Program: The benefits of Patrimonio Hoy accrue not only to the participants but to the community at large and our company.

Challenges Patrimonio Hoy faces two key challenges.

- The first, which is also a primary goal, is to replicate the model in other developing countries.
- The second is to integrate social and environmental features.
- To address these challenges, they have undertaken the following:
    - A pilot program to introduce energy-efficient appliances to raise consciousness of climate change while serving participants decreases energy usage and costs.
    - Research to analyze and update the business model for more effective scalability and to develop a plan to enter new geographic regions at full scale.
    - An initiative to provide additional business training and new microfinance products.
    - Feasibility studies for launching Patrimonio Hoy in other developing countries.

Their success with Patrimonio Hoy has encouraged the development of other social enterprises that provide market-based solutions to help low-income families to sustain themselves and contribute to the development of their communities.

The goal of CEMEX's Company Social Responsibility is to guarantee a sustainable social environment.

Business Ethics
Quality of life in the company
Linking with the company
Environment Economic
Development of the Communities

Findings and Suggestions

By looking into the various steps of organization taking in terms of corporate social responsibility, is unparalleled. The organization like CEMEX has been an example for others to improve the standard of employees by helping them in building their own employee's home and on the same parameters building the whole community. The various outcomes of the program at CEMEX are as:

Outcomes of the successful program: For example, indicators of the success of the program in Mexico alone include the following:

- Participants are able to build their homes or additions three times faster and at a third of the average cost to build a home in Mexico.
- Participants gain access to the credit markets. Since inception, Patrimonio Hoy has advanced more than USD135 million in micro credits.
- The market value of homes built through Patrimonio Hoy is approximately 20 percent higher as a result of the higher quality and functionality of the structures.
- The program creates jobs mainly among local masons and those trained as promoters; 95 percent of promoters are women, of which half had no previous working experience.
- Approximately one-third of participants use their homes, or extra rooms that they have built through their participation in Patrimonio Hoy, to build their own businesses.
- Improvement of local public school infrastructure, including classrooms, bathrooms, and sports facilities, with the active participation of the program participants.
- In all, Patrimonio Hoy helps us build long-term relationships and trust within underserved communities and increases our competitiveness within the low-income market segment.
- So far, Patrimonio Hoy has helped the Cemex bottom line by tripling the rate of cement consumed by its low-income, do-it-yourself home-builders. This amount has increased from 2300 pounds consumed once every four years, on average, to the same amount being consumed in 15 months.

When the CSR activity of a company is closely related to the company's underlying business, the company should link the corporate brand with the activity. The brand and the social impact will be strengthened. When a company has experienced negative publicity, it should note that any CSR activity may be seen as self-serving. Downplay the association between the brand and the activity. Employees volunteer in the community, the company must avoid overt publicity efforts. Let employees serve as "ambassadors" for the CSR activity and, by inference, for the company brand.

CONCLUSION

A growing multitude of organizations are finding innovative and prosperous ways to grow their business while simultaneously helping people in need and sustaining our fragile planet. The principles we have offered will hopefully inspire and guide many other organizations to identify unique, viable, and worthwhile opportunities to nurture their business prosperity, as well as the communities in which we and future generations live and work. CEMEX fosters positive, long-term relationships with its key stakeholders to address the pressing needs and concerns of society. Throughout its history, the company has sought to be a good corporate citizen with sustainability being an integral part of its business.

References

1. KPMG report, 2008
2. http://megselfhelp.gov.in/resources/SHG%20Concept%20-%20English.pdf
3. http://www.self-help-approach.com/Aboutus.aspx
4. http://www.forbes.com/sites/csr/2010/11/12/blazing-the-social-innovation-trail-cemex-continues-to-thrive/
5. http://www.cemex.co.uk/cemex-recognized-as-a-leader.aspx
6. http://www.cemex.com.eg/Sustainability/SocialResponsibility.aspx
7. http://www.scribd.com/doc/142311354/CEMEX
8. http://csrwestafrica.com/2011/07/08/csr-activities-and-corporate-brands/

13

Intrinsic Motivation: An Analytical Study in the Light of Jeevan Vidya and Its Application to Human Resource Management

Garima Jain
Faculty Trainee
Institute of Bank Personnel Selection, Mumbai
E-mail: clicktogarima@gmail.com

ABSTRACT

This article is an attempt to focus on intrinsic motivation in the light of Jeevan Vidya – which is a modern spiritual science of self-verification. Basing the employee training and retention on these principles, shall be quite helpful. A skilled employee who is laid down for behavioural issues can be "cured" permanently; also the amount of expenditure on trying to motivate the employee through rewards can also be cut down. The understanding of the mentioned principles can elevate the integrity of the employee as well as his/her commitment to the organization.

Considering that personality is the manifestation of the self, an understanding of the self as per Jeevan Vidya may prove helpful. The self may be defined as the aliveness of a human that co-exists with the body. When we look beyond the mechanical body of a person, we can realize something running those mechanisms. This something that remains with the body is called the self. This has also been called the consciousness. This consciousness feels sad, happy or elated. All the feelings reside here, i.e., in the self.

The following chart describes the dynamics of an individual –

Human = I (self) (In Co-existence with) Body

⇆

Information exchange between self and body

Need	Abstract (e.g.- feelings)	Physical objects
Need with respect to time	Continuous	Temporary
Need with respect to Quality/ Quantity	Qualitative	Quantitative (Limited)

The self needs abstract things like happiness, bliss, satisfaction, love, respect, and so on. The needs of the body are varied physical and chemical objects. Herein a point that can be noted is that the organizations can constructively fulfill the abstract needs of the employees that relate to feelings. These feelings are on a very different plane than the concrete needs of the body. An illustration in terms of honoring employees can prove useful. To honor a person, the concrete objects like flowers and gifts are **just symbolic**. The sense of fulfillment that an employee will have when serving an organization will not arise from his/her material gains from the service of the organization. The material gains that translate themselves into the needs of the body, satiate exactly those, the needs of the body. The real essence of honor lies somewhere else – it lies in how the organization treats the employee at large.

The self derives power from desire, thought and expectation—desire being the primary source. The desires may come from preconditioning (set of beliefs) or may arise from sensation based pleasures or from natural acceptance. The understanding of desire that comes from preconditioning , the understanding of what will a person be driven towards or away when operating under a particular set of beliefs (preconditioning) also, desire for the course would he take up to fulfill it is the major study of behavior and personality and basis of psychological predictions. This principle forms a base for performance appraisals. As these preconditionings or beliefs remain relatively unchanged throughout the lifespan of an individual it leads to the accuracy of predictions and results upon testing. Jeevan Vidya proposes that beyond the desires lie the power of the activities of realization and understanding. These have the power to change the preconditionings and the beliefs on the basis of natural acceptance (what an human naturally accepts without any external force) and thus the personality.

Until the self verifies things at its own right, the desire, thoughts and selections happen on the basis of preconditioning and so seem to be endless and contradictory, thereby creating conflicts (which may also be dealt with dysfunctionally) in thoughts and environment. The self-verification or validation can be done through self-exploration. In this process any information is taken to be as a proposal and these proposals are investigated and verified on an individual basis. This is guided by the natural acceptance of these proposals to the self.

This verification starts with identifying the gap between "What I am?" and "what I want to be?" When this question is investigated within, the answer to the former question is a matter of individual differences and perceptions, however what anyone wants to be remains constant, i.e., the desire of every human being is the same. Irrespective of varied individual factors everyone wants to be happy and live righteous lives. So the probable answers may be I am sad but I want to be happy, I am bad but I want to be good. To seek the correct path to happiness remains a constant and unchanged desire of everyone.

Even the people who claim the acceptance of being sad tend to have a vision that being sad in the present will help them (in some cases even guarantee) find some eternal happiness in the future. Most people who have resigned to the fact that happiness and its continuity is a utopian idea or cannot be accomplished through the correct path, have confessed that the desire remains the same—at the level of desire, it is to be happy and live righteous life. They choose to discard a desire for varied reasons, but the desire is there. This experiment/process has been vastly carried out with varied sets of people in the past decade and the results have been amazingly uniform. Thus, one thing that gets certain about gold is that it wants to be pure. As per this school, anything a human does has to be accepted by him as correct and leading to happiness or helping to maintain the state of happiness. Without this assurance in place no individual ever does anything.

The faculty within everyone that does not look for scriptures, instruments, or other people's opinions has been called natural acceptance. It is naturally acceptable to us to be happy. It is also naturally acceptable for us to be happy continuously. There is no scientific formula or preset involved here, and it is plain simple binary 0 or 1. The 0 stands for being unhappy and the 1 stands for being happy. All of us choose 1. Even the ones who choose 0, yield with some investigation that they will be ensured 1 through the 0. This yields objective answers in yes or no. This faculty resides in the self.

Considering the case of two salespersons who could not meet the set target. Employee A, who blows up his sales figure, assumes that this act will give him benefit that may lead to happiness and that falsifying isn't a bad thing . He/she may know that falsifying is a malpractice, but until he/she is convinced of the fact that it is alright if he/she falsifies (once or repeatedly), he/she will not indulge in the act of falsifying. He/she may agree to or accept some risk as a part and parcel of the trade or exchange with the desired object that gives him/her happiness. As per his/her perception, from his/her set of individual belief system, he/she is taking the path of happiness and the correct path as well. This is the basis of saying that all of us are the same. The one who is falsifying is doing so, because his preconditioning or belief has initiated in him the desire to cheat, with agreement to the fact that the act of falsifying isn't so incorrect considering his/her situation or the "unfair" appraisal policy of the company.

Another employee B who decides not to cheat will also refer to a set of beliefs that initiates in him/her the desire to be "honest". The beliefs create the difference in desires and actions. Conflicting beliefs lead to conflicting desires and the one that finds more support in the thought process wins the conflict. However, when passed through the test of self-verification on the basis of natural acceptance, both sets of people have the same desire – the desire to do something that is right in the given circumstance. Their definition of right – as far as based on natural acceptance, is the same for everyone, but when based on preconditioning will differ vastly. The decision of employee A is subject to the fact that at this situation and for this particular presentation, it is the right thing to do. As the circumstance changes, the decision also will change, as in this case it is based on artificial acceptance. For that employee to cheat, it is necessary that he/she gives ample importance to the presentation, to the remarks gained, to the positive by-product of remarks and less importance to the humiliation he/she may have to face. However, for him/

her not to falsify, needs only one criterion, the understanding and realization that falsifying is not the right thing for him/her to do.

Once that happens, the employee will ensure that he/she does not have to falsify. He/she will put in efforts to improve his/her selling skills and that will be a natural effort, when based on understanding and realization. On the basis of this understanding he/she will be able to decide on things correctly and the correct decision will lead to harmony and happiness – the effort will be natural. It will flow from within the individual and there shall be no force required. Also there will be no need of either a reward or an incentive – to motivate the employee in question.

References

1. Nagraj A., 1998, Jīvana Vidya Ek Parichaya, Jīvana Vidya Prakasan, Amarkantak.
2. Gandhi M. K., 1938, Hind Swaraj, Navjeevan Publishing House, Ahmedabad
3. The Teacher's Manual: A Foundation Course in Human Values and Professional Ethics, R. R. Gaur, R. Sangal and G. P. Bagaria, Excel Books, New Delhi.
4. A Foundation Course in Human Values and Professional Ethics, R. R. Gaur, Sangal R. and Bagaria G. P., Excel Books, New Delhi.
5. Muhammad Yunus, Banker To The Poor, Penguin Books, New Delhi.
6. Muhammad Yunus, Creating a World Without Poverty, Penguin Books, New Delhi.
7. Muhammad Yunus, Building Social Business, Penguin Books, New Delhi.
8. Pavan K. Varma, The Great Indian Middle Class, Penguin Books, New Delhi.

14

Relationship between Employee Motivation and Organizational Effectiveness

Rashmi Singh
Assistant Professor
Department of Management
Rama Institute of Engineering & Technology, Kanpur
E-mail:rashmi.hrexpert@gmail.com

K.P. Singh
Assistant Professor
Department of Management
Rama Institute of Engineering & Technology, Kanpur
E-mail:kps907@gmail.com

ABSTRACT

The purpose of this paper is to identify the factors that affect employee motivation and examine the relationship between organizational effectiveness and employee motivation. A model was designed based on the literature, linking factors of employee motivation with employee motivation and organizational effectiveness. Three hypotheses were built based on the literature and the models were tested in perspective of the previous studies and literature. The literature and various studies concluded that factors: empowerment and recognition have positive effects on employee motivation. More the empowerment and recognition of employees in an organization is increased, more will their motivation to work will enhance. Also there exists a positive relationship between employee motivation and organizational effectiveness. The more the employees are motivated to tasks accomplishment higher will the organizational performance and success. The study focuses on the practice and observance of the two central factors, empowerment and employee recognition for enhancing employee motivation which leads to organizational effectiveness. The organizations should design their rules, policies and organizational structures that give space to the employee to work well and appreciate them on their tasks fulfillment and achievements.

INTRODUCTION

It is a must for management, and other senior managers to think that each and every employee should have positive attitude for achievement of organization's common objectives, which only come through good leadership along with right kind of motivation practices and skills for achievement of results. To lead a person with right kind of motivation an organization should have clear vision in their mind along with and highly motivated, result oriented and achievement approach through which employee can do miracle for the organization. If an individual goals matches with the organization's goal, it would be fruitful for both employee and as well as for employer.

In the context of globalization, privatization and liberalization it is very challenging to design the behavior of employees in accordance with that of organization's requirement as workforce has lots of diversity. Workforce has diversity on the basis of race, religion, ethnicity, caste, nationality, language. Organizations have to understand human behavior on the basis of mental, physical, social and economic ground as well. The issue is how to study the behavior of human being who is working in an enterprise for leading, motivating and modernizing him in skillful employee. There are number of factors which influence a human for retort and respond in personal and professional life:

HUMAN BEHAVIOR AND NEEDS

Behavior of human being can be understood on the basis of his needs. Maslow (1954) suggested that human needs could be structured into five categories in a hierarchy of ascending order of prepotency and probability of appearance: (a) physiological; (b) safety and security; (c) belonging and love; (d) esteem; and (e) self-actualization in the form of basic need, social, environmental, ego, psychological, social needs, etc. Harvey (1973) has noted, from a policy point of view, nine areas of needs: (a) food; (b) housing; (c) medical care; (d) education; (e) social and environmental services; (f) consumer goods; (g) recreation; (h) neighborhood amenities; and (i) transport facilities. While these definitions of needs are functional and do provide a loose boundary for what may be considered need or no-need, they may not be able to differentiate the needy from the no-need groups. In this regard, Bradshaw (1972) has provided a methodology in making a 'real' need possible. His proposal was to first delineate four types of social needs, namely: (a) normative; (b) felt; (c) expressed; and (d) comparative, then to examine their presence in a given situation. The presence of all types of needs is equated to real need: (a) ***Normative need*** tends to be a desirable standard and is set by professionals, policy makers or social scientists, against which the actual standard is compared. Those below the standard are said to be in need of support and special services. (b) ***Felt need*** *is equated* to what people want. It can be defined easily by asking service users or potential users what they wish to have. (c) ***An expressed need*** is generally taken as equivalent to demand, as the unmet need. The notion is that one does not make a demand unless one feels the need. (d) ***Comparative need*** is measured by reference to a user already receiving the service in question. Therefore, a person is in comparative need if he or she has the same or worse characteristics as someone receiving the service.

Understanding human behavior is a complex task as every human being has got unique programming and his behavior can be understood by UPC (Understanding of human, Prediction of behavior, Control of behavior) Model & SOBA (S-stimuli, O-organize, B-behavior, and A-action) model. An individual is guided or influenced by its internal and external stimuli like social, political, economical, cultural, psychological stimuli. Individual then organize all these according to their own ways. Their behavior and action is based upon the stimuli.

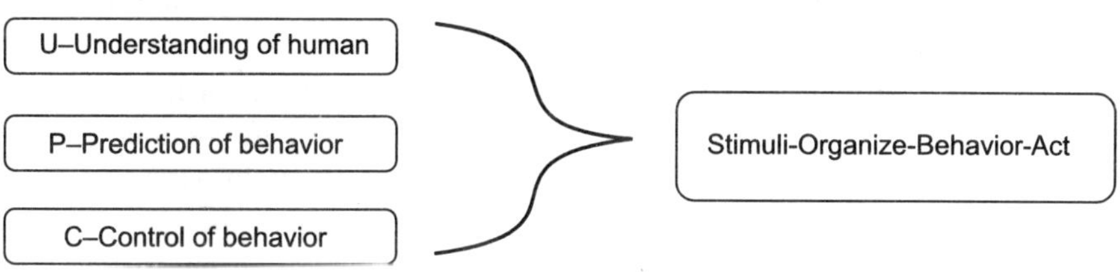

ORGANIZATION/PERSONAL GOAL

It is very critical and unpredictable that which kind of leadership is required for an employee and what are those motivating factors (Carrot, stick, job enlargement or job enrichment) monetary or non-monetary inducement which more influence an employee for achievements of goal. One person may be glad to get financial reward while another might not feel the same level of joy and may prefer satisfaction in terms of less pressure in the given job. Human behavior is the sum of total activities performed by human beings which is influenced by the stimuli such as personal, cultural, values, ethics, leadership and motivation along with skills having with employee as (communication, presentation, managerial, interpersonal, entrepreneurship, customer caring), etc.

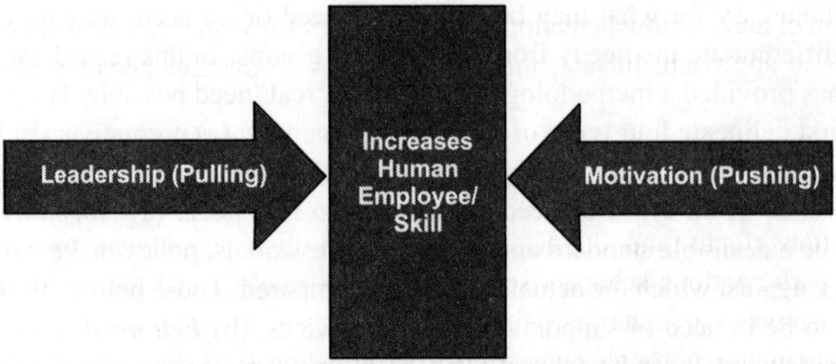

Employee can do miracle only if it is well directed and well equipped and having right direction of leadership (autocratic, bureaucratic, democratic and laissez-faire, etc). So like this way organization pull as well push their employee to achieve their goals.

MOTIVATION

According to Webster's New Collegiate Dictionary, a motive is "something a need or desire that causes a person to act". "Motivate" in turn, means "to provide with a motive," and motivation is defined as "the act or process of motivating". Consequently, motivation is the performance or procedure of presenting an intention that makes a person to capture some accomplishment (Shanks N. H.). Motivation is derived from the word "motivate", means to move, push or influence to proceed for fulfilling a want (Kalimullah et al., 2010).

Bartol and Martin (1998) describe motivation as a power that strengthens behavior, gives route to behavior, and triggers the tendency to continue (Farhad et al., 2011). This explanation identifies that in order to attain assured targets; individuals must be satisfactorily energetic and be clear about their destinations. In view of Bedeian, (1993) it is an internal drive to satisfy an unsatisfied need and the will to accomplish. Motivation is a procedure that initiates through a physiological or psychological want that stimulates a performance that is intended at an objective. It is the concluding product of interface among personality behavior and organizational distinctiveness (IRCO). It symbolizes those psychological procedures that found the stimulation, route, and determination of deliberate actions that are target business oriented (Farhad et al., 2011). Also motivation is a progression of moving and supporting goal-directed behavior (Chowdhury M.S. 2007). It is an internal strength that drives individuals to pull off personal and organizational goals.

Motivation is a set of courses concerned with a kind of strength that boosts performance and directs towards accomplishing some definite targets (Kalimullah et al., 2010). According to Barron (1983), it is an accrual of diverse routes which manipulate and express our activities to attain some particular ambitions. (Porter and Miles (1974) proved that the motivation boosts, expresses and continues. The motivation of an individual envelops all the motives for which he selects to operate in a definite approach. In fact, motivation is "inside another person's head and heart".

EMPLOYEE'S MOTIVATION

Organizations focus and do effort to empower their employees by different ways of participations schemes such as decision making and taking, designing policies, suggestion schemes, financial participation, participation at board level, participation through ownerships, participation through complete control, participation through staff or work councils, participation through joint councils and committees, participation though collective bargaining, The employee can be more productive, effective , understandable and controlled through job enlargement and job enrichment. Job enlargement means expanding the job by content-adding task elements horizontally, and job enrichment means that additional motivators are added to the job so that it is more rewarding. The purpose of job enlargement and job enrichment is to relieve the boredom of the worker which flows from excessive specialization in mass-production industries so that the job itself may be a source of self-satisfaction. Job enlargement and job enrichment do provide for workers' participation because they offer freedom and scope to them to use their judgment. So, these are some basic techniques through which one can motivate the employees whereas there are some motivational tools an theories that guide us to motivate the individual. One of the most popular and widely accepted theories is need hierarchy theory by Abraham Maslow. Maslow gave the theory of motivation based upon the human need assuming that human need goes in ascending order. As and when a need is satisfied, another need arises and individual tries to get that need that higher than that of the previous need.

It is imperative to say that only the theories of motivation will not help the managers to motivate their employee, they need to understand other techniques such as management by objective (MBO), flexible working hours, two-tier pay system, flexible benefits and the like. MBO is a formal set of procedures that begins with goal setting and contributes through performance review. In the process of motivating any employee managers have to understand whether monetary factors can motivate the employee or not. There are several factors other than that of monetary that motivates the employees like recognition, growth and self-respect, etc.

Employee motivation is one of the policies of managers to increase effectual job management amongst employees in organizations (Shadare et al., 2009). A motivated employee is responsive of the definite goals and objectives he/she must achieve, therefore he/she directs its efforts in that direction. Rutherford (1990) reported that motivation formulates an organization more successful because provoked employees are constantly looking for improved practices to do a work, so it is essential for organizations to persuade motivation of their employees (Kalimullah et al., 2010). Getting employees to do their best work even in strenuous circumstances, is one of the employees most stable and greasy challenges and this can be made possible through motivating them.

ORGANIZATIONAL EFFECTIVENESS

Composition of people which formulate independent business identity for some specific purpose is commonly known as organization and getting desired outcome within defined resources is treated as effectiveness. Organizational effectiveness is the notion of how effectual an organization is in accomplishing the results the organization aims to generate. It plays an important role in accelerating organizational development. It is the net satisfaction of all constituents in the process of gathering and transforming inputs into output in an efficient manner (Matthew et al., 2005). Organizational effectiveness is defined as the extent to which an organization, by the use of certain resources, fulfils its objectives without depleting its resources and without placing undue strain on its members and/or society(Mary et al., 1996). It is the maximum combined utility of the primary constituents (Matthew et al., 2005). The study is aimed to determine the factors that increase employee motivation and the relationship of organizational effectiveness with employee motivation.

FACTORS AFFECTING EMPLOYEES' MOTIVATION

No one works for free, nor should they. Employees want to earn reasonable salary and payment, and employees desire their workers to feel that is what they are getting (Houran, J., 2011). Money is the fundamental inducement, no other incentive or motivational technique comes even close to it with respect to its influential value (Sara et al., 2004). It has the supremacy to magnetize, maintain and motivate individuals towards higher performance. Frederick Taylor and his scientific management associate described money as the most fundamental factor in motivating the industrial workers to attain greater productivity (Adeyinka et al., 2007). Research has suggested that reward now cause satisfaction of the employee which directly influences performance of the employee (Kalimullah et al., 2010). Rewards are management tools that hopefully contribute to firm's effectiveness by influencing individual or group behavior. All businesses use pay, promotion, bonuses or other types of rewards to motivate and encourage high-level performances of employees. To use salaries as a motivator effectively, managers must consider salary structures which should include importance organization attach to each job, payment according to performance, personal or special allowances, fringe benefits, pensions and so on (Adeyinka et al., 2007). Leadership is about getting things done the right way, to do that you need people to follow you, you need to have them trust you. And if you want them to trust you and do things for you in the organization, they need to be motivated (Baldoni. J., 2005). Theories imply that leader and followers raise one another to higher levels of morality and motivation. Motivation is purely and simply a leadership behavior. It stems from wanting to do what is right for people as well as for the organization. Leadership and motivation are active processes (Baldoni. J., 2005). Empowerment provides benefits to organizations and makes sense of belonging and pride in the workforce. In fact, it builds a win-win connection among organizations and employees; which is considered an ideal environment in numerous organizations and their employees. Empowering can flourish virtual human capacities. Empowered employees focus their job and work-life with additional importance and this leads to constant progress in coordination and work procedures. Employees execute their finest novelties and thoughts with the sense of belonging, enthusiasm and delight, in empowered organizations. Adding up, they work with a sense of responsibility and prefer benefits to the organization (Yazdani, B.O. et al., 2011). From the literature, gathered for the study, the factors that enhance employee motivation are fair pay, incentives, special allowances, fringe benefits, leadership, encouragement, trust, respect, joint decision making, quality of supervision, adequate working relationships, appreciation, chances for growth, loyalty of organization, identification and fulfillment of their needs, recognition, empowerment, inspiration, importance attached to their job, safe working conditions, training and information availability and communication to perform actions.

OBJECTIVE OF THE STUDY

The main objective of the study is to analyze the impact of employees motivation on organizational effectiveness. The sub-objectives of the study are:

- To determine the factors that increase employees motivation.
- To examine the relationship between employees motivation and organizational effectiveness.

The conceptual framework of the study is:

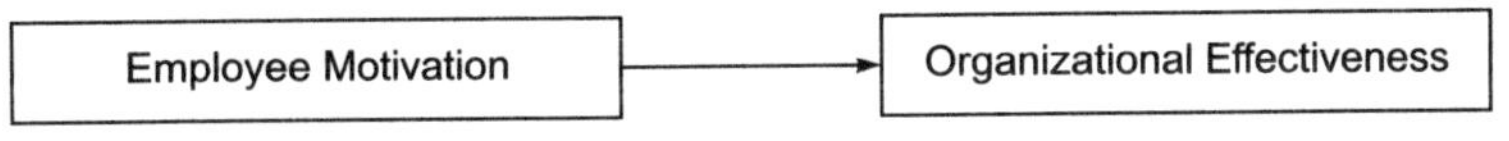

The following is the model of the study which will be further discussed and justified.

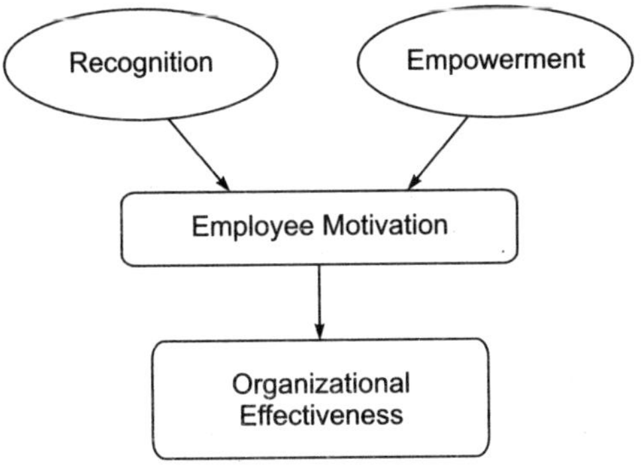

Hypotheses

Based on the literature and model the study is designed to test the following hypothesis:

- H1: There is an effect of recognizing employee's work on their motivation to work.
- H2: There is an effect of empowering employee's in tasks on their motivation to work.
- H3: There is a relationship between employee's motivation and organizational effectiveness.

RECOGNITION AND EMPLOYEE MOTIVATION

According to Maurer (2001) rewards and recognition are essential factors in enhancing employee job satisfaction and work motivation which is directly associated to organizational achievement (Jun et al., 2006). Kalimullah Khan conducted a study in which he examined the relationship between rewards and employee motivation in commercial banks of Pakistan. The study focused on four types of rewards of which one was recognition which he tested through Pearson correlation. The results showed that recognition correlates significantly (0.65) with employee work motivation (Kalimullah et al., 2010).

An empirical study was conducted in India to measure the impact of reward and recognition on job satisfaction and motivation. 125 questionnaires were distributed and filled by employees of different sectors. The results showed that there exists a significant ($r = 0.13$, $p < 0.05$) relationship between recognition and employee work motivation (Rizwan et al., 2010).

A study was conducted in India to examine the job satisfaction among bank employees in Kanpur. A structured questionnaire survey was used and data was gathered from 5 bank's employees. The value of correlation coefficient for recognition was 0.251 which shows that its relationship with job satisfaction is positive. Job satisfaction is directly associated with internal work motivation of employees that enhances as the satisfaction of employees increases (Salman et al., 2010). That is why a study says that deficiency of appropriate recognition and rewarding reduces employees work motivation and job satisfaction. Hence, administration of organizations and institutions should build up the arrangement for giving that rewards and recognition to enhance employee job satisfaction and motivational level (Reena et al., 2009). The above literature, studies and discussion fully supports first hypothesis that recognizing employees work increases their motivation to accomplish tasks and execute responsibilities towards them by the organization.

EMPOWERMENT AND EMPLOYEE MOTIVATION

According to (Bennis, 1989; Block, 1987; Kanter, 1977) empowerment is defined as an approach to leadership that empowers subordinate as a main constituent of managerial and organizational effectiveness (Honold, L, 1997). Bowen & Lawler (1992) expressed empowerment as a site to permit employees to formulate decisions (Amin et al., 2010). Empowering is giving authority and liberating potential of employees.

The main driving force of empowerment is having larger control over, how jobs are done and carried for more growth and productivity (Smith, B, 1997). According to Tannenbaum (1968), it is the study of internal organization power and control which illustrated that the distribution of power and control enhances organizational effectiveness (Honold, L,1997). Rappaport (1987) defined empowerment process as mastering on problems of organizations by people, organizations and societies (Amin et al., 2010). Empowering makes employees feel that they are appreciated and for making it possible continuous and positive feedback on their performance is essential (Smith, B, 1997). The above literature, studies and discussion fully supports second hypothesis that empowering employee's in tasks effects on their motivation.

EMPLOYEE MOTIVATION AND ORGANIZATIONAL EFFECTIVENESS

Employee satisfaction and motivation towards work refers to prospects of the employee about the organization and his approaches frontward his service (Ali et al., 2011). Organizational effectiveness refers to locating targets and attaining them proficiently in spirited and energetic surroundings (Constant, 2001).

A study was done to examine the relationship of organizational effectiveness and employee performance and motivation in the telecommunication and banking sector. A sample of 103 respondents was taken and Pearson correlation was applied. The results showed that there exists significant positive correlation (0.287) between employee motivation and organizational effectiveness.

The autocratic leadership styles, mechanistic design of organization and authoritarian rules as practiced in African organizations, are all where decision making is concerned only to top management and employees are just given orders to accomplish different tasks. In these types of organizational environment the employees may suppress innovativeness and their motivation hinders which has a direct negative effect on organizational performance, growth and effectiveness (Constant. D. et al., 2001). An internally satisfied, delighted and motivated worker or employee is actually a productive employee in an organization which contributes in efficiency and effectiveness of organization which leads to maximization of profits (Matthew. J. et al., 2009). Thus from the literature and various studies the third hypothesis is fully supported that there exists a positive relationship between employee motivation and organizational effectiveness.

CONCLUSION

Recognition and empowerment play an essential part in enhancing employee motivation towards organizational tasks. By appreciating the employees for their work done and giving them participation in decision making, internally satisfies them with their job, organization and organizational environment. Thus, their enthusiasm and motivation towards accomplishment of tasks increases.

Employee recognition and employee motivation towards organizational tasks have positive relationship between them as exhibited by the empirical studies conducted were positive. Thus, it is concluded that appreciation and recognition of employees and employees tasks fulfillment stimulates them towards working with more energy and dedication to the organization.

Employee empowerment and employee motivation towards organizational tasks have also direct and positive relationship. The motivated employees work best in the interest of the organizations which leads them towards growth, prosperity and productivity. Thus the employee motivation and organizational effectiveness are directly related. So the organizations should work out and make such policies and organizational structures that support employee recognition and empowerment.

References

1. Aydin, B., & Ceylan, A., (2009). Does Organizational learning capacity impact on organizational effectiveness? Research analysis of the metal industry. Development and Learning in Organizations, 23 (3), 21–23.
2. Sara L. Rynes, Barry Gerhart and Kathleen A. Minette 2004: The importance of pay in employee motivation: Discrepancies between what people say and what they do, Human Resource Management Volume 43, Issue 4, pp. 381–394.
3. Houran. J 2011: Impact of employee motivation on organizational effectiveness: European Journal of Business and Management www.iiste.org. ISSN 2222-1905 (Paper) ISSN 2222-2839 (Online) Vol. 3, No. 3.
4. Adeyinka,2007:Work Motivation, Job Satisfaction, and Organizational Commitment of Library Personnel in Academic and Research Libraries in Oyo State, Nigeria, Library Philosophy and Practice 2007, ISSN 1522–0222.
5. Shanks, N. H., Chapter 2, Management and Motivation [WWW page]. URL www.jblearning.com/catalog/samplefile.aspx?isbn=076373473X&filename=3473X_CH02_4759.
6. Yazdani, B. O., Yaghoubi, N. M., & Giri, E. S., (2011). Factors affecting the Empowerment of Employees. European Journal of Social Sciences, 20 (2), 267–274.
7. Baldoni, J., (2005). Motivation Secrets. Great Motivation Secrets of Great Leaders [WWW page]. URL http://govleaders.org/motivation_secrets.htm

8. Matthew, J., Grawhich, & Barber, L. K., (2009). Are you Focusing both Employees and Organizational Outcomes. Organizational Health Initiative at Saint Louis University (ohi.slu@edu), 1–5.
9. Honold, L., (1997). A Review of the Literature on Employee Empowerment. Empowerment in Organizations, 5 (4), 202–212.
10. Smith, B., (1997). Empowerment—the challenge is now. Empowerment in Organizations, 5 (3), 120–122.
11. Beugré, Constant, D., & Offodile, O. F., (2001). Managing for organizational effectiveness in sub-Saharan Africa: a culture-fit model. The International Journal of Human Resource Management, 12 (4), 535–550.
12. Chowdhury, M. S., (2007). Enhancing Motivation and Work Performance of the Salespeople: The Impact of Supervisors' Behavior. African Journal of Business Management, 1 (9), 238–243.

15

Changing Paradigm in HR Function: E-Recruitment

Mahak Shrivastava
Assistant Professor, Faculty of Management, JSSGIW, Bhopal
E-mail:s.mahak26@gmail.com

ABSTRACT

E-recruitment is a process of searching the candidates for employment and stimulating them to apply for job online in various organizations. The sources to find out a candidate can be internal or external depending upon the requirement of the job profile. The various trends in E-recruitment are outsourcing, poaching, and E-recruitment. Thus, various companies are adopting the E-recruitment strategies to get best employees for them. As we know, every organization needs the right manpower for sustainability so E-recruitment plays a very crucial role in every organization. The level of performance of an organization depends on the effectiveness of its E-recruitment function. Many of the biggest companies in the world are using software to recruit their workforce, if you take the time to fill in a job application, you might think someone would at least have the courtesy to actually look at it. But as more and more job applications are made online, companies are increasingly turning to computer programs to help manage the load. Thus, E-recruitment has got lots of importance in past 3-4 years as companies are adopting this strategy for new manpower need. The chapter aims to find out the current trends in E-recruitment and its uses and practice.

INTRODUCTION

E-recruitment plays very crucial roles of the human resource professionals. The effectiveness of E-recruitment functions shows the level of performance of the organization. The organization in this technological world needs to adopt new strategies for sustainability. Thus, organizations have to developed and follow E-recruitment strategies to hire the best talent and utilize their resources optimally. A successful E-recruitment strategy should be well planned and practical to attract more and good talent to apply in the organization.

Literature Review

The words e-recruitment, online recruitment, cyberuiting, or the Internet recruiting are synonymous. They imply formal sourcing of jobs online (Ganalaki, 2002). It is a complete process which includes job advertisements, receiving resumes and building human resource database with candidates and incumbents. Vidot (2000), suggested that e-recruitment is the use of the Internet to attract high quality candidates, screening of suitable profiles, streamlining the application and selection process.

According to Gerry Crispin, Principal of Staffing for CareerXroads, an HR consulting firm, "The use of the Internet for job searches has grown and will continue to grow." (as quoted by Vinky Sharma (2011) JBS, JIIT in his paper) Online recruitment market today is worth over $7.1 billion, according to HR.com. Online recruitment was rated the preferred way to find a job, with 78 per cent satisfied with the outcome compared to 54 per cent who opted for the traditional methods.

Objectives of the Study

- To study the HR function in E-recruitment.
- To study the uses of E-recruitment.
- To study the practices adopted in E-recruitment.

RESEARCH METHODOLOGY

Research Design

For this study the descriptive research design is used.

Data Collection

For this study the data has been collected from the secondary sources like websites, published and unpublished research articles, white papers, working papers and newspapers.

Meaning of E-recruitment

An online recruitment system automates an organization recruiting process by receiving service applications through the Internet. Online recruitment is the process of matching people to appropriate jobs, using the Internet. The most common form of online recruitment is the advertisement of job openings on job sites and corporate sites. This may generate a lot of responses, but simply attracting large numbers of potential candidates is only part of the online recruitment process. The real benefit of online recruitment is apparent when recruiters streamline the recruitment process by automation through HR software.

Advantages of using E-recruitment

E-recruitment has the potential to:

- Pace up the E-recruitment cycle and rationalize administration
- Allow organizations to make use of IT systems to manage vacancies more in effect and co-ordinate E-recruitment processes
- Decrease E-recruitment costs
- Achieve a wide pool of applicants

- Reach a forte pool of applicants
- Make internal vacancies broadly known from corner to corner multiple sites and separate divisions
- Provide the image of an up-to-date organizations, reinforcing employer branding and giving an indication of organizations culture
- Offer access to vacancies 24 hours a day, 7 days a week reaching a global audience
- Be a cost-effective way to construct a talent bank for future vacancies
- Help handle high volume job applications in a consistent way
- Provide more tailored information to the post and organizations, e.g., case histories of the 'day in the life' or self-assessment questionnaire or quiz to assess fit with role
- Be spontaneous for candidates as ease of use means there is the ability for applications to be instantaneous.

Using E-recruitment

Technology can be used:

- To publicize vacancies – on your organization's website, job sites, or on social networking sites
- To deal with the applications – email enquiries, emailed application forms/ CVs, online completion of application forms
- To select candidates – online testing, in order gathering
- To enhance company brand
- To create a personal connection with your talent pool.

HR Function: E-recruitment

There is growing evidence that organizations are using the Internet technology and the World Wide Web as a platform for recruiting and testing candidates. The IES survey of 50 organizations using e-recruitment reported that the primary drivers behind the decisions to pursue e-recruitment were to:

- Improve corporate image and profile
- Reduce recruitment costs
- Reduce administrative burden
- Employ better tools for the recruitment team.

Fifty-five per cent of respondents expected their organization to reduce its use of other recruitment methods in the future. The key limiting factors to e-recruitment most frequently reported were:

- The cultural approach of the organization towards recruitment
- The lack of knowledge of e-recruitment within the HR community

- Internet usage by target candidates
- Commitment of senior management.

Issues raised as causing concern with e-recruitment included the quantity and quality of candidates applying using web-based tools (e.g., organizations being inundated with CVs attached by email, many of whom were not suitable for the post), the relevance of shortlisting criteria (e.g., the validity and legality of searching by keywords), confidentiality and data protection, and ensuring diversity of applicants.

The trends in E-recruitment use suggest a changing landscape whereby in future the candidate is connected to the central system and there is involvement of the line manager in the process (see figure). In addition to the reported benefits such as cost efficiencies, the role of HR in this model is viewed as more of a facilitative role, in theory allowing time for recruiters to become involved in the strategic issues within resourcing.

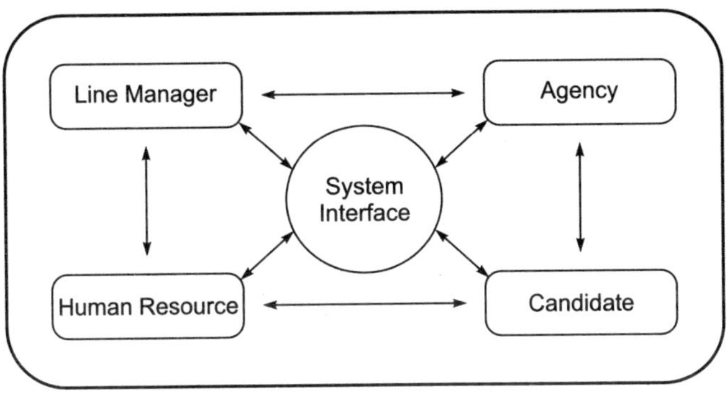

Source: IES

E-Recruitment: Hiring Process

The hiring process means carrying out a full series of functions in addition to simple recruitment. It means making a choice and deciding if the company feels that any of the candidates meet the requirements of the specific job and, if so, hiring that person. The next step is closing the deal and having the new employee join the company and fit in within the existing company culture. This means that once the company's hiring policies have been clearly defined, there is a process, which we call the "Hiring Process" that may be broken down into the following stages:

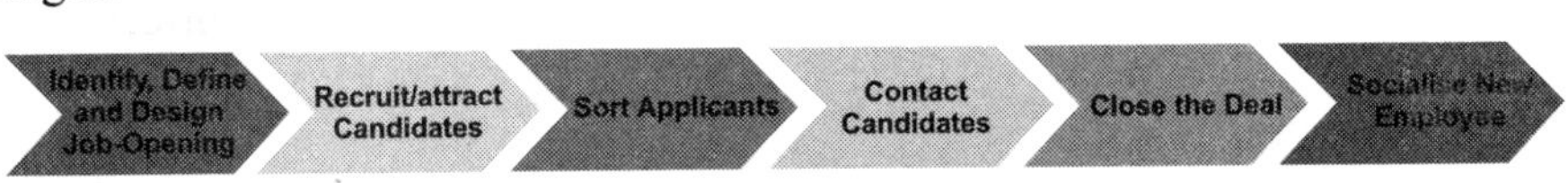

Source: International Refereed Research Journal, Vol.–III, Issue–3(2), July 2012 [36]

E-recruitment Methods

Advertising job openings, tracking the source of applications, and online enquiry forms, were the most frequently used methods for attracting candidates. In many cases, web-based technology in selection and assessment is only being used by the most selection-sophisticated organizations that can afford the high start-up and maintenance costs. The IES survey reported that, out of the 50 organizations surveyed:

- A large proportion were using online application forms (67 per cent)
- Only four per cent were using psychometric tests online.

There was wide variety in the extent to which online applications were structured, and also in how they were screened, e.g., electronically by keywords or manually. There exists a great deal of variation and less maturity in this part of the E-recruitment process in terms of application and use, than in the application of Internet technology at the attraction stage of the process.

In terms of applicant tracking and workflow systems, of the 50 organizations surveyed, 78 per cent received CVs and application forms online, 49 per cent used email response letters, with 39 per cent using progress-tracking systems. Only nine per cent provided status reports to hiring managers. (Source: Vinky Sharma, JBS, JIIT, Feb 2011 and IES)

Findings

As per the study conducted, there were various findings which are as below:

- E-recruitment is a better tool for employ recruitment.
- It helps in improving the image of the company and do brand building also.
- E-recruitment helps the organization in reducing recruitment costs.
- The candidate can easily access to the sites doing online recruitment.
- E-recruitment reduces the administrate burden.

Suggestions

There is a need to create awareness to the candidate who does not use the Internet.

- Respond promptly and sensitively to submitted forms.
- The software which been used should be tested thoroughly before launching it.
- The software should be simple so that the normal user can use it.
- Information given in online recruitment should be precise and correct.

CONCLUSION

The aims of this paper were to examine the overall thought of E-recruitment. It has been rightly said that recruitment is not only hiring the best amongst those who applied for a particular post rather it's the question to enroll the right candidate in one's human capital. E-recruitment has come out to be an important part of the recruitment strategy. It can be used to track and direct candidate applications, particularly among larger organizations. E-recruitment can provide some notable benefits in terms of efficiency and cost. In the wake of above discussion, a permanent improvement in understanding the technological issues related to e-recruitment is highly suggested. Future research should focus on verifying the identified advantages and disadvantages by using empirical tools such as time-studies. Thus, E-recruitment is vital now for many organizations to recruit a right person at a right job and at a right time in current scenario. Every organization should be allowed to make use of IT systems to manage vacancies more in effect and co-ordinate E-recruitment processes.

References

1. www.eE-recruitmentbuddy.com/articlesnews/showarticle/4,Thu 07 January 2010, Category: e-E-recruitment
2. http://www.dare.co.in/strategy/human-resources-E-recruitment/innovative-hiring-strategies.htm
3. *E-Recruitment: Is it Delivering?* Kerrin M, Kettley P. Report 402, Institute for Employment Studies, 2003. ISBN: 978-1-85184-329-9. PDF Download only: £8.00
4. http://www.ehow.com/about_6319257_definition-online-recruitment.html#ixzz2a2X3mwz2

16

New Paradise in Management Dynamics: Corporate Restructuring

Ankita Agarwal
Assistant Professor, Banshi Group of Education, Kanpur
E-mail:ankita6390agarwal@gmail.com

ABSTRACT

The term, "restructuring" means 'giving new structure or rebuild or rearrange'. In this perspective, 'corporate restructuring' is defined as a process of rearranging the organizational or business structure of the company for increased efficiency and profitable growth. Corporate restructuring can involve making dramatic changes to a business by cutting out or merging departments that often has the effect of displacing staff members.

OVERVIEW

Simply stated, corporate restructuring is a comprehensive process by which a company can consolidate or rearrange its organizational set up or business operations and strengthen its position so as to achieve its short-term or/and long-term objectives and establish itself as a synergetic, dynamic, continuing as well as successful independent corporate entity in the competitive environment.

In the words of Hon'ble Justice D.Y. Chandrachud "Corporate Restructuring" is the means that can be employed to meet challenges which confronts businesses.

The company will be restructured in following aspects:

- Financial (an ownership, capital mix and business mix);
- Assets (a asset mix of company);
- Production (products and services, and use of production facilities or technologies);
- Sales and purchases (oriented both on inputs and outputs of the organization);
- Organization (defining function roles and relations in business processes);
- Information (information systems in a complex concept);
- Personnel (human resources – volume, structure, quality).

Types of corporate restructuring

- Mergers/Amalgamation
- Acquisition and Takeovers

- Divestiture
- Demerger (spin off/split up/split off)
- Joint Ventures

Merger/Amalgamation: A merger is a combination of two or more businesses into one business. Laws in India use the term 'amalgamation' for merger. Amalgamation is the merger of one or more companies with another or the merger of two or more companies to form a new company.

Acquisitions and Takeovers: An acquisition may be defined as an act of acquiring effective control by one company over assets or management of another company without any combination of companies. When an acquisition is 'forced' or 'unwilling', it is called a takeover.

Divestiture: Divestiture means an out sale of all the assets of the company or any of its business undertakings/divisions, usually for cash (or for a combination of cash and debt) and not against equity shares.

Demerger: Demerger is a form of corporate restructuring in which an entity's business operations are segregated into one or more components. Demerger can take three forms: Spin-off, Split-up and Split-off.

Joint Venture: Joint venture is an arrangement in which two or more companies (called joint venture partners) contribute to the equity capital of a new company (called joint venture) in pre-decided proportion. For example, Maruti Suzuki.

List of some companies which had gone through the restructuring process:

Canon
Procter & Gamble (P&G)
Khadi Gram Udyog
Coal India
Kingfisher Airlines
It can be understood more clearly through case study of Procter & Gamble.

Corporate Restructuring Exercises by Procter & Gamble (P&G)

Issues: To gain insight into the common causes that contribute to steady decline over a period of time in the performance of a large multi-product multinational company of high repute.

Introduction: The US based Procter Gamble (P&G), one of the largest fast moving consumer goods (FMCG) companies in the world, was in deep trouble in the first half of 2000. The company, in March 2000, announced that its earnings growth for the financial year 1999-2000 would be 7% instead of 14% as announced earlier. The news led P&G's stock to lose $27 in one day, wiping out $40 billion in its market capitalization.

To add to this, in April 2000, P&G announced an 18% decline in its net profit for January – March 2000 quarter. For the first time in the past eight years P&G was showing a decline in profits. In the late 1990s, P&G faced the problem of stagnant revenues and profitability. In order to accelerate growth, the erstwhile P&G's President and CEO, DurkJager officially launched the Organization 2005 program in July 1999. Organization 2005 was a six-year long organizational restructuring exercise which included the standardization of work processes to expedite growth, revamping the organizational culture in order to embrace change, reduction in hierarchies to enable faster decision-making, and retrenchment of employees to cut costs.

With the implementation of the program, P&G aimed to increase its global revenues from $38 billion to $70 billion by 2005. But implementation was not so effective and this resulted in the decline of the company's revenues and profitability. After a brief stint of 17 months, Jager had to quit his post. In June 2000, Alan George Lafley took over as the new President & CEO of P&G. Under Lafley, P&G seemed to be on the right path. He was able to turn the company around through his excellent planning, execution and focus. With Lafley at the helm, P&G's financial performance improved. The company's share price shot up by 58% to $92 by July 2003, as against a fall of 32% in S&P's 500 stock index.

Background Note

Procter & Gamble was established in 1837 by William Procter, a candle maker, and his brother-in-law, James Gamble, a soap maker, when they merged their small businesses. They set up a shop in Cincinnati and nicknamed it "Porkopolis" because of its dependence on swine slaughterhouses. The shop made candles and soaps from the leftover fats of the swine. By 1859, P&G had become one of the largest companies in Cincinnati, with sales of $1 million. The company introduced Ivory, a floating soap in 1879 and Crisco, the first all-vegetable shortening in 1911. In the period between the 1940s and 1960s, P&G embarked on a series of acquisitions. The company acquired Spic and Span (1945), Duncan Hines (1956), Chairman Paper Mills (1957), Clorox (1957; sold in 1968) and Folgers Coffee (1963).

In 1973, P&G began manufacturing and selling its products in Japan through the acquisition of Nippon Sunhome Company. The new company was named "Procter & Gamble Sunhome Co. Ltd."

In 1988, the company started manufacturing products in China. P&G became one of the largest cosmetics companies in the US when it acquired Noxell (1989) and Max Factor (1991). After witnessing a period of significant organic and inorganic growth, P&G began to face several problems during the 1990s.

Excerpts

The 'Organization 2005' Program: In January 1999, Jager, a P&G veteran became the new CEO taking charge at a time when P&G was in the midst of a corporate restructuring exercise that started in September 1998.

Jager faced the challenging task of revamping P&G's operations and marketing practices. Soon after taking over as the CEO, Jager told analysts that he would overhaul product development, testing and launch processes. The biggest obstacle for Jager was P&G's culture. Jager realized the need to change the mindset of the P&G employees who had been used to lifetime employment and a conservative management style.

On July 1, 1999, P&G officially launched the Organization 2005 program. It was a program of six-year duration, during which, P&G planned to retrench 15,000 employees globally. The cost of this program was estimated to be $1.9 billion and it was expected to generate an annual savings of approximately $900 million per annum by 2004.

Change in Organization Structure: Till 1998, P&G had been organized along geographic lines with more than 100 profit centers. Under Organization 2005 program, P&G sought to reorganize its organizational structure from four geographically-based business units to five product-based global business units – Baby, Feminine & Family Care, Beauty Care, Fabric & Home Care, Food & Beverages, and Health Care.

The restructuring exercise aimed at boosting P&G's growth (in terms of sales and profits), speed and innovation and expedition of management decision making for the company's global marketing initiatives.

It also aimed to fix the strategy-formulation and profit-creation responsibilities on products rather than on regions. The global business units (GBUs) had to devise global strategies for all P&G's brands and the heads of GBU were held accountable for their unit's profit. The sourcing, R&D and manufacturing operations were also undertaken by the GBU.

Standardization of Work Processes: One of the major objectives of Organization 2005 program was to significantly improve all inefficient work processes of P&G including its product development, supply chain management and marketing functions. In order to achieve this objective, P&G undertook several IT initiatives including collaborative technologies, B2C e-commerce, web-enabled supply chain and a data warehouse project for supplying timely data to company's various operations located globally.

Revamping the Corporate Culture: The Organization 2005 program made efforts to change P&G from a conservative, lethargic and bureaucratic to modern, quick-moving and the Internet-savvy organization. The new structure was directed towards revamping the work culture of P&G so as to focus on its new Stretch, Innovation and Speed (SIS) philosophy. Emphasizing on innovation, Jager said, "Organization 2005 is focused on one thing: leveraging P&G's innovative capability.

The Mistakes Committed: The Organization 2005 program faced several problems soon after its launch. Jager had made efforts in January 2000 to acquire Warner-Lambert and American Home Products. Contrary to P&G's cautious approach towards acquisitions in the 1990s, this dual acquisition would have been the largest ever in P&G's history, worth $140 billion. However, the stock market greeted the news of the merger negotiations by selling P&G's shares, which prompted Jager to exit the deal.

Implementing Strategies to Revive P&G: In June 2000, Alan George Lafley, a 23-year P&G veteran popularly known as 'AG,' took over as the new President and CEO of P&G. The major difference between Lafley and Jager was their 'style of functioning.' Soon after becoming CEO, Lafley rebuilt the management team and made efforts to improve P&G's operations and profitability. Lafley transferred more than half of P&G's 30 senior most officers, an unprecedented move in P&G's history. He assigned senior positions and higher roles to women.

P&G Current Status: In 2003, Lafley continued his efforts to make P&G more adaptable to the dynamic changes in business environment. He challenged P&G's traditional perspective that all its products should be produced in-house. In April 2003, Lafley started outsourcing the manufacturing of bar soaps (including P&G's longest existing brand, Ivory) to a Canadian manufacturer. In May 2003, IT operations were outsourced from HP. Since Lafley became CEO, P&G's outsourcing contract went up from 10% to 20%. Lafley continued to review P&G's businesses and new investments with the aim of achieving sharper focus on its core businesses, cost competitiveness and improved productivity.

Analysis

The case discusses the Organization 2005 program a six-year long organizational restructuring exercise conducted by the US based Procter & Gamble (P&G), global leader in the fast moving consumer goods (FMCG) industry. The case examines in detail, the important elements of the restructuring program including changing the organizational structure, standardizing the work processes and revamping the corporate culture. The case elaborates on the mistakes committed by DurkJager, the erstwhile CEO of P&G and examines the reasons as to why Organization 2005 program did not deliver the desired results. Finally, the case discusses how Alan George Lafley, the new CEO, accelerated the initiatives under the Organization 2005 program and revived P&G's financial performance.

According to analysts, though Organization 2005 program was well planned, the execution of the plan was a failure. Analysts believed that Jager concentrated more on developing new products rather than on P&G's well-established brands.

Websites

1. www.google.com
2. www.corporate restructuring cases.in

17

Employer Branding: Need of the Hour

Sapna Tripathi
Assistant Professor, Dept. of Management, Axis Group of Institutions
E-mail: sapna.tripathi192@gmail.com

Deepali Gupta
Research Scholar, RIET, Kanpur
E-mail: deepaliguptadg@gmail.com

Anshuman Kushwaha
MBA Final Year, STEP-HBTI, Kanpur
E-mail: anshumanmba2010@gmail.com

ABSTRACT

The term 'employer branding' was first used in the early 1990s, and has since become widely adopted by the global management community. Employer brand denotes an organization's reputation as an employer. employer brand as "the image of your organization as a 'great place to work". Employer branding is concerned with enhancing your company's employer brand.

WHAT IS EMPLOYER BRANDING

The sum of a company's efforts to communicate to existing and prospective staff what makes it a desirable place to work and the active management of "a company's image as seen through the eyes of its associates and potential hires".

"Employer branding" denotes what people currently associate with an organization, employer branding has been defined as in other words, employer brand management addresses the reality of the employment experience and not simply its presentation. By doing so it supports both external recruitment of the right kind of talent sought by an organization to achieve its goals, and the subsequent desire for effective employee engagement and employee retention.

The effective employer branding and brand management requires a clear employer brand proposition or employee value proposition. You cannot simply assert your way to a new culture, no more can you assert your way to a strong brand, it needs to be consistently and continuously shaped and managed, which is one of the primary reasons many organizations have turned from the short-term engagement focus of internal branding initiatives to more long-term focus of employer brand management.

HOW TO BUILD THE EMPLOYER BRAND

Employer branding acts as a catalyst in making crucial decision about one's career. Successful employer branding aligns employees on a holistic and philosophical level bringing convergence on values, culture and vision. Retaining the brand's core values, key messages such as a great workplace, high potential for career growth, superior learning curve and more must emerge.

Developing and communicating your organization's culture your core value is a planned process with exposure to best practice in this space, engage more can assist you in effectively communicating your brand in the marketplace and successfully for talent.

You believe that time is money, and then take note. In a survey of more than 4700 talent acquisition decision makers, a reported 50 percent savings in cost per hire is associated with a strong employer brand.

According to Employer Brand International, "84 percent of companies believe a clearly defined strategy is the key to achieving employer branding objectives." In layman's terms, don't try to be something you aren't. Figuring out your culture isn't difficult.

Consider how the company interacts, behaves, and communicates. Incorporate surface interactions as well as the underlying aspects like attitudes, common goals, perspectives, standards, and beliefs.

An employer brand that conveys what a company *wants* to be, not what they are. The company culture that you want people to see should be a good mix of the two. Stay true to who you are as a company, while keeping a constant heading toward who you would like to become clear, authentic messages and offerings are what you should concentrate on.

When you have a clear message in mind, make it visible and get to the meat of creating an employer brand. And back to the beginning of this post, who has time for that? That's like asking, "Who has time to be good at their job?"

Employer branding has become such a huge part of recruiting today that it is now part of your job, whether you're concentrating on it or not. If you haven't started fostering a strong employer brand, you're not doing your job.

Employer Brand International's (EBI) 2012/2013 Global Research study found that 39% of companies plan to increase their investment in employer branding initiatives in 2013. The important consideration in this statistic is just how much of this investment will add value and how much will be wasted. For many companies it may lead to an outcome that many marketers are only too well aware of: half of their investment is wasted, they just don't know which half!

Making the case to measure return on investment of employer branding isn't the hard part. Figuring out what to measure is , EBI's 2011 global study found that retention rate (thirty-eight percent of companies surveyed use this metric) is the most common metric used to measure ROI of employer branding. Thirty-three percent use employee engagement, twenty-nine percent quality of hire, twenty-seven percent cost per hire and twenty-six percent use number of applicants. So which metric(s) should you use?

The key to which metrics you use to measure your ROI is to align the metrics with your business objectives. There is no point measuring the number of applicants if you are recruiting astronauts to send into space. If you are hiring for a new local store opening or an upcoming busy summer period you may focus your spend on employee referrals if your previous research has shown your employer brand metrics should be reliable and predictive. If you can identify the drivers of employer brand value and focus your investments on these activities aren't you more likely to receive the ongoing support of the executive to invest in employer branding? Following an employer brand strategic audit in 2012, a large Danish employer found they were spending sixty percent of their employer branding investment on University activities but only five percent of new hires were being recruited from this channel. Sure enough, investment was re-allocated to channels which were producing the best hires and this is where understanding what to measure can drive value.

EBI research shows the employer brand strategy is driven by the human resources department in 36% of companies and in 30% the responsibility is shared amongst more than one function. Based on this statistic it would be reasonable to expect that measures that have commonality amongst all departments contributing to the employer brand strategy are more likely to get closer to the true 'employer brand value creation' goal.

The link between creating employer brand value and financial (e.g., cost per hire, profit per employee, staff turnover cost) and non-financial measures (e.g., employee engagement, employee loyalty, employer brand awareness) is variable and must be evaluated on a case by case basis and re-evaluated over time as the strategy evolves.

Employer brand leaders should think like researchers and employ tactics to better understand their workforces. Conducting feedback and discussion group sessions and interviews with current and future employees will assist you to better understand what measure is driving the emotions behind why employees choose to join your company, why they stay and what would make them leave.

ALIGNMENT OF MEASURES TO OBJECTIVES

This means it's essential to make measurement a standard and cyclical part of your strategy depending on where you are in the evolution of your employer brand strategy. For example, if you've developed and launched your employer brand strategy in year one, you may be measuring employer brand awareness and/or alignment between departments responsible for the strategy. In year two, as you become more skilled at engaging with your target audience you may track conversion rates of your Facebook, Linkedin or Twitter followers who become members of your online talent community where they can receive more targeted communications based on their profile.

We all know the value of data, but what's important here is the value of data over time. Employer brand value is best measured as it is enhanced over time. That's why corporate sustainability has become such a hot topic in business as companies are fast realizing the impact on business performance through low levels of engagement and high staff turnover. This is one of the reasons why the practice of employer branding has a bright future.

It doesn't matter whether you have been managing your employer brand strategy for three years or three minutes, below is a ten-point action plan you can share and discuss amongst those responsible for your employer brand strategy to improve your measurement and ROI.

1. Clearly Define your Employer Branding Objective(s): Attracting and retaining the best talent may be a logical objective. The definition of clear objective(s) is critical as it guides the allocation of resources. Conducting a strategic audit of your employer brand is a good place to start to define your objectives and identify where your investments are best focused before you start spending big on creative and communications.

2) Understand the Key Drivers of Achieving Your Objective: This should be part of your audit process as well and may require revisiting the survey data you invested heavily in and now makes a great bookend on your bookcase! If you can identify the cause and effect of how you attract and retain the best talent, you can focus your efforts on these activities. If your research tells you your hiring manager satisfaction produces the best hires or the quality of your induction program results in the most effective sales people then you can start to implement your employer branding activities with a higher level of predictability.

3. Develop an Employer Brand Scorecard: Your scorecard should identify the financial and non-final measures that drive employer brand value. It should allow you to track and report on those measures most likely to impact on achieving your objectives.

4. Allocate Responsibility for the Measure(s): The responsibility for reporting on the performance should rest with the employee(s) responsible for the employer branding activity. Thirty-six percent of human resource departments are responsible for the employer brand strategy. However, thirty percent of responsibility lies in more than one department so it makes little sense for a HR leader to be responsible for measuring employer brand awareness if marketing is responsible for the external communication activities to extend the market reach of the company's employer value proposition (EVP) communications.

5. Obtain Baseline Data on Your Workforce: Measures are nothing without a baseline understanding of your audience. Start by gathering data on your current workforce to obtain a solid understanding of your target audience and who they are. Seek information on hobbies, commuting patterns, family situations, interests and behaviors. Go beyond demographics and search for patterns amongst subsets of employees. Your most talented young employees may all share an interest in gaming so use that to your advantage rather than send them to a full day of training on a topic unrelated to their interests!

6. Dispel Assumptions: Share the data with your leaders and dispel assumptions they have about the typical employee. Break down employee likes and dislikes. Share intuitive data about commonalities you found amongst 'A level' talent. Create new personas that are data-based and not assumption based.

7. Listening Closely to Employee Feedback and Observe Behaviors: Pay close attention to the channels your current employees use and map marketing strategies to their preferred channels. This will ensure you have tactics to allow for a deeper, richer perspective into how well your employer brand and EVP strategy is resonating with employees.

8. Evaluate your Progress: Business conditions aren't static, nor should your measures be! They're ever changing and more valuable when measured over time. Make comparisons and don't be afraid to report failures. They'll drive change and show you're paying attention to your investment.

9. If all Else Fails: If you are unable to convince your executives to invest in employer branding, consider the human element. In early 2012, found only three mentions online for the search terms "I love Dow Chemical." How many people love your brand? That alone can demonstrate how far back in the pack you are. Genuine feelings about a brand matter. Don't forget the power that human love (or hate) can bestow on your brand success.

Analysis

An employee value proportion is used to define an organization's employment offer. The marketing disciplines associated with branding and brand management have been increasingly applied by the human resources and talent management community to attract, engage and retain talented candidates and employees.

- Only 10% companies said they have a clearly defined employer branding strategy.
- 49% companies today see a problem in finding the right candidates to work for your company.
- 44% of companies felt that being creative and innovative as an employer is the challenge number one in employer branding.

- 41% of companies considered a commitment of managers for the challenge.
- 23% of employers check their ranking position in the research rankings of the best employers.

CONCLUSION

1. Apply Perfect Employer Branding Strategy

Well defined and implemented employer branding strategy has a significant impact on the attraction, engagement and retention of talent. The award in this category is intended for organizations that have successfully developed and implemented a strategy to employer branding in their company. The jury will look for consistency of the strategy and its impact on the cycle of operation of the employee in the company, from recruitment, through a process of on-boarding, to the engagement and retention. The evaluation will assess the creativity and uniqueness of the strategy.

2. Use Perfect On-Line Campaign

The rapid development of the Internet technology and continuously emerging new tools greatly assist employers in attracting the best talent to the organization. Using the online platform has changed the paradigm of traditional recruitment. The recruitment process is now firmly supported by social networks, videos, RSS, podcasts, blogs, multimedia presentations and e-recruitment platform. The jury will look for creativity and uniqueness of the campaign and the campaign relation to its objectives.

3. Use Perfect Off-Line Recruitment Campaign

Recruitment campaign off-line is often the first contact of the candidates and the chance to give the impression that may affect firm's interest in and acceptance of work by the candidate. Top employers in recruitment campaigns are able to capture the important connection of the employer, EVP, organizational culture and values of the target group of the campaign. The jury will look for creativity and uniqueness of the campaign and the campaign relation to its objectives.

4. Built Excellent Internal Image Campaign

Even the best prepared employer branding strategy, it will be only half-hearted and did not have the desired effect if it is intended only for external action, without internal employer brand strategy. The employer of choice ensures the involvement of employees in the process of promoting the image of the employer, inviting them to be ambassadors for the brand. The award in this category is intended for organizations that have successfully developed and implemented an internal strategy or partial employer branding campaign for your business. The jury will look for innovation strategy and its impact on the overall brand strategy for all employers. The evaluation will assess the creativity and uniqueness of the strategy.

Websites

1. www.google.com
2. www.employerbranding.org

18

Employees' Provident Fund Scheme as a Social Security for Employees

Archika Katiyar
Guest Faculty, UPTTI, Kanpur
E-mail: archikakatiyarmba@gmail.com,

Sadhika Katiyar
MBA Final Year, IBM, C.S.J.M. University, Kanpur
E-mail:mesadhikakatiyar@gmail

ABSTRACT

Social security protects not just the subscriber but also his/her entire family by giving benefit packages in financial security and healthcare. Social security schemes are designed to guarantee at least long-term sustenance to families when the earning member retires, dies or suffers a disability. Thus, the main strength of the social security system is that it acts as a facilitator—it helps people to plan their own future through insurance and assistance. The success of social security schemes however requires the active support and involvement of employees and employers. The Employees' Provident Fund & MP Act, 1952 is an important piece of labour welfare legislation enacted by the Parliament to provide social security benefits to the workers. At present, the Act and the schemes framed there under provides for three types of benefits—contributory provident fund, pensionary benefits to the employees/family members and the insurance cover to the members of the provident fund.

The Employees' Provident Funds Scheme 1952 (EPF)

Employee Provident Fund (EPF) is one of the main platforms of savings in India for nearly all people working in government, public or private sector organizations. This scheme comes under Employees' Provident Funds Act, 1952. It is now referred as the Employees' Provident Funds & Miscellaneous Provision Act, 1952 which extends to the whole of India except Jammu and Kashmir.

Employee Provident Fund

A provident fund is created with a purpose of providing financial security and stability to elderly people. Employee Provident Fund (EPF) is implemented by the Employees Provident Fund Organization (EPFO) of India. An establishment with 20 or more workers working in any one of the 180+ industries (given here) should register with EPFO. Typically 12% of the Basic, DA, and cash value of food allowances has to be contributed to the EPF account. EPFO is a statutory body of the Indian Government under Labour and Employment Ministry. It is one of the largest social security organizations in the world in terms of members and volume of financial transactions undertaken.

Administration

The 'Fund' shall be administered by the Central Board and other agencies discussed hereunder:

Central Board

The Central Board of Trustees, EPF is a statutory body constituted by the Central Government under the provisions of section 5A of the Employees' Provident Funds and Miscellaneous Provisions Act, 1952 (Act 19 of 1952).

It is a tripartite body administering the three schemes, namely:

- Employees Provident Fund Scheme, 1952
- Employees Pension Scheme,1995 (it replaced Employees Family Pension Scheme, 1971)
- Employees Deposit Linked Insurance Scheme, 1976

Framed under the Act, at present, Hon'ble Minister of Labour & Employment, Government of India is the Chairman of the Board.

The tenure of the Board is five years.

The constitution of the Board as per section 5A of the Act is as under:

1	Chairman		u/s 5A(1)(a)
2	Vice Chairman		u/s 5A(1)(a)
3	Central Provident Fund Commissioner, ex officio		u/s 5A(1)(aa)
4	Central Government representatives	5	u/s 5A(1)(b)
5	State Governments' representatives	15	u/s 5A(1)(c)
6	Employers' representatives	10	u/s 5A(1)(d)
7	Employees' representatives	10	u/s 5A(1)(e)

Functions of Central Board

Main functions of the Board are:

1. Administration of the funds created and vested with the Board and performing other works incidental thereto.
2. Delegation of administrative and financial powers as it may deem necessary for efficient administration of the schemes.
3. Appointment of officers and staff.
4. Maintenance of accounts of income and expenditure in prescribed form and manner.

5. Submission of audited accounts (with comments of CAG) and annual Report on performance of the organization to the government.

Executive Committee

The Executive Committee is a statutory committee, which is constituted from amongst the members of the Central Board of Trustees by the Central Government under section 5AA of the Act. Its purpose is to assist the Central Board of Trustees, EPF in the discharge of its functions relating to administrative matters. The term of the Committee is two-year and six months.

As per section 5AA, the constitution of the Committee is as under:

1	Chairman		u/s 5AA(1)(a)
2	Central Government representatives	2	u/s 5A(1)(b)
3	State Governments' representatives	3	u/s 5A(1)(c)
4	Employees' representatives	3	u/s 5A(1)(d)
5	Employers' representatives	3	u/s 5A(1)(e)
6	Central Provident Fund Commissioner, ex officio		u/s 5A(1)(f)

Regional Committee

The Regional Committees (Employees' Provident Fund) for the States are constituted under the provisions of Para 4 of Employees' Provident Fund Scheme, 1952.

The Chairman, Central Board of Trustees (Employees' Provident Fund) is the competent authority to constitute/reconstitute the Regional Committee (EPF) for the states under Para 4 of the Employees' Provident Fund Scheme, 1952.

The term of each Regional Committee is three years from the date of notification in the Official Gazette

1	Chairman	1	Under Para 4 (1) (a)
2	State Governments' representatives	2	Under Para 4 (1) (b)
3	Employers' representatives	2	Under Para 4 (1) (c)
4	Employees' representatives	2	Under Para 4 (1) (d)
5	Non-official members of CBT ordinarily resident in the state		Under Para 4 (1) (e)

How to become an EPF Member

To become an EPF member, one has to work in an establishment which is covered under EPF and MP Act, 1952.

- If 20 or more employees are working in an establishment, EPFO will cover that establishment.
- If employer and employees of an establishment desire, that establishment can voluntarily opt for EPF cover even if the employees employed therein are less than 20.

- If your establishment is not covered and at least 20 employees are working in that establishment, you can approach EPFO to cover it.

BENEFITS TO MEMBERS UNDER EPF SCHEMES

1. Provident Fund benefits

1. Employer also contributes to Members PF @ 12% (10% in case of sick industrial units, any establishment having accumulated loss equal to its entire paid up capital and any establishment in Jute Industry, Beedi Industry, Brick Industry, Coir Industry and Gaur Gum Factories.)
2. EPFO guarantees the Employer contribution and credits interest at such rates as determined by the Central Government.
3. Member can withdraw from this accumulations to cater to financial exigencies in life–No need to refund unless misused.
4. On resignation, the member can settle the account, i.e., the member gets his PF contribution, employer contribution and interest.

2. Pension Benefits

1. Pension to Member
2. Pension to Family (on death of member)
3. Scheme Certificate
    - This Certificate shows the service and family details of a member.
    - This is issued if the member has not attained the age of 58 while leaving an establishment and he applies for this certificate.
    - Member can surrender this certificate while joining another establishment and the service stated in the certificate is added with the service he is gaining from the new establishment.
    - After attaining the age of 50 or above, the member can apply for Pension by surrendering this scheme certificate (if total service is at least 10 years).
    - This is a better choice than Withdrawal Benefit, as a member dies holding a valid scheme certificate, his family will get pension (Death when NOT in service).

3. Withdrawal Benefit

- If not eligible for pension, member may withdraw the amount accumulated in his pension account.
- The calculation of this amount is based only on (i) Last average salary and (ii) Service (Not based on actual amount available in Pension Fund Account).

1. No amount is taken from Member to give Pension to the Member. Employer and Govt. contributes to Pension fund @8.33% and @1.16% respectively.

2. EPFO guarantees pension to members, even if the employer has not contributed to Pension Fund.

4. Death Benefits

1. Provident Fund Amount to Family (or to Nominee)
2. Pension to Family (or to Parent / Nominee)
3. Capital Return of Pension
4. Insurance (EDLI) amount to Family (or to Nominee)
    - No amount is taken from Member for this facility. Employer contributes for this.
    - Nominee is basically determined as per the information submitted by the member at this office through FORM-2.
    - Grant of exemption from the operation of the scheme/s framed under the Act to an establishment to a class of employees and to an individual employee, on certain conditions.
    - Penalties to employers/trustees of exempted Provident Fund who contravene the provision of the Act and the Scheme.
    - Appointment of inspector to secure compliance under the Act and the schemes framed thereunder.
    - Mode of recovery of moneys due from employers.

5. Special Occasions-EPF at Help

There are special occasions in your family or some emergency arises. In case of need of funds and no recourse, EPF comes handy as it gives option to withdraw from the corpus but within a certain limit and by meeting some specified conditions.

1. Goals—Marriage, Education need for Self, Child or any Sibling In case you have to arrange funds for any of the above need then from your EPF corpus you can withdraw up to 50% of your contribution. Not only this, you can take this benefit three times in your life. However, do remember that for availing this facility you should be in services for at least 7 years. You will have to provide valid documents like marriage card or proof of fee payable to the organization.

2. Your Dream House You can withdraw from your EPF account for house construction, repair or maintenance or for housing loan repayment. For all of these benefits, there are conditions specified by the organization. If you availed a housing loan and wish to make any repayment, then you can utilize up to 36 months wages from your EPF balance provided you have completed 10 years of service. Similarly, you can also withdraw up to 12 months' wages (only once) if you wish to do some alteration or repairing in your existing house. For this you should have completed 5 years of service (10 years for repairing). The number of years of service reduces to five years if you wish to purchase/construct a new plot/

house. The maximum you can withdraw is 36 month wages (24-month for plot) but only once. The best part here is that the house can be in name of your spouse or in joint ownership.

3. Medical Emergency EPF gives benefit for major surgical operations in a hospital or by those suffering from TB, leprosy, paralysis, cancer, mental derangement or heart ailment. You can withdraw up to six times of your salary or the entire contribution made till date, whichever is less. The funds can be utilized for self or family (spouse, children, dependent parents) treatment.

CONCLUSION

Employee Provident Fund is a very important tool of retirement planning. The tax-free interest (compounding) and the maturity ensures a good growth of your money. If continued for a very long term, it can help immensely in meeting ones retirement goal. But while fulfilling other goals or during emergencies, we fall short of funds even after taking all recourse and do force borrowing. At this moment EPF can be helpful due to certain benefits it provides which most of us are unaware of.

19

Employee Development and Its Effects on Employee Performance: A Conceptual Framework

Neetu Singh
Assistant Professor, Faculty of Management
Naraina Group of Institutions, Kanpur
E-mail: neetu_mba@yahoo.com

ABSTRACT

Employee is a key element of an organization. The success or failure of the organization depends on employee performance. Therefore, organizations are investing huge amount of money on employee development. This paper analyzes the theoretical framework and models related to employee development and its effect on employee performance. The key variable identifies relatedness between employee development and employee performance. Further discussion develops a proposed model which explains the relationship between employee development variables (employee learning, skill growth, self-directed, employee attitude) and employee performance variable. The employee performance effect on organizational effectiveness. The paper is divided in three parts. The introductory part provides brief overview related to employee development and its effect on employee performance. The second part analyzes the views and studies of the past researchers related to employee development and employee performance. In the end, paper presents the proposed model along with the discussion and conclusion.

INTRODUCTION

Employee development is one of the most important functions of Human Resource Management. Employee development means to develop the abilities of an individual employee and organization as a whole. Hence, employee development consists of individual or employee and overall growth of the employee as when employees of the organization would develop the organization, organization would be more flourished and the employee performance would increase (Elena 2000). Therefore, there is a direct relationship between Employee Development and Employee Performance. As when employees would be more developed, they would be more satisfied with the job, more committed towards the job and the performance would be increased. When employee performance would increase, this will lead to the organization effectiveness (Champathes, 2006).

Importance of Employee Development Activities

Employee development activities are very important for the employees, as the activities are performed, it indicates that organization cares about their employees and wants them to develop. Many of the organizations are investing in employee development. When organizations contribute towards the employee development activities, the employees work hard; utilize their full skills and efforts to achieve the goals of the organizations. There are many schools of thoughts. One school of thought says that employee development focuses on:

1. Self-Development
2. Self-Directed Learning

This concept indicates that employee development must be recognized by the employees who want to learn or who are willing to learn. When employees are willing to learn, they show their interest in the developmental activities, as a result they are more satisfied with the job which will lead to increase in employee performance . Employee development also depends upon the individual employee, how much curiosity to learn.

1. How much curiosity to learn an individual employee?
2. How to learn to develop themselves?

As when individual employee wants to learn, he would learn more and more, he would participate in many other activities such as attend seminars, workshops and others training sessions, either on the job or off the job. This indeed would lead to employee development, and employee development would lead to increase in employee performance. No matter how much expertise does a person have if person or employee is not willing to develop? No matter how much resources you provide employee would not be developed. So employee development is also a personal responsibility of the employees. Employees at all levels are involved in the developmental activities whether the upper level employees, middle or lower level employees (Antonacopoulou, 1996).

Challenges in Employee Development

As employee development depends upon the individual employee whether employee is willing to participate or not. Employee development also depends upon the organization culture, attitude of top management, and limited opportunities of promotion. (Elena, P. 2000; Antonacopoulou, 1996).

Organization Culture: If organization culture supports employees, it will encourage employees to participate in decision making, employees would develop more and performance would increase.

Attitude of Top Management: Top management attitude is another important factor that influences employee developmental activities. It depends on the sincerity and commitment of the top management.

Limited Opportunities of Promotion: If opportunities of promotion are limited then employees would not participate in the employee developmental activities.

Developmental Activities

Coaching: Coaching is an important activity for the employee development. Coaching is not formal. It involves treating employees as a personal partner in achieving both personal and organizational goals. Therefore, we can solve personal problems of the employees by providing coaching (Agarwal, 2006). When problems are resolved, this leads to increase in organizational performance as employees would be able to achieve organizational goals.

360 Degree Feedback and Developmental centers: 360 degree feedback and development centers are preplanned and are based on prior defined assessment criteria. As developmental centers are present in the organization or there are many developmental centers outside the organization and are very important as they provide training to the individual employee (Hazucha, 1993). How to be developed and employees can only be developed if they have a desire or motivation to be developed.

Developmental Appraisal: Developmental appraisal is an ongoing process for the employee development during the whole year. Basically, it is a compulsory part of the performance management. This appraisal will determine the weak area of employee where employee development is required in order to improve the employee performance (Kirkpatrick, 2006).

Investment in Perceived Developmental Activities of the Employees: The investment in perceived developmental activities of the employee are important in order to increase the employee performance. As investment in perceived developmental activities also provide the organization as a competitive advantage (Chay et al., 2003).

Competitive Advantage: Most of the organizations do not consider the employee developmental activities of much value. They only focus on achieving the goals of the organization. They do not care about the development of employees. So, if organizations would focus on employee developmental activities, this would help in enhancing the skills of the employees (Chay et al., 2003). As skills are enhanced, they would be able to develop their career and make realistic career plans and thus lead to increase the organizational effectiveness.

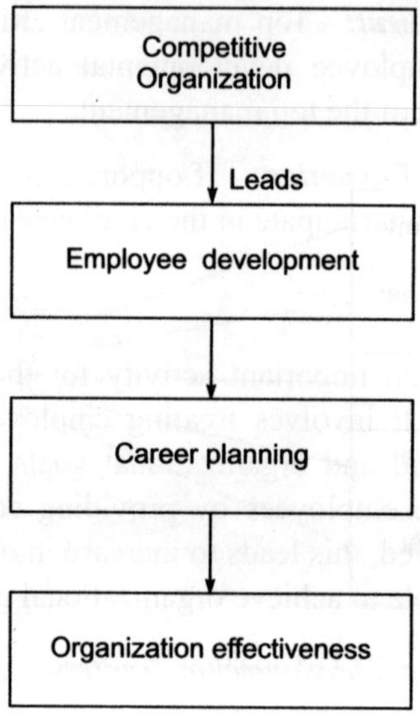

Competitive Focus Leads

Source: ChayHoon Lee and Norman T. Bruvold, (2003). Creating value for employees: investment in employee development, Int. J. of Human Resource Management, Vol. 14, No. 6, pp. 981–1000.

HR Practices on Employee Performance A large number of researchers have forwarded following classical theories (Husselid, Pfeffer, 1994; Arthur 1994). There are following major practices which affect employee performance:

- Organization
- Employee development
- Career planning
- Organization effectiveness
- Job autonomy
- Organizational support
- Training
- Distributive justice
- Procedural justice

Source: Hazucha, J., Hezlett, S. and Schneider, R. (1993), "The impact of 360-degree feedback on management skills development", Human Resource Management, Vol. 32, No. 2, pp. 325-51.

Five Major Practices

Autonomy

Organizational Support

Training
Distributive Justice
Procedural Justice

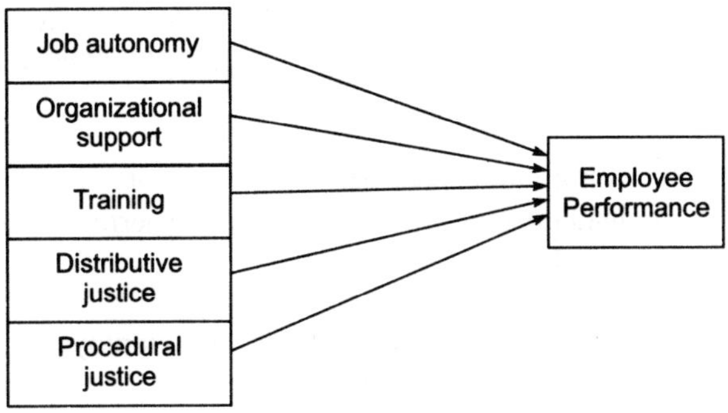

Five major practices

Source: Hazucha, J., Hezlett, S. and Schneider, R. (1993), "The impact of 360-degree feedback on management skills development", Human Resource Management, Vol. 32, No. 2, pp. 325–51.

Employee development is becoming an increasingly critical and strategic imperative for organizations in the current business environment (Sheri-Lynne, Parbudyal 2007). Following five variables of employee development will affect on employee performance:

Coaching
Training and development
Empowerment
Participation
Delegation

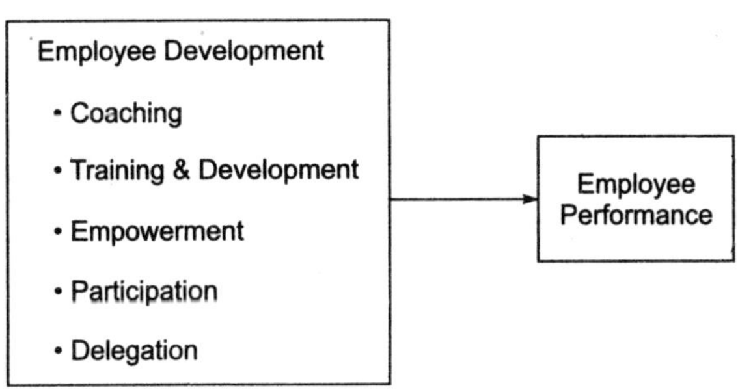

Coaching: Individuals are allowed to take the responsibility. They are treated as a partner to achieve personal and organizational goals. As goals are achieved, the performance is enhanced (Agarwal, 2006).

Training and Development: Training is the permanent change in behavior. Employee should be taught how to do a particular task? Development is a long-term process (Leibowitz, 1981).

Empowerment: Empowerment means to increase the capacity of the employee and also provide freedom of work which will build the confidence among the employees.

Participation: By letting employees participating in organization's policies or decision making can lead the employee to enhance the performance. They will be able to make more smart decisions.

Delegation: If managers delegate authority to the employees to perform the task what they want can also lead to enhance performance. Employees will do those activities which they can perform more easily. This will lead to achieve organizational goals and thus enhance organizational performance (effectiveness).

Proposed Model (Self Made): The proposed model is devised in the light of literature review of past researchers conducted in different studies related to employee development and employee performance. The proposed model is self made and explains the relationship between employee development and employee performance. Employee performance is a dependent variable and employee development is independent variable. Employee development variable is operationalized by the following sub variables;

Employee Performance
Skill growth
Employee learning
Self-directed
Employee attitude and behavior

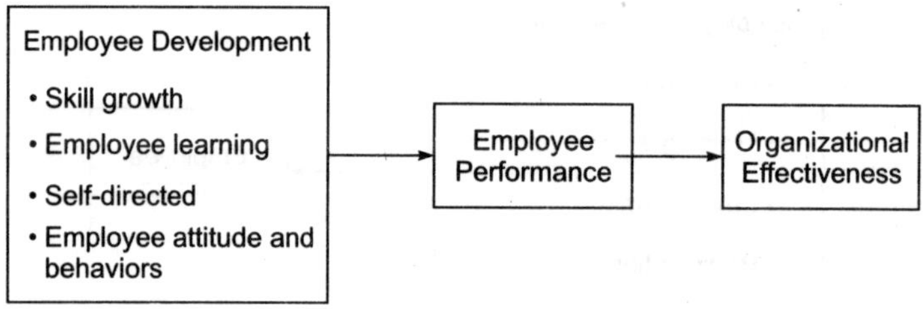

Proposed Model: Employee development and its effect on employee performance means employee productivity and output as a result of employee development. Employee performance will ultimately affect the organizational effectiveness.

Employee Learning: Employee learning explains the process of acquiring knowledge through curiosity to learn. It is a mindset who has anxiety to get information. Employee learning will increase the abilities and competency of the employee (Dixon 1999). The abilities and competencies are helpful in employee performance and productivity.

Skill Growth: It means to increase in the skill inventory level of an employee. The skill growth is possible through training and coaching. The skill level will affect the employee performance. Employee performance will affect the organizational effectiveness.

Self-directed: Employee development also depends upon the individual employee.

1. How much curiosity to learn an individual employee?
2. How to learn to develop themselves?

As when individual employee wants to learn, he would learn more and more, he would participate in many other activities such as attend seminars, workshops and others training sessions, either on the job or off the job. This indeed would lead to employee development, and employee development would lead to increase in employee performance (Elena P., 2000).

Employee Attitude and Behavior: Employee attitude and behavior refer to the responsiveness of an employee. When employee is nominated in different workshops, and training sessions, the employee attitude and behavior will determine the seriousness in training and development programs. The responsive employee will learn different skills which will increase the employee performance. Employee performance will affect the organizational productivity.

Employee Performance: Employee performance means employee productivity and output as a result of employee development. Employee performance will ultimately affect the organizational effectiveness.

Organizational Effectiveness: Organizational effectiveness refers to the achievement of overall organizational goals (Milkovich et al., 2004). Employee development leads to employee performance. Individual performance of an employee will lead to the organizational effectiveness.

Conclusion: Employee is a valuable resource (asset) of the organization. The success or failure of the organization depends on employee performance. Therefore, organizations are investing huge amount of money on employee development. The key variables identifies relatedness between employee development and employee performance. The paper presents the importance of the employee developmental activities, importance of investment in a human capital, and challenges in employee development. The further discussion develops a proposed model which explains the relationship between employee development variables (employee learning, skill growth, self-directed, employee attitude) and employee performance variable. The employee performance will affect on organizational effectiveness.

References

1. Antonacopoulou, E.P. and FitzGerald, L. (1996). Reframing competency in management development: a critique, *Human Resource Management Journal*, Vol. 6 No. 1, pp. 27–48.
2. Agarwal, R., C. M. Angst and M. Magni (2006). The performance effects of coaching: A multilevel analysis using hierarchical linear modeling, Robert H. Smith School of Business Research Paper Series.
3. Abbas Q. and Yaqoob S., (2009). Effect of Leadership Development on Employee Performance in Pakistan. *Pakistan Economic and Social Review,* Vol. 47, No. 2, pp. 269-292. Burgoyne, J. (1977),
4. Self-development, managerial success and effectiveness: some empirical evidence", *MEAD Journal*, Vol. 8 No. 2, pp. 16–20.
5. Champathes M. R. (2006), Coaching for performance improvement: The coach model. *Development and Learning in Organizations*, Vol. 20, No. 2, pp. 17–18.
6. ChayHoon Lee and Norman T. Bruvold, (2003). Creating value for employees: investment in employee development, *Int. J. of Human Resource Management*, Vol. 14, No. 6 pp. 981–1000.
7. Collins, D. and Holton, E.F. (2004). "The effectiveness of managerial leadership development programs: a meta analysis of studies from 1982 to 2001", *Human Resource Development Quarterly*, Vol. 15 No. 2, pp. 217–48.
8. David Preece, and Paul Iles, (2009). Executive development assuaging uncertainties through joining a leadership academy. *Journal of Personnel Review,* Vol. 38 No. 3, pp. 286–306 Emerald Group Publishing Limited.
9. Dixon, N. M., (1999). The organizational Learning Cycle: How we can Learn Collectively. Second Edition (4), Gower pp. 63–91.
10. Elena P. Antonacopoulou, (2000). Employee development through self-development in three retail banks. *Journal of Personnel Review,* Vol. 29 No. 4, pp. 491–508.
11. Ellinger and S. B. Keller (2003). Supervisory Coaching Behaviour, Employee Satisfaction, and Warehouse Employee Performance: A Dyadic Perspective in the Distribution Industry. *Human Resource Development Quarterly*, Vol. 14, Issue 4, pp. 435–458.

12. Fisher, D. Merron, K. and Corbert, W. (1987). "Human development and managerial effectiveness", Group and Organisational Studies, Vol. 12 No. 3, pp. 257–73.
13. Hazucha, J., Hezlett, S. and Schneider, R. (1993). "The impact of 360-degree feedback on management skills development", *Human Resource Management*, Vol. 32 No. 2, pp. 325–51.
14. Huselid, M.A. (1995). The Impact of Human Resource Management Practices on Turnover, Productivity, and Corporate Financial Performance, *Academy of Management Journal*, 38: 635–72.
15. Hwang, S. A. (2003). Training strategies in the management of knowledge. *Journal of Knowledge Management*, Vol. 7, No. 3, pp. 92–104.
16. Kirkpatrick, D. L. (2006), *Improving Employee Performance Through Appraisal and Coaching*. American Management Association Publication.
17. Leibowitz, Z. and Schlossberg, N. (1981). 'Training managers for their role in a career development system', *Training and Development Journal*, pp. 72–79.
18. Milkovich, George T. and John W. Boudreau (2004). The Changing Definition of Organizational Effectiveness, *Journal of Human Resource Planning*, Vol. 27.1, 2004. pp. 53–59.
19. Mwita, J. I. (2000), Performance management model: A system-based approach to system quality. *The International Journal of Public Sector Management*, Vol. 13, No. 1, pp. 19–37.
20. R. A. and Wilk, S. L. (1993). 'Investigation of the factors that influence employees participation in development activities', *Journal of Applied Psychology*, 78, 291–302.
21. Raymond A. Noe, (1996). Is Career Management Related to Employee Development and Performance? *Journal of Organizational Behavior,* Vol. 17, No. 2, pp. 119–133.

20

Cultivating Ethics and Human Values: A Case of Migrants

Ankita Sharma
Registrar, Dr. Virendra Swarup Education Foundation, Kanpur
E-mail:ankitasharma@vsef.org, 09453037350(m)

ABSTRACT

This paper discusses how gaps in both the data on migration and the understanding of the role of migration in livelihood strategies and economic growth in India, have led to inaccurate policy prescriptions and a lack of political commitment to improving the living and working conditions of migrants. Field evidence from major migrant employing sectors is synthesized to show that circular migration is the dominant form of economic mobility for the poor; especially the lower castes and tribes. The authors argue that the human costs of migration are high due to faulty implementation of protective legislation and loopholes in the law and not due to migration per se. The paper discusses child labour in specific migration streams in detail stressing that this issue needs to be addressed in parallel. It also highlights the non-economic drivers and outcomes of migration that need to be considered when understanding its impacts. The authors calculate that there are roughly 100 million circular migrants in India contributing 10% to the national GDP. New vulnerabilities created by the economic recession are also discussed.

BACKGROUND AND INTRODUCTION

Migration in India is not new. Historical accounts show that people have moved in search of work, in response to environmental shocks and stresses, to escape religious persecution and political conflict. However improved communications, transport networks, conflicts over natural resources and new economic opportunities have created unprecedented levels of mobility. But as we discuss in following sections, the increase in mobility is not fully captured in larger surveys often leading to erroneous conclusions about mobility levels in India.

Although significant in recent years, growth has been unequal in India (Balisacan and Ducanes 2005), characterized by industry in developed states such as Gujarat, Maharashtra and Punjab drawing labour from agriculturally backward and poor regions such as eastern Uttar Pradesh, Bihar, southern Madhya Pradesh, western Orissa and southern Rajasthan. High productivity agricultural areas ("green revolution areas") continue to be important destinations, but rural urban migration is the fastest growing type of migration as more migrants choose to work in better paying non-farm occupations in urban areas and industrial zones. Delhi and the states of Gujarat and Maharashtra are top destinations for inter-state migrant labour. Labour mobility has grown and will probably continue to grow once the economy recovers from the current crisis.

Migrant labour makes enormous contributions to the Indian economy through major sectors such as construction, textiles, small industries, brick-making, stone quarries, mines, fish and prawn processing and hospitality services. But migrants remain on the periphery of society, with few citizen rights and no political voice in shaping decisions that impact their lives (Kabeer 2005). Unlike countries in Southeast Asia and East Asia, the bulk of the migrant workforce in India has little or no education (Srivastava 2003). In fact migrants are poorly endowed all-round: they come from poor families where access to physical, financial and human capital is limited and where prospects for improving living standards are constrained by their inferior social and political status. Historically disadvantaged communities such as the Scheduled Castes, Scheduled Tribes and Other Backward Castes are heavily represented in migration. Poor migrants are absorbed in informal sector jobs, much maligned for being insecure, poorly paid and unproductive but offering the only option for labourers to improve their capabilities.

MAJOR MIGRANT EMPLOYING SECTORS

A search through published and grey literature on migration shows that there is large number of studies which portray a very different picture of migration. They show that circular migration is the main form of mobility for work and that such migration is higher among the poor and especially SCs and STs . They also show higher rates of migration among women and children.

All three sectors of the Indian economy, namely, agriculture, industry and services employ very large numbers of migrant workers. Field evidence shows that the major subsectors using migrant labour are textiles, construction, stone quarries and mines, brick-kilns, small-scale industry (diamond cutting, leather accessories, etc.), crop transplanting and harvesting, sugarcane cutting, plantations, rickshaw pulling, food processing including fish and prawn processing, salt panning, domestic work, security services, sex work, small hotels and roadside restaurants/ tea shops and street vending. We piece together available information on the numbers of workers involved and their contribution to the economy. There are gaps in the information and we have not been able to cover all sectors but we can convey the significance of migration to India's economy. Some of the sectors are strongly associated with specific migration streams (e.g., migration from western Orissa for brick kiln work in Andhra Pradesh and migration from Bihar for agricultural work in Punjab) which have differing recruitment and remuneration patterns and varying impacts on human development. A small number is discussed here to provide insights into the recruitment practices of companies and agents and how they circumvent the legal system to extract cheap labour in return for few obligations to migrant labourers and their families. The earnings and human development impacts of these migration streams are discussed wherever evidence has been available. These accounts also show that distinctions between migration, trafficking, bonded labour and child labour are often difficult to make because of the widespread use of child labour in agriculture, industry and services and the poor working conditions of migrants. The next part pulls together all the available evidence to analyse the implications of migration for human development and how policy distortions and implementation failures can be addressed.

INDUSTRY

Construction

The construction industry provides direct employment to at least 30 million workers in India (Chen 2007) but recent expansions (before the economic crisis) had resulted in a higher number: trade unions estimate that there were roughly 40 million migrant construction workers in India in 2008 (Sarde 2008). Although numbers would have gone down with the recent economic crisis there will nevertheless be a continuation of urban construction which will attract migrant workers. There is anecdotal evidence that some categories of returnee migrants from the Gulf have been absorbed in construction. Construction attracts both skilled workers (masons, carpenters) and unskilled workers , although there is some scope for upward mobility, poorer and lower caste/tribe migrants tend to remain in low-paid unskilled jobs. This is because of discrimination against them and being excluded from opportunities to gain skills. Women work mainly as unskilled workers.

Textile Industry

The textile industry in India (including the garment industry) is the largest foreign exchange earner among all other industrial sectors and provides direct employment to around 35 million people. A large proportion of these workers is migrants, judging from micro-studies (Unni and Bali 2006) but it is difficult to put a precise figure on the numbers. The textile industry is extremely complex in its structure, with handlooms and home-based production at one end of the spectrum, to capital intensive, large mills at the other. Small, privately owned power looms now dominate the industry. Yarn production is still in large mills but 78 per cent of the cloth production occurs in smaller power looms and handlooms. According to labour statistics published by the Labour Bureau 31% of the workers in the manmade textile industry were migrants.

Silk Industry

Sericulture is a labour-intensive industry and employs roughly 6 million people in different stages of production including rearing silk worms, reeling thread, twisting, dyeing, weaving, printing and finishing (Ministry of Textiles) in all its phases, namely, cultivation of silkworm food plants, silkworm rearing, silk reeling, and other post-cocoon processes such as twisting, dyeing, weaving, printing and finishing. It provides employment to approximately 6 million persons, most of them being small and marginal farmers, or tiny and household industry mainly in the hand reeling and hand weaving sections. Mulberry silk is produced extensively in the states of Karnataka, West Bengal and Jammu and Kashmir. About 85 per cent of the country's production is contributed by the Karnataka. Silk thread making and sari folding have now become notorious for employing large number of children.

Education

Children who migrate on their own or migrate with their parents miss school. There are no official estimates of the numbers of migrating children out of school but 6 million is now a widely accepted figure for India (AIF 2006). The inability to educate children perpetuates poverty beyond the present generation into the next one and the government of India recognizes the need to reach migrating children, at least through legislation. The underlying assumption is that educating the children of poor workers will interrupt the intergenerational transmission of poverty.

The scheme for universal primary education, the Sarva Shiksha Abhiyan (SSA) and the Education Guarantee Scheme and Alternative and Innovative Education (EGS & AIE) programme promise a number of facilities to make education more accessible to mobile children. These include mobile schools, examinations on demand; bridge courses, residential camps and drop-in centres for street and slum children.

Food

In India food grains are allocated to the States by the Food Ministry under the Targeted Public Distribution System (TPDS) on the basis of state poverty levels and on the directions of other ministries for welfare schemes (Rural Development and Human Resource Development). The food grains are provided to BPL (below the official poverty line) households through more than 400,000 Fair Price Shops covering 160 million families. The scale of this welfare programme makes it the largest distribution network of its type in the world, at least on paper (Saxena 2007). A Planning Evaluation Organisation study in 2005 found that about 58 per cent of the subsidized food grain did not reach the intended beneficiaries because of identification errors, nontransparent operation and corrupt practices in the implementation of TPDS. There are errors of wrong inclusion and of "ghost" cards and non-BPL households being included (Saxena 2007). Performance is geographically uneven with "backward" states such as Bihar and Jharkhand showing very poor results.

HUMAN DEVELOPMENT IMPACTS

Income data were available for both 2001/2 and 2006/7 for only 155 households with mobile earners (commuters, seasonal and permanent migrants) from 5 villages; the sample distribution by village is also reported. These households were drawn from 300 households surveyed in 2001/2. While all the households were migrating households in 2006/7, this was not the case in previous rounds where some were non-migrants.

Table 1 Distribution of Migrant Households in Sample Villages, 2006/07 Survey, Andhra Pradesh, India

Villages	*Frequency*	*Percent*
OP	24	15.5
VP	31	20.0
KO	33	21.3
GU	38	24.5
MD	29	18.7
Total	155	100.0

MIGRATION AND POVERTY STATUS IN AP

Head count income poverty was calculated using poverty lines of Rs 3100.68 per person per annum for 2001/2, and Rs 4028.65 per person per annum for 2006/7. These poverty lines were computed using GDP deflators and the Andhra Pradesh rural poverty line of Rs 292.95 per person per month for 2004/5. Households were first classified as poor and non-poor based on the poverty line for both 2001/2 and 2006/7. It was possible to trace the poverty status of the same households over a period of five years and those who remained poor in both periods were classified as chronically poor. Those who were poor in one of the periods i.e. 2001/2 or 2006/7 were regarded as vulnerable. Those who were not poor in both periods were classified as stable. Poverty was proportionately higher among the schedule tribes, marginal farmers and located proportionally more in poorly-connected villages (Akter et al., 2008).

Comparing the two rounds of 2001/2 and 2006/7 and by tracing the situation of the same households (using household ID) it was seen that the proportion of households with migrants in the category of poor had gone down from 45% to 29%. Using poverty transition matrices we calculate that the average mobility out of 100 households is 41; upward mobility is more than double the downward mobility. Upward mobility means movement from poor to non-poor and downward mobility is the opposite. In this period the crude probability of becoming poor given that a person was non-poor is 23% and the probability of escaping poverty given that a person was poor is 64%. It appeared from the quintile based analysis that over this period 36.2% moved upward and 34.1% downward; consistent with the developing country situation where immobility ranges from 30% to 40% over a five year period (Baulch and McCulloch 1998; Baulch and Hoddinot 2000).

Furthermore, the analysis shows that upward movement is the highest (45.2%) among the most experienced migrants (those who were already migrants in 2001/2 are taken here as the most experienced migrants). This indicates positive contribution of migration towards poverty reduction. More experienced people may be more resilient and are capable of using opportunities to move upward. Although upward movement is the highest in the experienced cohort, the poverty head count is still the highest (37.1%) in this group. This may be due to the fact that less poor households entered migration and commuting streams in later rounds as they became more attractive with rising wages and other factors.

POLITICAL PARTICIPATION

Questions related to political participation were included in the rabi 2002 questionnaire in Andhra Pradesh. A total of 360 households from 6 villages were interviewed to assess participation in socio-political/administrative forums and voting. Data were collected on a number of dimensions of political participation including attending meetings, raising issues, voting, campaigning and communicating with officials.

CONCLUSION

Sector reviews and case studies show that migrant labourers live and work in extremely difficult and dangerous conditions. They are on the margins of society both economically and socially and face unnecessary high costs and risks because of non-recognition at the policy level and faulty implementation of labour laws. Both secondary and primary data show that migration is an important route out of poverty. But the impacts of migration on poverty reduction and the contribution that migrants make to the economy are under-recognised. Our estimates show that migrants contribute around 10% to the National GDP.

Nearly all sectors employ migrant workers (including children) through a complex system of contractors and agents who are well-positioned to exploit illiterate and poor workers. Where workers have become more experienced and confident the hold of market intermediaries has weakened but in the absence of effective employment exchanges for the poor, agents and contractors provide vital information and job opportunities to people who would otherwise be unemployed in villages.

The lack of data and the laxity in implementing labour laws indicate an underlying lack of political commitment to improving the lives of migrant workers (adults and children). India seems to be struggling with being told by the ILO and labour unions on the one hand that labour laws need to be made more stringent but being told at the same time by neo-liberal economists that existing labour laws are too rigid and are stifling productivity. However, there has to be a level beyond which human rights violations will not be tolerated and India needs to take a stronger position on protecting migrant workers.

The immediate need is to change the policy level discourse on migration by reviewing key documents and policies and moving away from theory and language which portrays migration as bad and something that must be stopped.

References

1. AIF (2006) Locked Homes and Empty Schools. Zubaan/America India Foundation, New Delhi.
2. Action Aid (2008a) Bonded workers freed from Jaipur sari hellhole. Available at http://www.actionaid.org/india/index.aspx?PageID=3889
3. Action Aid (2008b) Just nuts: Supermarkets thrive on women cashew workers' poverty.Available at http://www.actionaid.org/india/index.aspx?PageID = 2819.
4. ActionAid (2005) From Hunger to Suffering … a Journey: Migrant Workers in the Brick Kilns.
5. Akter S, Farrington J, Deshingkar P, and Freeman A (2008). Livestock, Vulnerability and Poverty.
6. Dynamics in India, Discussion Paper (forthcoming). Targeting and Innovation. ILRI (International Livestock Research Institute), Nairobi, Kenya.Balisacan, A.M. and Ducanes, G.M. (2005) Inequality in Asia: A Synthesis of Recent Research on the Levels, Trends, Effects and Determinants of Inequality in its Different Dimensions.
7. The Inter-Regional Inequality Facility, London: Overseas Development Institute.
8. Baulch, B. and J. Hoddinot, 2000, 'Economic Mobility and Poverty Dynamics in Developing Countries', Journal of Development Studies, 36(6): 1-24.
9. Baulch B and McCulloch N (1998). Being Poor and Becoming Poor: Poverty Status and Poverty.
10. Transitions in Rural Pakistan, Working Paper 79, Institute of Development Studies, Sussex.
11. Borhade, A. (2007). Addressing the needs of seasonal migrants in Nashik, Maharashtra Disha Foundation/Population Council, New Delhi.

21

Job Satisfaction of Employees in Mumbai Refinery of Bharat Petroleum Corporation Limited

Tazyn Rahman
Dean, Jaipuria Institute, Ghaziabad (U. P.)
Email: tazyn08@gmail.com

ABSTRACT

The globalization in petroleum sector not only invites private sector companies in oil refining business but also sharp increase in employee turnover. The business environment saw many changes after the initial phase of deregulation. Retention of market share would be a serious threat with anticipation of the entry of new local (private) and global players in this sector. In order to "survive", Indian organizations and in particular, the petroleum sector are being forced to undergo massive changes. In this context, it would be important to identify the factors in the organizational environment that have the most positive impact on the performance of the organization. Among various factors, attitudes and feelings of the individuals regarding their jobs are very important. Job satisfaction is the result of various attitudes the employee holds towards his job, towards related factors and towards life in general. The importance of job satisfaction is that if the people are satisfied with their work, then there is an improvement in both the quality and quantity of production.

Job satisfaction is a topic which has received much attention from academicians, researchers, and practicing managers. Various studies have been conducted to find out the factors which determine job satisfaction and the way it influences productivity in the organization. Though there is no conclusive evidence that job satisfaction affects productivity directly since productivity depends on many variables, it is still a prime concern for managers. Job satisfaction is the mental feeling of favorableness which an individual has about his job. It is often said that "a happy employee is a productive employee." Job satisfaction is very important because most of the people spend a major portion of their life at their workplace. Moreover, job satisfaction has its impact on the general life of the employees also, because a satisfied employee is a contented and happy human being. A highly satisfied worker has better physical and mental well-being. The study tries to evaluate how human resource factors affect the satisfaction level of employees in Mumbaii Refinery in BPCL. It assesses how far welfare and financial factors motivate the employees in the company. The study also attempts to analyze the opinion of employees towards the work life in the company.

INTRODUCTION

Fieldman and Arnold defined job satisfaction as "the amount of overall positive effect or feelings that individuals have towards their jobs". At its most general level of conceptualization, job satisfaction is simply how content an individual is with his or her job. At the more specific levels of conceptualization used by academic researchers and human resources professionals, job satisfaction has varying definitions. Affective job satisfaction is usually defined as an unidimensional subjective construct representing an overall emotional feeling individuals have about their job as a whole. Hence, affective job satisfaction for individuals reflects the degree of pleasure or happiness their job in general induces.

LITERATURE REVIEW

David C. McClelland (1940) reveals three needs that motivate human behavior: power, affiliation and achievement. Every person has a need for any one of these needs. Locke (1976) stated job satisfaction as a pleasurable positive state resulting from one's job and job experience. Individuals show pleasurable positive attitudes when they are satisfied with their job.

Robert M. Hochheiser (1998) reassessed the meaning of the workplace and proposed a simple formula for success: "Forget the idea that hard work alone leads to success and instead focus on building good relationships". He asserts that the best way to win at work is to understand what is needed to support the egos of bosses, peers, and subordinates. Chris Stride, Toby D. Wall, Nick Catley (2008) presented widely used measurement scales of job satisfaction, mental health, job-related well-being and organizational commitment, along with benchmarking data for comparison. The benchmarking data is based on a sample of almost 60,000 respondents from 115 different organizations across a wide spectrum of industries and occupations. Information is given by occupational group, and is further broken down by age and gender. C. J. Cranny, Patricia Cain Smith, Eugène F. Stone (1992) reveals perceiving future opportunity can actually be more motivating than actually receiving a raise, getting promoted, or being given additional responsibilities.

Paul E. Spector (1997) summarizes the findings concerning how people feel towards work, including: cultural and gender differences in job satisfaction and personal and organizational causes; and potential consequences of job satisfaction and dissatisfaction. He provides with a pithy overview of the application, assessment, causes and consequences of job satisfaction. Joanna Penn (2008) teaches how to improve your position in your current employment, gaining more from your job, discovering more about yourself and what it is you would be happy doing, stress management and people management. Evren Esen (2007) examined in terms of industry and staff size as well as employee age and gender more than 20 indicators of job satisfaction including career advancement opportunities, benefits, the flexibility to balance life and work, and compensation. Elwood Chapman (1993) helps to determine employee level of satisfaction and then assists in making positive changes to increase both satisfaction level and quality of work.

OBJECTIVES OF THE STUDY

Employees are the main forces of an industry and their efficiency can move an organization to success. Only with a group of satisfied employees the company can lead into success. For employee satisfaction, the company must provide adequate welfare measures. By conducting a job satisfaction survey, we can analyze whether the employees are satisfied or not and also whether they are motivated by the general, welfare, financial and other related factors. This study aims to achieve the following objectives in this context:

1. To assess how far welfare and financial factors motivate the employees in Mumbai Refinery.
2. To determine the opinion of employees towards the work life in Mumbai Refinery.
3. To determine the various facilities provided by Mumbai Refinery.
4. To evaluate how human resource factors affect the satisfaction level of employees in Mumbai Refinery.
5. To conduct a brief study to analyse the various functions performed by these sections.
6. To suggest suitable measures to improve welfare measures in the organization.
7. To suggest any measures in jobs to increase the efficiency of the employees.

RESEARCH METHODOLOGY

Both primary and secondary data are used for the study. The primary data are collected by using questionnaire method. Secondary data are collected from books, journals, company manuals, company website, company magazines and informal talk with the officers and the employees. The survey was conducted in four departments of Mumbai Refinery under Bharat Petroleum Corporation Limited, namely, Human Resource Development (HRD) Department, Maintenance Department (MD), Captive Power Plant (CPP) and Finance & Accounts (F & A). The total number of employees in 4 departments are 290.

- Human Resource Development - 38
- Maintenance Department - 72
- Captive Power Plant - 98
- Finance & Accounts - 82

Out of the total 290 employees, 100 employees were selected as sample. The questionnaires were distributed to the respondents in the selected sample.

ANALYSIS AND INTERPRETATION OF DATA

Table 1 Gender-wise Response to the Survey

Gender	*Respondents*	*Percentage*
Male	78	78
Female	22	22

Source: Primary data through questionnaire

From the above table & graph, it can be interpreted that out of 100 respondents of different age profile, male represented 78% of the sample while 22% were females.

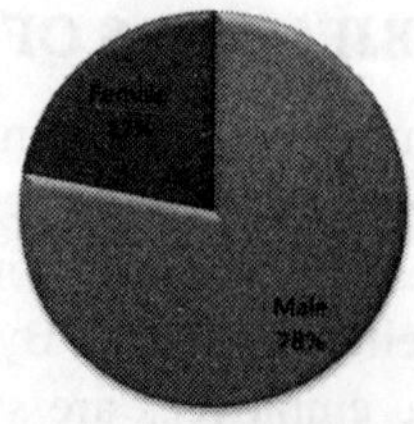

Employee Response on Job Security

The graph shows that 90% of the employees are satisfied. 41% have excellent opinion about job security whereas 49% have good opinion about job security When adequate job security is provided to the employees it will motivate them to do their work and increase productivity.

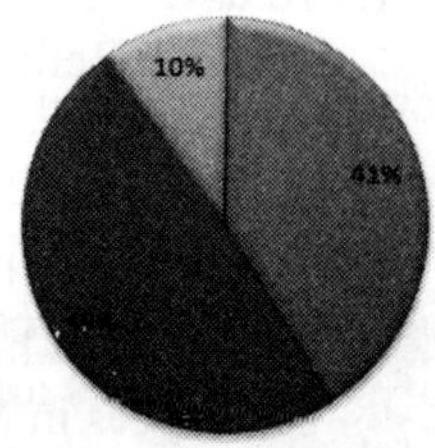

Source: Primary data through questionnaire

Employee Response on Communication

The graph depicts that 88% of the employees are satisfied about their communication with subordinates. Regarding communication with superiors, 76% of the employees are satisfied. Good communication among employees has a positive impact on job satisfaction.

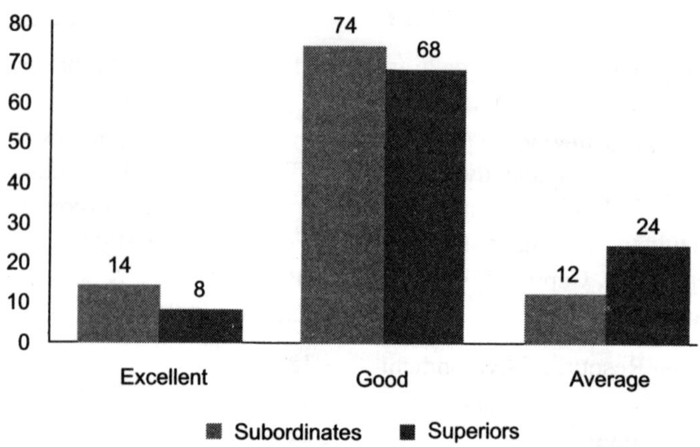

Source: Primary data through questionnaire

Employee Response on Interpersonal Relationship

The chart shows that 78% employees are satisfied with respect to the interpersonal relationship existing in the organization. Rest 22% are dissatisfied. Interpersonal relationships among employees serve as a source of support, comfort, advice and assistance to the individual group members and it will have a positive impact on job satisfaction.

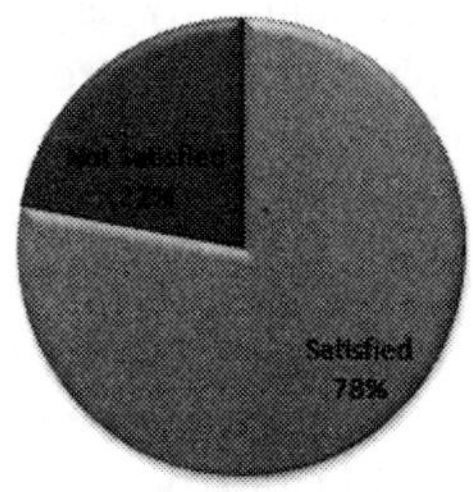

Source: Primary data through questionnaire.

Employee Response on Training & Development

Mumbai Refinery Limited provides various types of training such as apprenticeship training, refresher training, etc., which improves the performance of the employees and thus results in better production. The table below reflects that 62% of the employees are satisfied of which 53% have a good opinion. But rest 38% of them are not so satisfied with the training and development facilities provided.

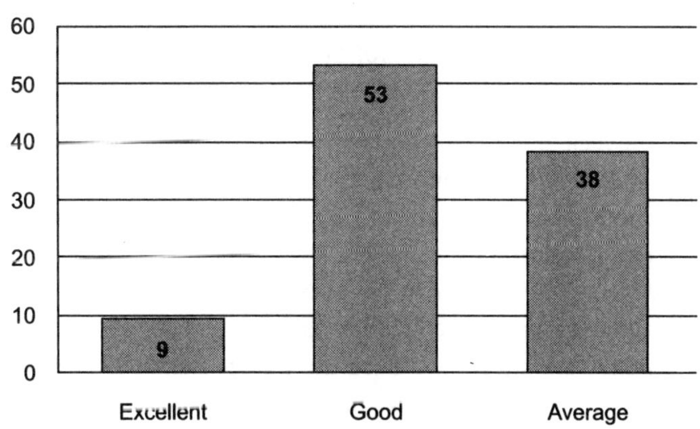

Source: Primary data through questionnaire

FINDINGS OF THE STUDY

The following are the major findings of the study:

1. Mumbai Refinery provides adequate job security to the employees which motivates them to do their work.
2. The employees are free from various tensions regarding their family security and thus they devote more time for their work.
3. Career development in the company is limited only to ambitious and achievement oriented employees for improving their skills.
4. Mumbai Refinery provides good salary package, incentives and leave travel facilities to employees, which energizes them to work more and reduce labour turnover. However, majority of the employees are of the view that the promotion policies adopted by the company should be revised.
5. The employees are highly satisfied with the medical benefits provided by the company. They are satisfied with the sick, casual, maternity and personal leave provided to them.
6. The canteen facility and the club facilities in the form of music, sports, games and theatre of Mumbai Refinery are excellent. However majority of the employees feels that the transportation facilities should be improved.
7. The employees are satisfied with housing facilities and concessional rate of interest offered on loan of housing, vehicle and education.
8. The company gives adequate importance to its retired employees through its medical benefit scheme and pension package.

SUGGESTIONS

Based on the above findings, the following recommendations are made for improving job satisfaction among employees in Mumbai Refinery.

1. The employees should be given an opportunity to participate in decision-making so that the decisions can be smoothly implemented.
2. The promotion policy should be time bound and uniform in order to keep the morale of the employees high.
3. Incentives may be provided to employees who successfully complete courses under company's education assistance scheme.
4. The company should re-introduce the transportation facility to its officers which will reduce cost over-run and savings in income.
5. The management can assist the employees in building their career by identifying critical jobs accordingly to their qualifications and by allocating additional/higher responsibilities to enrich their skills.

6. There is an urgent need for adoption and implementation of suggestion schemes. The grievance handling system should be made more efficient and the company should see that complaints are solved quickly.
7. There is a need to improve the career development opportunities. This reduces boredom, monotony and job dissatisfaction.
8. Mumbai Refinery should give more emphasis on training and development programmes. Job rotation system should be improved with a view to develop multiple skills in employees and create greater job interest and career options.
9. More and more opportunities should be provided to employees to promote interpersonal relationships and communication.

LIMITATIONS OF THE STUDY

1. Due to the busy work schedule of the employees, the responses may not be sincere and hence invalid.
2. Though the study aims at examining the job satisfaction, the depth analysis was restricted to the selected unit of Mumbai Refinery. All units could not be covered due to large size of the organization.
3. The data for the present study is collected from only middle and lower level employees.
4. Due to lack of time and considering the resources available, the study was limited to four departments and 290 employees only.
5. Some respondents hesitated to give the actual situation. They feared that management might take action against them.

CONCLUSION

The main conclusion drawn from this study is that, employees are satisfied with their work and working environment. The management has taken the best efforts to maintain cordial relationship with the employees. From the study, the researcher has come to know that most of the employees were satisfied with the welfare measures provided by company. There is more safety for employees like job security. This job satisfaction study was a procedure by which employees report their feelings towards their job and work environment. It helped as a powerful diagnostic instrument for assessing employee problems. As mentioned earlier that "if the people are satisfied with their work, then there is an improvement in both the quality and quantity of production" and this statement is proved true in company performance in year 2011 – 12, in which the company was able to achieve an all time record breaking production of 127% of its installed capacity.

BIBLIOGRAPHY

Journal

1. Jha, P. and Pathak, G.W. 2003. "A Comparative study of job satisfaction in the post-liberalization scenario among executives of private and public sector organizations". Indian Management Studies Journal, Vol. 7, pp. 21–31.
2. Reddy, K.S. and Rajasekhar, K.S. 1990. "Job satisfaction, job involvement and work involvement of permanent and temporary employees", Indian Journal of Applied Psychology, Vol. 28 No. 1, pp. 5–10.
3. Mohan, V. and Chauhan 1999. "A comparative study of organisational Role stress amongst managers of government, public and private sectors", Journal of Indian Academy of Applied Psychology, Vol. 25 No. 1-2, pp. 45–50.
4. Srivastava, S.K. and Pratap, S. 1984. "Perception of job satisfaction and organisational climate", Perspectives of Psychological Research, Vol. 7, pp. 41–43.

Conference/Symposium Papers

1. Ali, N. and Akhtar, Z. 1999. "Job satisfaction as related to organisational climate among bank officers", Paper presented in 4th international & 35th IAAP conference at Anand (Gujarat), May 27–29.
2. Srivastava, S.K. 1994. Correlational study of organisational climate and need satisfaction with job involvement. Paper presented in Asian and XXXII IAAP Conference at A.M.U., Aligarh. Feb. 27–29.

Books

1. Buhler, Patricia, Scott, Jason (2009), 'The Employee Satisfaction Revolution: Understanding and Unleashing the Power of a Satisfied Workforce', Prestwick House, Inc.
2. Boucher, Jane (2004), 'How to Love the Job You Hate: Job Satisfaction for the 21st Century', Beagle Bay Books.
3. Cranny, C. J, Smith, Patricia Cain, Stone, Eugène. F (1992), ' Job satisfaction: how people feel about their jobs and how it affects their performance', Lexington Books.
4. C.B. Mamoria: Personnel Management, Himalaya Publishing House.
5. Davis L.E.: Job satisfaction research (The Post Industrial view – Industrial relations).
6. Drever. J: Dictionary of Psychology (Penguin books, Middlesex) 1998.
7. Esen,Evren (2007), 'Job Satisfaction', Society for Human Resource Management.

8. Hochheiser, Robert M. (1998) 'Its a Job Not a Jail: How to Break Your Shackles When You Can't Afford to Quit', Simon & Schuster.
9. Hoppocke. R: Job satisfaction (Harper, New Yark) 1996.
10. K. Ashwathappa: Human Resource & Personnel Management, Tata Mc Graw Hill Publications, New Delhi
11. Locke G.A.: What is job satisfaction (Organizational behavior and human performance)
12. P. Subba Rao: Human Resource Management & Industrial Relations, Himalaya Publishing House.
13. Rowan, Sophie (2008) 'Happy at Work: Ten Steps to Ultimate Job Satisfaction', Pearson Education Limited.
14. Spector, Paul. E (1997) 'Job Satisfaction: Application, Assessment, Causes, and Consequences', Sage Publications.
15. Stride, Chris, D. Wall, Toby, Catley, Nick (2008) 'Measures of Job Satisfaction, Organisational Commitment, Mental Health and Job Related Well-being', John Wiley and Sons.

Website www.bharatpetroleum.com

22

Green Marketing: An Analysis of Consumer Behaviour Towards Green Products

Ghazala Shoeb
Scholar, Shobhit University
E-mail: gazala.shoeb@gmail.com

Amima Shoeb
Assistant Professor
Faculty of Commerce & Management Studies
Rama University Uttar Pradesh Kanpur
E-mail: amimashoeb89@gmail.com

Satish Chandra Ojha
Assistant Professor
STEP-HBTI, Kanpur
E-mail: satish2011@gmail.com

ABSTRACT

The term Green Marketing is the buzzword used in industry which is used to describe business activities which attempt to reduce the negative effect of the products/services offered by the company to make it environment-friendly.

Environment-friendly, so called green marketing has become a discussion subject and companies are constantly trying to find the best ways to reach the customers with their green message. Customers are becoming more demanding and they have started to pay more attention to the environment. Increasing awareness on the various environmental problems has led a shift in the way consumers go about their life. There has been a change in consumer behavior towards a green lifestyle. People are actively trying to reduce their impact on the environment.

This paper attempts to analyze the consumer behavior towards green products on customer satisfaction and environmental safety using comprehensive literature review. As a result, this paper can be used by researchers who need to find out the impact of green marketing on customer satisfaction, challenges and environmental safety.

INTRODUCTION

A majority of people believe that green marketing refers solely to the promotion or advertising of products with environmental characteristics. Terms like phosphate-free, recyclable, refillable, ozone-friendly, and environment-friendly are some of the things consumers most often associate with green marketing. Thus, green marketing incorporates a broad range of activities, including product modification, changes to the production process, packaging changes, as well as modifying advertising. Green marketing is growing rapidly and consumers are willing to pay a lot for green product. There has been little analysis of the impact of this new market on the consumers and the environment so far. Green marketing affects all areas of our economy, it does not just lead to environmental protection but it also creates new market and job opportunities. Companies that are environmental stewards stand a chance of gaining many satisfied and loyal customers.

The growth of green marketing research dates back to1980s when there was emergence of concept of green marketing. Early literature indicates green marketing to be an approach which indicated signs of shift in consumer attention to green product. At that time green marketing research concentrated on the shift in consumer consumption of green products.

Literature Review

The American Marketing Association (AMA) held the first workshop on ecological marketing in 1975. 1980 was the first time green marketing came into existence. AMA defines green marketing as the marketing of products that are presumed to be environmentally safe. It incorporates several activities such as product modification, changes to production processes, and packaging, advertising strategies and also increases awareness on compliance marketing amongst industries. Business Dictionary defines green marketing as promotional activities aimed at taking advantage of changing consumer attitude towards a brand. These changes are increasingly being influenced by a firm's policies and practices that affect the quality of the environment and reflect the level of its concern for the community. It can also be seen as the promotion of environmentally safe or beneficial products.

Environmental marketing, more popularly known as green marketing or sustainable marketing can also be defined as the effort by a company to design, promote, price and distribute products in a manner which promotes environmental protection (Polonsky, 2011). Green marketing is 'all activities designed to generate and facilitate any exchanges intended to satisfy human needs or wants such that the satisfaction of these needs and wants occurs, with minimal detrimental impact on the natural environment'(Polonsky, 1994).This definition is much broader and incorporates much of the traditional components of the conventional marketing definition and also includes the protection of natural environment. Today green marketing is a vital component of marketing research which began due to increasing media exposure and pressure on firms to present ecofriendly behaviour. The growth in green marketing over the years has been promoted by adoption of product packaging and presenting to the public these improvements. Over the years there has been a subtle shift from practicing environmental marketing practices as a result of compulsion identified as a result of legislations and pressure from environmental groups to genuine efforts to improve sustainable marketing plans and behaving in an eco-responsible manner (Polonsky and Rosenberger, 2001).

Today's marketplace is increasingly attractive for marketers of green products. Consumers are expected to double their spending on "green" products, reaching $500 billion in 2009 (CBS News, 2008) and many consumers state that they are willing to pay a price premium for these products (Wüstenhagen, 1998; Vlosky *et al.*, 1999; Veisten, 2007). Recent studies indicate that 93 per cent of consumers stated they have participated in tremendous efforts to sustain environment (Hartmann Group, 2007), 37 per cent felt highly concerned about the environment (California Green Solutions, 2007). Kals *et al.* (1999) identified that the motivational instrument that protects the natural environment is the human feeling of nature.

NEED FOR GREEN MARKETING

"Green' is the buzzword that is gaining popularity among the current generation. A number of businesses right from private entities such as Wal-Mart trying to push the concept of organic food to public entities like the London governments Congestion Charge are all aimed at improving the environment by promoting 'Green' products and issues. 87% of people from various nations like Brazil, Canada, China, France, Germany, India, UK and US have shown an interest in reducing their impact on the environment, according to a survey by McKinsey (2007).

According to First and Khetriwal (2008), the concept of green branding is almost unexplored by green marketers. Yet, several studies demonstrate that the growing environmental awareness of consumers have encouraged them to be more inclined towards brands that seemed to be environmental friendly (Eagly and Kulesa, 1997; Swenson and Wells, 1997). Brands can change consumer attitudes to greener consumption (Travis, 2000; Pickett-Baker and Ozaki, 2008). Likewise, Ottman (1998) has stated affective marketing has the power to shift passive green consumers who are keen to pay premium prices for environmental products to greener consumption patterns. Effective green positioning involves brand communication and differentiation based on functional attributes and emotional benefits (Aaker, 1996; Hooley *et al.*, 1998; Kotler, 2000; Hartmann *et al.*, 2005). According to Pickett *et al.* (1995), if green brand attributes are not well communicated, environmentally sustainable products will not be commercially successful. Similarly, other researchers have suggested that green positioning is an important element in the success of green branding strategies (Coddington, 1993; Meffert and Kirchgeorg, 1993). A car brand, for example, may be considered environmentally sound if the models cause significantly lower emissions than competitors.

UNDERSTANDING CUSTOMERS' RESPONSIVENESS TOWARDS GREEN PACKAGING AND ECO-LABELING

As argued by Barber (2010), as people are becoming more aware of the damage caused to the environment, environmental concerns of the industry have been identified as a critical issue that packaging companies must contend. The concept of being environment friendly or green will have an effect on all parts of the business from the conception of products to the use and subsequent disposal of the products by customers (Prahalad and Hamel, 1994). According to Delia (2010), packaging can be considered ecological depending on the degree of environment pollution. Furthermore, Morris *et al.* (1995) have stated that specific products claims on product labels like "eco-friendly", "recyclable", "biodegradable" and "ozone-friendly" used by marketers enabled companies to communicate the environmental benefits of products to their customers. Packaging is one of the key components that can provide a competitive advantage in the marketplace for many consumer products and even a low investment in changing the package can drive significant gains in brand sales compared to advertising and promotion activities (Barber, 2005, 2010).

THE EFFECT OF GREEN ADVERTISING ON CONSUMER PURCHASING PATTERNS

Pickett-Baker and Ozaki (2008) found that, except for cleaning products, most consumers cannot identify greener products. This may be because most green messages labels are falling flat and not making an impression in the minds of shoppers (Green Biz Staff, 2009). Hence, green communication is a major area of weakness for green marketers. Carlson *et al.* (1993) have affirmed a parallel rise in environmental advertising accompanied by greater consumer interest in the environment. In fact, advertising terms such as "recyclable, environment-friendly, ozone safe, biodegradable" can be seen regularly in green advertisements and consumers are often exposed to such messages, whilst some of these messages also pertained to consumer resistance (D'Souza, 2005).

Green branding communication strategies should be aimed at associating the brand with pleasant, emotional imagery of nature, while presenting information on environmentally sound product attributes. However, Rose (2002) has affirmed that although some manufacturing companies cannot influence consumer choice towards green products, yet, they can shape green consumption patterns in the way the products are being offered and marketed. Similarly, marketers should emphasize ecological knowledge in their organizations, their products offerings and their advertising campaigns in order to achieve the goal of changing consumer purchasing behaviour (Mendleson, 1994).

FOUR P'S OF GREEN MARKETING

When companies come up with new innovations like eco-friendly products, they can access new markets, enhance their market shares, and increase profits. Just as we have 4P's, product, price, place and promotion in marketing. We have 4p's in green marketing too, but they are a bit different.

Green Product

The products have to be developed depending on the needs of the customers who prefer environment-friendly products. Products can be made from recycled materials or from used goods. Efficient products not only save water, energy and money, but also reduce harmful effects on the environment. Green chemistry forms the growing focus of product development. The marketer's role in product management includes providing product designers with market-driven trends and customer requests for green product attributes such as energy saving, organic, green chemicals, local sourcing, etc., For example, Nike is the first among the shoe companies to market itself as green. It is marketing its Air Jordan shoes as environment-friendly, as it has significantly reduced the usage of harmful glue adhesives. It has designed this variety of shoes to emphasize that it has reduced wastage and used environment-friendly materials.

Green Place

Green place is about managing logistics to cut down on transportation emissions, thereby in effect aiming at reducing the carbon footprint. For example, instead of marketing an imported mango juice in India it can be licensed for local production. This avoids shipping of the product from far away, thus reducing shipping cost and more importantly, the consequent carbon emission by the ships and other modes of transport.

Green Promotion

Green promotion involves configuring the tools of promotion, such as advertising, marketing materials, signage, white papers, websites, videos and presentations by keeping people, planet and profits in mind. British Petroleum (BP) displays at gas station with its sunflower motif and boasts of putting money into solar power. Indian Tobacco Company has introduced environment-friendly papers and boards, which are free of elemental chlorine. Toyota is trying to push gas/electric hybrid technology into much of its product line. It is also making the single largest R&D investment in the every-elusive hydrogen car and promoting itself as the first eco-friendly car company. International Business Machines Corporation (IBM) has revealed a portfolio of green retail store technologies and services to help retailers improve energy efficiency in their IT operations. The center piece of this portfolio is the IBM SurePOS 700, a point-of-sale system that, according to IBM, reduces power consumption by 36% or more. We even see the names of retail outlets like

"Reliance Fresh", Fresh@Namdhari, Fresh and Desi, which while selling fresh vegetables and fruits, transmit an innate communication of green marketing.

Green marketer can attract customers on the basis of performance, money savings, health and convenience, or just plain environment friendliness, so as to target a wide range of green consumers.

Consumer awareness can be created by spreading the message among consumers about the benefits of environment-friendly products. Posting of profiles related to green marketing on social networks creates awareness within and across online peer groups. Marketing can also directly target the consumers through advertisements for product such as energy saving Compact Fluorescent Lamps, the battery-powered Reva car, etc.

Additional social marketing "P's" that are used in this process are:

- ***Public:*** Effective Social Marketing knows its audience, and can appeal to multiple groups of people. "Public" is the external and internal groups involved in the program. External public include the target audience, secondary audiences, policymakers, and gatekeepers, while the internal public are those who are involved in some way with either approval or implementation of the program.

- ***Partnership:*** Most social change issues, including "green" initiatives, are too complex for one person or group to handle. Associating with other groups and initiatives to team up strengthens the chance of efficacy.

- ***Policy:*** Social marketing programs can do well in motivating individual behavior change, but that is difficult to sustain unless the environment they are in supports that change for the long run. Often, policy change is needed, and media advocacy programs can be an effective complement to a social marketing program.

- ***Purse Strings:*** How much will this strategic effort cost? Who is funding the effort? Are few such questions to be answered.

CHALLENGES AHEAD

1. Green products require renewable and recyclable material, which is costly.
2. It requires a technology, which demands huge investment in R & D.
3. Water treatment technology, which is too costly.
4. Majority of the people are not aware of green products and their uses.
5. Majority of the consumers are not willing to pay a premium for green products.

CONCLUSION

Green marketing should not neglect the economic aspect of marketing. Marketers need to understand the implications of green marketing. Green marketing to some extent strengthen company's image in the mind of respondents.

Thus, green marketing should look at minimizing environmental harm, not necessarily eliminating it. Green marketing covers more than a firm's marketing claims. While firms must bear much of the responsibility for environmental degradation.

Firms can have a great impact on the natural environment; the responsibility should not be theirs alone. Ultimately, it is consumers who demand goods, and thus create environmental problems. It appears that consumers are not overly committed to improving their environment and may be looking to lay too much responsibility on industry and government.

It is clearly evident from review of literatures that the majority of the consumers still lack 'green' knowledge and because of such low awareness towards green products organizations are still not pushing towards developing more green products nor are they working hard on green packaging. Organizations still believe that marketing aspects such as developing a proper supply chain, packaging, pricing, etc., take precedence over green marketing initiatives. Companies are also starting to educate the masses with an increase in advertising that puts emphasis on green products and how they are more beneficial for the consumers. This kind of advertising goes a long way in educating the masses and promoting the concept of green products among the people. With more and more consumers willing to pay a little extra towards green products, organizations are taking notice of the demands and behavior and attitude of the consumers.

Recommendations

Green marketing is a continuous process that requires constant inputs from the suppliers, government legislations and policies and the people. This is required so that the business's green marketing strategy can be aligned to the target markets and so it can gain a sustainable competitive advantage. The current study will provide a valuable insight to both practitioners and theoreticians who want to understand environmentally conscious individuals. Since the success of green products depend on the consumers adopting or changing their attitude and behavior towards such products, it is imperative that green marketers identify all the factors that encourage cooperation.

References

1. Aaker, D.A. (1996), *Building Strong Brands*, The Free Press, New York.
2. Barber, N. (2005), "Wine label design, information and bottle packaging: influence on wine buying behaviors", Master's thesis, Purdue University, West Lafayette, IN.
3. Barber, N. (2010), "Green wine packaging: targeting environmental consumers", *International Journal of Wine Business Research*, Vol. 22, No. 4, pp. 423-44.

4. Coddington, W. (1993), *Environmental Marketing: Positive Strategies for Reaching Green Consumers*, McGraw-Hill, New York.
5. Carlson, L., Grove, S., Kangun, N. (1993), "A content analysis of environmental advertising claims: a matrix method approach", *Journal of Advertising*, Vol. 22, No. 3, pp. 27–40.
6. California Green Solutions (2007), "Green consumer research outlines the challenge".
7. CBS News (2008), "A closer look at 'green' products manufacturers are making more environment-friendly products, but not all stand up to the test".
8. Delia, D. (2010), "Review concerning the functions of packaging".
9. D'Souza, C. (2005), "Green advertising effects on attitude and choice of advertising themes", *Asia Pacific Journal of Marketing and Logistics*, Vol. 17, No. 3, pp. 51–66.
10. Eagly, A.H., Kulesa, P. (1997), "Attitudes, attitude structure, and resistance to change", in Bazermann, M.H., Messick, D.M., Tenbrunsel, A.E., Benzoni, K.A. (Eds), *Environment, Ethics, and Behaviour*, The New Lexington Press, San Francisco, CA, pp. 122–53.
11. First, I., Khetriwal, D.S. (2008), "Exploring the relationship between environmental orientation and brand value: is there fire or only smoke", *Business Strategy and the Environment*, Vol. 19, No. 2, pp. 90–103.
12. Green Biz Staff (2009), "Most green labels fail to catch shoppers' eyes, survey finds".
13. Hartmann Group (2007), *The Hartman Report on Sustainability: Understanding the Consumer Perspective*, Hartman Group, Bellevue, WA.
14. Hooley, G., Saunders, J., Piercy, N.F. (1998), *Marketing Strategy and Competitive Positioning*, Prentice Hall, Hemel Hempstead, 2nd ed.
15. Kals, E., Schumacher, D., Montada, L. (1999), "Emotional affinity toward nature as a motivational basis to protect nature", *Environmental and Behaviour*, Vol. 31, No. 2, pp. 178–202.
16. Mckinsey. (2007). Mckisey and Company Inc.
17. Meffert, H., Kirchgeorg, M. (1993), *MarktorientiertesUmweltmanagemet*, Schaeffer-Poeschel, Stuttgart.
18. Morris, L., Hastak, M., Mazis, M. (1995), "Consumer comprehension of environmental advertising and labeling claims", *The Journal of Consumer Affairs*, Vol. 29, No. 2, pp. 328–51.
19. Mendleson, N. (1994), "Environmental marketing business partnering at AFC-developing strategic alliances, environmental marketing: critical success strategies for reaching the green consumer", *Proceedings of the 1994 Conference, Sydney, 22-23 February*, pp. 87–103.
20. Ottman, J.A., Stafford, E.R., Hartman, C.L. (2006), "Avoiding green marketing myopia: ways to improve consumer appeal for environmentally preferable products", *Environment*, Vol. 48, No. 5, pp. 22–36.

21. Polonsky, Michael Jay. 1994. "A Stakeholder Theory Approach to Designing Environmental Marketing Strategy." Unpublished Working Paper.
22. Polonsky, M. J., & Rosenberger, P. J. III. (2001) Reevaluating green marketing: a strategic approach, Business Horizons, 44(5), 21-30. http://dx.doi.org/10.1016/S00076813(01)80057-4
23. Polonsky, M. J. (2011). Transformative green marketing: Impediments and opportunities. Journal of Business Research, 64(12), 1311-1319. http://dx.doi.org/10.1016/j.jbusres.2011.01.016
24. Pickett-Baker, J., Ozaki, R. (2008), "Pro-environmental products: marketing influence on consumer purchase decision", *Journal of Consumer Marketing*, Vol. 25, No. 5, pp. 281–93.
25. Prahalad, C.K., Hamel, G. (1994), "Strategy as a field of study: why search for a new paradigm?", *Strategic Management Journal*, Vol. 15, No. S2, pp. 5–16
26. Wüstenhagen, R. (1998), "Pricing strategies on the way to ecological mass markets", *Partnership and leadership: building alliances for a sustainable future*, proceedings of the 7th International Conference of the Greening Industry Network, Rome, 15-18 November, pp. 1–24.
27. Rose, B. (2002), *Introduction of Brand Green: Mainstream or Forever Niche*, Green Alliance, London.
28. Swenson, M.R., Wells, W.D. (1997), "Useful correlates of pro-environmental behaviour", in Goldberg, M.E., Fishbein, M., Middlestadt, S.E. (Eds), *Social Marketing, Theoretical and Practical Perspectives*, Lawrence Erlbaum, Mahwah, NJ, pp. 91–109.
29. Travis, D. (2000), *How Successful Brands Gain the Irrational Edge: Emotional Branding*, Prima Publishing, Washington, DC. http://blogs.siliconindia.com/nayan/MARKETING_MIX_OF_GREEN_MARKETING-bid-uQo5nC9M98069957.html

23

Evolution and Challenges of Green Marketing

Sunil Shukla
Associate Professor, GHS-IMR, Kanpur
E-mail:drsunilghs@yahoo.co.in, 09415718899(m)

Ashish Kumar Shukla
Assistant Professor, Bareilly University
E-mail: ashish59.2009@rediffmail.com, 09889703530(m)

ABSTRACT

In today's business world environmental issues plays an important role in marketing. Almost all the governments around the world are concerned about green marketing activities that they have attempted to regulate them. For example, in the United States (US) the Federal Trade Commission and the National Association of Attorneys-General have developed extensive documents examining green marketing. There has been little attempt to academically examine environmental or green marketing. This article introduces the terms and concepts of green marketing, briefly discusses why going green is important and also examines some reasons that organizations are adopting a green marketing philosophy. It also focuses on some of the problems with green marketing.

INTRODUCTION

Many people believe that green marketing refers solely to the promotion or advertising of products with environmental characteristics. Generally, terms like Phosphate Free, Recyclable, Refillable, Ozone Friendly, and Environmental Friendly are some of the things consumers most often associate with green marketing. In general green marketing is a much broader concept, one that can be applied to consumer goods, industrial goods and even services. For example, around the world there are resorts that are beginning to promote themselves as "ecotourism" facilities, i.e., facilities that specialize in experiencing nature or operating in a fashion that minimizes their environmental impact. Thus, green marketing incorporates a broad range of activities, including product modification, changes to the production process, packaging changes, as well as modifying advertising. But to define green marketing is not a simple task. The terminology used in this area has varied meanings, it includes: Green Marketing, Environmental Marketing and Ecological Marketing. While green marketing came into prominence in the late 1980s and early 1990s, it was first discussed much earlier. The American Marketing Association (AMA) held the first workshop on "Ecological Marketing" in 1975. The proceedings of this workshop resulted in one of the first books on green marketing entitled "Ecological Marketing".

Green marketing is defined as "**Green or Environmental Marketing consists of all activities designed to generate and facilitate any exchanges intended to satisfy human needs or wants, such that the satisfaction of these needs and wants occurs, with minimal detrimental impact on the natural environment**."

This definition incorporates much of the traditional components of the marketing definition, that is "All activities designed to generate and facilitate any exchanges intended to satisfy human needs or wants" Therefore, it ensures that the interests of the organization and all its consumers are protected, as voluntary exchange will not take place unless both the buyer and seller mutually benefit. The above definition also includes the protection of the natural environment, by attempting to minimize the detrimental impact this exchange has on the environment. This second point is important, for human consumption by its very nature is destructive to the natural environment. So green marketing should look at minimizing environmental harms, not necessarily eliminating it.

IMPORTANCE OF GREEN MARKETING

Man has limited resources on the earth, with which she/he must attempt to provide for the world's unlimited wants. There is extensive debate as to whether the earth is a resource at man's disposal. In market societies where there is "freedom of choice", it has generally been accepted that individuals and organizations have the right to attempt to have their wants satisfied. As firms face limited natural resources, they must develop new or alternative ways of satisfying these unlimited wants. Ultimately, green marketing looks at how marketing activities utilize these limited resources, while satisfying consumers wants, both of individuals and industry, as well as achieving the selling organization's objectives. When looking through the literature there are several suggested reasons for firms increased use of Green Marketing. Five possible reasons are as follows:

1. Organizations perceive environmental marketing to be an opportunity that can be used to achieve its objectives.
2. Organizations believe they have a moral obligation to be more socially responsible. Governmental bodies are forcing firms to become more responsible.
3. Competitors' environmental activities pressure firms to change their environmental marketing activities.
4. Cost factors associated with waste disposal, or reductions in material usage forces firms to modify their behavior.

OPPORTUNITIES

All types of consumers, both individual and industrial are becoming more concerned and aware about the natural environment. In a 1992 study of 16 countries, more than 50% of consumers in each country, other than Singapore, indicated they were concerned about the environment. A 1994 study in Australia found that 84.6% of the sample believed all individuals had a responsibility to care for the environment. A further 80% of this sample indicated that they had modified their behavior, including their purchasing behavior, due to environmental reasons. As demands change, many firms see these changes as an opportunity to be exploited. It can be assumed that firms marketing goods with environmental characteristics will have a competitive advantage over firms marketing non-environmentally responsible alternatives. There are numerous examples of firms who have strived to become more environmentally responsible, in an attempt to better satisfy their consumer need. McDonald's replaced its clam shell packaging with waxed paper because of increased consumer concern relating to polystyrene production and Ozone depletion. Xerox introduced a "high quality" recycled photocopier paper in an attempt to satisfy the demands of firms for less environmentally harmful products.

This is not to imply that all firms who have undertaken environmental marketing activities actually improve their behavior. In some cases firms have misled consumers in an attempt to gain market share. In other cases firms have jumped on the green bandwagon without considering the accuracy of their behavior, their claims, or the effectiveness of their products. This lack of consideration of the true "greenness" of activities may result in firms making false or misleading green marketing claims.

SOCIAL RESPONSIBILITY & GREEN MARKETING

Many firms are beginning to realize that they are members of the wider community and therefore must behave in an environmentally responsible fashion. This translates into firms that believe they must achieve environmental objectives as well as profit related objectives. This results in environmental issues being integrated into the firm's corporate culture. Firms in this situation can take two perspectives; (1) they can use the fact that they are environmentally responsible as a marketing tool; or (2) they can become responsible without promoting this fact. There are examples of firms adopting both strategies. Organizations like the Body Shop heavily promote the fact that they are environmentally responsible. While this behavior is a competitive advantage, the firm was established specifically to offer consumers environmentally responsible alternatives to conventional cosmetic products. This philosophy is directly tied to the overall corporate culture, rather than simply being a competitive tool. An example of a firm that does not promote its environmental initiatives is Coca-Cola. They have invested large sums of money in various recycling activities, as well as having modified their packaging to minimize its environmental impact. While being concerned about the environment, Coke has not used this concern as a marketing tool. Thus, many consumers may not realize that Coke is a very environmentally committed organization. Another firm which is very environmentally responsible but does not promote this fact, at least outside the organization, is Walt Disney World (WDW). WDW has an extensive waste management program and infrastructure in place, yet these facilities are not highlighted in their general tourist promotional activities.

GOVERNMENTAL PRESSURE

As with all marketing related activities, governments want to "protect" consumers and society; this protection has significant green marketing implications. Governmental regulations relating to environmental marketing are designed to protect consumers in several ways by less production of harmful goods or by-products; 1) modify consumer and industry's use and/or consumption of harmful goods; or 2) ensure that all types of consumers have the ability to evaluate the environmental composition of goods.

Governments establish regulations designed to control the amount of hazardous wastes produced by firms. Many byproducts of production are controlled through issuing of various environmental licenses, thus modifying organizational behavior. In some cases governments try to "induce" final consumers to become more responsible. For example, some governments have introduced voluntary curb-side recycling programs, making it easier for consumers to act responsibly. In other cases governments tax individuals who act in an irresponsible fashion. For example, in Australia there is a higher gas tax associated with leaded petrol.

COMPETITIVE PRESSURE

Another major force in the environmental marketing area has been firms' desire to maintain their competitive position. In many cases firms observe competitors promoting their environmental behaviors and attempt to emulate this behavior. In some instances this competitive pressure has caused an entire industry to modify and thus reduce its detrimental environmental behavior. For example, it could be argued that Xerox's "Revive 100% Recycled paper" was introduced a few years ago in an attempt to address the introduction of recycled photocopier paper by other manufacturers. In another example when one tuna manufacture stopped using driftnets the others followed suit.

COST OR PROFIT ISSUES

Firms may also use green marketing in an attempt to address cost or profit related issues.

Disposing of environmentally harmful byproducts, such as polychlorinated biphenyl (PCB) contaminated oil are becoming increasingly costly and in some cases difficult. Therefore firms that can reduce harmful wastes may incur substantial cost savings. When attempting to minimize waste, firms are often forced to re-examine their production processes. In these cases they often develop more effective production processes that not only reduce waste, but reduce the need for some raw materials. This serves as a double cost savings, since both waste and raw material are reduced. In other cases firms attempt to find end-of-pipe solutions, instead of minimizing waste. In these situations firms try to find markets or uses for their waste materials, where one firm's waste becomes another firm's input of manufacture. One Australian example of this is a firm who produces acidic waste water as a byproduct of production and sells it to a firm involved in neutralizing base materials. The last way in which cost or profit issues may affect firms' environmental marketing activities is that new industries may be developed. This can occur in two ways: 1) a firm develops a technology for reducing waste and sells it to other firms; or 2) a waste recycling or removal industry develops. For example, firms that clean the oil in large industrial condensers increase the life of those condensers, removing the need for replacing the oil, as well as the need to dispose of the waste oil. This reduces operating costs for those owning the condensers and generates revenue for those firms cleaning the oil.

STRATEGIC IMPLICATIONS OF GREEN MARKETING

Green marketing subsumes green products as well as greening firms. Managers need to identify what ought to be green: systems, processes or products? A research model has been developed for the purpose of this study. This consists of five major sets of variables, namely, Antecedents, Mediators, Strategy, Outcomes and Moderators. Antecedent are all those factors affecting firm's environmental orientation, which subsequently shapes marketing strategy. According to political economy paradigm, there are four groups of antecedent factors, namely, external polity, i.e., socio-political and regulatory system in which the firm operates, external economy, i.e., prevailing and prospective economic environment surrounding the firm, internal polity, i.e., the way power, authority are handle within the firm and internal economy, i.e., the way existing resources are allocated to produce sufficient and satisfactory output. The antecedents have an impact on firm's values, belief and attitude towards environmentalism and related aspects, which acts as a mediator on environmental marketing strategy. Environ-marketing strategy provides the central construct of the model, comprising environmental adjustments of the traditional marketing mix elements (product, price, promotion and place) to a specific target market setting. Enviro-marketing strategy implementation will have certain financial, market, customers and competitive outcomes for the organization with regard to its marketing performance. Finally, the effect of strategic factors on marketing performance is controlled by a number of moderators, which can be found either internally, i.e., organizational size, scope of operations, etc., or externally, i.e., industry type, industry growth rate, etc. to the organization.

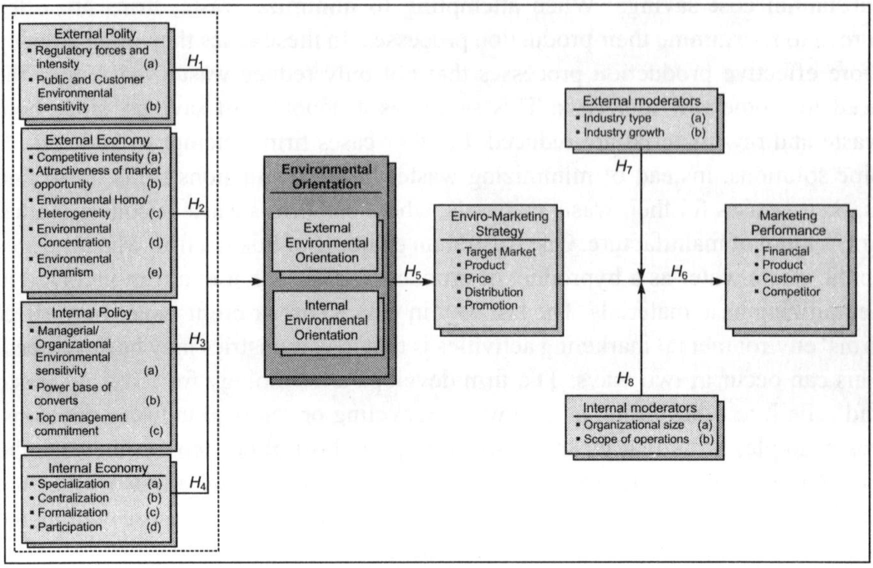

Figure: A Political Economy Model of Environ-Marketing Strategies

Source: "Antecedents and Consequences of Environ-marketing Strategy: A Political Economy Perspective" by Constantinos N. Leonidou, Doctoral Student, Leeds University Business School, University of Leeds, U.K.

With the help of this model the marketing managers will be able to better understand the critical forces that drive organizations to become environmentally oriented, their association with marketing strategy formulation will be established and the ultimate impact on marketing performance will be demonstrated.

GREEN MARKETING CASES

1. Philips Light's "Marathon"

Philips Lighting's first shot at marketing a standalone *compact fluorescent light* (CFL) bulb was Earth Light, at $15 each versus 75 cents for incandescent bulbs. The product had difficulty climbing out of its deep green niche. The company re-launched the product as "Marathon," underscoring its new "super long life" positioning and promise of saving $26 in energy costs over its five-year lifetime. Finally, with the U.S. EPA's Energy Star label to add credibility as well as new sensitivity to rising utility costs and electricity shortages, sales climbed 12 percent in an otherwise flat market.

2. Electronics Sector

The consumer electronics sector provides room for using green marketing to attract new customers. One example of this is HP's promise to cut its global energy use 20 percent by the year 2010. To accomplish this reduction below 2005 levels, The

Hewlett-Packard company announced plans to deliver energy-efficient products and services and institute energy-efficient operating practices in its facilities worldwide.

3. Car Sharing Services

Car-sharing services address the longer-term solutions to consumer needs for better *fuel* savings and fewer traffic tie-ups and parking nightmares, to complement the environmental benefit of more open space and reduction of *greenhouse gases*. They may be thought of as a "time-sharing" system for cars. Consumers who drive less than 7,500 miles a year and do not need a car for work can save thousands of dollars annually by joining one of the many services springing up, including Zip Car (East Coast), Flex Car (Washington State), and Hour Car (Twin Cities)

4. Introduction of CNG in Delhi

New Delhi, capital of India, was being polluted at a very fast pace until Supreme Court of India forced a change to alternative fuels. In 2002, a directive was issued to completely adopt CNG in all public transport systems to curb pollution.

5. Coca-Cola Joins Green-Marketing Rush

Coke's campaign broadens the definition beyond environmentalism, centering on the concept of "sustainable well-being." The first two executions, for example, don't focus at all on environmentalism and instead paint the soft-drink giant as a corporate good guy concerned with meeting consumer needs and supporting worthy local education and sports programs.

Some More Cases

1. McDonald's restaurant's napkins, bags are made of recycled paper.
2. Coca-Cola pumped syrup dircctly from tank instead of plastic which saved 68 million pound/year.
3. Badarpur Thermal Power station of NTPC in Delhi is devising ways to utilize coal ash that has been a major source of air and water pollution.
4. Barauni refinery of IOC is taken steps for restricting air and water pollutants.

KEYS TO SUCCESSFUL GREEN MARKETING

Green Marketing Can Win More Customers If You Do It Right

Show potential customers that you follow green business practices and you could reap more green on your bottom line. ***Green marketing*** isn't just a catchphrase; it's a marketing strategy that can help you get more customers and make more money. But only if you do it right.

For green marketing to be effective, you have to do three things; be genuine, educate your customers, and give them the opportunity to participate.

1. Being Genuine means that

(a) that you are actually doing what you claim to be doing in your green marketing campaign and

(b) that the rest of your business policies are consistent with whatever you are doing that's environmentally friendly. Both these conditions have to be met for your business to establish the kind of environmental credentials that will allow a green marketing campaign to succeed.

2. Educating Your Customers isn't just a matter of letting people know you're doing whatever you're doing to protect the environment, but also a matter of letting them know why it matters. Otherwise, for a significant portion of your target market, it's a case of "So what?" and your green marketing campaign goes nowhere.

3. Giving your Customers an Opportunity to Participate means personalizing the benefits of your environmental friendly actions, normally through letting the customer take part in positive environmental action.

Let's put the three essential elements of a successful green marketing campaign together by looking at an example.

Suppose that you have decided that your business will no longer use plastic bags to wrap customer purchases. You know that the traditional plastic bag takes about one thousand years to decompose and want to do your part to stop the proliferation of plastic bags in landfills. You feel that this is the kind of environmental action that will be popular with potential customers and a good opportunity to do some green marketing.

To be genuine, you have to ensure that none of your business practices contradict your decision not to use plastic bags. What if customers who happen to walk behind your store see an overflowing trash bin filled with paper, cardboard and plastic bottles? Obviously, he or she will decide that you don't care as much about recycling as you say you do in your green marketing.

Not using plastic bags appears to be environmental no-brainer, but you will still need to educate your target market. Did you know that a single use plastic bag takes about one thousand years to decompose? I didn't until I researched this article and probably a fair number of otherwise environmentally conscious people don't either. This one little fact about plastic bags could be used as part of your green marketing campaign – all by itself it lets the people know why single use plastic bags are environmentally disastrous and that you and your business care about the environment.

And the third element? By shopping at your store, the customer is taking action to protect the environment by preventing at least one single use plastic bag from going into a landfill. It doesn't sound like much, but he or she gets the satisfaction of physically doing something that fulfills their beliefs. You can also reinforce your customers' green decisions and increase their participation by offering them additional related actions, such as buying cloth bags to use for future purchases.

SOME PROBLEMS WITH GREEN MARKETING

There are a number of potential problems that must overcome. One of the main problems is that firms using green marketing must ensure that their activities are not misleading to consumers or industry, and do not breach any of the regulations or laws dealing with environmental marketing. Green marketing claims must clearly state environmental benefits. A problem faced by the firms is that those who modify their products due to increased consumer concern must contend with the fact that consumers' perceptions are sometimes not correct. For example, the McDonald's case where it has replaced its clam shells with plastic coated paper. There is ongoing scientific debate which is more environmentally friendly. Some scientific evidence suggests that when taking a cradle to grave approach, polystyrene is less environmentally harmful if this is the case McDonald's bowed to consumer pressure, yet has chosen the more environmentally harmful option. When firms attempt to become socially responsible, they may face the risk that the environmentally responsible action of today will be found to be harmful in the future. Take for example the aerosol industry which has switched from CFCs (chlorofluorocarbons) to HFCs (hydro fluorocarbons) only to be told HFCs are also a greenhouse gas. Some firms now use DME (di-methyl ether) as an aerosol propellant, which may also harm the ozone layer. Given the limited scientific knowledge at any point, it may be impossible for a firm to have made the correct environmental decision. This may explain why some firms, like Coca-Cola and Walt Disney World, are becoming socially responsible without publicizing the point. They may be protecting themselves from potential future negative backlash; if it is determined they made the wrong decision in the past. While governmental regulation is designed to give consumers the opportunity to make better decisions or to motivate them to be more environmentally responsible, there is difficulty in establishing policies that will address all environmental issues. For example, guidelines developed to control environmental marketing address only a very narrow set of issues, i.e., the truthfulness of environmental marketing claims. If governments want to modify consumer behavior they need to establish a different set of regulations. Thus governmental attempts to protect the environment may result in a proliferation of regulations and guidelines, with no one central controlling body.

Reacting to competitive pressures can cause all "followers" to make the same mistake as the "leader." Mobil Corporation who has followed the competition and introduced "biodegradable" plastic garbage bags, as because technically these bags were biodegradable, the conditions under which they were disposed of did not allow biodegradation to occur. Mobil was sued by several US states for using misleading advertising claims. Thus, blindly following the competition can have costly ramifications.

The push to reduce costs or increase profits may not force firms to address the important issue of environmental degradation. End-of-pipe solutions may not actually reduce the waste but rather shift it around. While this may be beneficial, it does not necessarily address the larger environmental problem, though it may minimize its short term affects.

Ultimately, most waste produced will enter the waste stream, therefore to be environmentally responsible organizations should attempt to minimize their waste, rather than find "appropriate" uses for it.

CONCLUSION

Green marketing covers more than a firm's marketing claims. While firms must bear much of the responsibility for environmental degradation, ultimately it is consumers who demand goods, and thus create environmental problems. One example of this is where McDonald's is often blamed for polluting the environment because much of their packaging finishes up as roadside waste. It must be remembered that it is the uncaring consumer who chooses to disposes of their waste in an inappropriate fashion. While firms can have a great impact on the natural environment, the responsibility should not be theirs alone. It appears that consumers are not overly committed to improving their environment and may be looking to lay too much responsibility on industry and government. Ultimately green marketing requires that consumers want a cleaner environment and are willing to "pay" for it, possibly through higher priced goods, modified individual lifestyles, or even governmental intervention. Until this happens it will be difficult for firms alone to lead the green marketing revolution. It must not be forgotten that the industrial buyer also has the ability to pressure suppliers to modify their activities. Thus, an environmental committed organization may not only produce goods that have reduced their detrimental impact on the environment, they may also be able to pressure their suppliers to behave in a more environmentally "responsible" fashion. Final consumers and industrial buyers also have the ability to pressure organizations to integrate the environment into their corporate culture and thus ensure all organizations minimize the detrimental environmental impact of their activities.

References

1. Crane, A. (2000), "Facing the backlash: green marketing and strategic re-orientation in the 1990s", Journal of Strategic Marketing, Vol. 8, No. 3, pp. 277–96.
2. Elkington, J. (1994), "Towards the sustainable corporation: win win business strategies for sustainable development", California Management Review, Vol. 36, No. 2, pp. 90–100.
3. Mintel (1991). London, The green consumer report.

4. Ottman, J.A. (1993), Green Marketing: Challenges and opportunities, NTC Business Books, Chicago, IL.
5. Porter, M.E., Van der Linde (1995), "Green and competitive: ending the stalemate", Harvard Business Review, Vol. 73, No. 5, pp. 120–33.
6. Shelton, R.D. (1994), "Hitting the green wall: why corporate programs get stalled", Corporate Environmental Strategy, Vol. 2, No. 2, pp. 5–11.
7. Smithe, T. (1998), "The Green Marketing Myth: Tending out Goats at the Edge of Apocalypse, university of Toronto press, TorontoWong, V., Turner, W., Stoneman, P. (1996), "Marketing strategies and market prospects for environmentally-friendly consumer products", British Journal of Management, Vol. 7, No. 3, pp. 263–81.
8. Polonsky, M. J. "An Introduction to Green Marketing." Electronic Green Journal 1, No. 2 (November 1994).
9. Ottman, J. A. (Jan2004) "Empower to the people" Inbusiness.
10. Prakash, A. (May2002) " Green Marketing, public policy and managerial strategy".
11. Business Strategy and The Environment, Bus.Strat.Env.II, pg 285–297.
12. Ottman JA, Stafford ER, Hartman CL,(June-2006)" Avoiding Green Marketing Myopia", The Environment, Vol. 48, No. 5, pp. 22–26.
13. Frankel, C. 1992. "Blueprint for green marketing", marketing executive review, pp. 2(5): 22–23. Approach." Business Horizons 34(4): pp. 92–98.
14. Carlson, Les, Stephen Grove and Norman Kangun (1993),"
15. A Content Analysis of Environmental Advertising." Journal of Advertising Vol. 22(3), pp. 27–38 (2006).
16. The ICFAI Journal of Environmental Economics, Vol. IV, No. 4, Nov. 6, "Down to Earth", March 15, 2007 issue.
17. Saxena Rajan (2006, 3rd Edition), Marketing Management, New Delhi, Tata McGraw-Hill Publishing Co. Ltd.

24

A Study on Buying Motives and Preferences of Gold Jewellery Buyers

Preeti Srivastava
Assistant Professor
Department of Business Management
Sherwood College of Engineering Research & Technology, Barabanki
Email: srivastava.preeti369@gmail.com

Raman Kumar
Assistant Professor
Department of Business Management
Sherwood College of Engineering Research & Technology, Barabanki
Email: raman.kr24@gmail.com

ABSTRACT

Gold has always been an auspicious metal in India for all occasions. It is the most preferred metal that Indian consumers like to buy on auspicious events, especially wedding. Despite the rising and fluctuating price of gold, people from across all class are buying this valuable metal as per their capability on different occasions and festivals. The purpose of this research is to find out buying motive and purpose of gold jewellery with special reference to Lucknow city. The objective of the study is to get the feedback about various factors affecting buying behaviour of jewellery product, identify the brand awareness and buying attitude of the customers in purchasing of gold at the branded and non-branded jewellery retail stores. The descriptive research design has been used in this study.

INTRODUCTION

We ourselves have changed a lot since our independence in almost every way. Even our day-to-day life is not the same as we lived in past including food habit, life style, wearing, fashion, culture and so on so forth. However, when we observe and try to find some common habits or consumption in past as well as in present time, it seems to be also true that gold has always been an inseparable part of our lives. The preference and willingness for buying jewellery of different types and designs have gradually changed but gold in any form especially gold jewellery is still there with all of us. The changing lifestyle, fashion, trend, art-of-living have paved a way to an entirely different life. The new opportunities and threats of life lead us to think beyond the assumption and traditional approaches in all respect including spending pattern, taste, motives, preference and attitude towards earning and consumption as well.

This gives birth to an organized jems and jewellery industry. The changing consumer behaviour has also significant impact on jewellery industry, which is a relatively new industry although it derives from ancient activities such as goldsmith. Jewellery has been made to put on nearly every body part, from hairpins to toe rings and many more types of jewellery. Jewellery is one of personal embellishment, manifesting itself as anklets, rings, necklaces, earrings, nose-pin and bangles/bracelets, etc. Jewellery may be made from any material, usually gemstones, precious metals (silver, gold, platinum), beads, or shells. Factors affecting the choice of materials may include cultural differences and the availability of the materials and others price, trend and fashion, etc. Jewellery is sometimes bought as an investment to create wealth. Some jewellery throughout the ages may have specifically been as an indication of a social group while traditional jewellery is usually made with gemstones and precious metals, such as silver or gold.

ABOUT GOLD JEWELLERY

The earliest gold jewellery dates from around 6000 years ago. Whenever man has found gold he has fashioned it into a jewel, worn it as a symbol of status or power, or given gold jewellery as a public declaration or intimate celebration of his love to a woman who has then worn it, loved it and handed it down through countless generations.

BUYING BEHAVIOUR

Consumers are individuals with likes and dislikes. When the predominance of people in a particular group feel one way or another about a product, service, entity, person, place or thing, it is said to be a generalized consumer attitude that could affect the marketing of that person, product or entity in positive or negative ways.

THE EMERGENCE OF BRANDED/ORGANIZED GOLD JEWELLERY

Before the liberalization of the Indian economy in 1991, only the Minerals and Metals Trading Corporation of India (MMTC) and the State Bank of India (SBI) were allowed to import gold. The abolition of the Gold Control Act in 1992, allowed large export houses to import gold freely. Exporters in export processing zones were allowed to sell 10 per cent of their produce in the domestic market. In 1993, gold and gold ornaments mining were opened up for private investors and foreign investors were allowed to own half the equity in mining ventures.

ORGANIZED VS TRADITIONAL JEWELLERY RETAILERS

Among the more notable of the Gitanjali Group's departure from traditional jewellery trade has been its strategy of branding. It's another strategy of layered distribution, using superstores, departmental stores and franchised retail. It is very first consumer brand, Gili, was also India's first jewellery brand, now a super-brand with several product variants and a growing global franchise. Mehul Choksi, chairman of Gitanjali Group, says people are a lot more conscious of quality today and prefer to buy from organized retailers who can guarantee quality and are more transparent.

Jewellery retail in the country has largely been an unorganized affair with 85% of the market still controlled by local and regional players. While the market might be growing at 15% a year, the organized part is speeding ahead clocking a growth of 40-50% a year.

Balram Garg, managing director and chief executive officer of Delhi based PC Jewellers says that there is a big shift from unorganized to organized jewellery retail. PC Jewellers had a turnover of Rs 3000 crore in 2011-12. It plans to expand its presence from 30 stores currently to about 50 by 2014.

Tribhovandas Bhimji Zaveri plans to invest Rs 1200 crore over the next two years to ramp up its retail presence significantly, from 21 stores today to about 57 across tier I and tier II cities. The chief executive officer R.K. Nagarkar says that they are willing to expand pan India now.

INDIAN GOLD JEWELLERY INDUSTRY

Indian gold jewellery industry is the largest globally, valued at USD 40 billion (including recycled volumes), driven by a gamut of cultural, social and demographic factors. India along with China is the two largest consumers of gold, with jewellery constituting bulk of the yellow metal consumption. IRCA research (Indian Gold Jewellery Industry–Transforming into an organized retail play) also predicts that the domestic gold jewellery retail industry is witnessing a structural transformation with organized retailing gaining prominence. Contribution of organized retail to total jewellery consumed in India has grown to 18% from less than 5% (largely over the past decade), aided by the widening retail network of organized players and shifting consumer preferences towards organized / branded jewellery.

LITERATURE REVIEW

India is the largest market for gold jewellery in the world, representing a staggering 746 tons of gold in 2010. Indian consumers are actively engaged in considering their next piece; 75% of women say they are constantly searching for new designs. Whilst over 50% of gold jewellery is bought for weddings, the wedding anniversary has now become the most inspirational occasion for receiving gold today, extending a couple's relationship with gold beyond the marriage ceremony.

The festival of Dhanteras, the most auspicious day in the calendar just before Diwali, has traditionally created a strong seasonal surge in sales. However, the strategic development of the AkshayaTritiya festival in May, together with leading trade partners, has seen phenomenal recent success; sales during that period grew over 28% in the last year.

India's culture and mythology embrace gold. And India's traditions of unparalleled craftsmanship and skill are exemplified by the country's gold jewellery manufacturing, with the majority of pieces still made meticulously by hand. Each region's symbols and designs are reinterpreted in gold which is overwhelmingly high in cartage.

The biggest reason for the change in consumers' mindset is the lack of gold's standardization. Since, hallmarking was not made mandatory in India, jewellers do not accompany any certificates with jewellery items and most of the business is done purely on trust between jewellers and consumers in remote Indian cities. In big cities, however, organized retails have changed consumers' mindset drastically in the last couple of years. Organized retail offers various choices of design, cut and polish which allure consumers more. As a consequence, modern means of jewellery sales are gradually taking over businesses of traditional jewellers, said Mehul Choksi, chairman of Gitanjali Gems, which has witnessed over 40 per cent growth in branded jewellery sales last year.

Consumers' tastes have changed from more of classic design for occasional wearing and store value to sophisticated modern design for one jewellery for all occasions. Unlike limited and mostly age old designs by inherent family jewellers, the modern branded retail chains offer jewellery for every occasion. Therefore, most of footfalls in Monday's branded retails get converted into a customer for long life, said an official with the country's largest jewellery retailer, Tanishq. As a consequence, global organized retails which contributes 15 per cent of $80-billion overall jewellery sales have been growing at 35-40 per cent against the family jewellers' growth rate between 5-10 per cent.

Gold jewellery is an integral part of weddings in India, and is considered a necessity with wedding related demand accounting for substantial portion of overall jewellery demand, especially in the South. Jewellery demand has also been supported by the increasing appetite for gold jewellery from rural and non-urban markets which constitute a major chunk (about 70%) of the total consumption. Gold has also served as a means of savings especially for the rural sector, owing to the lack of any major alternative investment options supported by its anti-inflationary characteristics.

Jewellery consumption over the past decade has recorded a strong growth upwards of 15% driven increasingly by organized retail. Rising quality awareness of customers has also provided a fillip to the organized retail segment, which is banking on its 'reliability' and 'quality' to compete against the highly fragmented unorganized jewellers. Organized players have steadily chipped away market share from smaller/unorganized retailers by addressing the need for enhanced experience of a demanding customer base, which is marked by shifting demographic and socio-economic profiles.

OBJECTIVES OF THE STUDY

The objective of this paper is to know the reasons behind buying gold jewellery. Since gold is not an invaluable metal, it does have other impacts on people besides cultural and fashion influences. Therefore, the paper aims at knowing the following important facts mentioned as under:

- To know buying motives of gold jewellery.
- To study the brand awareness of jewellery in Lucknow city.
- To compare the consumer preference between the branded and non-branded jewellery.
- To identify the factors affecting changing consumer preference for gold jewellery.

RESEARCH METHODOLOGY

The present study is based on primary as well as secondary data. To collect the primary data, interviews were conducted with customers at Tanishq, Gitanjali and traditional jewellery stores located in Lucknow. The primary data was collected by personal contact through a set of questions with consumer at the stores. 57 customers out of 75 from above-mentioned jewellery retail stores gave fruitful information to meet the objective of the study. To analyse the buying behaviour and motives of gold jewellery of buyers from Lucknow, random sampling method is used to select the respondents for collecting data. The secondary data is collected from journals, textbooks and through the Internet.

LIMITATIONS

There is no study without limitations. Thus, the study of this paper has been done with the following limitations:

- There was time constraint for this paper and hence some important aspect of the research could not be incorporated in this research.
- The data gathered from people of Lucknow could not be very correct as every customer is composed of unique characteristics and set of likings and dislikings. Besides, information may also depend on their awareness and interest.

Result and Discussion

- Gold is still a very popular and preferred valuable metal available to consumers of Lucknow. This metal is not only considered spiritual and religious thing but one of the good investment options too.
- The key trends in the jewellery market of Lucknow are the changing taste and preferences of the consumers, huge impact of festive season sales, escalating brand awareness, quality consciousness, emergence of new distribution channels in form of organized players and inclination towards branded jewellery.
- The analysis of factors explains reasons behind the growth of gold in the jewellery industry. These reasons include an increasing disposable income, luxurious lifestyle, and growing number of working women, fostering new talent and income as well. The key challenges could be noticed in terms of factors such as large market of unorganized players, involvement of huge working capital, dependency on import for raw materials and a labour intensive market, etc.

Table 1: Respondents Details

	Responded	*Not Responded*	*Total Respondents*
No. of Respondents	57	18	75
% of Responded	76	24	100

- 76% respondents have answered to the desired questions for the objective of study.
- The rest of respondents did not respond well and hence resulted in unsuitable information.

Table 2: Jewellery Buying Motives

Motives	*Buyers' Response*	*% of Buyers' Response*
Interest	14	24.56
Cultural	33	57.89
Marriage	52	91.23
Fashion	14	24.56
Status symbol	6	10.53
Future investment value	29	50.88
Traditional festivals	6	10.53

- It has been found that occasions like marriage, cultural influences and future investment value are the main and crucial motives for buying gold jewellery.

- The result shows that marriage is the most important motive and reason for buying the gold jewellery followed by cultural (Dhanteras and Akshaya Tritiya) and future investment value.

Table 3: Influencing Factors for Buying Gold Jewellery

Factors	*Buyers' response*	*% of Buyers' response*
Quality	34	59.65
Variety	19	33.33
Design	29	50.88
Fashion	15	26.32
Status symbol	8	14.04
Uniqueness	17	29.82
Services	10	17.54
Assurance	6	10.53
Brand image	13	22.81
Purity	26	45.61
Offers & discounts	13	22.81

- The study reveals that buyers are quite quality conscious. The result also unveils buyer's concerned about quality followed bylatest design, purity variety and uniqueness. Surprisingly, brand image is not one of the main motives of buying jewellery.

Table 4: Current Status of Buyers

	Branded	*Traditional*	*Both*	*Total*
No. of Respondents	19	37	1	57
% of Responded	33.33	64.91	1.75	100.00

- The research study also shows that jewellery buyers still prefer traditional stores to branded stores for purchasing gold jewellery on most of the occasions.

Table 5: Brand Awareness

Brands	*Awareness*	*% of Awareness*
Tanishq	52	91.23
Gili	25	43.86
D'damas	37	64.91
Ashmi	23	40.35
Oyzterbay	5	8.77

Contd.

Trendsmith	6	10.53
Zaveri	25	43.86
PC Jewellers	31	54.39
Sia	10	17.54
Orra	18	31.58
Eros	15	26.32

- The highest brand awareness is for Tanishq. Whereas D'damas, Gili, Ashmi brands are also popular brands of Gitanjali group. PC Jewellers has also good recognition among gold jewellery brands after Tanishq and D'damas.
- Major players in Lucknow jewellery market are Tanishq, Gitanjali Group, P C Jewellers and Traditional Jewellery stores. TATA's Tanishq has maintained an upper hand in terms of revenues followed by other players in the market.
- Tanishq is a well-known name among jewelly buyers and people are more aware about Tanishq than any other branded jewellery retailer. On the contrary, Tanishq is one of its three jewellery brands, others being Zoya and GoldPlus but the latter two have very less awareness in the market.
- Gitanjali is less famous than Tanishq. However, brands like Gili, D'damas, and Asmi has greater awareness level among customer than that of Tanishq.

Table 6: Investment Preference

	Branded	*Traditional*	*Does Not Matter*	*Total*
No. of Respondents	20	23	10	53
% of investment preference	35.09	40.35	24.56	100

- Respondents prefer to go for traditional jewellery when it comes to their investment preferences.

CONCLUSION

Lucknow has an enormous opportunity for gold jewellery. Buying gold jewellery is considered a rational decision due to its inherent future investment value. However, status symbol and traditional festivals are also significant factors encouraging purchasing of gold and gold jewellery. There are many occasions including festive and wedding time when gold jewellery is bought at any price. People are price sensitive but at the time of wedding and festivals like Dhanteras and Akshaya Tritiya, people do not escape from buying gold jewellery. The demand for fashionable jewellery, viz. lightweight, custom-made and designer collections are always there by young buyers. Rising price of gold has also compelled people to think about and encouraged to invest in gold as gold jewellery. Gold jewellery is also being bought for gift purpose on relative's wedding and on auspicious occasions. Though a large portion of people are still buying from traditional jewellery stores, they are now planning to switch to branded jewellery for better quality assurance and guarantee, resale and residual value and status symbol.

References

1. Potluri, Rajasekhara Mouly, Ansari, Rizwana and Challagundla, Srilakshmi (2013). A Study on Spending Patterns and Buying Motives of Indian Gold Consumers, Journal of Distribution Science: July, 2013. Vol. 11, pp. 31–37.
2. Kumar, S. and Varadaraj, Dr. S. (2013). A Study on Buying Behaviour of Women Customer's towards Jewellery Products with Special Reference to Tirupur City, Indian Journal of Applied Research: May, 2013. Vol. 3, Issue: 5.
3. Walia, Karan; Kaur, Inderpreet and Kaur, Gurjeet (2013), Customer Perception Regarding Branded Jewellery, Asian Journal of Research in Marketing: April, 2013. Vol. 2, Issue 2
4. Bamalwa, Bachraj, chairman of the All India Gems and Jewellery Trade Federation (GJF) and partner of Nemichand Bamalwa & Sons (2011), Akshaya Tritiya Spreads Good Fortune All Around, Solitaire International: June, 2011, pp. 47–51.
5. Huma Tariq, Donelda S. McKechnie, Jim Grant, Janice Phillips: Shopping for gold a ritual experience. American University of Sharjah, United Arab Emirates.
6. http://www.seminarsonly.com/Engineering-Projects/Marketing/Jewellery-Buying-Preference.php
7. http://articles.economictimes.indiatimes.com/2012-08-29/news/33476383_1_gold-jewellery-gitanjali-group-jewellery-collection
8. http://www.gold.org/jewellery/about_gold_jewellery/
9. http://www.gold.org/jewellery/markets/india/
10. http://www.business-standard.com/article/markets/organised-retail-takes-over-traditional-jewellery-biz-111041900033_1.html
11. http://www.icra.in/Files/ticker/SH-2013-H1-1-ICRA-Jewellery.pdf
12. http://articles.economictimes.indiatimes.com/2013-01-01/news/36094055_1_gitanjali-group-retail-presence-tribhovandas-bhimji-zaveri
13. http://www.icra.in/Files/ticker/SH-2013-H1-1-ICRA-Jewellery.pdf

25

Factors Affecting Impulse Buying Behavior in Malls: A Consumer Study with Special Reference to Kanpur City

Smita Dron
Assistant Professor
STEP-HBTI, Kanpur
dsmitadron@yahoo.com

Rohit Dron
System Engineer
Power Grid Corporation London (U.K.)
E-mail: rohitdron@gmail.com

ABSTRACT

"Retailing is the final step in the distribution of merchandise—the last link in the supply chain connecting the bulk producers of commodities to the final consumers." One undergoing this process is referred to as Retailer. Retailing includes diverse products such as apparel, footwear, consumer durables, financial services and leisure. However, in India retail trade remains in the backward state but at the same time is poised to expect a rapid growth in tandem with the economic growth. India's $350-400 bn retail market –$ 7.5 bn organized retail is growing about 25-30% annually against economic growth of around 8% a year. With this onset many players are entering the market with various products and strategies to cash upon this development in retail sector, thereby increasing competition. Similarly, there are various retail formats coming up to grab the opportunity in the retail sector. One of the most prominent retail formats coming up is "Shopping Malls" which can be defined an arrangement of retail stores and providing the right mix of shopping, food courts and entertainment and parking facilities. The retail space is shared by anchor stores and other retailers (tenants), who will pay the developers of the mall-rent or lease payment for putting up the shop within the mall premises. Sarang Panchal, Executive Director Customized Research ACNielsen South Asia says, "With increase in the sheer numbers of malls and modern format stores shopping has almost become a national pastime in our country especially in the cities. Strong economic growth along with booming young adult populations with unprecedented levels of disposable incomes has made people more conscious of the latest trends and fashions. No one wants to be left behind, Indian consumers are ever willing to upgrade their knowledge where latest trends are concerned

and these definitely helped in increasing the footfalls in all these modern malls mushrooming across the city."

INTRODUCTION

An impulse purchase or impulse buy is an unplanned or otherwise spontaneous purchase. One who tends to make such purchases is referred to as an impulse purchaser or impulse buyer. Impulse buying disrupts the normal decision making models in consumers' brains. The logical sequence of the consumers' actions is replaced with an irrational moment of self gratification. Impulse items appeal to the emotional side of consumers. Some items bought on impulse are not considered functional or necessary in the consumers' lives. Preventing impulse buying involves techniques such as setting budgets before shopping and taking time out before the purchase is made. The retail sector has been grown drastically over the years and there are large number of Shopping Malls and various other retail formats coming up in Metros, Tier I and II cities giving tight competition to the existing ones. And because of this, the retailers are the main focus today and they are totally engrossed in knowing their customer and consumer.

There are several malls coming up in metros. The success of mall in tier I cities is definitely influencing tier II cities and smaller towns to replicate the mall model. Thus, the next logical step for a retailer is to tap this huge latent demand in tier II cities and establish a strong presence in such cities. And this can be seen in case of a second tier city like Kanpur where recent market research shows that Kanpur is likely to grow at a phenomenal rate in the coming 2-3 years as the retails revolution rocks India. With a projected growth rate of around 18% in the retail sector, Kanpur is a large town with a good consumption and has enough potential. It is one of the cities where Pantaloons opened before Big Bazaar and is now one of the better performing stores. Kanpur has a lot to offer for retail development and after initial research I found it a good market to foray into. It has a huge young customer belt because a number of educational institutes are there. The industrial sector is also growing. The city has the highest number of self employed people and therein lies Kanpur's uniqueness.The city is home to SMEs engaged in leather, cotton and wool production, flour and refined oil mills, and chemical industries. According to estimates, more than 40 percent of the people in Kanpur are self employed.

Shopping Malls in Kanpur are well planned, inspired by international ideas of retailing. Along with the shopping experience, recreation and entertainment are integrated, thus giving a complete family experience. The previous concept of shopping malls was different in Kanpur, the purpose of it was to accommodate many small shops, and the place was stuffy with cheap articles. But the concept is gradually changing in Kanpur with the upcoming of shopping malls.

People get all types of products like garments, toys, bags, jewelry, shoes, gift items, crockery, etc. under one roof. The Shopping Malls in Kanpur also have arrangement for entertainment, as they have multiplexes and hang out places for families and visitors. These are the number of Malls in Kanpur.

- The Mega Mall, Adjacent to the City Center (Rotomac Industries), The Mall
- The Rave @ Moti, Adjacent to The Moti Lal Padam Pat Udyog, Sarvodaya Nagar
- The Rave 3, Parvati Bagla Road, Kanpur
- The Z Square Mall, Opposite Christ Church College, The Mall, Kanpur
- Somdutt Plaza Parade, The Mall, Kanpur
- Nadri Bazar, Swaroop Nagar
- Vishal Mega Mart, GT Road near Coca Cola Chauraha, Kanpur
- SGM Parade
- SGM Gurudev Palace

Impulse Purchases

"Impulse buying has been considered a pervasive and distinctive phenomenon in the American lifestyle and has been receiving increasing attention from consumer researchers and theorists (Youn & Faber, 2000, p.179)". Often retail purchase involves unplanned or impulse purchases. The grocery consumers generally ignore print advertisements before shopping and in many cases the grocery shopping is unplanned. Surveys indicate that a significant number of grocery shoppers do not prepare a list before shopping. A study found that impulse purchases represented between 27% and 62% of all department store purchases (Bellenger et al., 1978). Rook and Hoch (1985) assert that most people have experienced an impulse purchase. Other research findings support this assertion revealing almost 90% of respondents have made grocery purchases on impulse occasionally (Welles, 1986), and between 30% and 50% of all purchases can be classified by the buyers themselves as impulse purchases.Today's research suggests that impulse buying behavior is much more complex than previously conceptualized. This behavior stems from the desire to satisfy multiple needs that underlie many types of buying behavior (Hausman, 2000).

OBJECTIVES OF THE STUDY

Objective of this research paper is to analyze and understand the impulse buying behavior of consumers in organized retailing environment especially in malls. Sub objectives are to study factors affecting the Impulse Buying Behavior and to assess the role of in-store advertising on consumer buying patterns.

RESEARCH METHODOLOGY

Type of Research: Descriptive research.

Population of the Study: The population of the study comprised of residents of Kanpur.

Sample Size: Sample consisted of 100 respondents of age group (18-35).

Sampling and research tool used: Convenient sampling method was adopted to fill the questionnaire by personal interaction with the customers visiting to retail stores in malls.

Data Analysis and interpretation: Data was analyzed using the excel sheet, calculating out the various percentages.

DATA ANALYSIS AND INTERPRETATION

PLANNED SHOPPING

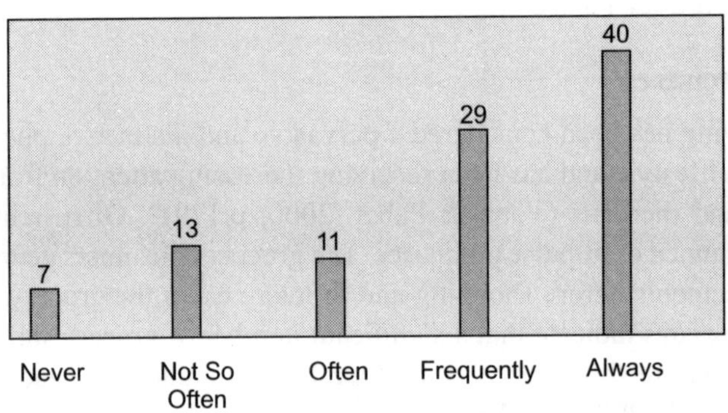

A significant number of the respondents, i.e., 40% said that they always planned their shopping whereas, 29% said that they frequently plan their shopping followed by very few people (7%) who said that they never plan their shopping.

INFLUENCE OF POP DISPLAYS ON THE PURCHASE DECISION

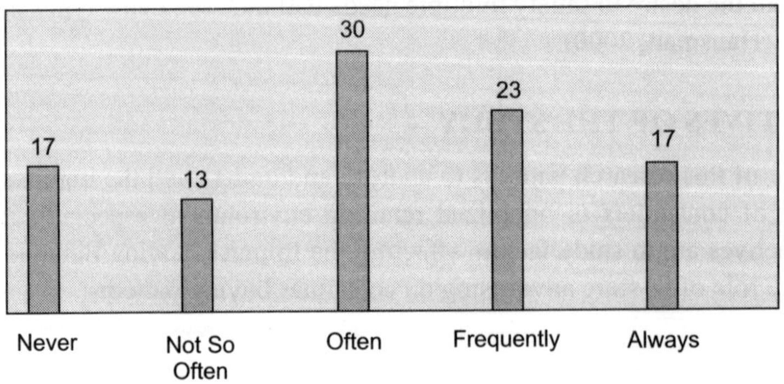

30% of the respondents said that their purchase decision often gets influenced by the Point-of Purchase displays, 23% said that their purchase decision frequently gets influenced by the P.O.P. displays whereas 17% of the respondents said that they always get influenced by the displays.

ATTRACTIVE WINDOW DISPLAYS MOTIVATE TO ENTER THE STORE

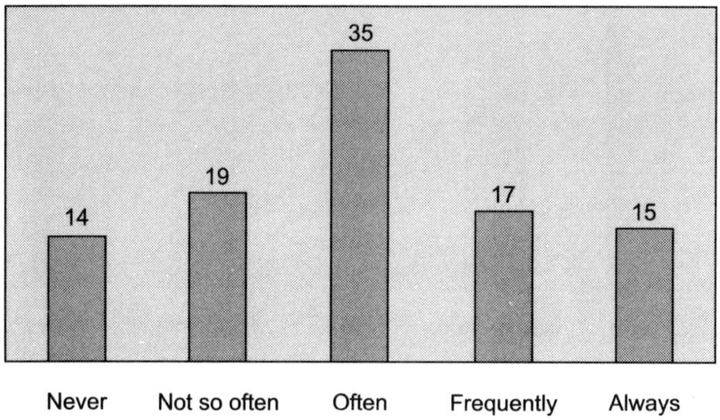

A significant 35% of the respondents said that attractive displays often motivated them enter a store followed by 17% who said that they frequently entered a retail outlet when attracted by displays. However, 14% of the respondents said that they never got influenced to enter a retail outlet due to attractive displays.

ATTRACTIVE DISPLAYS LEAD TO UNPLANNED PURCHASE

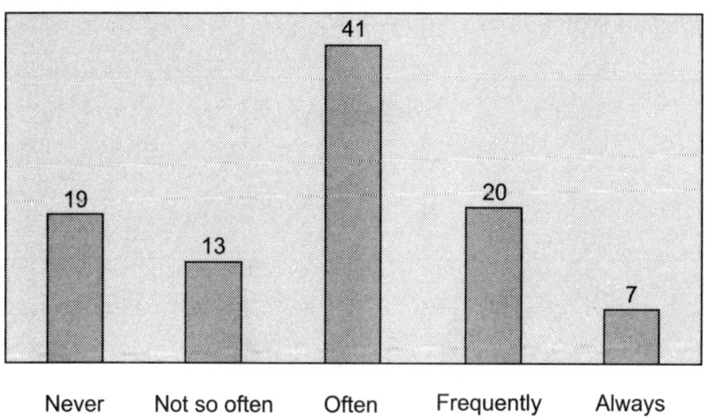

A significant number of respondents, i.e., 41% said that they got influenced by the attractive displays and often made purchases that they had not planned for, followed by 20% who said that it frequently happened that attractive displays made them make unplanned purchases. 19% of the respondents said that they never got influenced by attractive displays.

ATTRACTIVE DISPLAYS CHANGE THE BRAND DECISIONS

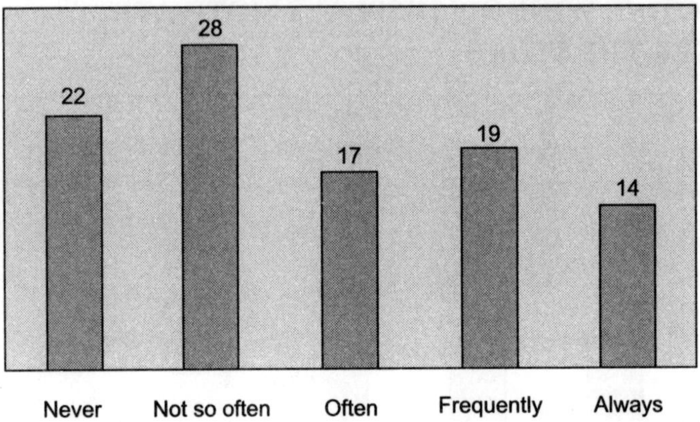

28% of the respondents said that their brand decisions not so often got influenced by attractive displays whereas 19% said that their brand decision frequently got influenced by attractive displays. 22% said that they never changed their brand decisions at the retail outlet.

BRAND DECISIONS TAKEN INSIDE THE RETAIL OUTLET

In order to study the impact of displays consumer responses for brand decisions for grocery items taken inside the retail outlet for different product categories were taken, analysis of which is as given below:

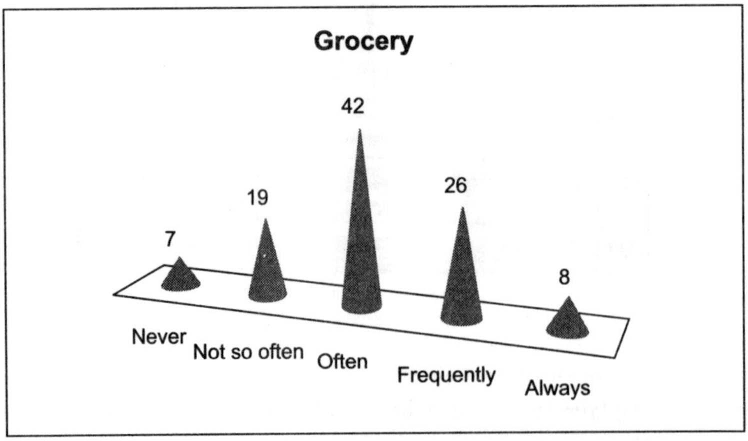

42% of the respondents said that they often took brand decision for grocery items inside the retail outlets, 26% frequently took brand decision for grocery items inside the retail outlets and 19% did not do it so often.

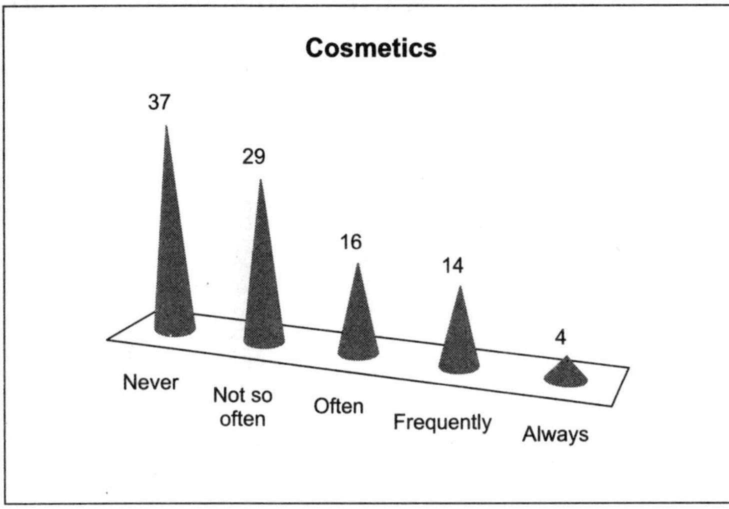

For cosmetics, 37% respondents never took their brand decision inside the retail outlet, 29% did not do it so often and only 14% of the respondents said that they frequently decided the brand of cosmetics to be purchased inside the retail outlet.

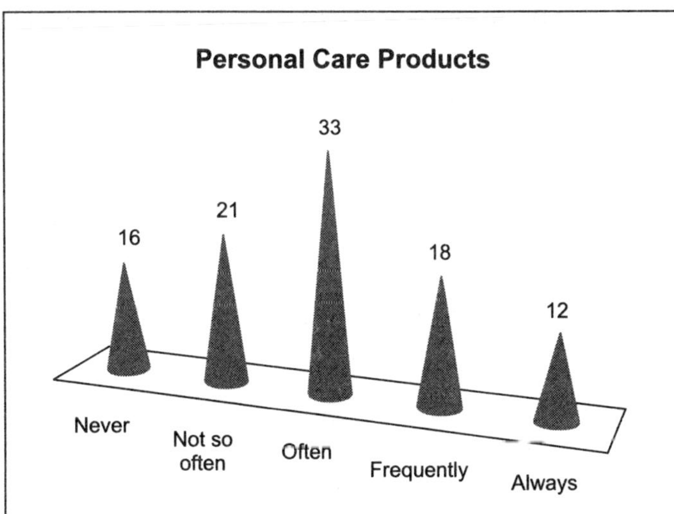

In case of personal care products a significant 33% of respondents said that they often took their brand once inside the retail store with 18% frequently doing so. However, 21% of the respondents said that they did not often take their brand decisions for personal care products inside the store whereas 16% of the respondents said that they never did so.

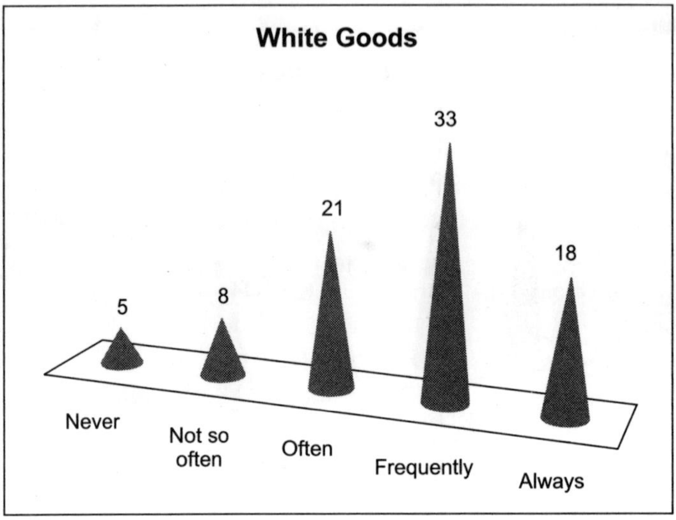

For white goods 33% of the respondents said that it frequently happened that they took the brand decision while in a retail store whereas 21% often and 18% of the respondents always took brand decisions inside the retail outlet.

IMPORTANCE OF DISPLAYS ON PURCHASE DECISIONS

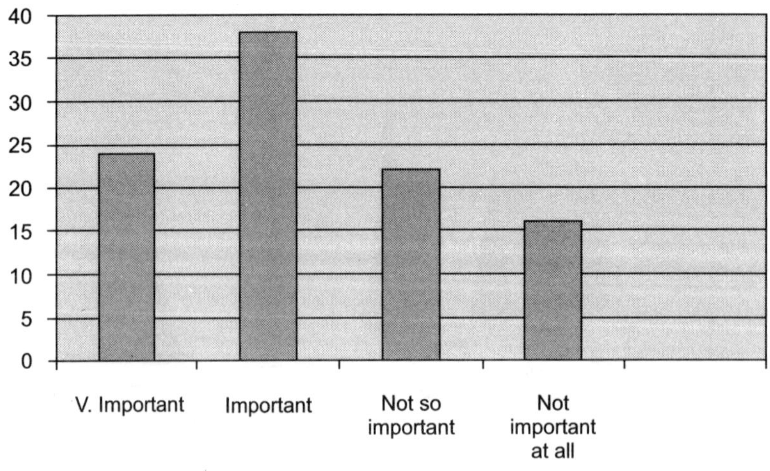

38% of the respondents said that displays have an important role to play in influencing the purchase decision, whereas 24% said that displays were very important in influencing the purchase decision. A significant 22% of the respondents were also of the view that displays are not important followed by 16% who did not find displays important at all.

FINDINGS

1. Attractive window displays lead to an increase in footfalls in the store.
2. Most of the respondents said that POP displays lead to purchases.
3. Though attractive displays motivated a significant number of respondents to make purchases but very few changed their brand decisions due to these displays. This shows that displays do not influence the brand decision quite often.
4. It was also found that impulse purchases were a common feature in case of groceries.
5. In case of cosmetics the brand decision rarely got influenced at the retail outlet which implies that for cosmetics the consumers are generally hard core loyal and frequently purchase cosmetics in a planned manner.
6. In case of personal care products the brand decision often got influenced by the attractive displays and variety of brands available at the retail outlets.
7. Most of the respondents took their brand decision for white goods inside the retail outlet which implies that P.O.P. displays may have an impact on the consumer brand decision to some extent.

SUGGESTIONS

1. Since impulse purchase is very common for grocery items, therefore, retailers should allot the premium shelf space to the products with comparatively higher margins.
2. Displays lead to increased footfalls and impulse purchases being one of the special characteristics of retailing, therefore, to have increased daily average sales attractive P.O.P. material should be used to attract consumers and motivate them to enter the retail outlet.
3. Since the brand decision for white goods is generally taken inside the retail outlet therefore, the product and its different variations should be attractively displayed. This is important not only to a retailer alone but also to the manufacturer also because a good brand not attractively displayed may lose to the competitor's well displayed brand.
4. In order to have attractive display of the product range available at a retail outlet, clutter should be avoided. The P.O.P. items used should be in accordance to the standard of the target segment.
5. Window displays should be able to convey the available product range to the consumers so as to attract the target customer to enter the outlet.
6. Since Brand loyalty for cosmetics is high, therefore, each brand should be given a proportionate shelf space so as to draw the attention of customers with different brand preferences.

CONCLUSION

Displays definitely have an impact on consumer purchase decision and in the long term affect the retail sales by and large. If the in-store displays are professionally managed it can help the organization to en-cash the feature of impulse purchases in retailing. Attractive displays is one of the main reasons for the growth of the retail sector at such a fast pace. A well designed store with proper P.O.P. displays gives the customers a chance to compare the product, feel it, check it and finally purchase it. Displays leading to purchases also strengthen the view that marketers create needs or rather make the customer feel the need for a product. Attractive displays have a vital role to play when consumers go for unplanned shopping and also help in creating customer awareness for products as well as different brands available in the market. Thus, it is concluded that displays definitely play a major role in the growth of retail business.

References

1. Berman Berry & Evans R. Joel, Retail Management–A Strategic Approach, PHI Pvt. Ltd., New Delhi, 2005. pp 456–463.
2. http://www.fas.usda.gov/info/factsheets/China/distribution.html, retrieved on 27 February, 2011
3. www.ibef.org "Retail", December, 2010, retrieved on 27 February, 2011.
4. www.business-standard. com, "FDI or no FDI, global retail has a local ally" retrieved on 27th February, 2011.

26

Consumer References towards Motorcycles Purchases Decision: An Empirical Analysis of Rural Lucknow

Yasir Arafat Elahi
Assistant Professor (Business Administration)
Oman College of Management and Technology
P.O. Box 680, P.C. 320, Barka, Sultanate of Oman
URL: www.omancollege.edu.om
dr.yaelahi@gmail.com

Anisur Rehman
Senior Lecturer, Department of Business Management
Faculty of Management and Research, Integral University, Lucknow
E-mail: anisur.rehman11@gmail.com

ABSTRACT

Two-wheeler vehicles ownership in India is increasing at a high rate due to fast economic growth. Majority of Indians, especially the youngsters prefer motorcycles rather than cars. It is the world's second largest manufacturer of motorcycles after China and there are eight key players in the Indian markets that produced 13.8 million units in 2010-11. As per estimates, the rural market now accounts for around 45% of total domestic motorcycle sales volumes. We present a survey of people in rural Lucknow, a representative rural area of northern India, to analyze preferences of consumers in the Indian rural market. Understanding rural consumer behavior in the present scenario is extremely important as it is no longer a simple task. Unless a marketing manager has the knowledge of the factors that affect rural consumers purchasing patterns, he cannot formulate his best sale policies and advertising policies.

The situation of few motorcycles manufacturers in India has changed with the entry of other competitors, especially after liberalization and globalization. The foreign collaboration saw production going up tremendously due to the availability of many alternative choices, consumer preferences and needs changed. Hence, this study makes an attempt to know the changes in the motorcycles markets and buying motives of motorcycles buyers in rural areas.

INTRODUCTION

India is the second largest producer of two-wheelers in the world and stands next to China and Japan in terms of production and sales respectively. Majority of Indians, especially the youngsters prefer motorbikes rather than cars. Capturing a large share in the two-wheeler industry, bikes and scooters cover a major segment. Motorcycles are considered to be the favorite among the youth, as they help in easy commutation. The two- wheeler industry has shown impressive growth of over 10% for four year till 2006-07. In 2007-08 there was a drop in agricultural output which resulted in slow growth but a boost came after the Sixth Pay Commission recommendations. Major players in the market including Hero Motor Corp, Honda, Bajaj Auto, TVS, Suzuki, Yamaha, Mahindra, Royal Enfield and LML are striving hard to capture the two-wheeler market-share.

Indian Two-Wheeler Industry: Sales and Market Figures

Indian two-wheeler industry saw a slight growth of 1.04% during the April-May period of 2013 compared against the same period of 2012. A total of 2,374,253 units were sold during the period as 2,349,814 units were sold in April-May 2012. Hero Motor Corp is the biggest manufacturer in Indian market who sold 1,035,823 units during April-May 2013.

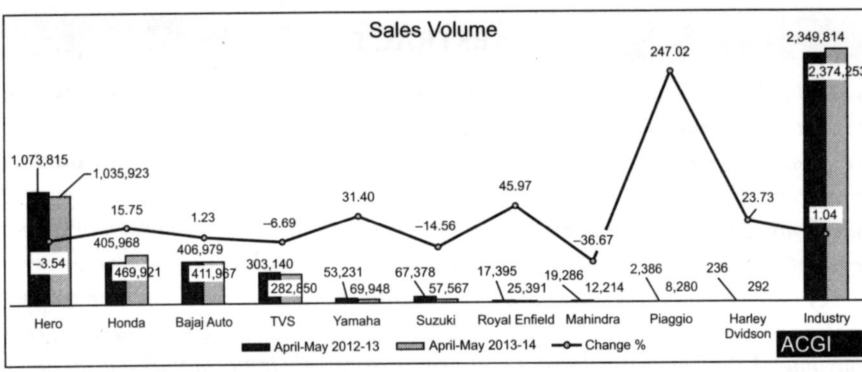

Figure 1: Indian Two-Wheeler Industry Sales Volume (Source: ACG)

The period April-May of 2013 saw the share of Hero came down to 43.63%. Honda gains some shares and put them at second place replacing Bajaj. Honda holds 19.79% share as per April-May 2013 while Bajaj has now 17.35% share.

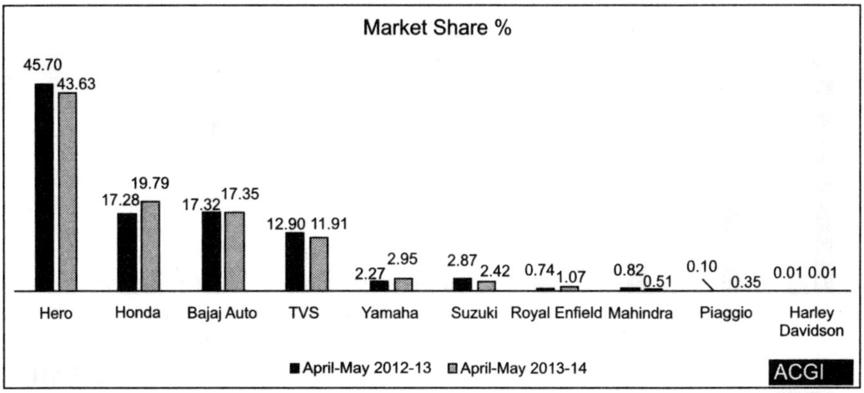

Figure 2: Indian Two-Wheeler Industry: Market Share (Source: ACG)

Indian Motor Cycles Industry: Sales and Market Figures

Sales of Hero declined by 7.27% while Yamaha also saw their sales went down by 9.39%. Apparently Honda registered 21.33% growth.

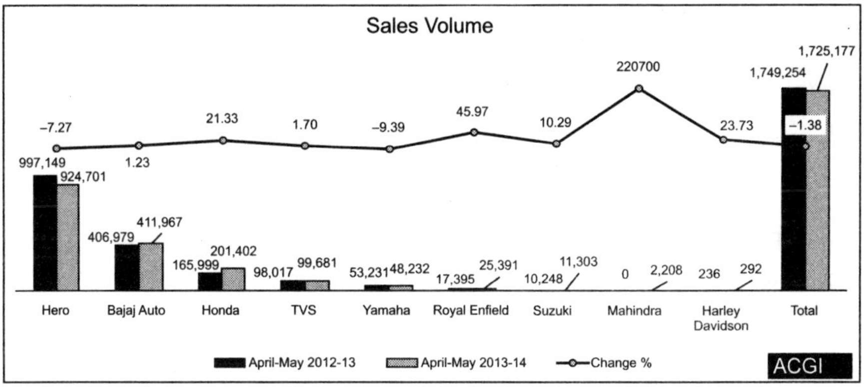

Figure 3: Indian Motor Cycles Industry Sales Volumes (Source: ACG)

Triggered by the decline of sales Hero's share in motorcycle segment came down to 53.60% for April to May period of 2013. Their former partner Honda with improved share of 11.67% stays at third place in terms of sales in Indian two-wheeler market.

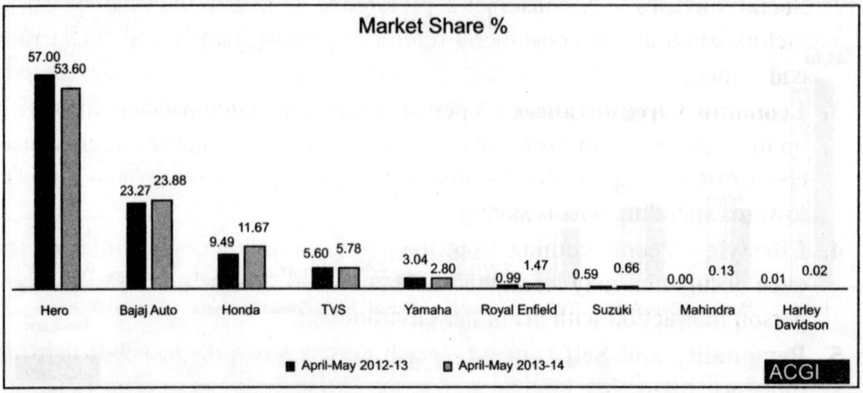

Figure 4: Indian Motor Cycles Industry: Market Share (Source: ACG)

From Figure 5 it is clear that there is an increase in the demand of motorcycles in India as well as abroad. The last four year data reveals that there is growth in sales of motorcycles except for the current year 2012–13. This is mainly due to increasing inflation in India and also due to increase of fuel prices globally.

Motorcycles Volumes/Units	*2009–10*	*2010–11*	*2011–12*	*2012–13*
Sold	7,341,122	9,013,888	10,096,062	9,305,708
Exported	1,102,978	1,474,678	1,847,517	1,723,961
Total	8444100	10488566	11943579	11029669

Figure 5: Yearly Sales figure of Motorcycles (Source: ACG)

From Figure 6 it is clear that there is an increase in the percentage growth of motorcycles demand in India as well as abroad. There is a negative growth in export of motorcycles for the current year 2012–13.

Motorcycles Growth %	*2009–10*	*2010–11*	*2011–12*	*2012–13*
Sold	25.9%	22.8%	12.0%	0.9%
Exported	13.6%	33.7%	25.3%	–0.6%

Figure 6: Yearly Growth figure of Motorcycles (Source: ACG)

Factors Influencing the Consumers Preference

Consumer behaviour or buyers' attitude is a process by which an individual decides what, when, how, whether or not, from whom to purchase goods and the service.

The various factors affecting the consumer's preference are as follows:-

1. **Cultural Factors** - Cultural factors such as buyer's culture, sub-culture and social class identification bear in depth and wide influences of consumer preference.

2. **Social Factors** - A consumer's preference is also influenced by social factors, such as the consumer's reference groups, family and social roles and status.
3. **Economic Circumstances** - A person's economic circumstances also affect up to great extent in his product choice. People's economic circumstances consist of their spendable income, saving, borrowing power and attitudes towards spending versus saving.
4. **Lifestyle** - People coming from the same sub-culture, social classes and even occupation may lead quiet different life. Lifestyle portrays the whole person interaction with his or her environment.
5. **Personality and Self-concept** - Each person has a distinct flair that will influence his or her buying preference. A person's personality is usually described in terms of such trait as self-confidence, dominance, autonomy, deference, sociability defensiveness and adoptability.
6. **Psychological Factors** - A person's buying choice is also influenced from major psychological factors like motivation, perception, learning, beliefs and attitudes.
7. **Brand Loyalty** - To be truly brand loyal the consumer must hold a favorable attitude towards the brand in addition to purchasing it repeatedly. One may be forced to purchase a particular brand repeatedly because other brands may not be available unable to find a suitable replacement though he is not liking the unfavorable substitutes.

Literature Review

Indian Two-Wheeler Report (2013) elucidates facts on the Indian two-wheeler industry, supplemented by the latest statistics. The report emphasizes on Indian two-wheeler industry over next 5 years and also provides overview of various segments of the industry, regulatory issues, trade scenario and overall performance of the domestic market. The report gives details of the some key players in the two-wheeler industry.

Last year, Honda Motorcycle & Scooter India Pvt Ltd sold 2.33 lakh two-wheelers a month against Bajaj's sales of 2.12 lakh units a month. Hero, the market leader, sold 5 lakh units a month. TVS, the fourth player, is way behind with sales of 1.8 lakh units a month. **(As per timesofindia.indiatimes.com › Business, Jun 26, 2013).**

ICRA Report (2013) states that the domestic two-wheeler industry is expected to report moderate volume growth of around 4-5 per cent in 2012-13. The two-wheeler industry, however, has clocked a compounded annual growth rate (CAGR) of 21.8 per cent over the last three years. The report further adds that over the medium term, the two-wheeler industry is expected to report a volume CAGR of 8-9 per cent, to reach a size of 22-23 million units (combining domestic and exports) by 2016-17.

Faiz Ahmed Shaikh (2011) in his research paper titled "A critical analysis of Consumer buying behavior of two-wheelers" reviews the current marketing practices in the two-wheeler industry and their impact on consumer.

Anuj Kumar Kanojia (2011) in his research paper titled "Analyzing the State Of Competition in Indian Two-Wheeler Industry" shows the oligopolistic nature of the Indian two-wheeler industry and the propensity of the major players to increase their share. The study also reveals that urban and rural segments have different preferences in purchasing two-wheelers.

Anjan Ghosh, Subrata Ray, Jitin Makkar (ICRA 2011) in their research paper titled "Two-wheeler Industry: Growth Drivers Intact" stated that two-wheeler is the most affordable mode of private transport in India. Entry of new players into the Indian market has enriched product offerings and brought in new technologies. Urbanization has drawn rural people in contact with cities and towns at a steady pace. The need for mobility in most Indian cities and towns therefore has increased substantially and the available public transport system is not sufficient.

Sunila George (IIM Bangalore), Raghbendra Jha (ANU, Canberra), Hari K. Nagarajan (IIM Bangalore and NCAER, Delhi), 2001 in their research paper titled "The Evolution and Structure of the Two-wheeler Industry in India" studies the evolution of the competitive structure of the two-wheeler industry in India.

Virupaxi Bagodi and Biswajit Mahanty (2008) in their research paper titled "Two-wheeler service sector in India: factors of importance for sustainable growth" identified important factors to achieve customer satisfaction in two-wheeler service industry.

RESEARCH METHODOLOGY

Problem Statement

The study is about the activities of the rural consumers with respect to their opinion about the best quality of motor cycles and their preference towards the purchase of motor cycles. The research also analyzes the rural consumer's income level, advantage and disadvantage of vehicle, price of the vehicle, quality because these factors also determine the purchase factor. Convenient sampling technique is adopted to collect primary as well as secondary data. Personal interview technique is adopted to collect the data. For the purpose of effective study, all types of motor cycles have been taken into consideration. The collected data will be interpreted through tables for better and clear understanding.

Research Objective

- To identify those attributes which are highly determinate for purchasing motor cycles vehicles in rural areas of Lucknow.
- To measure the performance of selected motor cycles companies through appraisal of the customer satisfaction level.

- To suggest some considerable points for the expansion of motor cycles industry in rural areas of Lucknow.

Sources of Data Primary and Secondary Data

Primary Data was collected with the help of Final year MBA students.

Sample Size The survey was conducted from April to July 2013 in Lucknow, India. 150 respondents of four Tehsils of Lucknow District were surveyed in a different time period based on convenience sampling from different segments of people. The sample constitutes of Business men, Employees, Professionals, Students, etc. Questionnaires were used to get feedback from target sample.

Choice of Location Lucknow, located in Northern India is the capital of Uttar Pradesh has one of the highest populations of all cities in Uttar Pradesh. It is the largest city of Uttar Pradesh, second largest metro of North and Central India after Delhi and 11th largest city of India. With an estimated population of 6.4 million in 2012, the city is projected to double its population by 2022. A very high percentage of the total population (36.37 percent) resides in rural areas, i.e., almost 1.93 million. Having experienced a large growth of motorcycles ownership on account of its economic growth, this city is ideal for the present study. Being comparatively less influenced by globalization, the rural area preserves many typical Indian characteristics like the traditional joint family set up.

Sample Size and Survey Method Questionnaires were given to 150 Respondents in the in rural areas of Lucknow for purpose of carrying out the project. History of the motor cycles companies were narrated the best to the knowledge of the student's researcher to make the project effective and fruitful. Perfectly structured questionnaire has been used to accumulate the essential primary data. The interviews conducted and the information was gathered in person. The answers thus obtained were documented.

The study is about the activities of the rural consumers with respect to their opinion about the best quality of motorcycles and their preference towards its purchase. The research is also analyzing the rural consumer's income level, advantage and disadvantage of vehicle, price of the vehicle, quality because these factors also determine the purchase factor.

Limitations of the Study The study is based on the Consumer Preference towards the various types of Motorcycles in rural Lucknow only. The research is mainly concentrated on the attitude of rural consumers. The researcher has relied upon the oral facts given by the respondents. Hence, the research finding are not generalized.

Table 1 Profile of the Respondents

Age	*Category of Respondent*	*Number*	*Percentage*
Age (Year)	Less than 20 yrs	25	16.7
	20-35 yrs	64	42.7
	35-50 yrs	43	28.7
	Above 50 yrs	18	12
	Total	150	
Income (Monthly) Rs.	Less than 8,000	17	11.3
	8,000-12,000	43	28.7
	12000- 20,000	56	37.3
	Above 20,000	34	22.7
	Total	150	
Occupation	Farmer	64	42.7
	Business	36	24
	Private job	23	15.3
	Government job	27	18
	Total	150	
Educational Qualifications	Illiterate	19	12.7
	Below Class 10	36	24
	Class 10/12	48	32
	Graduate	32	21.3
	Post-Graduate	15	10
	Total	150	

Some Primary Data Findings

1. Normally 60% of the respondents were having income more than 12,000 per month.
2. 42.7% respondents were in the age group of 20-35 years, 28.7% are in the age group of 35-50 years. Therefore 70% of the respondents were in the age group of 20 -50 years.
3. 42.7% respondents were farmers and 24% respondents were performing small business activities like retailing, trading, brokering, etc.
4. Almost 53% of the respondents were having class 10 as their prior education qualification.

Table 2 Brand Preference of Motorcycles

S. No.	*Brand*	*Frequency*	*Percentage*
1	Hero	53	35.3
2	Honda	31	20.7
3	Bajaj	28	18.7
4	TVS	13	8.7
5	Suzuki	11	7.3
6	Yamaha	8	5.3
7	Royal Enfield	4	2.7
8	Mahindra	2	1.3
		150	100

From the above, it is evident that Hero is the market leader as per the brand preference of rural consumers. Honda and Bajaj are close together for the second and third place.

Garrett's Ranking Technique

Garrett's ranking technique was used to find out the most significant factor which influences the consumers to buy motorcycle. The consumers were asked to assess ten factors influencing their decision to buy motorcycle on its own significance. Each consumer was instructed to indicate the importance of the influencing factor by giving rank 1 to the most important factor, rank 2 to the second important factor and so on.

Based upon the ranks assigned by the sample consumers, the order of important factors influencing the consumers to buy motorcycle is identified. Garrett's Ranking Technique is calculated as percentage score and the scale value is obtained by employing Scale Conversion Table given by Henry Garrett.

The Percentage Score is calculated as:

$$\text{Percentage score} = 100\,(R_{ij} - 0.5)\,/\,N_j$$

where

R_{ij} = Rank given for the ith variable by j^{th} respondents
N_j = Number of variable ranked by j^{th} respondents

The percentage score for each rank from 1 to 10 are calculated. The percentage score thus obtained for all the ten ranks are converted into scale values using Scale Conversion Table given by Henry Garrett. The scale values for first rank to tenth rank are 81, 70, 63, 57, 52, 47, 42, 36, 29 and 18 respectively. The score value (fx) is calculated for each factor by multiplying the number of respondents (f) with respective scale values (x). The total scores are found by adding the score values (fx) of each rank for every factor. The mean score can be calculated to know the order of preference given by the respondents for the factors. Based on the mean score, the overall ranks are assigned for each. The ranking analysis of the factors influencing the consumers to buy motorcycle through Garrett's Ranking Technique is shown in Table 3. The factors having highest mean value is considered to be the most important factor.

Table 3 Factors Influencing in buying Motorcycles (Garrett Ranking Analysis)

	Rank	*1*	*2*	*3*	*4*	*5*	*6*	*7*	*8*	*9*	*10*		
Factors	*Scale Value (x)*	*81*	*70*	*63*	*57*	*52*	*47*	*42*	*36*	*29*	*18*	*Total Score*	*Rank*
Comfort	*f*	5	6	10	10	11	11	15	17	16	49		
Level	*fx*	405	420	630	570	572	517	630	612	464	882	5702	10
After Sales service		13	12	10	14	13	13	18	18	28	11		
		1053	840	630	798	676	611	756	648	812	198	7022	6
Affordable Price		24	17	21	24	21	11	7	8	5	12		
		1944	1190	1323	1368	1092	517	294	288	145	588	8749	3
Engine Capacity		12	4	11	23	22	29	17	17	9	6		
		972	280	693	1311	1144	1363	714	612	261	108	7458	5
Mileage		33	22	35	8	12	14	6	8	7	5		
		2673	1540	2205	456	624	658	252	288	203	90	8989	1
Maintenance		20	18	34	29	16	7	10	9	5	2		
Cost		1620	1260	2142	1653	832	329	420	324	145	36	8761	2
Brand Image		18	45	12	15	18	7	7	8	13	7		
		1458	3150	756	855	936	329	294	288	377	126	8569	4
Finance Options		10	6	4	7	13	30	31	23	11	15		
		810	420	252	399	676	1410	1302	828	319	270	6686	8
Dealer's		6	7	8	8	9	10	19	20	34	29		
Behaviour		486	490	504	456	468	470	798	720	986	522	5900	9
Advertisement		9	13	5	12	15	18	20	22	22	14		
		729	910	315	684	780	846	840	792	638	252	6786	7
Total		150	150	150	150	150	150	150	150	150	150		

Note: x = scale value, f = number of respondents and fx = score value.

From Table 3, it is clear that most of the respondents consider mileage as the main factor which influences them to purchase motorcycles and it is rank first with a score of 8989 points. The basic reasons were regular hike in fuel prices and low income of rural respondents.

It is also evident that maintenance cost ranked second as they are also considered important factor by motorcycle customers while purchasing their brand quality. Rural respondents do not want to purchase motorcycles with high maintenance cost.

Pricing is also considered an important factor while purchasing motorcycles and it is ranked third. Motorcycle models with a price between Rs. 40,000-50,000 comprise the executive segment, which is largely concentrated around the 100-125 cc models were mainly demanded by rural consumers

Brand image is ranked fourth by the respondents. Hero, Honda and Bajaj were capturing almost 75% of the rural market share.

Engine capacity is ranked fifth by the respondents. Rural consumers prefer to have motorcycles strong and powerful enough to face undeveloped road challenges.

After sales service is an important factor and was ranked sixth by the respondents. Companies have to maintain good service standards in order to be successful in rural market. Regular supply of spare parts and technological advancement in delivering service are the key to success.

Advertisement is ranked seventh by the respondents. Rural consumers prefer to have print advertisement as an informative tool for giving information about the two wheeler vehicles.

Finance options is ranked eighth as there is a diminishing importance of finance availability in rural market. Here the buyers rely less on the organized financing sector and there is a shift in the purchase pattern of buyers. Till 2006-07, around 50% of all motorcycles purchased were financed but now the share has come down to around 25% in 2010-11.

Dealer's behaviour is ranked ninth by the respondents. The dealers must emphasize on good and healthy relationship with the rural consumers.

Comfort level is ranked last by the respondents. Rural consumers are going for their purchase in pursuit of mileage, price, maintenance cost, brand image, etc. They are least bothered about comfort level in motorcycles purchase.

CONCLUSION

Automobile industry is providing large number of employment opportunities both directly and indirectly. It also increases the economic stability of a country and encourages small scale industries (ancillary units). Automobile industry increases the export and import of a country which helps to earn foreign exchange. The various structural positives associated with the domestic motorcycle industry including favourable demographic profile, moderate motorcycle penetration levels (in relation to several other emerging markets), under developed public transport system, growing urbanization, strong replacement demand and moderate share of financed purchases remain intact; as also the large opportunity available to grow presence in overseas markets, mainly Africa and Latin America.

The status of the rural consumer's behavior regarding the decision for motorcycles purchase was recognized. There is a constant improvement of earning among the rural consumer's. The rural consumer's were found to be clear and aware regarding the purchase. This study focuses on those attributes which are very important for success of motorcycle companies in rural market. Motorcycle companies can gain market leadership only if they understands the rural consumer needs and final solution that delights rural consumer through superior value, quality and service.

References

1. Anjan Ghosh , Subrata Ray, Jitin Makkar, Two-wheelers Industry: Growth Drivers intact, (ICRA), June 2011.
2. Anuj Kumar kanojia, Analyzing the State of Competition in Indian Two-Wheeler Industry, Competition Commission of India, New Delhi, 2011.
3. Ardiyok, S. "Aftermarket theories in Competition Law and Regulation on Motor Vehicles, International Journal of Business, Management and Economics, Vol. 1, No. 2, 2005.
4. Automotive Component Manufacturers Association of India (ACMA). 1998. Automotive Industry in India, Facts and Figures 1997-1998. Mumbai.
5. Bajaj auto Ltd – Riding towards darkness: 23rd March 2011.
6. B.N. Goldar and S.C. Aggarwal, Trade Liberalization and Price-Cost Margin in Indian Industries, 2005.
7. Faiz Ahmed Shaikh, A Critical Analysis of Consumer buying behavior of two-wheelers, Indian stream Research Journal, 2012.
8. G. S. Dangayachy and S. G. Deshmukhy, Practice of manufacturing strategy: evidence from select Indian automobile companies, 2001.
9. Government of India. 1980. Sixth Five Year Plan (1980-85). New Delhi: Planning Commission.
10. Government of India. 1985. Seventh Five Year Plan (1985-90). New Delhi: Planning Commission.
11. Government of India. 1992. Eighth Five Year Plan (1992-97). New Delhi: Planning Commission.
12. Joshi, V., Little, I. 1996. India's Economic Reforms: 1991-2001. New Delhi, Oxford University Press.
13. Rishikesha T. Krishnan & Ganesh N. Prabhu, Creating Successful New Products: Challenges for Indian Industry, 31 July 1999.
14. Shapiro, C., "Aftermarkets and Consumer Welfare: Making Sense of Kodak", Antitrust Law Journal, Vol. 63, 1994.
15. Sunila George (IIM Bangalore), Raghbendra Jha (ANU, Canberra), Hari K. Nagarajan (IIM Bangalore and NCAER, Delhi), The Evolution and Structure of the Two-wheeler Industry in India, 2001.
16. T.A. Bhavani and N.R. Bhanumurthy, The State of Competition in the Indian Manufacturing Sector, Institute of Economic Growth, March 2007.
17. Two-wheeler industry in India, enrich.ch-india.com, 07 April 2009 53.

18. Virupaxi Bagodi, Biswajit Mahanty (2008), Two-wheeler service sector in India: factors of importance for sustainable growth, in (ed.) Emerald Group Publishing Limited, pp.21-27.

Websites

1. *www.icra.in/Files/ticker/SH-2013-Q2-1-ICRA-Two-Wheeler.pdf*
2. www. *timesofindia.indiatimes.com* › Business
3. http://articles.economictimes.indiatimes.com/2010-12-16/news /27622928_1_munjal-family-hero-honda-indianpromoters
4. http://en.wikipedia.org/wiki/Hero_Honda_Split
5. http://www.content4reprint.com/cars-and-trucks/motorcycles/the-two-wheeler-industry-in-india.htm
6. http://economictimes.indiatimes.com/news/news-by-industry/auto/two-wheelers/indian-bike-makers-to-take-onchinese-counterparts-on-africa-roads/articleshow/8919169.cms
7. http://economictimes.indiatimes.com/news/news-by-industry/auto/two-wheelers/honda-to-boost-bike-capacityin-india-to-4-million-units-by-2013/articleshow/8581921.cms
8. http://articles.economictimes.indiatimes.com/2009-10-30/news /27649118_1_vehicle-sales-bajaj-autoindonesian-market
9. http://articles.economictimes.indiatimes.com/2003-06-04/news /27562354_1_indian-automobile-industry-autoindustry-today-multi-axle
10. http://www.slideshare.net/vikasmisar/advertising-two-wheeler-industry-ppt
11. http://www.slideshare.net/bharatbookseo/research-report-on-indian-two-wheeler-industry
12. http://www.automobileindia.com/two-wheelers/bikes/
13. http://www.allfreeessays.com/topics/indian-two-wheeler-industry-2010/0
14. http://www.imaginmor.com/automobileindustryindia.html
15. http://www.mospi.nic.in/stat_act_t3.htm
16. http://www.economictimes.indiatimes.com › News ›
17. http://www.*cci.gov.in/images/media/ResearchReports/AnujInt200711.pdf*
18. http://www.*icra.in/Files/.../Two-Wheeler%20Industry%20Note,%20 June%202011.p...*

27

Reputational Capital as an Ethical Questioning of Technological Innovation

The Case of MONSANTO

José G. Vargas-Hernández
Salvador Ortiz Sánchez
University Center for Economic and Managerial Sciences
University of Guadalajara
jvargas2006@gmail.com, jgvh0811@yahoo.com, josevargas@cucea.udg.mx

ABSTRACT

Introduction of transgenic crops as an alternative to solve the problem of food deficiency in most economies represents an area of opportunity for the development of biotechnology which in recent decades has pioneered Monsanto. Through literature review and a qualitative analysis of the main theoretical approaches that explain the behavior and strategies of expansion and growth of the company, checking the assumption that the active participation of society in the evidence of damage caused determine the strategic value of corporate reputation of leading transnational disputes, uncertainty and distrust regarding their products and processes, assuming that a danger to the health of the population and the environment in general.

INTRODUCTION

In recent decades, society's concern has focused on demographic matters primarily associated with strong population growth, mainly in developing countries; whose threat to natural resources and the environment in general, provide serious consequences (socio-economic) not only in those economies, but also in other developed nations.

The impacts of population growth have been problematic after market changes and the heavy losses in the production of agricultural fields, as a result of strong drought and frost problems. From the perspective that there is not sufficient access to nutritious foods that reduce the rate of malnutrition in the population who are at all stages of life, the problem has been classified as food insufficient and unsustainable.

In this way, the implementation of public policies and new alternatives based on actions that favor attention deficiency problem in food production is a challenge in each of the economies taking care not mainly relying on imports of basic grains. So, before that problem, numerous studies suggest that Genetically Modified (GM) crops represent a viable option that can contribute to increased yields and agricultural production, without being necessary to increase the area under cultivation, forest rescuing the imminent logging and deforestation to expand agricultural land.

The rescue alternative of ecosystem pointed to the investment and development of GM crops, and that agriculture biotechnology enables to obtain healthier foods with better flavor and reduced pesticide use, increased crop yields, better management of water and reduced greenhouse gas emissions and other benefits, which not only supports to farmers, but also benefits families and consumers in general. For this reason, companies like Monsanto are at the forefront of technology and pose to be found in the best position to contribute to the global challenges faced by society today, generating enough food for the growing population which is increasing every day in an effort to abate hunger and extreme poverty by developing sustainable agriculture.

BACKGROUND

Today, sustainable agriculture has been presented as a solution to the problems of food shortage facing most economies around the globe. Companies like Monsanto, Bayer, Syngenta and DuPontPioneerAmerican, have expressed to their preparedness to reduce poverty and ensure food security through processes such as genetic improvement. The seed business by itself is quite competitive, and unlike many others, the purchase of the input is performed annually at seasonal or peak period and depending on the good or bad experience in the harvest, which will determine the purchase of the same or another seed for the next season, ensuring competition and constant innovation of the company.

While the leading biotechnology that has been at the forefront and the public focus has been Monsanto, it has been mainly in regard to such innovation and improvement of agricultural seeds. Because anti-biotechnology activist groups and unfair competitors or follower companies that have taken pains to make propaganda against, trying to prove that the success is due to anti-competitive behavior and further damaging the company's reputation.

Reputational capital is a valuable tool that the company develops over time and can make decisions about which products to buy, where to invest and where to work. In this way, the strategic value of reputation characterizes the company making it attractive or not and expanding their options not only for managers, but for the general consumers. In the business environment, corporate reputation can be considered as an intangible asset and strategic organization capable of representing a proof of competitiveness of the firm. Kaplan & Norton (1996) suggest that proper management of intangible assets may be favorable to business relationship with customers, ensuring the loyalty of existing ones and offering services which allow customers cleave segments and other market areas.

PROBLEM DELIMITATION

Thus, in an environment that historically technological contributions and achievements of Monsanto have represented achronological sum of mistakes. Because the bad reputation of the company, the innovations achieved not only generates uncertainty in the population, but a full assurance that their contributions represent a danger to humanity.

JUSTIFICATION

In the context in which Monsanto is developing, it is in the best position to meet the demand for food of growing world population and fight hunger through the development of sustainable agriculture, not only supplying the agricultural sector with seeds, but products of biotechnology, agrochemical and technology in general.

However, one of the main contributions of Monsanto and perhaps the most representative made lately, has been the production of GM foods. Against this production of GM foods, several international environmentalist organizations have struggled since its inception. The GM foods are the same ones that Greenpeace (2011) has defined as living with a technique artificially created by inserting a plant or animal genes of viruses, bacteria, plants, animals and even humans, in order to produce an insecticidal substance or give resistance to herbicides.

This invention has been the trigger for society to turn against Monsanto's activities, arguing that the production of this type of seed varieties not only limits natural native varieties of the region, but also pollutes wildlife, reduces biodiversity and chemically contaminate soil and groundwater. Missouri´s firm through its actions and creations, historically has been involved or has been responsible for various adverse events:

- In the beginning, Monsanto made strategic alliances with one of the most controversial groups in history: Monsanto became one of Coca-Cola's main suppliers, mainly of saccharin and other sweeteners.
- Participated in the production of the first nuclear bomb used during World War II, and then operated an American plant of nuclear in the early 80's.
- The creation of the pesticide DD Tin 1944. The substance was banned in countries like Hungary, Norway, Sweden and the U.S. itself.
- Monsanto acted as a supplier of Agent Orange to the U.S. Army during the Vietnam War, substance which killed around 400,000 people, causing damage to around half a million babies in the following years.
- Creating the growth hormone "bovine somato tropin" (BST), used in countries like Brazil, United States and Mexico. Its use has been banned in the rest of the world to be linked with health problems, such as cancer.

- Monsanto through a vertical integration strategy, founded in 1980 the company NutraSweet, building a monopoly of poisons and no calorie sweeteners.
- Reduction in seed variety. Using horizontal integration (buying organic seed companies) Monsanto over the years has been commissioned to market only exclusive products they produce.
- Using genetic and toxic methods of bees on crops.
- Creating herbicides "non-selective" as Roundup (the patent expired in 2000) whose main ingredient is Glyphosate that kills plants by inhibiting their ability to generate aromatic amino acids.

Given these developments, Monsanto has acquired the title of the worst company in the world, so without making value judgments, such appointment is based on the market power that the company has, since despite this, its sales and global presence foster its growth and power.

ASSUMPTION

Despite the deniability strategy and conduct a carry on whitewash of responsible image, according to Delgado (2006), the more powerful the technology, the consequences can be profound. Then, the bad reputation of Monsanto creates uncertainty and mistrust in society in regard to innovations, assuming its actions are the cause of danger to people and the environment in general.

THEORETICAL FRAMEWORK

The connotation of the literature review arises regarding theoretical models, by which it is possible to understand the behavior of Monsanto in these 112 years, determined by the realization of important strategic alliances with other TNCs, purchases and acquisitions of firms that have facilitated some processes execution and reduce its competition. Similarly, the theoretical conception of the various expansion strategies implemented by the leading producer of (Genetically Modified Organism) GMOsis identified by the link between reputation management and the ability to create value for the firm, understanding the nature of reputation as enterprise resource.

Strategic Alliances

According to Hitt, Horkisson & Kim (1997), in business, formalizing a partnership is carried out in response to a particular strategy that might well be addressed with the implementation of another strategy.

Thus, Tallman & Shenkar (1994) propose that an alliance can conceive how a managerial process and organizational issues arising from whether economic or not, and by means of a cost-benefit assessment of the process of this alliance.

Incidentally, Das & Teng (1997) determined that proper management of the alliance is a necessary process, though not sufficient, for the success of the same, whose decision should be made based on formalization of the strategy to continue the business, since according Ariño & de la Torre (1998), these partnerships evolve while the company strategy does.

Therefore, according to McKelvey (1997) and Alcázar & Martínez (2004), the evolution of a company that has strategic alliances with other companies, is designed simultaneously with the changing environment. Thus, a match between the goal of the alliance and strategies of the companies involved is made based on the competitive environment, institutional and organizational in which they operate.

Vertical Integration

Currently, companies face some problems that can lead to aggravated constraints which hinder the achievement of goals or objectives thereof, being necessary to resort to various strategies to obtain new advantages over the competition.

According to Villarreal & Gomez (2009), integration is a strategy that allows increasing the benefits and profits of organizations by improving processes, adding value and increasing profitability, allowing better opportunities to stay in the industry. Business integration can occur vertically, one in which the firm attempts to control the successive stages of the value chain of the product, or by way of horizontal integration, one in which it fosters cooperation with competitors in the same stage of the value chain.

According to Colangelo (1995), vertical integration produces higher yields than horizontal integration. However, Hill & Gareth (2005), state that horizontal integration increases the profitability as it tends to reduce costs. By contrast, vertical integration according to Mpoyi (2003), can determine the degree to which the company controls the production and distribution. Similarly, the sequence of activities is the process which provides value to the product, which is described by the principle of the value chain by Porter (1990).

Acquisitions

Among the strategies used by firms to gain size and generate competitiveness, there are activities such as the purchase of a company by another, also known as acquisition, whose cause according Zozaya (2007), is mostly facing threats or seize market opportunities.

According to Abellán (2004), the combination of interests of the various actors involved in the management of the firm can lead to be chosen by the strategy of a merger or acquisition. At company level, acquisitions often have significant impact on variables to determine the success and value of the firm, such as employment, stock price, market power, profits and/or profitability, growth rate, productivity and technological performance to name a few.

Intangible Assets

In business management, intangible assets were introduced in the late 90's by Richard Hall. Intangible asset scan be understood as business factors represented by an idea or knowledge that can drive the organization into positions where it is possible to achieve competitive advantages. In this respect, contributions like Itami (1991) consider organizational in tangibles by way of invisible assets, there levant factors such as technology, brand image, consumer confidence, organizational culture, and management capabilities.

Tissen, Andriessen & Deprez (2000), conceived of intangible assets through business skills that allow them to generate sustainable competitive advantages, arguing that the proper management of these skills can create economic value for the firm. WhileLev (2001), refers to intangible assets as assets arising from knowledge. Kaplan & Norton (2004), understood as determining factors for achieving the strategic objectives set by the companies.

While, according to the different views of these assets, it is difficult to define a single approach, it can be possible to steer it in three main groups common to any corporate entrepreneurship:

- Human capital includes skills, attitudes and aptitudes of firm personnel.
- Organizational capital includes items related intangible knowledge held by the company from its daily management.
- Relational capital includes the status of relations of the firm with its stakeholders.

Based on the diversity of ideas described above, from positions such as accounting, strategic knowledge management, information technology and human resources, it is noteworthy that all relate to the concept of intangible assets, knowledge and intellectual capital.

Intellectual Capital

In terms of strategic management, a pioneer in promoting the concept of intellectual capital was Stewart (1991), who referred to this concept considering the sum of elements of the human factor in the company, able to provide a competitive advantage market. In this regard, Edvinsson & Malone (1997) refer to intellectual capital by way of knowledge that can be transformed into inventions, technologies, processes and software, providing added value to the company. Mean while, Hand & Lev (2001) refer to this concept, by its origin from three main areas, innovation, organizational practices and human talent.

Thus, according to various theoretical approaches, it can be identified that the terms of intangible assets and intellectual capital are often used interchangeably. However, it is prudent to mention that the existence of intangible resources not necessarily refers to the intellectual capital of the firm, since it is usually considered only the culmination of the management process, determining even the generation or destruction of firm value.

Generating Business Value

According to Mandel, Hamm & Farrell (2006), over 50% of the market value of the companies in the Fortune ranking of 500 is made up of intangible assets. Therefore, most of the wealth and growth of the developed economies are due to intangible asset management. In the field of business, to determine the value of a firm is one of the great challenges, this due to the nature of the resources and liabilities intangible, difficult to quantify objectively in the financial statements.

Barney (1991) considers the resource-based view and the business capabilities of intangible resources of the firm, which can create competitive advantages and thus create value for the company, provided that:

- The resource provides financial value to the organization,
- Only some organization shave, that is, there are few,
- There source is inimitable, and
- There are no substitutes on the market.

Thus, it is possible to attribute a monetary value to the competitive advantages of the firm, since this process represents a quantifiable measure of the value recognized by investors.

Business Reputation

In the organizational sense or at firm level, Fombrun (1996) mentions that reputation is an intangible asset of companies that represents the identity and transmits signature hall marks by which succeeds in changing behavior of their stakeholders. Therefore, the degree of perception of the name of the firm, having customers, investors, suppliers, creditors, employees and the general public are called organizational reputation. Thus, the institutional reputation refers to the way in which external agents conceive of corporate reputation, i.e. how they see, hear and opinions regarding the target company, either locally or internationally. According to Villafañe (2004), it is possible to identify three organizational dimensions around the concept of reputation:

- Axiological Dimension: Within which it incorporates the cultural values of the organization, corresponding for the ethical question about the relationship with third parties and being a socially responsible company,
- Corporate Dimension of Service: In which are included commitments arising in the course of time in relation to the key players, and
- Management Corporate Dimension: Corresponding to the proactive attitude.

According to Costa (2004), reputation arises from the history of the company, on the credibility of its organizational objective and the means to achieve this goal by making use of resources such as corporate culture, based on the recognition that the company makes of its identity.

Factors Influencing Construction Business Reputation

While organizational reputation represents a certain strategic value to the company, the difficulty of it lies in measuring the impact it creates in every organization. Hillenbrand & Money (2007) raise some reputational models about the analysis of such an intangible asset, emphasizing the theoretical and conceptual foundations for the various interest groups, whose value appreciates or it is lost over time. Fombrun (2001) proposes five basic principles to generate organizational prestige:

- The Principle of Differentiation: Positioning in the minds of the stakeholders.
- The Principle of Concentration: The clear focus of the actions and communications on the subject of interest from trading.
- Principle of Consistency: The integration and coordination of organizational initiatives, to involve stakeholders.
- Identity Principle: Carry out a performance, public or private, in accordance with the principles and values that govern the existence of the organization.
- Principle of Transparency: Maintaining strong levels of communication with stakeholders, and the people in general over the daily management of the organization.

Meanwhile, Villafañe (2004) refers to the need for hand social interests and business on maximizing profits for reinvestment. Business viability depends on factors such as ethics and sustainability. Corporate reputation then is measured by:

- Financial economic results.
- Quality of commercial offer.
- Corporate culture and work quality.
- Ethics and corporate responsibility.
- Innovation.
- Global dimension and international presence.

While the principles of reputational assets is about building conceptual parameters that allow the perception to be forwarded to the stakeholders, factors refer to specific quantifications that determine the levels of perceived reputational to keep stakeholders.

Technological Innovation

According to Moreno (1985), innovation is understood from the definition of technology. It is described from the use of knowledge to produce goods or provide services. However, in the theory of innovation there are two main approaches conceived. One is tracked to the technical question in which tangible objects encompass a humanistic approach that relates to the transformation of objects for the benefit of mankind, for meeting the needs of the population, as well as greater control over the environment.

According to Escorsa (2003), technological innovation focuses primarily toward obtaining results, mainly characterized by:

- Having a novelty character to satisfy the needs of the population.
- Include the introduction of a technical change in products and services.
- Provide a socially visible utility.

Similarly, according to Pérez (2005), technological innovation can be seen as a process that starts from an idea, based on the identification of a need for the development of a product or service commercially accepted.

In an innovative approach to processes, the strategy of "Technology Brokering" and building social capital, whose main exponent is Hargadon (2003), argues that technological innovation is related to the social metaphor of Burt (2000), who proposes that the social structure is a type of capital that creates a competitive advantage to achieve the goals set by groups or individuals. However, the change in scientific development and application of techniques for the generation of technologies with commercial validity, involves a series of steps that inter relate with other activities incurring in vanishing points that encourage inter connections.

Contextual Framework

While almost since the origin of mankind, according to Delgado (2006), biology through a series of processes and mechanisms of trial and error has been used as a tool to transform nature by various techniques. With respect to agricultural development, the contribution of Mendel's laws set the tone for these lection process improvement and subsequently cross linking "manual" between compatible species bringing hybridization (Bisang, Campi, & Cesa, 2009).

According Solbrig (2004), invention and idea of carrying out the modification of the characteristics of living organisms for specific purposes of the interest is shown technological development for thousands of years.

Since the application of biotechnology in the production focuses on natural resources, it is important to highlight the significant competition in innovation and scientific complexity that generates about the universe framing the technological development and taking shape in a small number of companies that generate these advances, such Monsanto is the case. In that perspective, though, the transnational of Missouri was founded in 1901, its expansion began in 1928 through the acquisition of companies in the chemical and textile industry. It was until 1981 when it established as a focus of biotechnology research and in 2000 it achieved consolidation dedicated exclusively to the agrochemical industry.

Today, according to Pérez & Medina (2008), Monsanto has over 14,000 employees and has presence in countries on five continents, including: Argentina, Germany, Australia, Austria, Bangladesh, Belgium, Brazil, Bulgaria, Canada,

Chile, China, Colombia, Croatia, CzechRepublic, Denmark, Ecuador, France, Greece, Guatemala, Honduras, Hungary, India, Indonesia, Ireland, Italy, Japan, Jordan, Kenya, Korea, Malawi, Malaysia, Mexico, Netherlands, newZealand, Nicaragua, Pakistan, Paraguay, Peru, Philippines, Poland, Portugal, Romania, Russia, Senegal, Singapore, Slovakia, South Africa, Spain, Sri Lanka, Sweden, Switzerland, Taiwan, Thailand, Turkey, Uganda, Ukraine, United Kingdom, United States, Venezuela, Vietnam and Zimbabwe.

As in most of those countries where environmental advocacy groups are leading protests and demonstrations by countless violations on genetic manipulation of natural products (transgenic), loss of biodiversity, market monopoly, violation of food sovereignty, movement and displacement of peoples and land concentration, among others, are leading campaigns on the history and impact of the company.

Method

In the present study, it was conducted a review of novel electronic materials and critical of the current situation of the company, supported by a qualitative analysis of the main theoretical approaches that explain the behavior and strategies taken by Monsanto.

Analysis of Results

The global expansion strategy has allowed Monsanto to seize food problems of the population, taking into account their strengths and favorable conditions obtained from experience by acquiring other companies and integrating both vertically and horizontally organizations on five continents, transforming key processes and providing technology.

The growth and expansion strategy that Monsanto has been characterized by allying with dubious companies like Coca-Cola than in Asian countries is called "toxic-tail", accused of selling harmful products that cause cancer and poison people, water and earth. The Nutra Sweet Company is in the segment of carbonated beverages that produce carcinogens. Calgene, Inc., a leader in plant biotechnology, and Dekalb Genetics Corp., the second largest producer of seed corn "improved" in the United States, or by dubious good intentions by buying business-oriented organic seed production.

The human health problems and environmental pollution arising from the errors in products and processes have evolved in reliability problems to the company, expressed through a series of contingencies that discuss the positioning and consolidation of quality in biotech innovations Monsanto. While social controversies and conflicts of value arising on the development of the company are the result of the interests of various groups: Scientists and technologists, entrepreneurs and investors, farmers, politicians, and citizens in general, have led to important and significant ethical judgments and mobilizations against transnational, based mainly on how to operate the company.

The main accusations against transnational include human rights violations and ancestral rights of indigenous peoples, compulsive evictions, unlawful coercion, murder, looting of commons, destruction of the territories where they operate, destruction of native forest, effects on the health of populations, impacts on local sovereignty, national and popular, violation of labor rights, concentration, privatization and foreign ownership of land. According to Proceso de Justicia Popular (2012), as demonstrations against such activities, the multinational has had to face a number of complaints and prosecutions carried out around the world, such as:

- The complaint filed by the association Eauxet Rivièresde Bretagnein 2001 by announcing that its Roundup product was efficient and had no risks for the environment.
- The complaint by the residents of Anniston (Alabama) in 2002, for polluting the water sources of the village with the chemical PBC.
- A law suit in 2004 for 350 million dollars for the use of as part a mein their sweeteners despite its toxic effect to the brain.
- A complaint in 2004 in Andhra Pradesh by the use of infants in "horrendous conditions" in cotton seed fields.

As a protest, in order to manifest and protest against the company, there have been several demonstrations and popular resistances.

- The campaign in Mexico: "Without corn there is no country" ("Sin Maíz no hay País") firmly rejects GM maize, and advocates for the defense of the Mexican countryside, protection of Mexican corn, food sovereignty and the reactivation of the Mexican countryside.
- The campaign led by the Peasant Association Scimitar River Valley (Asociación Campesina del Valle del río Cimitarra). "Monsanto Mata" in Colombia.
- The Campaign in Latin America, "Latin American Network for GMO-Free" ("Red por una América Latina Libre de Transgénicos"), to declare the Andeanregion, the center of origin of potato, transgenic potato free.
- The network of civil society organizations and people's movements lead the "Campaign for a GMO-FreeBrazil" ("Campaña por un Brasil Libre de Transgénicos").
- Global Protest against Monsanto on behalf of more than 200,000 people in 40 countries on May 25, 2013 by the indignation of the inaction of the governments to the detrimental effect with GM products and their production without any impediment.

By way of response, Monsanto has directed its strategy faking transparency through the "green washing", where by attempts to convince the public that favor the preservation of the environment, and convincing politicians that their activities are popular support.

CONCLUSION AND RECOMMENDATIONS

Due to the larger social interest in reducing risks to the environment and human health, the relationship between society and techno-scientific power further conflict, has become controversial. The controversies generated around innovations in the development field denote that the industrial model characterized by ignorance and little or no participation of the society in which only the evidence of damage already caused to health or the environment is a cause justifiable for the modification or withdrawal of such technological inventions, is no longer adequate.

Given the technological development, issues such as prevention and accountability represent moral obligations by Global Bioethics, so that genetic modification seen as a cultural intervention must be assessed in context.

References

1. Abellán, D. (2004), *Mergers and Acquisitions: a survey of motivations.* Documento de trabajo 0401. Universidad Complutense de Madrid.
2. Alcázar, F. M. & Martínez F. S. (2004), *El proceso de alianzas estratégicas desde el enfoque de la teoríaevolutiva de alianzas.InvestigacionesEuropeas de Dirección y Economía de la Empresa.*Universidad de Cádiz. Vol. 10(3), pp.189–207.
3. Ariño, A. & De la Torre, 1. (1998).Learning from Failure: Towards an Evolutionary Model of Collaborative Ventures. *Organization Science*, Vol. 9, 306–325.
4. Barney, J. B. (1991). Types of Competition and the Theory of Strategy: Toward an Integrative Framework. *Academy of Management Review*, Vol.11(4), pp. 791–800.
5. Bisang, R., Campi, M., Cesa, V. (2009).*Biotecnología y desarrollo. ComisiónEconómicaparaAmérica Latina y el Caribe (*CEPAL). NacionesUnidas, Santiago de Chile.
6. Burt, R. S. (2000). The network structure of social capital. *Pre-print parauncapítulo en Research in Organizacional Behavior.* Vol. 22.Eds Robert I. Sutton, Barry M. Staw., Greenwich, CT: JAI Press.
7. Costa, J. (2004).*La Imagen de Marca.* UnFenómeno Social. Paidós. Madrid (España).
8. Colangelo, G. (1995). Vertical vs. Horizontal integration: pre-emptive merging. The *Journal of Industrial Economics*, Vol. XLIII, No. 3, septiembre, pp. 323–337.
9. Das, T.K. &Teng, B. (1997).Sustaining Strategic Alliances: Options and Guidelines.*Journal of General Management*, Vol. 22(4), 49–64.
10. Delgado, D. C. J. (2006).Cambiosrevolucionarios y cuestionamientoséticos en lasciencias de la vida: los enigmas de la vidadiseñada. Capítulo final dellibro*Bioética y medioambiente.* Editorial Félix Varela. La Habana.

11. Edvinsson, L. & Malone, M. S. (1997). *Intellectual Capital.Realizing Your Company's True Value by Finding Its Hidden Brainpower*.HarperBusiness, 1st Ed. NY (USA).
12. Escorsa, P. (2003). *Tecnologia e Innovación de la empresa*.Ediciones UPC.
13. Fombrun, C. J. (1996). Reputation: Realizing Value from the Corporate Image. *Harvard Business School Press.* Boston MA (USA).
14. Fombrun, C. J. (2001). Corporate Reputation, Its Measurement and Management.*Thexis, Vol.* 18, No. 4, pp. 23–26.
15. Greenpeace, (2011).*¿Quéesuntransgénico? Agriculturasustentable y transgénicos*. Recuperado de http://www.greenpeace.org/mexico/es/Campanas/Agricultura--sustentable--y-transgenicos/Y-tu-sabes-lo-que-comes/Lo-que-esta-en-tu-comida-y-no-te-dicen/Que-es-un-transgenico/
16. Hargadon, A. (2003). *How break trhroughs happen. The surprising thruth about how companies innovate*, Boston, Massachusetts, Harvard Business school press.
17. Hand, J. M. & Lev, B. (2001).*Intangible Assets: Values, Measures*, and Risks. Oxford University Press. Oxford (UK).
18. Hill, C. W. & Gareth, R. J. (2005).*Administraciónestratégica: unenfoqueintegrado*. McGraw Hill, México.
19. Hillenbrand, C. & Money, K. (2007). Corporate Responsibility and Corporate Reputation: Two Separate Concepts or Two Sides of the Same Coin?*Corporate Reputation Review*, Vol. 10(4), pp. 261–277.
20. Hitt, M., Horkisson, R.E. y Kim, H. (1997). International Diversification: Effects on innovation and Firm Performance in Product-Diversified Firms. *Academy of Management Journal*, Vol. 40, n° 4, pp. 767–798.
21. Itami, H. (1991). *Mobilizing Invisible Assets.Harvard University Press*. Cambridge MA (USA).
22. Kaplan, R. S. and Norton D. P., (1996). *The Balanced Scorecard: Translating Strategy Into Action,*Boston, MA: Harvard Business School Press.
23. Kaplan, R. S., & Norton, D. P. (2004). Measuring the Strategic Readiness of Intangible Assets.*Harvard Business Review*, Vol. 82(2), pp. 52–63.
24. Lev, B. (2001). *Intangibles: Management, Measurement, and Reporting*. The Brookings Institution. Washington D.C. (USA).
25. Mandel, M.; Hamm, S. & Farrell, C. J. (2006). Why The Economy is a lot stronger than you think. *BusinessWeek,*ProQuest, No. febrero 13 2006, pp. 62–70.
26. Mckelvey, W. (1997).Quasi-natural Organization Science.*Organization Science*, vol. 8(4), pp. 352–380.
27. Moreno, P. F. (1985), *Introducción al desarrollotecnológico*. Sena.
28. Mpoyi, R. T. (2003). Vertical Integration: Strategic Characteristic and Competitive Implications. *Competitiveness Review*, Vol. 13, No. 1, pp. 44–55.

29. Pérez, G. S. & Medina, H. (2008). Informesobrelasactividades de Monsanto. *Eco Portal.* http://www.ecoportal.net/Temas_Especiales/Transgenicos/Informe_de_investigacion_sobre_las_operaciones_de_Monsanto_en_Argentina
30. Pérez, M. C. B. (2005). *Modelo de innovacióntecnológicabasado en enfoques de redes socio técnicas: estudio del caso Montana.* Universidad de los Andes. Maestría en Ingeniería Industrial.
31. Porter, M. E. (1990). The Competitive Advantage of Nations: Cover Story. *Harvard Business Review*, No. 2, pp. 73–93.
32. Proceso de Justicia Popular (2012).Juicioético a lastransnacionales: Caso Monsanto NOA. En: http://juicioalastransnacionales.org/2012/11/caso-monsanto-noa/
33. Solbrig, O. (2004). Ventajas y desventajas de la agrobiotecnología, en Bárcena y otros., Los Transgénicos en América Latina y el Caribe. Un debate abierto, CEPAL NacionesUnidas, Santiago de Chile.
34. Stewart, T. A. (1991). Brainpower: How intellectual capital is becoming America's most valuable asset. *Fortune Magazine*, No. Junio 2001, pp. 44–60.
35. Tallman, S.B. &Shenkar, O. (1994).A Managerial Decision Model of International Cooperative Venture Formation.*Journal of International Business Studies*, first quarter, 91–113.
36. Tissen, R.,Andriessen, D. &Deprez, F. L. (2000).*El Valor delConocimiento.* Pearson Education S.A. Madrid (España).
37. Villafañe, J. (2004). *La Reputación: Claves del Valor Intangible para Las Empresas. Pirámide.* Madrid (España).
38. Villarreal, S. F. M. & Gómez, R. J. G. I. (2009). La integración en laspequeñas y medianasempresasfabricantes de muebles de la ciudad de Durango, México. *Contaduría y Administración.* UNAM. No. 227, enero-abril.
39. Zozaya, G. N. (2007). *Las fusiones y adquisicionescomofórmula de crecimientoempresarial.*Ministerio de Industria, Turismo y Comercio. Dirección General de Política de la PYME. Madrid.

28

Recognising Ethical Issues in Global Business

Meenal Yadav
Associate Professor, LBSIMDS, Lucknow
E-mail: meenal.yadav@gmail.com

ABSTRACT

Ethics have become an organizational priority. In the 21st century, ethics is neither a luxury nor an option. The globalized business environment has brought about business uncertainties, changing demographics, and a push for diversity that has resulted into corporate business cultures that are less homogeneous and increasingly competitive. The malpractices that we continue to see in business world are centered upon the self-indulgent, introspective and myopic perspectives of the business organizations that are not able to transform their thoughts to consider all possible perceptions and ramifications of their actions.

The chapter therefore finds its relevance in the day-to-day violations of business ethics in the globalized business environment and contends that business organizations must take responsibility of these violations or omit at their own peril.

INTRODUCTION

The real threat to business is from within, from poor ethical *standards and lack of integrity that can do incalculable harm. History has proven repeatedly that business ethics, shared value and corporate governance determine the longevity of an enterprise...*

—Azim Premji

The recognition of ethical behavior is absolutely essential for the functioning of the economy. A series of major financial scandals involving Enron, WorldCom, Lehman Brothers and the 2008 global financial crisis are often cited as an illustration of the moral shortcoming and have raised deep concerns about ethics in business. These scamps impact not only on their immediate stakeholders, but entire economies and industries.

A socially and environmentally ethical approach ensures a company's ability to thrive in the long-term by protecting its reputation, its license to operate, its supply chain, its relationships with partners and its ability to recruit talent. But despite codes of practice, regulatory oversight and ever increasing public pressure, many firms routinely ignore ethical considerations and make short-term gains. Enron's bankruptcy has had enormous adverse affect upon its employees and its investors, the actions of executives within Johns Manville led to the death of many of its hourly workers, and Pacific Gas polluted the groundwater and injured its neighbors.

The final loser in the ethical mess of today's 21st century age is no doubt society. We cannot do business as a culture if trust is lost, values have no meaning, and everything has to be solved through litigation. Good reputations and solid ethical decisions in business create value. While some firms consistently fail to consider ethical factors, others have given themselves a competitive edge by establishing strong credentials in this area. For instance, in the nineties Toyota boosted its global standing with pioneering work on the hybrid Prius model. Coca-Cola thought it commercially worthwhile to take a minority stake in the UK fruit drinks firm Innocent, which boasts that it gives away a tenth of all its profits. And McDonald's is investing heavily in activities aimed at associating it with ethical and environmental awareness as it rebuilds its brand and attempts to overcome decades of negative publicity.

Ethical leadership and corporate social responsibility requires a continuing commitment to behave ethically and contribute to economic development while improving the quality of life of the workforce, their families, the local community, and society as a whole.

Ethical behavior is the lubricant that keeps the economy running. Without that lubricant, the economy would operate much less efficiently—less would be available to consumers, quality would be lower, and prices would be higher.

Thus, for the good of everyone—including profit-making companies—it is vitally important that business be conducted within an ethical framework that builds and sustains trust.

BUSINESS ETHICS: THEORETICAL FRAMEWORK

The debate on cultural and ethical values in business has moved from one extreme to another in the past 50 years. Economists in the 1970s, foremost among them Milton Friedman, argued that the role of business was solely to make money. At the opposite pole today, many businesses prosper by publically founding themselves on ethical values. In fact, driving a business based on cultural and ethical values now looks like a model of the future. In such a scenario certain standards are required to govern how organizations go about their business operations; these standards are called ethics and are applied to any and all aspects of business. Ethics goes beyond the legal requirements for a company and is, therefore, about discretionary decisions and behavior guided by values.

Business ethics is a wider term that includes many other sub-ethics that are relevant to the respective field. For example, there is financial ethics for finance and accounting, ethics in HR for human resource department and the like. Some of the key issues addressed in current codes of business ethics are bribery and corruption; gifts and hospitality; conflicts of interest; diversity; health and safety, environmental stewardship and political donations and lobbying.

Nowadays almost all organizations lay due emphasis on their responsibilities towards the society and the nature and they call it by different names like corporate social responsibility, corporate governance or social responsibility charter. In India, Maruti Suzuki, for example, owned the responsibility to maintain a large number of parks and ensuring greenery. Hindustan Unilever, similarly started the e-shakti initiative for women in rural villages. Globally also many corporations have bred philanthropists who have contributed compassion, love for poor and unprivileged. Bill Gates of Microsoft and Warren Buffet of Berkshire Hathaway are known for their philanthropic contributions across globe. Many organizations, for example, IBM as part of their corporate social responsibility have taken up the initiative of going green, towards contributing to environmental protection.

It is not that business did not function before the advent of business ethics; but there is a regulation of kinds now that ensures business and organizations contribute to the society and its well-being.

THE ETHICAL DIMENSION OF DIFFERENT FUNCTIONAL AREAS OF BUSINESS: CAPACITY BUILDING

Integrity and unflinching commitment to values is what builds the backbone of a strong business. As an organizational priority, ethics will not only affect decision making but also institutional culture. To achieve this ideal, there must be an alignment process that integrates business ethics with mission, vision, values, strategies and goals. *What is required is the 'capacity building' towards deeper ethical behavior'.*

For capacity building dimensions of different functional areas of business should be dealt effectively and they are discussed as under:

The Ethical Dimension of HRM

'The entire concept of HRM is devoid of morality.'(Hart, 1993: 29)

Ethics sometimes fall by the wayside when organizations do not have a solid value-based culture starting from the top and working its way down. When this occurs, it is typically HR that is called to get involved. Issues such as sexual harassment toleration, knowingly hiring illegal immigrants, violation of privacy, biased performance reviews, wage and hour violations for the sake of saving overtime money, terminating whistle-blowers for reasons totally unrelated to performance, and tolerable discrimination. Lying for the sake of personal, corporate and shareholder gain. It appears that an underlying theme in all HR-involved workplace issues is a management culture that fosters ethical ignorance – or at the very least knowingly allows an action to happen – even when the organization flaunts a Code of Ethics.

The negative effects of ethical violations within an organization can be enormous. Energy levels at work drop, gossip and rumors abound, attendance floats, turnover excels, clients lose trust, and profits decrease to the point of extinction.

It is argued (Winstanley and Woodall, 2000) that HRM holds the moral 'stewardship' of organizations. It is interesting therefore to consider the special role of HRM in the generation of an ethical and moral climate in organizations in general. Much of the recent focus on business ethics has been directed against financial corruption, especially a concern with accounting standards.

Ethics tries to create a sense of right and wrong in the organizations and often when the law fails, it is the ethics that may stop organizations from harming the society or environment.

The Ethical Dimension of Finance

There is a strong business case for running companies in an ethically responsible way and for finance professionals to facilitate this. Of the 28 companies that fell out of the world leading S&P500 index in the past ten years, comparatively few casualties were claimed by shifts in technologies and markets. More were victims of massive fraud (as with Enron and WorldCom) or had leaders who'd failed to create a sustainable business model. This was evident most graphically in the financial services industry, with the likes of Lehman Brothers, Bear Stearns and Wachovia choosing huge short-term gains at the cost of their long-term survival. The financial crisis has certainly highlighted the need for capital market decision making to reflect long-term considerations. The fashionable drive to maximize shareholder value has seen investors and business leaders combine in a quest for short-term advantage. Today, it could be seen that one of the duties of a tough CEO is to resist such pressure by delivering more realistic financial results in the short-term, if need be.

The Ethical Dimension of Marketing

Marketing professionals with a backbone reap great rewards, including a solid career with the potential for advancement. Each facet of marketing has ethical danger points as discussed below.

Market Research

Some ethical problems in market research are the invasion of privacy and stereotyping. The latter occurs because any analysis of real populations needs to make approximations and place individuals into groups. However, if conducted irresponsibly, stereotyping can lead to a variety of ethically undesirable results.

Market Audience

Selective marketing is used to discourage demand from so-called undesirable market sectors. Another ethical issue relates to vulnerable audiences in emerging markets in developing countries, as the public there may not be sufficiently aware of skilled marketing ploys.

Ethics in Advertising and Promotion

Today an advertiser who fails to tell the truth offends against morality in addition to the law.

The advertising of certain products may strongly offend some people while being of interest to others. For examples, advertising of condoms has become acceptable in the interests of AIDS-prevention, but is nevertheless seen by some as promoting promiscuity.

To market ethically and effectively one should be reminded that all marketing decisions and efforts are necessary to meet and suit the needs of customers, suppliers, and business partners.

The Ethical Dimension of Supply Chain Management

An efficient supply chain is responsive to changing priorities by keeping costs in line, schedules on time and, more importantly, giving companies the room to scale for growth. The supply chain cannot be divorced from corporate social responsibility (CSR) concerns about the environment, health and safety. CSR advocates have always argued that companies have an ethical responsibility that isn't constrained by geographic and political borders, or even cultural traditions.

The experience of Nike in the 1990s illustrates this quandary acutely. Nike was driven by a desire to assemble products at a fraction of the cost of producing them in the United States. The company selected few contractors outside U.S. and drafted a code of conduct for its contractors and this code outlined best practices in the areas of safety standards, environmental regulation and worker insurance, and suppliers were required to certify that they were following the code and local regulations but there was no effort, of course, to determine if contractors complied with the code, and, eventually, Nike's factories came under attack for their workplace practices, including the use of child laborers. Watching its reputation sullied by stories of abuse, Nike began to see its profits dip.

By exhibiting a genuine commitment to social responsibility and ethical business practices, corporations have the power to not only transform their organizations but also their supply chains.

ETHICAL INITIATIVES OF BUSINESS

Organizations recognize that effective business ethics programs are good for business performance. Firms that develop higher levels of trust function more efficiently and effectively and avoid damaged company reputations and product images.

Following are the few ethical initiatives of business:

• ***Not Giving or Accepting Bribes:*** Sam Walton, the late founder of Wal-Mart, prohibited company buyers from accepting so much as a cup of coffee from suppliers. The Wal-Mart policy is black and white and leaves no room for interpretation.

• ***Fairness and Honesty:*** Fairness and honesty are at the heart of business ethics and relate to the general values of decision makers. Business persons are expected not to harm customers, employees, clients, or competitors knowingly through deception, misrepresentation, coercion, or discrimination.

• ***Communications:*** False and misleading advertising, as well as deceptive personal-selling tactics and product labeling anger consumers and can lead to the failure of a business.

• ***Plagiarism:*** In business, an ethical issue arises when an employee copies reports or takes the work or ideas of others and presents them as his or her own. A manager attempting to take credit for a subordinate's ideas is engaging in another type of plagiarism. Several well-known musicians, including Michael Jackson, George Harrison, and Michael Bolton, Annu Malik , Pritam have been accused of taking credit for the work of others.

• ***Relations with Owners and Shareholders:*** A business's responsibilities to its owners and investors, as well as to the financial community at large, include maintaining proper accounting procedures, providing all relevant information to investors about the current and projected performance of the firm, and protecting the owners' rights and investments. In short, the business must maximize the owners' investment in the firm.

• ***Employee Relations:*** Employees expect businesses to provide a safe workplace, pay them adequately for their work, and tell them what is happening in their company. They want employers to listen to their grievances and treat them fairly.

• ***Consumer Relations:*** A critical issue in business today is business's responsibility towards customers. The *right to safety,* the *right to be informed,* the *right to choose and the right to be heard* assures the fair treatment of consumers.

• ***Environmental Issues:*** Environmental responsibility has become a leading issue in the last decade as both business and the public acknowledge the damage done to the environment in the past. Many small and large companies are trying to eliminate wasteful practices. Auto makers, such as General Motors and Honda, are developing automobiles that run on alternative fuels—electricity, solar power, natural gas, and methanol. Many businesses have turned to *recycling,* the reprocessing of materials—aluminum, paper, glass, and some plastic—for reuse.

Procter & Gamble uses recycled materials in some of its packaging and markets refills for some of its products, which creates less packaging waste.

• ***Community Relations:*** Many businesses simply want to make their communities better places for everyone to live and work. Big corporate houses like Microsoft, Infosys, Reliance, ITC, etc. have started several initiative programs for health, education , rehabilitation, etc. around the globe.

ETHICAL DEFICIT: WHERE DOES INDIA INC STAND ON THIS BURNING ISSUE?

Ethics form the foundation of how companies function but people are realizing that ethics alone aren't good enough. The new buzz word is being a principled business, and that involves being ethical, along with a healthy dose of sustainability thrown in.

Adi Godrej, chairman, Godrej Group believes that to be successful in the long run, all aspects of a business need to be looked at. These are ethical business practices, strategy, sustainability and consumer centricity. According to him all four factors are crucial for long-term success.

Farhad Forbes, director, Forbes Marshall echoes that ethics are something that are a part of normal culture and way of working, not something one can switch on and off. It should be a part of philosophy.

Anju Shenoy, director—ethics and compliance—at Dell makes a point that they are committed to making ethics personal by ensuring each team member understands what is expected of them and providing them with the tools and resources to be successful. Speaking in the same lines Krish Shanker, executive director, HR, Bharti Airtel mentions that values are important as they help guide employees in how to behave in different situations.

Dev Bajpai, executive director—legal and company secretary—Hindustan Unilever strongly states that corporates around the world are facing an ethics deficit and the role of ethics in the workplace has never been as relevant as it is right now.

Rajeev Dubey, president (group HR & after market) & member, group executive board, Mahindra & Mahindra appreciates the core belief of his company which emphasizes on ethics, since ethics leads to sustainability. At The Coca-Cola Company, the aim is to lead by example and to learn from experience.

WORLD'S MOST ETHICAL COMPANIES: HONOREES, YEAR 2013

The Ethisphere Institute, an international think tank, has announced its seventh annual list of the World's Most Ethical Companies. The 2013 list includes 138 organizations.

2013 WORLD'S MOST ETHICAL COMPANIES

Name	*Country*	*Times on List*
Accenture	Ireland	5
Adobe Systems	U.S.	3
AECOM Technology Corp	U.S.	2
Aflao Inc.	U.S.	6
Alcoa	U.S.	3
Alyeska Pipeline Service Company	U.S.	1
American Express	U.S.	6
Applied Materials, Inc.	U.S.	1
Aramark	U.S.	2
Arthur J. Gallagher and Co.	U.S.	1
Baptist Health South Florida	U.S.	2
Becton Dickinson	U.S.	6
Best Buy Co., Inc.	U.S.	4
Blue Cross Blue Shield of North Carolina	U.S.	1
Blue Shield of California	U.S.	1
British Land pec	UK	2
CH2M HILL	U.S.	4
Cisco Systems	U.S.	5
Colgate-Palmolive Company	U.S.	2
Coloplast	Denmark	1
Commell Faut	Israel	3
Concurrent Technologies	U.S.	1
Costco	U.S.	2
CRH plc.	Ireland	4
Cummins Inc.	U.S.	5
Deere & Company	U.S.	6
Dun $ Company	U.S.	3
Eaton Corporation	U.S.	6
eBay Inc.	U.S.	2
Ecolab, Inc.	U.S.	6
EDP Energias de Portugal	Portugal	1
Electrolux	Seden	2
Encana Corporation	Canada	2
ENMAX Corporation	Canada	1
Ethical Fruit Company Ltd	UK	1
Fluor Corporation	U.S.	6

Ford Motor Company	U.S.	3
Freescale Semiconductor, Inc	U.S.	5
Gap Inc	U.S.	5
General Electric Co.	U.S.	6
Granite Construction Inc.	U.S.	3
Hasbro, Inc.	U.S.	1
Henkel AG & Co. KGaA	Germany	5
Henry Schein, Inc.	U.S.	1
Hitachi Data Systems	U.S.	2
Holland America Line	U.S.	1
Honeywell International Inc.	U.S.	3
Hospital Corporation of America	U.S.	3
Intel Corporation	U.S.	2
International Paper	U.S.	6
Johnson Controls, Inc.	U.S.	6
Jones Lang LaSalle Inc.	U.S.	5
Juniper Networks	U.S.	2
Kao Corporation	Japan	6
Kellogg Company	U.S.	4
Kennametal Inc.	U.S.	1
Kesko	Finland	2
Kimberly-Clark Corporation	U.S.	1
Kimpton Hotels	U.S.	2
L'ORÉAL	France	3
ManpowerGroup	U.S.	3
Marks and Spencer	UK	4
Marrott International, Inc.	U.S.	5
Medicis Pharmaceutical	U.S.	2
Microsoft	U.S.	2
Milliken & Company	U.S.	6
National Australia Bank	Australia	2
National Grid	UK/U.S.	2
Natura Cosmeticos	Brazil	3
Nippon Yusen Kabushi Kaisha	Japan	5
NiSource Inc.	U.S.	1
Nobis	U.S.	4
Northumbrian Water Group	UK	2
Novation	U.S.	1
NYSE Euronext	U.S./Netherlands	3

OfficeMax	U.S.	1
Old National Bank	U.S.	1
Panama Canal Authority	Panama	2
Patheon Enterprises	U.S.	1
Parsons Corporation	U.S.	3
Patagonia	U.S.	6
Paychex, Inc.	U.S.	4
PepsiCo	U.S.	6
Petco	U.S.	1
Portugal Telecom	Portugal	1
Premier Farnell plc	UK	2
Premier Inc	U.S.	5
Rabobank	Netherlands	6
Realogy Corporation	U.S.	1
Ricoh	Japan	4
Rockwell Automation	U.S.	4
Rockwell Collins	U.S.	3
Royal Philips	Netherlands	6
Safeway Inc.	U.S.	2
Salesforce.com	U.S.	6
SCA-Svenska Cellulosa AB	Sweden	5
Schneider Electric	France	2
Seabourn	U.S.	1
Sempra Energy	U.S.	3
Shiseido Co	Japan	1
SingTel	Singapore	2
Solae, LLC	U.S.	3
Sompo Japan Insurance Inc.	Japan	3
SONAE	Portugal	2
Spectra Energy Corp	U.S.	1
SRA International, Inc.	U.S.	1
Standard Chartered Bank	UK	6
Starbucks Coffee Company	U.S.	6
Statoil	Norway	2
Stonyfield	U.S.	5
StoraEnso	Finland	5
SwissRe	Switzerland	5
Symantec Corporation	U.S.	5
Target	U.S.	6

Tata Steel Ltd	India	1
Ten Thousand Villages	U.S.	5
Teradata Corporation	U.S.	3
Texas Instruments	U.S.	6
The Aerospace Corporation	U.S.	5
The Co-operative Group	UK	2
The Hartford Financial Services Group	U.S.	5
The Mosaic Company	U.S.	1
The Progressive Group of Insurance Cos	U.S.	1
The Rezidor Hotel Group	Germany	3
The Timken Company	U.S.	2
Thomson Reuters	U.S./UK	4
Thrivent Finanacial for Lutherans	U.S.	1
Timberlan	U.S.	4
Time Warner lnc.	U.S.	5
T-Mobile USA, lnc.	U.S.	4
Tokio Marine Holdings, lnc.	Japan	1
TSYS	U.S.	1
Umicore	Belgium	2
University Hospitals	U.S.	1
UPS	U.S.	6
Vestas Wind	Denmark	2
Waste Management	U.S.	5
Wegmans	U.S.	4
Westpac Group	Australia	1
Weyerhouser Company	U.S.	3
Whole Foods Market, lnc.	U.S.	4
William E. Connor & Associates Ltd.	U.S.	1
Wipro Ltd	India	1
Wisconsin Physicians Service Insurance	U.S.	3
Xerox Corporation	U.S.	6

Source: Ethisphere Institute

COMPANIES WITH THE WORST ETHICAL RATINGS FOR THE YEAR 2013

Covalence Ethical Quote is a reputation index tracking the world's largest companies on environmental, social, governance (ESG), CSR, ethics and sustainability has rated the 12 Least Ethical Companies in the World.

1. Monsanto Company
2. Halliburton company
3. Chevron Corp
4. Freeport–McMoRan Copper & Gold Inc
5. Phillip Morris International Inc
6. Occidental Petroleum Corporation
7. Ryanair Airline
8. Syngenta AG
9. Grupo Mexico SA De CV
10. Total SA
11. Mediaset Spa
12. Brrick Gold Corporation

CONCLUSION

The last two decades have been especially revealing. We have witnessed businesses succumb to poor ethical standards, impacting not only on their immediate stakeholders, but entire economies and industries. A common reason attributed to the falling trust in business is that the latter is trained to act primarily in its own interests with little consideration for the larger good. The 2008 global financial crisis is often cited as an illustration of this moral shortcoming. Naturally, there is a crisis of confidence in the values of business organizations; there is a crisis of confidence in their ability to lead; and there is a crisis of confidence in their moral right to continue to do business.

Business ethics is the application of ethical values to business behavior. It is upon the global business managers to develop, skillfully, business ethics codes that are relevant to today's global challenges to enable them become corporate leaders in the current competitive business environment.

From Indian perspective, there is an equally deep and urgent need to go beyond compliance enforced by standards. Last year, the Ministry of Corporate Affairs announced the National Voluntary Guidelines (NVG) outlining the social, environmental and economic responsibilities businesses must work towards. Global business organizations need to investment in and adopt proactive approaches towards ethical safeguards, strategies that are acceptable to all stakeholders for purposes of dealing with complex ethical dilemmas and maintaining guidelines.

References

1. Arthaud-Day, M. L. (2005). Transnational corporate social responsibility: a tri-dimensional approach to international CSR research. *Business Ethics Quarterly*, Vol. 15, No. **(1):** 1–22.
2. Apel ,Karl-Otto (1990). La position de Karl-Otto Apel s'appuie sur un essai de réfutation des thèses de Karl Popper." Stuttgart.

3. Bartlett, C. A., Ghoshal, S. and Birkinshaw, J. (2004). *Transnational Management. Text, Cases, and Readings in Cross-border Management, 4th Ed.* Boston, MA: McGraw-Hill Irwin.
4. Bowie, N. E. (1996). Relativism, culture and moral. In Donaldson, T. and Werhane, P. H. (Eds), *Ethical Issues in Business: A Philosophical Approach, 5th Ed.* Upper Saddle River, NJ: Prentice-Hall: 91–5.
5. Brownlie, D., Saren, M., Wensley, R. and Whittington, R. (1999). *Rethinking Marketing: Towards Critical Marketing Accounting.* London: Sage.
6. Gopalkrishnan, R. I. (2001). International exchanges as the basis for conceptualizing ethics in international business. *Journal of Business Ethics,* Vol. 31, No. **(1)**: 3–24.
7. Kotler, P. and Armstrong, G. (2004). *Principles of Marketing, 10th Ed.* New Delhi: Prentice-Hall of India.
8. John Maxwell, *There's No Such Thing as Business Ethics* (Boston: Warner Books, Inc., 2003).
9. Parker, B. (1998). *Globalization and Business Practice: Managing Across Boundaries*. London: Sage Publications.
10. Sheth, J. and Sisodia, R. (1999). Revisiting marketing's law-like generalizations. *Journal of the Academy of Marketing Science,* Vol. 21, No. **(1)**: 71–87.
11. Sheth, J., Gardner, D. and Garrett, D. (1988). *Marketing Theory: Evolution and Evaluation.* New York: Wiley.
12. Values," *Handbook of Workplace Spirituality and Organizational Performance*, eds. R. A. Giacolone and C. L. Jurkiewicz (New York: M. E. Sharpe Press, 2003): 29–45; and David Ulrich and Norman Smallwood, *Why the Bottom Line Isn't! How to Build Value Through People and Organization* (New Jersey: John Wiley & Sons, Inc., 2003).
13. Guthrie, D. (2012, Jan.) Paying More than Lip Service to Business Ethics. Forbes, 21–30.
14. Silverstein, K. (2013, May) Enron, Ethics And Today's Corporate Values. Forbes, 36–43.
15. Smith, J. (2013, Jun) The World's Most Ethical Companies. Forbes, 16–24.
16. http://forbesindia.com/article/third-anniversary-special/azim-premji-capacity-building-helps-ethical-behaviour/32932/1
17. http://ethisphere.com/worlds-most-ethical/wme-honorees/
18. http://www.forbes.com/2012/03/09/building-sustainable-and-ethical-supply-chains/
19. http://www.managementstudyguide.com/values ethics.htm

29

The Changing Paradigm in Retail Sector with Special Reference to the New Policy of FDI

Suchita Shukla

Assistant Professor, STEP-HBTI, Kanpur

E-mail: suchi_vs@yahoo.com

ABSTRACT

India has been placed at the first position in the category of countries with the best opportunity for investment in retail sector. The increasing disposable incomes among the Indian middle class and increasing young population have been cited as the main reasons for such attractive optimism. Retailing in India is one of the pillars of its economy and accounts for 14 to 15 percent of its GDP. The Indian retail market is estimated to be US $450 billion and one of the top five retail markets in the world by economic value. India is one of the fastest growing retail markets in the world, with 1.2 billion people.

In late 2012, Government of India permitted FDI upto 51% in multibrand retailing with its prior approval and 100% in single brand retailing thus further liberalizing this sector. Rise in purchasing power, growing consumerism and brand proliferation has led to retail modernization in India. This in turn would act as a major catalyst in the development of a country through upgradation of technology, managerial skills and capabilities in various sectors. Further, FDI in the retail can also expand markets by reducing transaction and transformation costs of business through adoption of advanced supply chain and benefit consumers and suppliers (farmers). On the other hand, some side-effects like employment losses, promotion of unhealthy competition among organized domestic retailers resulting in exit of small domestic retailers from the market and distortion of urban cultural development cannot also ignored.

In the light of the above, the present paper is an exploratory study on the recent policy changes and makes a modest attempt at developing an insight as to what are the benefits and drawbacks of FDI in retail sector. The approach applied for the analysis in this paper includes secondary literature review, and major reliance is placed on books, journals, newspapers, online databases and study of case studies on impact of FDI in retail in other emerging markets.

INTRODUCTION

Retail is the sale of goods and services from individuals or businesses to the end-use. A retailer purchases goods or products in large quantities from manufacturers directly or through a wholesale, and then sells smaller quantities to the consumer for a profit. Retailing defines the direct interface between the manufacturers and the end users.

Retailing is one of the oldest businesses that human civilization has known and forms an important social institution because about 30 per cent of what a customer spends, goes on products and services that they buy from retailers. Of late the retailing industry in India has bloomed with much coveted success causing positive impact on not only the national economy but globally also it is being recognized as the sunrise industry.

OBJECTIVE OF THE STUDY

- ✓ To study and analyze the new Foreign Direct Investment (FDI) policy in retail as proposed by Indian government.
- ✓ To highlight the potential impact of FDI regulation in retail on this sector.
- ✓ To assesses the benefits and challenges from opening up of FDI in retail for various stakeholders.

LITERATURE REVIEW

Foreign Direct Investment (FDI) refers to capital inflows from abroad that is invested in or to enhance the production capacity of the economy. Foreign investment in India is governed by the FDI policy announced by the Government of India and the provision of the Foreign Exchange Management Act (FEMA) 1999. The Ministry of Commerce and Industry, Government of India is the nodal agency for motoring and reviewing the FDI policy on continued basis.

FDI is there in India since 1991 when Indian Government announced the policy of liberalization. According to the latest data released by the Department of Policy and Promotion (DIPP) the FDI inflow during 2008-09 (from April 2008 to March 2009) stood at approximately US$ 27.3 billion. Needless to say, but FDI has obviously proved to be very beneficial for the overall development of the Indian economy and inter alia has resulted in increased capital flow, improved technology, notable management expertise and favourable access to international markets (Gupta, 2010).

The Indian retail industry is mainly divided into:

1. Organized and
2. Unorganized

Organized retailing refers to trading activities undertaken by licensed retailers, that is, those who are registered for sales tax, income tax, etc. These include the corporate-backed hypermarkets and retail chains, and also the privately owned large retail businesses.

Unorganized retailing, on the other hand, refers to the traditional formats of low-cost retailing, for example, the local kirana shops, owner manned general stores, paan/beedi shops, convenience stores, hand cart and pavement vendors, etc.

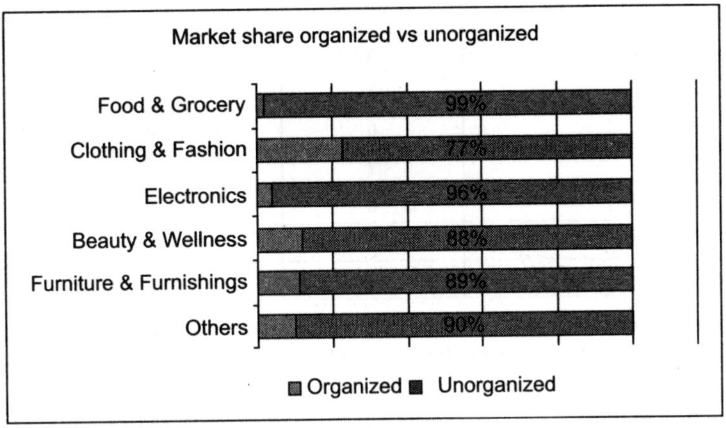

As part of the economic liberalization process set in place by Industrial policy 1991, the Indian government has opened the retail sector to FDI slowly through a series of steps. Until 2011, the Indian Central Government denied Foreign Direct Investment (FDI) in multi-brand retail, forbidding foreign groups from any ownership in supermarkets, convenience stores or other retail outlets. Even single-brand retail was limited to 51% ownership and a bureaucratic process.

However, in late 2012 the Government passed a cabinet note and permitted FDI upto 51% in multibrand retailing with prior Government approval and 100% in single brand retailing thus further liberalizing the sector. The new FDI policy implies greater autonomy in functioning for foreign single-brand retail players who can now own 100% of their Indian stores, up from the previous cap of 51% with only the stipulation that they will have to source 30% of their goods from small and medium-sized Indian suppliers.

According to A.T. Kearney's Global Retail Development Index (GRDI) 2012, India is the 5th most favorable destination for international retailers. Of the total Indian retail market, 8% constitutes the organized retail segment which is estimated to grow at a rate of almost 30% by 2015, and hence at a much faster pace than the overall retail market which is forecast to grow by 16% in the same period. India currently has a small penetration within the organized retail segment as compared to other emerging markets such as China, which has a penetration of more than 20% within organized retail according to the Global Retail Index report by the World Retail Conference. As a result of the new FDI policy, Indian retail market is estimated to exceed US$ 750 billion by 2015, according to the

India Retail Report 2013 (IRIS Research), presenting a strong potential for foreign retailers planning to enter India.

S.No.	Country	2012 Rank	2011 Rank	Change
1.	Brazil	1	1	0
2.	Chile	2	2	0
3.	China	3	6	+3
4.	Uruguay	4	3	-1
5.	India	5	4	-1
6.	Georgia	6	Unranked	N/A
7.	UAE	7	8	+1
8.	Oman	8	Unranked	N/A
9.	Mongolia	9	Unranked	N/A
10.	Peru	10	7	-3

Sources: Euromoney, Population Data Bureau, International Monetary Fund, World Bank, World Economoic Forum, Economist Intelligence Unit, Planet Retail: A.T. Kearney analyst.

PRESENT FDI POLICY FOR RETAIL SECTOR IN INDIA

The Ministry of Commerce and Industry, Government of India is the nodal agency for monitoring and reviewing the FDI policy on continued basis and changes in sectoral policy/ sectoral equity cap. The FDI policy is notified through Press Notes by the Secretariat for Industrial Assistance (SIA), Department of Industrial Policy and Promotion (DIPP). The foreign investors are free to invest in India, except few sectors/activities, where prior approval from the RBI or Foreign Investment Promotion Board (FIPB) would be required.

1. India will allow FDI of up to 51% in multi-brand sector.
2. Single brand retailers such as Apple and Ikea, can own 100% of their Indian stores, up from previous cap of 51%.
3. FDI up to 100% for cash and carry wholesale trading and export trading allowed under the automatic route.
4. The retailers (both single and multi-brand) will have to source at least 30% of their goods from small and medium sized Indian suppliers.
5. All retail stores can open up their operations in population having over 1 million. Out of approximately 7935 towns and cities in India, 55 suffice such criteria.
6. Multi-brand retailers must bring minimum investment of US$ 100 million. Half of this must be invested in back-end infrastructure facilities such as cold chains, refrigeration, transportation, packaging, etc. to reduce post-harvest losses and provide remunerative prices to farmers.

7. The opening of retail competition (policy) will be within parameters of state laws and regulations.
8. Any additional product categories to be sold under single brand retail must first receive additional government approval.

RESEARCH METHODOLOGY

In this paper the researcher has adopted analytical, descriptive and comparative methodology. The approach applied for the analysis is basically of secondary literature review, and for this major reliance has been placed on books, journals, newspapers, online databases and on the views of other writers on this topic.

STAKEHOLDERS OF FDI IN RETAIL

The proposed FDI in retail is expected to impact various stakeholders of India's retail sector. Key amongst these are the government, farmers, manufacturers/ MSMEs, unorganized trade and retailers, organized trade and retailers, and the Indian consumers. The benefits and limitations of FDI in retail would affect the various stakeholders for various reasons that are summed below.

BENEFITS OF FDI IN RETAIL SECTOR

(i) High Potential: Since the organized portion of retail sector is only 2-3%, thereby creating lot of potential for future players. Though, retail sector in India enjoys an extremely high growth rate at present, the contribution of retail sector to the GDP in India is hovering around 33-35% as compared to around 20% in USA.

(ii) High Employment Generator: The retail sector employs 7% of workforce in India, which is right now limited to unorganized sector only. Once the reforms get implemented this percentage is likely to increase substantially. Organized retail will need more workers.

(iii) Improved Technology: In the sphere of processing, grading, handling and packaging of goods and further technical developments in areas like electronic weighing, billing, barcode scanning, etc. could be a direct consequence of foreign companies opening retail shops in India,. Further, transportation facilities can get a boost, in the form of increased number of refrigerated vans and pre-cooling chambers which can help bring down wastage of goods.

(iv) Healthy Competition will be boosted and there will be a check on the prices (inflation): Retail giants such as Wal-Mart, Tesco, Target and other global retail companies already have operations in other countries for over 30 years, till date, they have not become monopolies rather they have managed to keep a check on the food inflation through their healthy competitive practices.

(v) Create Transparency in the System: The intermediaries operating as per mandi (market) norms do not have transparency in their pricing. According to some of the reports, an average Indian farmer realizes only one-third price, of what the final consumer pays. Another aspect of this would be intermediaries and mandi system will be evicted, hence directly benefiting the farmers and producers, and the prices of commodities will automatically be checked.

(vi) Quality Control and Control over Leakage and Wastage: Though India is the second largest producer of fruits and vegetables, it has a very limited integrated cold-chain infrastructure. Lack of adequate storage facilities causes heavy losses to farmers, in terms of wastage in quality and quantity of produce in general, and of fruits and vegetables in particular. Cost conscious and highly competitive retailers will try to avoid spillage and wastages and it will be their endeavour to make quality products available at lowest prices, hence making food available to the weakest and poorest segment of Indian society.

(vii) Cheaper Production Facilities: FDI will assure operations in production cycle and distribution. Due to economies of operation, production facilities will be available at a cheaper rate and thus resulting in availability of variety products to the ultimate consumers at a reasonable and cheaper price. Consumers in the organized retail will have the opportunity to choose between a number of internationally famous brands with pleasant shopping environment, huge space for product display, maintenance of hygiene and better customer care.

(viii) Heavy Flow of Capital Will Help in Building up the Infrastructure for the Growing Population: India is already operating in budgetary deficit. Neither the government of India nor domestic investors are capable of satisfying the growing needs (school, hospitals, etc.) of the ever growing Indian population. Hence, foreign capital inflow will enable us to create a heavy capital base.

There will be sustainable development and many other economic issues will be focused upon: According to the Indian Government's stipulation, foreign companies have to source a minimum of 30% of their goods from Indian micro and small industries. This will encourage the domestic manufacturing by creating a big effect for employment and technology upgradation and income generation.

LIMITATIONS OF FDI IN RETAIL SECTOR

(i) Lack of Competitors: A.T. Kearney's study on global retailing trends found that India is least competitive as well as least saturated markets of the world.

(ii) Highly Unorganized: The unorganized portion of retail sector is only 97% as compared to US, which is only 20%. The retail sector in India does not enjoy industry status, thereby making difficult for retailers to raise funds. Mckinsey study claims that the productivity of retail sector in India is also very low as compared to its international peers.

(iii) Shortage of Talented Professionals: The retail trade business in India is not considered reputed profession and is mostly carried out by the family members (self-employment and captive business). Such people are not academically and professionally qualified.

(iv) Indirectly Leads to Increase in Real Estate Cost: It is obvious that the foreign companies which enter into India to open up their malls and stores will certainly look for places in the heart of the cities. There shall be a war for place, initiated among such companies. It will result in increase in the cost of real estate in the cities that will eventually affect the interest of the ordinary people who desire to own their houses within the limit of the cities.

(v) Current Independent Stores will be Compelled to Close: This will lead to massive job loss as most of the operations in big stores like Wal-Mart are highly automated therefore requiring fewer workforces to carry on their operations. This will affect 50 million small merchants in India directly.

(vi) Big Players can Knock-out Competition: They can afford to lower prices in initial stages, become monopoly and then raise price later.

(vii) Negative Impact on Culture: Aspects of foreign culture and lifestyles may be adopted by Indian youth and they may develop inappropriate consumption pattern, not suited to our cultural environment.

(viii) Remember East India Company: It entered India as trader and then took over politically.

(ix) The Government has not been able to build Consensus: Profit distribution and investment ratios are also not fixed yet.

CONCLUSION

After careful analysis of the benefits and limitations of FDI in retail, it can be concluded without doubt that foreign investment in retail has an impact that goes beyond its direct investment impact. It is a force multiplier that would boost the socio-economic development of the entire country if implemented wisely and carefully. Therefore, the findings drawn by this study are in line with the views of Ravi Aron, Johns Hopkins University professor that "*opening up FDI will not only lead to a greater variety of products for sale and increased consumer choice, but also penetrate deep into the hinterland of Indian economic activity and do much to improve the country's "shunned sectors" — infrastructure and logistics*".

It is estimated that the arrival of foreign retail chains would have twofold impact on the Indian economy. First, companies would set up supply chains and logistical capabilities, spurring significant improvements in the infrastructure needed to, ship, store and deliver products (covering all aspects of value chain and supply chain activities, including storage, warehousing, and information-intensive operations). Second, their entry and expansion would induce domestic competitors to invest in infrastructure and logistics, as well as greatly speed up the emergence of product standards (especially in perishables and personal consumables), and begin the process of bypassing monopsony buyers and traders that dominate procurement in many product categories in India today. Therefore, with the implementation of this policy all stakeholders will stand to benefit whether it is government, farmers, manufacturers/MSMEs, unorganized trade and retailers, organized trade and retailers, or the Indian consumers.

References

1. "Aam bania is more powerful than the aam aadmi". The Times of India. 4 December 2011.
2. A. T. Kearney's Global Retail Development Index (GRDI) 2012.
3. Department of Industrial Policy and Promotion, 2010. "Foreign Direct Investment (FDI) in Multi-Brand Retail Trading," Discussion paper.
4. "Discussion paper on FDI in multi-brand Retail Trading", Department of Industrial Policy and Promotion July 6, 2010
5. Impact of organized retailing on the unorganized sector (ICRIER September 2008) Foreign and domestic investment in retail sector, Standing Committee on Commerce, May 13, 2009.
6. "FDI Policy in Multi-Brand Retail". Ministry of Commerce, Government of India. 28 November 2011.
7. "FDI in Retail: misplaced expectations and Half-truths", Sukhpal Singh, Economic and Political Weekly December 17, 2011.
8. "Rise in supermarket and their development implication" IFPRI Discussion Paper, Thomas Reardon and Ashok Gulati, February 2008.
9. Retail Global Expansion: A Portfolio of Opportunities". A.T. Kearney, 2011.
10. "Winning the Indian consumer". McKinsey & Company. 2005.

Websites

1. www.bms.co.in
2. www.dipp.nic.in
3. www.legalserviceindia.com
4. www.manupatra.com
5. www.scribd.com

6. www.cci.in
7. www.rbi.org.in
8. www.dipp.nic.in
9. www.legallyindia.com
10. www.icsi.edu
11. www.retailguru.com

30

Managing Women Education in India: Proposed Management Strategy for Improvement

Arup Jyoti Bhattacharya
IOFS, Indian Ordnance Factory, Kanpur
E-mail:arup-jt@rediffmail.com

ABSTRACT

Women education in India has made a good progress in last decade. However, a lot is still required and a long path yet to proceed. Managing women education in India is really complex owing to a wide diversity, awareness about literacy, poverty, wide disparity between urban and rural India, etc. This paper has analyzed various parameters of women education in India in the last decade (2001 to 2010) and proposed some suitable management approach for further development. The trend in education sector in India during 2011-13 has also been considered to propose the suitable methodology.

INTRODUCTION

Women education in India during the last decade gained some momentum. The progress of women education has been measured based on certain parameters.

(i) Increase in female literacy rate
(ii) Enrolment of women in primary and secondary education
(iii) Gender ratio in the number of teachers
(iv) Women in professional courses.

Based on the trend of progress in various parameters, it has been explained that there is a difference between urban and rural development. The progress in women education reflects the bright picture of urban development. The condition of women education in rural area still remains in shadow.

To manage the combined development of urban and rural education of women, the management technique that has been proposed is system approach. Particularly the system dynamics could be applied to implement a better strategy.

MEASURES TAKEN IN EDUCATION SYSTEM IN THE LAST DECADE IN INDIA

After 1976, according to the Constitutional amendment, education system in India started to prosper by means of co-operation and reallocation of responsibility between Center and State. In 1986, National Education Policy (NPE) was framed and same was adopted in 1992. In 2004, several reforms took place in education policy and system.

The Government took various initiatives in education systems like “Sarba Sikshya Abhiyan”, “Mid-day Meal”, “Education Guarantee Yojana”, etc. To promote education in backward classes “Mahila Samakhya Yojana” was implemented. In the year 2007-08, the budget allotted for this scheme was Rs. 34 crore. Special drive was taken for teachers’ training.

According to the Census-2001, in 47 districts in our country, the literacy rate for women was less than 30%. Among those districts, most of them belong to UP, Bihar, Jharkhand and Orissa. Suitable measures were taken to overcome the same. Mostly the women between the ages 15 and 35 years were given special attention. Initiatives were made for education to aged people as well as disabled persons.

According to the 93rd Constitution Amendment Act, 2006, special provision of vocational training was made in education for backward classes and backward citizens. In spite of various remarkable measures by the government of India, a long path is still ahead of us to travel.

ANALYSIS OF PROGRESS IN WOMEN EDUCATION IN LAST DECADE

1. Increase of Female Literacy Rate: Now the following graph shows the increase of female literacy rate in 2011 over 2001 in percentage, state-wise.

Chart 1: Increase of Female Literacy Rate in 2011 over 2001 in percent

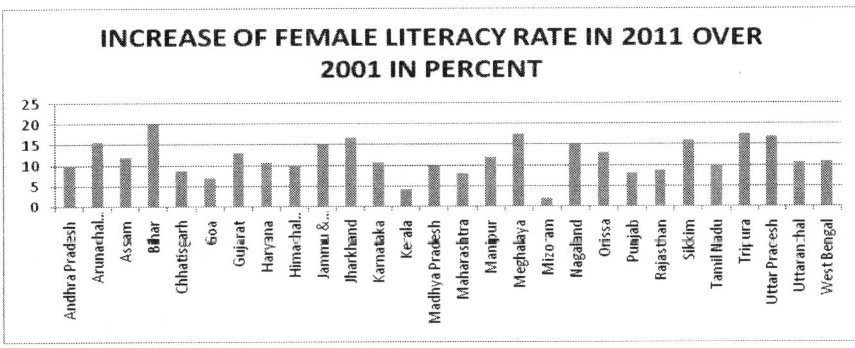

The above graph shows that the increase of female literacy rate in 2011 over 2001 is more than 15% which took place in Bihar, Auranachal Pradesh, J&K, Jharkhand, Meghalaya, Sikkim, UP, Nagaland. This is indeed a remarkable achievement in the states. However, the all-round improvement both in urban and rural sector could be also be assessed based on the following graph.

Chart 2: Difference between Urban and Rural Female Literacy Rate in percent

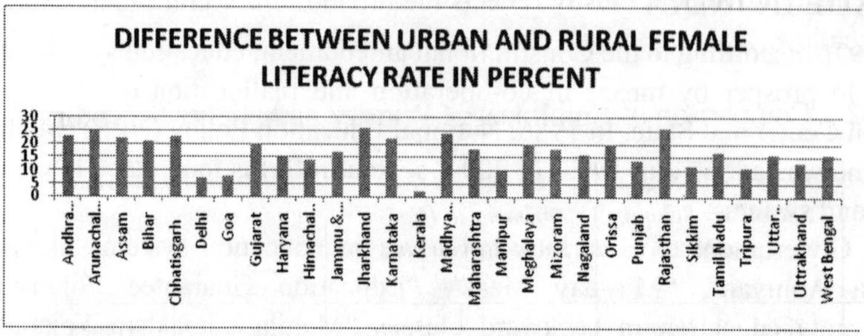

The balanced development in literacy is found in three states – Kerala, Goa and Delhi. The educational progress in Bihar, UP took place mostly in urban area.

2. Enrolment of Women in Primary and Secondary Education

In the last decade, there is a gradual increase in number of women enrolment in school education in primary section (I to V)

Table 1 Enrolment in School Education in Primary Section (I to V)

Year	*Total*	*Women*
2001–02	113883060	50263565
2002–03	122397715	57313336
2003–04	128266291	59905868
2004–05	130763067	61088524
2005–06	132048727	61552233
2006–07	133719922	62632501
2007–08	135470561	64381014
2008–09	134566314	64472422

But the percentage of women enrolled in primary section with respect to total number of enrolment remains almost same over the decades. However, percent of women with respect to the total students enrolled in higher secondary (IX to XII) shows a marginal increase. The trend as per Graph 3 and data in Table 2 could be analyzed as:

(i) There is a continuous improvement in total enrolment in education in primary section.

(ii) Number of women going to higher secondary level has increased.

(iii) The ratio of women to total enrolment remained almost constant, which implies that the improvement in women enrolment has also maintained the growth trend. But, on the other hand, it can also be concluded that the progress is limited to a confined population only.

(iv) The improvement has not been reflected in all the corners of our country. The improvement mostly reflects the urban India. Rural India is still under shadow.

Table 2 Comparison of Enrolment of Primary and Higher Secondary School

	Enrolment in Higher Secondary School only		*Enrolment from Primary to Higher Secondary School in Total*		*Total Drop out in Primary and Secondary together*		*Drop out % - Women w.r.t Total*
Year	*Total*	*Women*	*Total*	*Women*	*Total*	*Women*	
2001–02	30507215	12063696	193841678	83209637	16,33,34,463	7,11,45,941	44
2002–03	33214100	13718507	207964581	94255409	17,47,50,481	8,05,36,902	46
2003–04	35009349	14396677	217072644	98167510	18,20,63,295	8,37,70,833	46
2004–05	37075386	15388506	223845364	101485843	18,67,69,978	8,60,97,337	46
2005–06	38386019	16095563	227893970	103486371	18,95,07,951	8,73,90,808	46
2006–07	39938127	16950579	233500485	106707185	19,35,62,358	8,97,56,606	46
2007–08	44475476	19319218	243727224	112912480	19,92,51,748	9,35,93,262	47
2008–09	45646427	19952917	241911360	113393830	19,62,64,933	9,34,40,913	48

Chart 3: Percent of Women with Respect to the Total

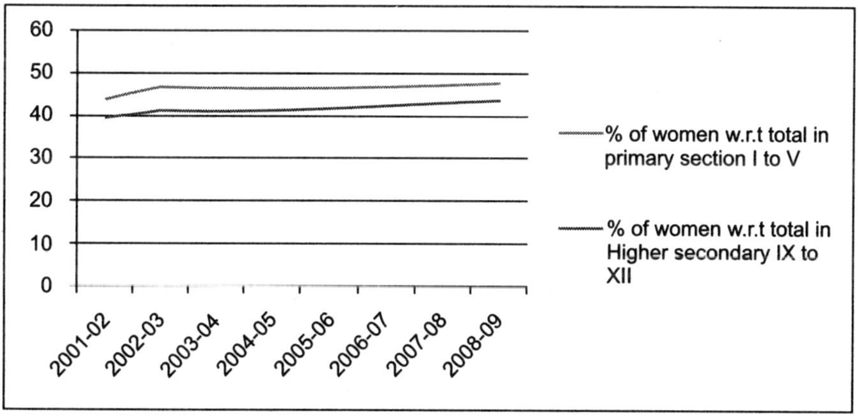

3. Gender Ratio in the Number of Teachers

During the last decade, there is a growing trend of women teacher. But the difference between the total number of teachers and women teachers has also been increased. For a balanced society and development of women power, the male to female ratio of teachers also should be improved.

Table 3 Number of Teachers in Primary/High School/Higher Secondary

	Primary Section		*High School*		*Higher Secondary Section*	
Year	*Total*	*Women*	*Total*	*Women*	*Total*	*Women*
2001-02	1928075	715214	1018795	383577	758700	236724
2002-03	1912931	746356	996054	380151	1037455	431962
2003-04	2096858	836966	1071660	407912	952818	366537
2004-05	2160666	842006	1082878	415331	1000112	385843
2005-06	2183479	857839	1122876	427325	1031779	393868
2006-07	2323286	920409	1173030	451847	1074930	407725
2007-08	2315081	1027031	1175058	446830	951817	348511
2008-09	2362849	1047981	1214347	457549	1214347	337940

Chart 4: Number of Teachers in Institutes (approved)

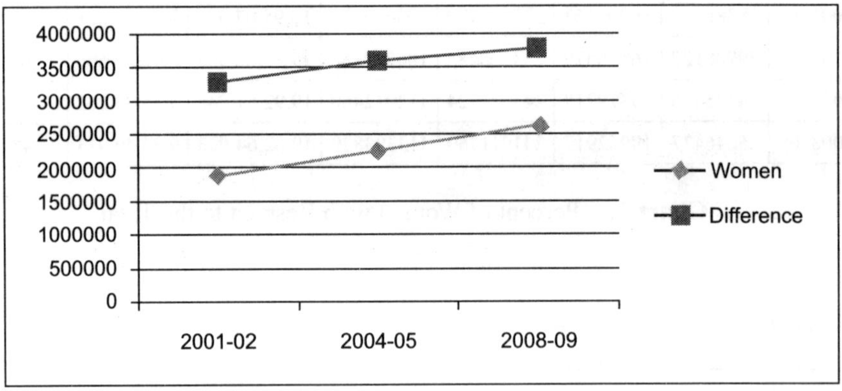

4. Women in Professional Courses – Engineering and Medical

Chart 5: Total Vs Engineering Vs Medical Students of Women in Higher Studies

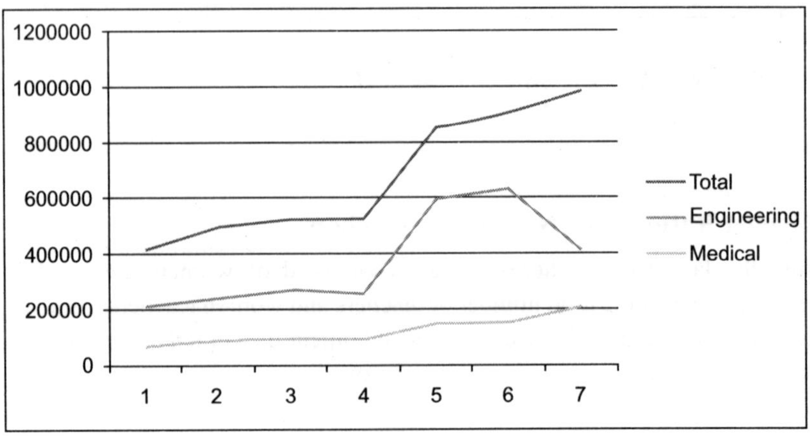

The above chart depicts that there is a drastic growth in higher studies and professional courses done by women. Medical course shows a steady growth trend. In engineering there is drastic variation is number because of economic ups and downs in world job market.

Coming to the total number of scholars in school and university level, women show their excellency in last decade.

Table 4 Number of Scholars in all Recognized Institutes

Years	*Total*	*Women*
2001-02	194530371	83354410
2002-03	208736223	94395722
2003-04	217891392	98268819
2004-05	224711627	101597406
2005-06	228803760	103614450
2006-07	234440825	106993069
2007-08	243727224	112912480
2008-09	241911360	113393830

Chart 6: Growing Trend in Women Scholars

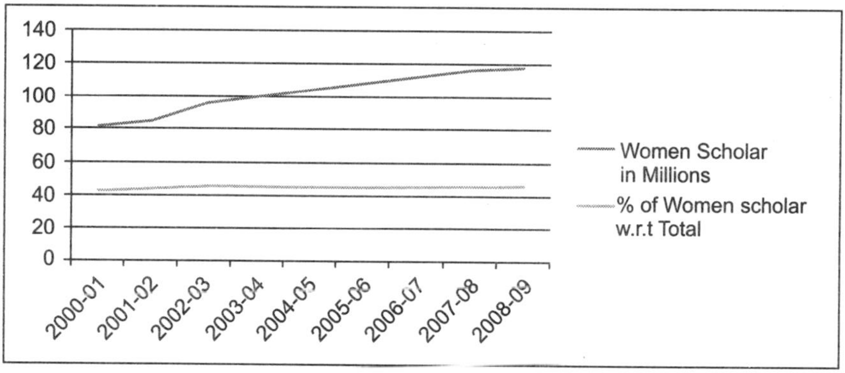

The following table shows the number of female students enrolled in universities for higher studies.

Table 5 Enrolment in Universities (other than Standalone University) for the year 2010-2011

COURSE	*FEMALE*	*TOTAL*	*Percent w.r.t Total*
PH.D	21023	57346	37
POST GRAUATE	399078	995742	40
UNDER GRADUATE	714621	1951245	37
P.G DIPLOMA	27461	80373	34

Proposed Management Strategy for Further Improvement

1. Rural Development of Women Education – System Approach The analysis of women education in the last decade implies a bright picture in some aspects but on the contrary, there is a dark side that overall improvement both in urban and rural sector has not been observed. Most of the states are utilizing the resources in urban development but rural progress particularly in terms of women education has not yet been boost up. Following chart indicates the state-wise expenditure in rural development in percent (%) in terms of Rs. lacs with respect to the total expenditure in all sectors for 2010-11.

Chart 7: Percent of Rural Development w.r.t Total in Rs. Lacs for 2010-11

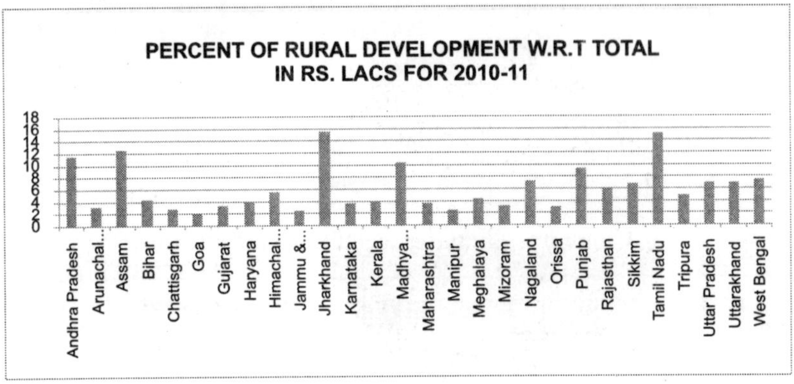

Only Assam, Jharkhand and Tamil Nadu have spent more than 12% of total expenditure in rural development.

System approach of management can give a better strategy in this case. Urban and rural development should not be treated in an isolated way. Any kind of development in transport, infrastructure should be implemented in equal pace in both urban and rural sectors. Similarly, education especially women education, should be developed in all the corners of our country.

2. Growth of Educational Institute – Approach of System Dynamics

In the last five years, there is a trend of exponential growth in educational institutes by private players particularly in engineering and management colleges. Any kind of exponential growth implies that there may be some faults in the system. Exponential growth may look apparently attractive but ultimately the system collapses if the drawbacks are not properly identified and rectified. System dynamics, a powerful management tool indicates the above concept. For the sudden growth of educational institutes, the approach of system dynamics can provide better guidelines to overcome the upcoming challenges.

Coming to the scenario of MBA institutes in India (AICTE Approved), the following chart shows that the institutes are not uniformly distributed across the country. The institutes are concentrated in some of the states or zones. Particularly in eastern zone, the number of institutes is considerably lesser in number than the northern part. South, central and western parts have a steady growth trend comparatively.

To analyze the above situation in the light of system dynamics, it could be stated that the sudden growth in number of management institutes may have bad teaching quality and improper education. This will also affect the women education in that zone. Steady growth of institutes in all the area should be maintained.

Chart 8: AICTE Approved MBA Institutes across the country

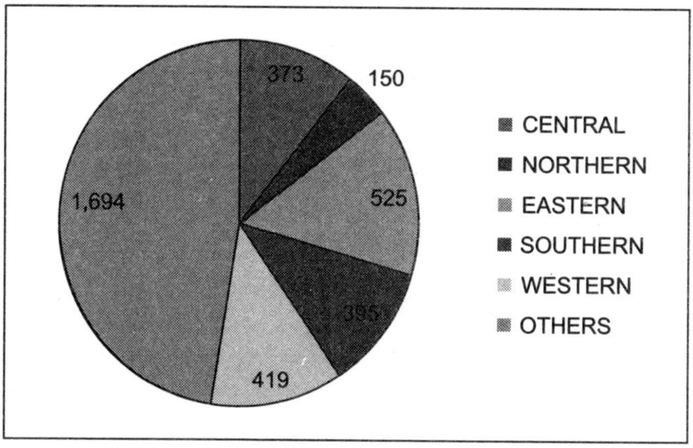

CONCLUSION

The prosperity of India belongs to women education. The number of male in the age group of 18-23 years in our country is 7,27,79,214, whereas that of female is 6,55,50,024 according to the report of 2012. This difference not only indicates an alarming situation but also insists on the women education. If the large number of population is kept away of higher education, ultimately the loser would be our country only. The success of women education will come when the all-round development would take place. The urban and rural development could not be kept isolated. Both urban and rural development should be treated as an integrated system. System dynamics approach should be applied to keep balance in development. Any kind of drastic change should be monitored and controlled. Women education in India will bring the real prosperity of our country.

References

1. "Bharat 2010" by Ministry of Information and Broadcasting, Chapter: "Shiksha" pg. 243-282 in Hindi Version.
2. All Indian Survey of Higher Education, year 2010-11 (Provisional) published by Ministry of Human Resource Development, Govt. of India in the Year 2012.
3. Statistical year Book India, 2012 by Ministry of Statistics and Programme Implementation, Govt. of India
4. Website of Ministry of Human Resource Department.
5. Website of AICTE accessed in August 2013.

31

Women Awakening in Present Education in India

Rita Singh Rathore
Principal, BJSGP PG College, Unnao
E-mail: rathore.ritasingh@rediffmail.com

ABSTRACT

Education in India falls under the control of both the Union Government and the states, with some responsibilities lying with the Union and the states having autonomy for others. The various articles of the Indian Constitution provide for education as a fundamental right. Most universities in India are controlled by the Union or the State Government.

The number of literate women among the female population of India was between 2–6% from the British Raj onwards to the formation of the Republic of India in 1947. Concerted efforts led to improvement from 15.3% in 1961 to 28.5% in 1981. By 2001 literacy for women had exceeded 50% of the overall female population, though these statistics were still very low compared to world standards and even male literacy within India. Recently the Indian government has launched Saakshar Bharat Mission for Female Literacy. This mission aims to bring down female illiteracy by half of its present level.

While the educated Indian women workforce maintains professionalism, the men outnumber them in most fields and, in some cases, receive higher income for the same positions. The education of women in India plays a significant role in improving livings standards in the country. A higher women literacy rate improves the quality of life both at home and outside of home, by encouraging and promoting education of children.

Nowadays Indian women like Kiran Mazumdar-Shaw, Chanda Kocchar, Akhila Srinivasan, Ekta Kapoor, Jyoti Nayak, Naina Lal Kidwai, Ritu Kumar, Ritu Nanda, Sahnaz Hussain, Priya Paul, Preetha Reddy, Ranjana Kumar, Simone Tata, Indira Nooyi, Vidya Manohar, Sonia Gandhi, Anu Aga, Indu Jain, Neelam Dhawan, Sunita Williams, Kalpana Chawala, etc. and so many other names are known as world level fame of our country.

The Indian women are no longer treated as showpieces to be kept at home. They are also enjoying the impact of globalization and making an influence not only on domestic but also on international sphere. Women are doing a wonderful job striking a balance between their house and career.

INTRODUCTION

Education in India: is provided by the public sector as well as the private sector, with control and funding coming from three levels: central, state, and local. The Nalanda University was the oldest university-system of education in the world. Western education became ingrained into Indian society with the establishment of the British Raj.

Education in India falls under the control of both the Union Government and the states, with some responsibilities lying with the Union and the states having autonomy for others. The various articles of the Indian Constitution provide for education as a fundamental right. Most universities in India are controlled by the Union or the State Government.

India has made progress in terms of increasing primary education attendance rate and expanding literacy to approximately two-thirds of the population. India's improved education system is often cited as one of the main contributors to the economic rise of India. Much of the progress, especially in higher education and scientific research, has been credited to various public institutions. The private education market in India is merely 5% although in terms of value is estimated to be worth $40 billion in 2008 and $68–70 billion in 2012.

However, India continues to face stern challenges. Despite growing investment in education, 25% of its population is still illiterate; only 15% of Indian students reach high school, and just 7% graduate. The quality of education whether at primary or higher education is significantly poor as compared with major developing nations. As of 2008, India's post-secondary institutions offer only enough seats for 7% of India's college-age population, 25% of teaching positions nationwide are vacant, and 57% of college professors lack either a master's or PhD degree.

As of 2011, there are 1522 degree-granting engineering colleges in India with an annual student intake of 5,82,000, plus 1,244 polytechnics with an annual intake of 265,000. However, these institutions face shortage of faculty and concerns have been raised over the quality of education.

WOMEN'S EDUCATION IN INDIA

Women have a much lower literacy rate than men. Far fewer girls are enrolled in the schools, and many of them drop out. Conservative cultural attitudes prevents some girls from attending school. The number of literate women among the female population of India was between 2–6% from the British Raj onwards to the formation of the Republic of India in 1947. Concerted efforts led to improvement from 15.3% in 1961 to 28.5% in 1981. By 2001 literacy for women had exceeded 50% of the overall female population, though these statistics were still very low compared to world standards and even male literacy within India. Recently the

Indian government has launched **Saakshar Bharat Mission for Female Literacy**. This mission aims to bring down female illiteracy by half of its present level.

Sita Anantha Raman outlines the progress of women's education in India:

Since 1947 the Indian government has tried to provide incentives for girls' school attendance through programs for midday meals, free books, and uniforms. This welfare thrust raised primary enrollment between 1951 and 1981. In 1986, the National Policy on Education decided to restructure education in tune with the social framework of each state, and with larger national goals. It emphasized that education was necessary for democracy, and central to the improvement of women's condition. The new policy aimed at social change through revised texts, curricula, increased funding for schools, expansion in the numbers of schools, and policy improvements. Emphasis was placed on expanding girls' occupational centers and primary education; secondary and higher education; and rural and urban institutions. The report tried to connect problems like low school attendance with poverty, and the dependence on girls for housework and sibling day care. The National Literacy Mission also worked through female tutors in villages. Although the minimum marriage age is now eighteen for girls, many continue to be married much earlier. Therefore, at the secondary level, female dropout rates are high.

Sita Anantha Raman also maintains that while the educated Indian women workforce maintains professionalism, the men outnumber them in most fields and, in some cases, receive higher income for the same positions.

Education of women in India plays a significant role in improving livings standards in the country. A higher women literacy rate improves the quality of life both at home and outside of home, by encouraging and promoting education of children, especially female children, and in reducing the infant mortality rate. Several studies have shown that a lower level of women literacy rates results in higher levels of fertility and infant mortality, poorer nutrition, lower earning potential and the lack of an ability to make decisions within a household. Women's lower educational levels is also shown to adversely affect the health and living conditions of children. A survey that was conducted in India showed results which support the fact that infant mortality rate was inversely related to female literacy rate and educational level. The survey also suggests a correlation between education and economic growth.

In India, it was found that there is a large disparity between female literacy rates in different states. For example, while Kerala actually has a female literacy rate of about 86 percent, Bihar and Uttar Pradesh have female literacy rates around 55-60 percent. These values are further correlated with health levels of the Indians, where it was found that Kerala was the state with the lowest infant mortality rate while Bihar and Uttar Pradesh are the states with the lowest life expectancies in India. Furthermore, the disparity of female literacy rates across rural and urban areas is also significant in India. Out of the 29 states in India, 6 of them have female literacy rates of below 60 percent. The rural state Rajasthan has a female literacy rate of less than 12 percent.

BUSINESS WOMEN/ENTREPRENEURS

Many Indian women have made remarkable growth in the field of business and other areas besides the above-mentioned constraints.

Women entrepreneurs may be defined as the women or group of women who initiate, organize and co-operate a business enterprise. Government of India has defined women entrepreneurs as an enterprise owned and controlled by a woman having a minimum financial interest of 51% of the capital and giving at least 51% of employment generated in the enterprise to women.

Women are enjoying the impact of globalization and making an influence not only on domestic but also on international sphere. Women are doing a wonderful job striking a balance between their house and career. Here are a few: *(The lists consists of no political figure and concentrates only on business leaders and organizational heads).*

1. Dr. Kiran Mazumdar-Shaw, Chairman & Managing Director of Biocon Ltd., who became India's richest woman in 2004, was educated at the Bishop Cotton Girls School and Mount Carmel College in Bangalore. She founded Biocon India with a capital of Rs.10,000 in her garage in 1978 – the initial operation was to extract an enzyme from papaya. Her application for loans were turned down by banks then – on three counts – biotechnology was then a new word, the company lacked assets, women entrepreneurs were still a rarity. Today, her company is the biggest biopharmaceutical firm in the country.

Dr. Kiran Mazumdar-Shaw

2. Ekta Kapoor, Creative Head of Balaji Telefilms is the daughter of Jeetendra and sister of Tushar Kapoor. She has been synonymous with the rage of soap operas in Indian TV, after her most famous venture *'Kyunki Saas Bhi Kabhi Bahu Thi'* which was aired in 2000 on Star Plus. Ekta dominates Indian Television.

At the 6th Indian Telly Awards 2006, she bagged the Hall of Fame award for her contributions.

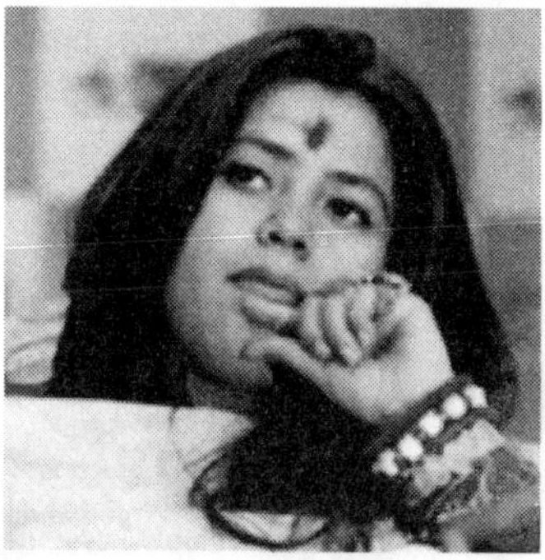

Ekta Kapoor

3. Neelam Dhawan, Managing Director, Microsoft India leads Microsoft India. She is a graduate from St. Stephens College in 1980, and also passed out from Delhi's Faculty of Management Studies in 1982. Then she was keen on joining FMCG majors like Hindustan Lever and Asian Paints, both companies rejected Dhawan, as they did not wish to appoint women for marketing and sales.

Neelam Dhawan

She has become a pioneering figure in the IT industry of India. Neelam Dhawan has been working in the Indian IT field for the last twenty-two years. She is the new Managing Director of Microsoft India. Before coming to Microsoft, she worked in all the top IT companies in India such as HP, IBM and HCL.

4. Naina Lal Kidwai, was the first Indian woman to graduate from Harvard Business School. Fortune magazine listed Kidwai among the world's top 50 Corporate Women from 2000 to 2003. According to the Economic Times, she is the first woman to head the operations of a foreign bank in India. (HSBC)

Naina Lal Kidwai

5. Indu Jain, the multifaceted lady used to be the Chairman of the Times Group— The most powerful and largest media house India has known. Indu Jain is known by many different identities such as that of spiritualist, humanist, entrepreneur, an educationalist but most prominently she played the role of the Chairman of Times Group. Indu Jain is the perfect picture of the successful Indian woman entrepreneur.

Indu Jain

6. Priya Paul, she has a bachelor's degree specializing in Economics from Wellesley College, USA. She entered her family business and is currently the Chairperson of Park Hotels.

Priya Paul

7. Simone Tata, *has been instrumental in changing a small subsidiary of Tata Oil Mills* into the largest cosmetic brand in India – LAKME, synonymous today with Indian Fashion. She became a part of Lakme during 1961 and has been responsible for turning the company into one of the biggest brands of fashion in India. At present she is the Chairperson of Trent Limited, a subsidiary of Tata Group.

Simone Tata

8. Mallika Srinivasan, currently the Director of TAFE–Tractors and Farm Equipment, India, was honoured with the title of Businesswoman of the Year during 2006 by the Economic Times. She joined the company in 1986 and has since been responsible for accelerating turnover from 85 crores to 2900 crores within a span of 2 decades.

Mallika Srinivasan

9. Preetha Reddy, Managing Director of Apollo Hospitals, Chennai, one of the largest healthcare conglomerates of India, is one of the pioneer businesswoman of India in the segment of healthcare industry.

Preetha Reddy

10. Ranjana Kumar, currently Vigilance Commissioner in Central Vigilance Commission, after her retirement as the Chairperson of NABARD- National Bank for Agricultural and Rural Development, is a prominent Indian Banker. When the Government of India appointed her as the Chairperson and Managing Director of The Indian Bank, she became the first woman to become head of a public sector bank in India. At that time of her appointment, The Indian Bank was saddled with huge losses and during her tenure she ensured the turn around of The Indian Bank.

Ranjana Kumar

Women like these are an inspiration for all other women who strive to achieve great heights in their lives. Taking them as our role models each one of us can be there where they are right now. All we need have is faith in ourselves, confidence and above all a fixed aim that we need work towards.

The 21 Leading Businesswomen in India

1.	**Akhila Srinivasan,** Managing Director, Shriram Investments Ltd
2.	**Chanda Kocchar,** Executive Director, ICICI Bank
3.	**Ekta Kapoor** Creative Director, Balaji Telefilms
4.	**Jyoit Naik,** President, Lijjat Papad
5.	**Kiran Mazumdar-Shaw,** Chairman and Managing Director, Biocon
6.	**Lalita D. Gupte,** Joint Managing Director, ICICI Bank
7.	**Naina Lal Kidwai** Deputy CEO, HSBC
8.	**Preetha Reddy,** Managing Director, Apollo Hospitals
9.	**Priya Paul,** Chairman, Apeejay Park Hotels
10.	**Rajshree Pathy,** Chairman, Rajshree Sugars and Chemicals Ltd.
11.	**Ranjana Kumar** Chairman, NABARD
12.	**Ravina Raj Kohli,** Media personality and ex-President, STAR News
13.	**Renuka Ramnath,** CEO, ICICI Ventures

14.	**Ritu Kumar,** Fashion Designer
15.	**Ritu Nanda,** CEO, Escolife
16.	**Shahnaz Hussain,** CEO, Shahnaz Herbals
17.	**Sharan Apparao,** Proprietor, Apparao Galleries
18.	**Simone Tata,** Chairman, Trent Ltd.
19.	**Sulajja Firodia Motwani,** Joint MD, Kinetic Engineering
20.	**Tarjani Vakil,** former Chairman and Managing Director, EXIM Bank
21.	**Zia Mody,** Senior Partner, AZB & Partners

Despite all the social hurdles, many women have become successful in their works. Recently, Forbes, one of the famous international business magazines, has published a list of most powerful women in various fields such as, politics, business. Indian women were also included in the list. Here are the names:

11. Indra Nooyi- 4th position- Chief Executive—designate, Pepsi Co.

This Madras born woman was a straight "A" student in her school. Nooyi did her bachelors from Madras Christian College and MBA from Indian Institute of Management, Calcutta. Nooyi then went to USA and attended Yale University. From Yale, she obtained degree on management. This brilliant corporate woman started her career in Boston Consulting Group and moved on to Motorola and Asea Brown Boveri. She joined Pepsi Co. in 1994. She turned the company into a bold risk taker. In 1998, Pepsi acquired Tropicana. In 1997, Pepsi started its own fast food chain. In 2001, she became President of Pepsi Cola. Wall Street Journal included her name in their top 50 women to watch in 2005. Fortune magazine declared her 11th most powerful women in business.

12. Sonia Gandhi-13th position—President, Congress Party

She was born in Italy and had a normal upbringing. In 1964, she went to Cambridge to study English and met Rajiv Gandhi. The two fell in love and got married in 1968. Sonia's entrance into politics was accidental. In 1991, after the assassination of Rajiv Gandhi, she was approached by the Congress Party leaders but she refused. She finally joined politics in 1998 by taking over the charge of Congress Party. Her opponents tried to ruin her image by labeling her as a foreigner, but with her timely decision to give up the position of Prime Minister to Dr. Manmohan Singh, after winning the general elections of 2004, she outmatched her opponents.

13. Lalita Gupte & Kalpana Morparia—93rd position—Joint Managing Directors, ICICI Bank

Kalpana Morparia and Lalita Gupte are Joint Managing Directors of ICICI Bank, the second largest bank of India. Lalita Gupte holds a Master's Degree in Management Studies from Jamnalal Bajaj Institute of Management Studies. She joined ICICI Bank in 1971. Her reason behind success is her supportive family. She got great support from her husband and in laws.

Ms. Kalpana Morparia is a graduate in law from Mumbai University. She joined ICICI in 1975 as a senior legal officer. In 1996, she became General Manager. She became Executive Director in 2001. In 1999, for her contribution in Finance and Banking sector in India, Indian Merchants' Chamber awarded her.

14. Vidya Manohar Chhabria– 95th position—Chairman, Jumbo Group

The wife of late Manohar Rajaram Chhabria, is now leading Jumbo Group, a Dubai based $1.5 billion business conglomerate. She became chairperson of the company after the death of her husband in 2002. She runs the business with the help of her three daughters. She was ranked 38th most powerful women by the Fortune magazine in 2003.

In another article, Forbes also mentioned some other names:

15. Anu Aga-Chairperson (former) Thermax Group

Like Vidya Manohar Chabaria, this woman also became the Chairperson of Thermax Engineering after the death of her husband Rohinton Aga. The company's condition was critical at that time. Its share price dipped to Rs. 36 from Rs. 400. Anu Aga, the then Director of Human Resource, Thermax, was compelled to take charge of the company. In order to make the company profitable, she brought a consultant from abroad and restructured the company. The strategy worked and the company saw profit again. She stepped down from the post of chairperson in 2004. Now, she spends most of her time in social activities. Bombay Management Association awarded her Management Woman Achiever of the Year Award 2002-2003.

16. Sulajja Firodia Motwani— Kinetic Motor

This beautiful woman is the Joint Managing Director of Kinetic, and the Managing Director of Kinetic Finance. Her grandfather founded this company. He was a very well-known figure in the Indian auto industry. Sulajja did her MBA in America. Later, she worked in Barra International, a California based investment consultancy firm, for four years and then returned to India and joined her family business. She travels a lot around India and likes to deal face to face with people. This is how she tries to understand the market in her country.

India has seen many women leaders in the form of rulers, administrators, freedom fighters and politicians in spite of being a very religiuos country practicing Sati, Jauhar and Pardha.

List goes here…

1. Maharani Jhansi Lakshmi Bai
2. Kittur Rani Chenamma
3. Rani Durgavati
4. Rani Avantibai
5. Rani Jalkari Bai
6. Rani Ahilyabai Holker
7. Rani Rashmoni
8. Begum Hazrat Mahal
9. Bhikaji Cama
10. Aruna Asaf Ali
11. Rani Gadinliu
12. Annie Besant
13. Durga Bai Deshmukh
14. Kasturba Gandhi
15. Kamala Nehru
16. Indira Gandhi
17. Meera Behn
18. Sarojini Naidu
19. Vijayalaxmi Pandit
20. Rukmini Laxmipathi
21. Rajkumari Amrit Kaur
22. Rani Jilabai
23. Rani Tarabai
24. Mai Bhago Ju
25. Minakshi Ammal
26. Sonia Gandhi
27. J. Jayalalitha
28. Mayawati

29. Mamata Banerjee
30. Vasundhara Raje Scindia

CONCLUSION

Women in India still have travel a long path. The joint efforts of Government and NGOs will go a long way in women awakening through education in India. Above all women have to have strong will to grow.

References

1. Bibhudatta Pradhan (19 July 2007). "Patil Poised to Become India's First Female President". Bloomberg.com. Retrieved 20 July 2007.
2. "Human Development Report; Sustainability and Equity". United Nations Development Programme. 2011. p. 139.
3. "The Global Gender Gap Report 2012". World Economic Forum. pp. 10-11.
4. "Rajya Sabha passes Women's Reservation Bill". Chennai, India: The Hindu. 10 March 2010. Retrieved 25 August 2010.
5. [hindu.com/2010/03/10/stories/2010031050880100.htm "Rajya Sabha passes Women's Reservation Bill"]. The Hindu. Retrieved 25 August 2010.
6. Jayapalan (2001). *Indian society and social institutions*. Atlantic Publishers & Distri.. p. 145.ISBN 978-81-7156-925-0.
7. "Women in History". National Resource Center for Women. Retrieved 24 December 2006.
8. Really Old School," Garten, Jeffrey E. New York Times, 9 December 2006.
9. India achieves 27% decline in poverty, *Press Trust of India* via *Sify.com*, 2008-09-12.
10. India still Asia's reluctant tiger, by Zareer Masani of *BBC Radio 4*, 27 February 2008.
11. Special Report: The Education Race, by *Newsweek*, 18–25 August 2011 issue.
12. "Science and Technology Education". Press Information Bureau. Retrieved 2009-08-08.
13. How To Save The World's Back Office, by Sramana Mitra of *Forbes*, 03.14.08.
14. "Women in India: How Free? How Equal?". United Nations. Archived from the original on 2006-09-11. Retrieved 2006-12-24.
15. "In India, Can Schools Offer Path Out of Poverty?". 2010-05-14. Retrieved 2010-06-23.
16. S. Chandrasekhar and A. Jayaraman, District Level Analysis of the Total Fertility Rate Using Indian Census Data (viewed on 9 March 2011), http://paa2004.princeton.edu/download.asp?submissionId=41578

17. Women Education in India, (viewed on 9 March 2011), http://www.slideshare.net/siddharth4mba/women-education-in-india
18. Literacy Rate and Gender Gap in Sechduled Castes in India, (viewed on 9 March 2011), http://www.capabilityapproach.com/pubs/NavjeetKaur.pdf
19. Nutrition in India, Viewed on 11 March 2011, http://www.icosgroup.net/static/foodsec/text/accscnun_indiacasestudy.pdf
20. Landscaping Women's Empowerment through Learning and Education in India, A study, Viewed on 11 March 2011, http://dasra.org/n/forwebsite/factsheet/Landscaping_Women_Empowerment_Report.pdf

32

Talent Management: A Study at B-Schools

Indu Shukla
Assistant Professor
Department of Management
RIET, Kanpur
E-mail: ap.indushhukla@gmail.com

Ajaynath Dubey
Assistant Professor
Dr. VSICS, Kanpur
Email: dubey.ajay@rediffmail.com

ABSTRACT

Attracting, developing and retaining qualified employees and building a culture of engagement and productivity is essential for success of any organization which is termed Talent Management. Like the corporate world, the education sector is also discovering the need for talent management and its retention to meet the new quality standards demanded by the society and the next generation. There has been a rapid growth in the number of educational institutions in India and this has posed some serious challenges. The growth in the number of institutions has created more opportunities to the youngsters to enter the arena of academics. This has also led to a high attrition rate even in the education sector which was unheard earlier. With more and more B-Schools and MBA institutions being established, the excellence of B-Schools depends on the kind of people able to enlist and retained as its faculties. It is the faculty that sets the tone of an educational institution to move forward. The acquisition of faculty has become a major challenge for B-Schools, yet a much bigger challenge is that of a high turnover, since a number of faculty members switch institutions. The sudden loss of these knowledge pool impacts existing academic plans of institution in a negative manner. This has resulted in a scenario where institutions are vying with each other to attract and retain the best available faculty talent. Therefore, it is of utmost importance that institutions should design and pursue policies/mechanisms so as to compete well in marketplace to attract and retain the best faculty talent.

The present paper is an endeavour to understand and suggest possible ways of acquiring and retaining talent in educational institutions. The study is undertaken to ascertain the measures taken by the employers towards talent management as well as the expectations of the teaching fraternity by conducting a primary research.

INTRODUCTION

Globalization has become a universal reality. India is striving to compete in globalized economy in all areas. The dynamic nature of global business is putting an ever-increasing pressure on institutions/universities to be constantly on the lookout for exceptional talent in a market where demand far exceeds supply. But for academics it is extremely serious and sincere in its true sense because it is not only concerned with the society and country at large but with the entire human civilization. The three pillars of any higher education institution are quality of faculty, infrastructure facilities and learning environment. But one of the major issues for higher education is ensuring the continued excellence of its faculty, to continuously improve and compete in the future as the number and diversity of students is increasing. Creating an institutional environment that values the recruitment and retention of an excellent and diverse faculty is more important than ever. This has made talent management one of the most pressing issues facing all organizations and institutions. Pressing imperatives, such as increasing turnover as the economy improves, globalization of education systems, aggressive competition and long-term foresight which creates costly monetary and academic consequences for institutions and academic departments, have intensified the need to acquire, develop, deploy, motivate and retain key talent.

In the broadest possible terms, it is the strategic management of the flow of talent through an organization. Its purpose is to assure that the supply of talent is available to align the right people with the right jobs at the right time based on strategic objectives although 'The Talent War' is looming over the organizations and academic institutions. Hence, talent management is a lot more than yet another HR process. It is a mind set that goes beyond the rhetoric towards a holistic and integrated approach to leveraging the greatest competitive advantage from people. Talent management is about those thoughts and actions that, consistently, over time, become institutional culture. Talent management is more than something to do; it is something to be, a way of working and achieving both short- and long-term success. It is a belief that talent differentiates organization culture and breeds competitive advantage, with benefits for both the individual and the organization.

An empirical study was conducted to ascertain talent management initiatives in higher education institutions by the managements and the requirements and responses of the teaching fraternity.

LITERATURE REVIEW

Teacher attrition has been a topic in the education literature for many years. It has been claimed that teacher attrition is a major problem in our schools. As many as 20% to 50% of new teachers decide to leave the profession in the first three to five years (Ewing, 2001; Ewing & Smith, 2002). Teaching is usually considered a vocation, one involving a long-term career path. Manuel (2003, p. 142) states that teaching isn't usually a drop in, drop out or revolving door type profession. Huberman as early as 1989 established that those who leave the profession usually do so in the first five years of entering the profession. For new teachers, how they survive the first year, if they do, can be a significant factor in decisions about remaining in or leaving the profession (Lang, 1999). For example, a 2003 Victorian Department of Education and Training Report reported that in the United States, a third of teachers leave the profession within three years and almost half within five years. In Britain, a 2003 survey by the University of Buckingham found that 30 per cent of British teachers who left teaching that year had been in the profession for less than five years (Hogan, 2007). The problem of faculty turnover has afflicted all disciplines, particularly in the last ten to twenty years. The market for PhDs outside academia has grown along with the dispersion of knowledge-based activity throughout the economy (Bowen and Schuster, 1986). Those with advanced degrees have proven their employability in a variety of fields. Considering that professors are paid roughly 25% to 30% less than similarly educated professionals, there is cause to worry that an increasing number of faculty will leave for the private sector (Bell, 2001).

The benchmark study of faculty mobility was conducted by Caplow and McGee and published in 1958 as **"The Academic Marketplace"**. Thirty years later, Burke replicated their study, producing "The New Academic Marketplace" in 1988. Burke found that the market for professors had become radically different over those three decades. Beginning teachers are leaving their jobs at an alarming rate that harms both the school, especially urban ones, and student performance (Ingersoll & Smith, 2003; Howard, 2003). Remaining employees are often forced to shoulder increased workloads without a rise in pay. Heightened turnover often has a demoralizing effect on those who remain, as well as a negative effect on prospective employees. More concretely, high turnover is associated with low job satisfaction, poor productivity, and high stress among employees (Olsen, 1993). Nienhuis (1994) describes faculty as mobile, loyal to the discipline rather than the institution. Considering the indications of an upward swing in both components, it is safe to assume that faculty turnover is causing greater problems for many administrators. Faculty who leave voluntarily tend to be characterized by a high achievement orientation (Barnhart, 1995). Bowen and Schuster's American Professors: A National Resource Imperilled, combining several studies, reports a 4% annual rate of attrition in early 1980s.

OBJECTIVES OF THE STUDY

The main objectives of the study are:

- To understand the reasons for the spiralling attrition rates of staff in B-schools.
- To understand management's and teachers' perspectives of talent management.

SCOPE OF STUDY

The study can help in designing strategies so as to acquire, develop and retain talents for an institution. The study will also help in formulating an approach to prioritize the initiatives that institutions need to take for faculty satisfaction and to attain leadership in higher education through talent management.

RESEARCH METHODOLOGY

Descriptive research with convenience sampling through non-probability method has been undertaken for conducting the study.

SOURCE OF DATA

A questionnaire was prepared and data was collected from both management and the faculty members of B-schools in Kanpur and data available on websites and available literature. Information has obtained from 15 heads of institutions/ management and 30 faculty members employed in these institutions in the age group of 25 to 35 years.

CRISIS OF TALENT IN B-SCHOOL

The three pillars of any higher education institution are: quality of faculty, infrastructure facilities and learning environment. With the increasing demand-supply gap, organizations are facing immense war for talent. Like business and industry, education field too is discovering the need for talent so as to meet the new quality standards demanded by the society and is also facing leadership crisis. As is also published by American Association of Collegiate Schools of Business (AACSB) in August 2002 a status report on management education with the alarming title —Management Education at Risk. This report, presented as the follow up to the landmark Porter and McKibbin report of 1988, paints a picture of the business school environment, identifies its main driving forces, and draws some conclusions. The report identified five main issues regarding the general context of management education and the changes that are taking place in this context, namely, the demand for management education, the supply of management education, globalization, technology and resource scarcity. Additionally, it pays attention to issues concerning doctoral education, the relevance of business curricula, and the convergence of degree and non-degree education. As the MBA program became more attractive during the 1980s and 1990s, fewer candidates applied to doctoral programs, preferring instead to go for an MBA degree. And those who had completed their MBA program found it more attractive to re-enter the job market rather than apply for a doctoral program. Furthermore, upon graduation, close to 40 per cent of PhD graduates opted for a career in industry, where compensation packages are often higher and the risk of failing to achieve promotion is lower. In other words, as the demand for highly qualified faculty went up the supply went down, producing an upward pressure on compensation packages for newly hired and existing faculty, particularly those with a strong record. Central in the report is the observation that the marketplace of management education is becoming ever more heterogeneous, giving way to novel marketing strategies and new competitors. In such an environment, attracting and retaining faculty are activities of crucial importance to the longer term well-being of the business schools. This claim is supported by the outcomes of the research by Stumpf et al. (2002) on academic change and leadership. This research shows that deans of 273 US business schools found the imminent shortage of doctoral faculty to be the most important challenge that was facing their business schools in the near future. Disconcertingly, some of the most disturbing observations in this AACSB report exactly relate to recruitment and retention of faculty by business schools. The number of recently earned doctorates in business is rather low compared to the social sciences and the humanities and only 62 percent plans to pursue a career in education (Business Week, 2004).Within the next few years, the shortage of business doctorates is expected to be 1142 rapidly climbing to a shortage of 2419 in 2013(AACSB, 2003). Together with the observations that (1) doctoral enrolments are not expected to increase in the near future, (2) foreseeable faculty retirements, and (3) increasing student enrolment on undergraduate levels in particular, it is clear that business schools will be faced with even enlarging faculty shortages in the coming years AACSB, 2002) As the AACSB sums it up, this faculty shortage may be leading to a decline in research productivity and intellectual vibrancy of existing faculty.

UGC AND AICTE NORMS FOR FACULTY STRUCTURE AND BENEFITS

The knowledge, skills, attitudes and values of staff are aspects which greatly contribute to their own individual effectiveness as well as to institutional performance. In addition to the norms on pattern and structure of staff, guidelines should also emphasize on the process of recruitment, development as well as appraisal.

The ratio of Professors to Associate Professors to Assistant Professors in a UG College shall be in the ratio, ordinarily of 1:2:6. The ratio of Professors to Associate Professors/Assistant Professor in a PG college shall be in the ratio ordinarily of 1:2. This is to provide for situations where the institution may not be able to identify programs to ensure appropriate senior faculty at the U.G. level also. The desirable student to teacher ratio for engineering degree program for the model curriculum will be 10:1. However, it should not be allowed to rise beyond 15:1.

Benefits

Increments: Each annual increment shall be equivalent to 3% of the sum total of pay in there levant Pay Band and the AGP as applicable for the stage in the Pay Band.

Pay 'Fixation Formula: The pay 'fixation formula' recommended by 6th Central Pay Commission as accepted by the Central Government shall be adopted for technical teachers.

Allowances: Allowances such as Leave Travel Concession, Special Compensatory Allowances, Children's Education Allowance, Transport Allowance, House Rent, Allowance, Deputation, Allowance, Travelling Allowance, Dearness Allowance, area based Special Compensatory Allowance, etc. as applicable to teachers and library and physical education cadres, shall be at par with those accepted by the Central Government for Central Government employees.

Study Leave: AICTE shall revise its guidelines in respect of granting study leave with pay for acquiring M. Tech. and Ph.D. in the relevant branch/discipline while in service by relaxing the number of years to be put in after entry while keeping in mind the availability of vacant positions for teachers and other cadres in technical institutions, so that a teacher and other cadres entering service without Ph.D. or higher qualification could be encouraged to acquire these qualifications in the relevant disciplines at the earliest rather than at a later stage of the career.

Sabbatical Leave for Teachers: To encourage interface between technical education and industry, the Committee recommends that a faculty member in an engineering college should be given a sabbatical leave for six months for working in industry after the completion of six years of teaching. Such leave, however, shall be available to a teacher only twice in his/her teaching career.

Research Promotion Grant: AICTE shall prescribe a scheme with appropriate guidelines for providing by way of appropriate 'start up grants' to teachers and other cadres taking up research in all disciplines including basic recommendations of sixth Central Pay Commission and shall be applicable from 1.09.2008

DATA ANALYSIS

Table 1

Reasons	***Respondents***			
	Yes	***Percentage***	***No***	***Percentage***
Staying in the same institution since joining the service	12	40	18	60
Joined service by choice	24	80		
Joined service by chance	6	20		

Table 1 highlights that 80% of the respondents have come to teaching by choice whereas only 20% are in this profession by chance. 40% of the teachers are staying in the same institution since their joining date whereas 60% have changed institutions. This trend shows the dissatisfaction and high attrition rate among teaching fraternity employed ininstitutions.

Reasons for Changing the Institution

Table 2

Reasons	***Respondents***	***Percentage***
Imbalance in workload	6	33
Low salary	18	100
Lack of encouragement for initiatives taken	15	83
No recognition of talents	18	100
College environment is not conducive for growth	16	89

Table 2 suggests that almost 100% of the respondents changed institutions when there was no recognition of talents or when the environment did not support growth. 83% changed the institution when their initiatives were not encouraged. 100% because of low salary and 33% because there was imbalance in the workload. One or more than factor influenced their decision for change.

Talents Possessed by Teachers

Table 3

Reasons	***Respondents***	***Percentage***
Communication skill	30	100
Good body language	27	90
Leadership skills	21	70
Counselling skills	24	80
Other skills (sports, dance, drama, music, etc.)	18	60

Table 3 shows that 100% of respondents possessed good communication skills, 90% possessed good body language, 70% possessed leadership skills, 80% of them possessed counselling skills and 60% were skilled in other areas like sports, dance, music, etc.

Institutional Contribution and Co-operation

Table 4

Reasons	*Respondents*			
	Yes	*Percentage*	*No*	*Percentage*
Institution is a platform to showcase the talent	30	100		
Institutional encouragement to improve the talent	6	20	24	80

Table 4 shows that 100 percent respondents believe that college is a platform to showcase the talent but only 20 percent say that their college encourages them to improve their talent.

Methods of Talent Development

Table 5

Reasons	*Respondents*	*Percentage*
Financial incentives	21	70
Permission to partake in conferences and workshops	24	80
Exemption from clerical work	30	100

Table 5 shows, 100% of the respondents are of the view that their talents could develop if they were given exemption from clerical work in college. 80% are of the opinion that conferences and workshops help in development of talent and 70% opine that financial incentives encourage them.

Management Opinion on Talent Management

Table 6

S. No.	*Management Opinion*	*No. of respondents*	*%*
1.	Responsibility of the head of the institution to (a) Appoint the staff (b) Developing the staff (c) Retaining the staff	 15 15 15	 100 100 100
2.	Attracting right kind of personnel	15	100
3.	High priority for talent management	15	100

Contd.

4.	Methods of identifying the talent: (a) By competency (b) By results (c) By potential	 15 15 15	 100 100 100
5.	Talent development activities carried out by the institutes Regular FDPs Participating/organizing seminars and conferences	15 15	100 100
6.	Talent retention activities (a) Acquiring new talents (b) Leverage existing talents (c) Retain current potential	 15 15 15	 100 100 100
7.	Recruitment methods in your institute are efficient Yes	15	100
8.	Employee turnover in the respective institution – Yes No	03 12	20 80
9.	Losing best employees to the competitors Yes No	03 12	30 80
10.	Is the institution attracting right kind of personnel to facilitate itsgrowth Yes No	12 03	80 20

Table 6 throws light on the attitude and beliefs of the management. A significant 80% of the principals/head of institutions think that they have the best recruitment policies and are able to attract the right kind of teachers. They also believe that they are not losing their best employees to their competitors. Unfortunately the teachers' opinion shows us that they are constantly in search of better employer.

DISCUSSION

On the basis of the above-mentioned literature it is clarified that teachers play a vital role in processing raw products into a finished goods that the corporates demand. Quality teaching is the only technique that makes it possible to transfer knowledge and understanding from teacher to a student that helps the student in decision making after scanning the circumstances and environment. Teacher's excellence is not only essential in moulding and refining the behavioral traits of students but also the characteristics and performance of faculty members, like the number of PhDs on a school's faculty, international profile of faculty, and research output by faculty, plays weighty role in modern business school rankings. Therefore, it is clear that a profile of faculty is not only beneficial for individual's development but also indirectly enhances the goodwill and maintains standards to an institution like, benchmarks we have IMD, IIM, XLRI; etc Therefore, it is of utmost importance that educational institutes should design and pursue policies/mechanisms so as to compete well in marketplace to attract and retain for them the best faculty talent. Future business school affluence hence depends on a principal area of attention within the human resources management function. For deans/directors of business schools it is paramount to develop effective retention policy based on an understanding of the factors that are relevant with respect to faculty retention strategies. This situation demands that management should identify the reason/s for this frequent change of employment by employees. Once reason/s has been identified, management can then devise retention strategies that will help in keeping essential employees for a rather longer tenure. It is therefore imperative for management to reduce, to the minimum, the frequency at which employees, particularly those that are crucial to its operations leave.

Institutions should establish a clear talent management policy and apply them while recruiting teachers. A dedicated/passionate teacher is not looking only for monetary benefits but also conducive work environment and encouragement for their talents and skills. Therefore, a proper environment conducive for the growth of teachers should be created by the management. A sincere effort should be made to identify and encourage their skills. Teachers should be completely exempted from clerical/administrative work. Managements should continuously obtain feedback from the teachers in order to find out if there is any gap in the plans and actions of talent management policies. Teachers should learn and improve their skills by making SWOT analysis of themselves.

LIMITATIONS

The study has the limitation of time. The response of on the questionnaire is taken from two parties, i.e., management and faculty. The third party of this system, i.e., student could not be obtained. The responses of management and faculty members may be biased in their favour.

CONCLUSION

This study was undertaken to establish the importance and the priorities given by the managements and the heads of the institutions to talent management and if the teachers were happy with the talent management policies of their employers. The employers felt that they are doing their best to retain and develop talents while on the contrary the teachers feel that something more and better is expected of the managements and heads of institutions. At this juncture, it becomes very important for both the managements and the teachers to assume responsibility and take sincere steps to bridge this gap. Managements should think beyond appointment of teachers for a limited salary and mere completion of syllabus. Teachers on the other hand, should also realize their responsibilities and concentrate on learning, improving and updating their skills. Many of the institutions in Kanpur are doing well not only because of the talent of their teachers but also because of the increasing number of students who can now afford to join these institutions. The strength of the higher education institutions will start dwindling as is happening at present, resulting in their closure if the institutions are not manned by qualified/ talented/skilled teachers.

Hence, talent management is imperative for educational institutions. In fact, it is high time that talent management initiatives are taken up by the managements of institutions.

References

1. Lyons Richard, "Achieving Effectiveness from Your Adjunct Faculty".
2. Office of Academic affairs, "Faculty Recruitment and Retention", Task Force Report - May 2001.
3. Van Ummersen, Claire A, "No Talent Left Behind: Attracting and Retaining a Diverse Faculty", Change: The Magazine of Higher Learning, Vol. 37, No. 6, p. 26, Nov-Dec 2005.
4. "Flexible and Accommodating Faculty Retention Policies and Programs", Loyola Marymount University, 2009.
5. "Talent Management Trends in Higher Education" People Admin, 2009.
6. Agarawal Jaiprkash, (2007), "Talent Management in self-finanancing institutions", 2nd International Conference, G.L.A. University, Mathura.
7. Gappa, J and D. Leslie (1993). "The Invisible Faculty: Improving the Status of Part-Timers in Higher Education". San Francisco: Jossey-Bas.
8. Kumar Manoj, (2006),"Attracting and Retaining Faculty in Technical Educational Institutions, 4th AIMS International Conference IIM Indore.
9. www.aicte-india.org

33

Current Scenario of Management Education in India

Rashi Saxena
Lecturer, A.I.T.H., Kanpur
E-mail: rash_saxena@rediffmail.com

ABSTRACT

Management education is considered elitist. It attracts young men and women which are usually motivated by the positive consequences associated with management education. In India, higher education especially management education is witnessing a exponential growth in terms of number of institutes imparting management education which are usually termed Business School. This paper tries to explore the present situation of management education in India. This paper also studies the trends prevailing in management education in India, and tries to find out implication of management education in India on industry and individuals. Further, it tries to study emerging issues of management education, and to find implementation of possible direction and policy towards improvement of management education in India. This paper will fill gap between existing literatures as not much of work has been done in this area.

INTRODUCTION

The development of management education can be traced back to 18th century. From 18th century to 21st century, management education has seen lot of changes and development. Management education in India is predominately a derivative of western management thought and practice. Occasionally, management schools draw some inferences from Indian epics, shastras and practices. It may be worthwhile to notice that management itself as a discipline has evolved from fundamental disciplines of philosophy, psychology, economics, accounting, computer science, mathematics, statistics and industrial engineering. In India, management education is seen as elitist. Often, young men and women are attracted to management education not because they need some education, exposure and experience to create something wonderful and hence useful to society but are usually motivated by the positive consequences associated with management education. 21st century India witnessed a sea change in its educational system. Process of liberalization, privatization, and globalization has not only replaced traditional approach with a more efficient professional approach; but also introduced new age courses in accordance with industry demand which have more economic value in today's time.

Management education is one among those which got a new dimension with this changing time. Initially, Marketing, Finance and Human Resource Management were considered functional areas of management, but now management education covers much more functional area like Operations, Information Technology, International Business.

India has witnessed a continuing growth in this sphere of education because of the rising demand of trained management graduates. Management education has become one of the most sought after education today as a result of this; private sector has entered in Indian management scenario and invested an immense amount for this. Management education in India is not very old, after the establishment of the IITs, there was dire need for similar establishments in the field of management education. Thus, came into existence the Indian Institute of Management Ahmedabad (IIMA), followed soon after by one in Kolkata (IIMC). Starting with the establishment of 4 Indian Institutes of Management Calcutta (1961), Ahmedabad (1962), Bangalore (1973), Lucknow (1984), now management education is being offered as full time/part time MBA programs by some leading universities in the country. Recently and particularly during the last 4-5 years the country has witnessed a tremendous growth in the founding of management institutions most of them in private sector offering management programs in different functional areas of management. Concurrently, there is a mushrooming of B-schools in the country (over 2500 institutes, of which about 1940 are certified by the All India Council for Technical Education (AICTE)), leading to issues of quality.

Review of Studies

Management education in India was initiated just after independence with establishment of Indian Institute of Management since then various changes, challenges, issues and implications have been pointed out. Sangeeta Sahney et al. (2004) pointed Indian educational system has been subjected to fast, radical, and ever revolutionary change over recent years. Panandiker, V. A. (1991) pointed out that knowledge and knowledge- creation will be far more central to the management education of the future rather than technology. He further added that humans will live not by bread and car alone but far more by knowledge, wisdom and ideas. This fundamental transformation of management education is both inevitable and necessary because the present consumption patterns of mankind can only take him thus far in its evolution and no further. We are therefore going to experience in the next decade altogether different focus of organizations and management systems. It will, therefore, be necessary to anticipate and study some of their contours so that we design appropriate system of management education as early as possible. Sahu K.C. (1991) emphasized that values are of utmost importance and are inseparable irrespective to any form of education, Management education should produce persons with such value orientation, who, through example of dedicated hard work in a spirit of service, can change the attitude of the people they manage towards work, and towards each other to ensure quality of life and of work life. Margaret McNamara et al. (1990) stressed on action learning in management education as management institutes are often criticized for focusing more on theory and on quantitative analysis while neglecting interpersonal relationship and quantitative finding. It is often stated that management education should be experience-based, active, problem oriented and modified by feedback and action learning serves the purpose. A. Gill (2003) emphasized due to globalization and advancement in information technology the role played by management education in enhancing country knowledge base has been placed under a sharper focus thus it has become imperative to look at management education from the market oriented perspective and take a strategic view to better align business.

Education with the requirement of the global market. Basu Sharma et al. (1996) pointed out that internationalization of management has been promoted along several dimensions such as curricula challenge, research activites with both contents and outlet being relevant and executive development programs. It seems that educational institutions and supplementary providers of management education have no choice but to rise to the challenge of global competition. Management education in India is at crossroads with the dawn of new millennium there has been exceptional growth in management institutes, to upgrade their competencies the financial autonomy will be the key and academic autonomy would be the major drivers. Chowdhry, K. (1977) wrote in his article that after independence, a combination of events, people and government policies came together in a unique way to professionalize management education in India. As a result of this unique interaction several institutions of management came into being in the 1950s and 1960s. Since the very first institute for imparting management education was set up almost five decades has passed, during this period management education has been subject to radical and revolutionary changes. Management education can be more meaningfully viewed as a process, rather than a program with twin objectives first, change in role behavior and second, effective influence of individual practising managers upon their organization. Management education in India today has acquired the characteristics of a commodity, to be bought and sold in markets like other commodities.

Research Issue

From the above review of studies, we have taken the following research issues which are different from earlier management thinkers, practitioners and researchers.

1. To find the present situation of management education in India after financial turbulence of USA and the case like Satyam in India.
2. To study the trends prevailing in management education in India.

3. To find out implications of management education of India on industry and individuals.
4. To study emerging issues of management education and its approach towards the development of curriculum needs of industry.
5. To find implementation of possible direction and policy towards improvement of management education in India.

Present Situation in India

Today managers are in great demand in every sector of economy. India needs a huge reservoir each year of people who are trained for business and for management and demands is to last for coming years. But it is matter of concern whether the demand is for what they have been taught. In management education, quality has become a necessity. To make India an intellectual capital of the world, we have to create a dynamic environment, which can encourage superior quality management education colleges and effort should be made to breathe life into management education. Government has taken initiatives in this direction by giving node to 7 more IIMs taking the total number of the premier management school to 14. India already has 11 functional IIMs in Ahmedabad, Bangalore, Kolkata, Lucknow, Indore, Kozhikode, Shillong, Tiruchirappalli, Ranchi, Raipur and Rohtak remaining three are to setup in state of J&K, Uttarakhand and Rajasthan. Apart from IIMs management education is offered by university's own department in campus, affiliated colleges of universities in same place or the whole state, now technical universities have been given this role. Moreover, autonomous institutes approved by AICTE, universities running distance education programs and open mode like IGNOU, Delhi University, Kurukshetra University, ICFAI and several others are also offering courses in management. Some recognized institutes and universities are also offering 3 years part time program in evening faculty for working executives. Foreign universities having collaborations in India and those having students exchange program with limited-time studies abroad are also imparting management education. New private universities like ICFAI (a national brand), Amity and several others are also coming up.

According to annual report (2009-2010), published by Ministry of Human Resource Development, there were 20 universities and 500 colleges at the time of independence. At present, there are 504 universities and university-level institutions (as on 31.12.2009) 243 state universities, 53 state private universities, 40 central universities, 130 deemed universities, 33 institutions of national importance established under Acts of Parliament five institutions established under various State legislations. There are 25,951 colleges of which, 7362 are recognized under 2(f) and 5997 colleges recognized under section 2(f) and declared fit to receive grants under section 12(B) of the UGC Act, 1956). Table (1) shown below shows growth of AICTE approved technical institutes in last five years. In 2008-2009 the number of institutes increased at an exceptional rate, thus can be called the golden year in respect to establishment of institutes. In last 5 years the number of AICTE approved colleges has increased by almost 70% in total in various disciplines, whereas number of management institutes has seen growth of 90% in terms of number of institutes and growth of 123% in terms of intake.

Management Education after Financial Crisis and Satyam Incident

Western corporate world is infatuated with operational efficiency and not necessarily effectiveness. Today organizations center more on performance rather than organizational purpose which is perhaps the root cause of the morality crisis, governance issues, and slipshod behavior of corporate citizens in the overall global context. Financial crisis in U.S. and Satyam incident in India has raised issues against management education. Western management education is based on the principle of 'individual excellence' and on the concept of the 'economic man'. Financial crisis was the result of greed of economic man and opportunism which is the direct result of way management education is being imparted. The modern management education in India stresses on performance and very little on purpose. It equips the young men and women to generate wealth and does not provide them the capacity to enjoy and share this wealth. It motivates individuals to accomplish their objectives with or without regard to means. The criticisms directed at management education generally revolve around two claims: first, that the crisis was brought about by managers educated in business schools which do not pay enough attention to social responsibility, ethics and governance; and, second, that some theories or models are taught at management school could be held responsible for the crisis, such as the principal-agent model or the portfolio model in finance. On other side episode like Satyam has given rise to new controversy and forced to make comparison like Satyam vs Enron, PWC vs A.C. Nielson and Ramalinga Raju vs Kenneth Lay and has questioned acumen and ethics of business managers. The future will see changes in business schools curriculum and management research. Future research will include questions of diagnosis and prediction and this will help in explaining and preventing future global economic meltdowns. Moreover the need to teach business within a global context will be more emphasized. Economic impacts are felt around the world whenever a major economy experiences challenges. It is also clear that developing economies like India need the attention and expertise from business school educators. Business education should fully encourage and stress the importance of socially responsible and honest conduct. Changes in curriculum, particularly in MBA programs, will cover ethics, governance, sustainability and corporate social responsibility to greater extent and will be imparted more rigorously. While more could certainly be done to further the integration of those issues with the functional areas of management. There is certainly room to stress integrative thinking, the importance of a global outlook and the development of responsible leaders. Other more significant changes inspired by the crisis could affect executive education and the development of specialized masters programs. Undergraduate programs might be also impacted. Complication of financial markets, coupled with the dynamics of globalization and the demands for responsible behavior will, together, lead to a number of interesting new programs and specializations at both the undergraduate and postgraduate levels. To conclude, it can be expected that management education to be marginally impacted. And, finally, it may lead to real innovations that might result in development of specialized masters programs on one hand, and new multidisciplinary collaborations on the other. Further, it brings a hidden opportunity for business schools to contribute to the development of better organizations and institutions, and thus to serve society for the greater good.

Trends in Management Education in India

The management education plays an essential role in today's dynamic business environment. The rapid trend of globalization and technological changes have made difficult for organizations to survive in the competitive world. As a result the importance of management education has been increased manifold. There are more than 2000 B-schools in India where students pay a massive sum hoping to find their dream career after completing their programs. Unfortunately, these business schools are not even able to place more than 50% of student except few top B schools. This is really an issue for concern and various reasons can be attached to it. These reasons can be explained from institutes imparting education, from student seeking education, and affiliating authorities. Quality has deteriorated from both ends, institutes imparting education and student gaining education. There are fundamental issues of student input quality. In addition, there are fundamental issues of academic delivery quality as most run-of-the-mill colleges spend less than 10 percent of their revenues on actual academic delivery. Most college owners complain of not being able to have enough admission in spite of investing on college infrastructure and startup costs. And those that are able to fill capacity they admit anyone who applies for admission thus resulting in poor input, leading to poor placements. After the introduction of ranking system for business schools, business schools opted proactive approach in making changes, although they focused primarily on product tinkering, packaging and marketing. A study on management education has shown that there will be a fundamental shift in business school product offerings away from traditional MBA programs and the trends of evolution of management education indicate that knowledge creation is becoming more student based (Friga, Bettis and Sullivan, 2003). This will result in various changes such as closer interaction among industry, students and faculty. It is clear that management education will emerge as one of the main distinct of higher learning, due to its growing demand. It has been stated that business schools, if they have to survive, have to focus on research to solve problems of enduring importance and to build such curricula that can actually prepare students to be effective in practicing the profession.

Emerging Issues of Management Education in India

This section discusses a number of issues that are relevant to management education in generally and management education in India in particular. Management education in India has not changed as per the requirement of the industry need and before this gaps widen enough; proper steps need to be taken. In this section we aim to disuses various emerging issues of Management Education in India which can helps us getting rid of this gap and produce managers as per requirement of industry and society, respond to challenges that comes with dynamics of internationalization There have been various committees that suggested improvements in management education, their has been no noteworthy changes.

1. Dedicated Governmental Body for Management Education

In India, governance of technical and management education is looke after by All India Council for Technical Education and its subsidiary the Board of Management Studies. Since both technical and management education have different requirement, so it definitely call for different body which could specifically look for issues related to improvement in management education which should be accountable for enabling independent institutional mechanism to specifically deal with management education that could lead to enhancement of standard of management education and give a new drive to management education. As stated in an article by Mr. R. Gopalakrishnan, a National Task Force on management education should be appointed that could look into the possibility of formation of All India Council of Management Education quite independent of AICTE. Issues like quality of faculty and research, interaction with industry and academia to produce world-class managers, and other issues of importance should also be addressed.

2. Quality of Faculty

AICTE and University Grants Commission have given sanctioning and affiliation to large number of institute, but were unable to produce competent faculty to teach in management courses, which created a demand supply gap and resulted in low standard quality of faculty. Institutes are engaged in appointing new faculty members on low salaries and heavy teaching load which further deteriorate their quality and they are left with no time for further development, and involving part time faculty which had little or no involvement with the institutes. Generally, they give lecture prepared from textbooks or their company based experience. The quality of management remained inferior in the sense that they paid not enough attention to application of knowledge, understanding of concepts, development of managerial skills institutions.

3. Curriculum Design and Developing Material Relevant to the Indian Context

Developing a curriculum is a challenging task and has to be continuously updated to keep pace with the advancements. Curriculum should be change driven and periodically reviewed to match the industry needs. But in most of Indian universities and B-School it takes years to get syllabus revised due to bureaucratic setup and private B-School also don't show much enthusiasm towards revision of syllabus because it may call for appointing new faculty and updating existing faculty which could be a costly issue. Institutes imparting management education should ensure to revise their syllabus. Course content need not just be latest but also country specific. We don't have much of Indian specific case studies which could help in bringing the congruence and rationality between what is taught and what is practice.

4. Emphasizing Research

The management institutions do not provide conducive environment that is supportive to research. Management institutes need to work in this direction. Research not only leads to updating of knowledge in concerned subject, but also leads to knowledge creation. Promoting a research culture in a management institutes requires change of mindset on the side of management. They need to look beyond just making money. Management institutes should inculcate proper motivation and interest among faculty for research. This can be done by providing incentives to faculty involved in research, giving due weight age to research activities and providing a good library support system. University Grants Commission has already taken step in this direction by giving due weight age to research and publication for promotions. This need to be extended and implemented not only in government universities and institutes, but all institutes imparting business education.

5. Corporate Governance for B-Schools

Corporate Governance has been buzz words for last few months especially after financial turndown in U.S.A. and Satyam case in India. Lack of corporate governance system in management institutes is one of the major reasons for fall of quality management education. Corporate governance has to be made a part of accreditation. Government must take the governance of management education away from AICTE and a strong monitoring system and statutory reporting on the lines of SEBI, handled by independent management specialists should be enforced. There is a need to introduce independent audit committees for managing the B-Schools. Corporate governance should include mandatory disclosure by institutions on faculty qualification, books and journals in library, computer labs, placement records and other required information that could be useful for student while choosing institutions. According to UGC norms institutes have to display this all information on the Internet but there is big difference between actual and information displayed on the Internet or filed with concerned statutory bodies. Corporate governance should ensure a heavy penalty for any such deviation. The AICTE has little muscle to discover these and other misdeeds. Very rarely have disobedient institutions been made answerable or penalized. Institutes are imparting courses on corporate governance, but they hardly practice.

6. Triad of Academic Industry

Development of industry interaction is an evolutionary process. Industry interaction has to be emphasized to greater extent so that student can be exposed to real problems and exposure of industry. In present curriculum student are exposed to six to eight weeks training which is not adequate to understand dynamics of industry in this world of liberalization and globalization. This need to be increased say to full semester. Assessment should also be based on internship authenticity and learning. As stated earlier enhancement of industry exposure which will lead to enhancement of experiential learning. Exposing students to real life situations which are more complex, demanding, critical, messy, will bring them closer to reality. Faculty interaction with executives should be enhanced by increasing participation of industry experts in academics either by appointing them as full time faculty or part time faculty. Institutions should be encouraged to arrange tie ups with business houses. If you talk about top notch B-Schools their strengths lies in their industry liaisoning.

7. Customization of Specializations

Customization is the need of a day. Every industry has its on set of challenges and dynamics, and it requires specific skill set and expertise. This could be only done by bringing specialization in concerned field. Management Education today is not just confined to areas as marketing, Finance and Human Resource Management, its requirement is felt in growing areas of business such as hospital management, disaster management, infrastructure management, ITES which needs faculty specialization curricula customization, specific material development. Though some B-Schools has taken initiative in extending boundaries of management education by introducing courses in disaster management. Aviation management, financial services. But their course contents are questionable as they are using material designed for other context in these courses without examining its contextual validity. These business need customized course content specially designed for the course, specialized faculty and material development. These factors are hardly paid any heed thus contributing to poor quality management education in India.

8. Multiple Perspectives

Management education is a value laden field, but its value is deteriorating not just because the way it is imparted, but also due to its nature. Management education needs to inculcate multiple perspectives since technological, organization and personal perspectives could differ. Linstone pointed out management is all about grappling with multiple perspectives. Management education need reconstruction with emphasis on explicitly imparting education in regard to political, ethical and philosophical nature of management practice and managers need to attend to interpersonal relationships, feeling, stress, emotional outburst, politics, and difference in opinion and like. Above discussion tells us need for manager to connect to wide array of duties which can only be done if management education is imparted aiming multiple perceptive.

9. Exposing to Real Business Issues

As stated earlier there is need for enhancing industry exposure which will lead to enhancement of experiential learning. Exposing students to real-life situations which are more complex, demanding, critical, messy, will bring them closer to reality. When it comes to decision making, experience that lies with decision maker is detrimental. One of the issues that management education has to consider is the manner in which experiential learning elements could be enhanced.

10. Inculcating a Global Mindset

Learning is a relative concept. Today success depends how fast you are enhancing your knowledge, sharpening your skills and pace of your learning. In globalization era where information is increasing at pace of Pico seconds mastering knowledge and skills have become essential. If India needs to compete globally we need manager with world-class talent which calls for developing a new approach of imparting teaching and learning. Global mindset need to be developed. This means that each business school should create a differentiated mix of teaching and training to develop not managers but global managers.

CONCLUSION

In the above sections we discussed present scenario prevailing in management education in India, trends and contemporary issues faced by management education in India. The outcome of all this is that management education appear to be more relevant than ever in the "global era". The ultimate challenge of management education approaches is to become more practical oriented and industry focus reason being theory-based developments and teachings are worthless, due to the fact that they will be of little use in concrete situations when a management issue arises. Management education needs to be holistic, targeted and customized with aim to remove the gap that exist between industry requirements and academic curriculum focusing on attitude, corporate awareness, grooming and developing managerial skills. Industry interaction has to be strengthened by inviting senior person from industry to deliver lecture and ensuring student get associated with live industry projects. Learning needs to student-centric resulting in development in all areas such as analytical reasoning, lateral thinking, and solving case studies and as such. Mentoring and carrier counseling has to be introduced Most B-schools claim to have it but only as a lip service. If management education in India has to really extend its image on international scenario beyond AIM's, institutes, industry and government has to work in alignment to improve quality of management education.

References

1. Angehrn, A. & Nabeth, T. (1997) "Leveraging Emerging Technologies in Management Education: Research and Experiences", European Management Journal, Vol. 15, No. 3, pp. 275–285.
2. Bandyopadhyay, R. (1991) "Indian Management Education: Need for a Constructive Debate", Economic and Political Weekly, Vol. 26, No. 48, pp. M118-M122.
3. Baumgartel, H. J., Pathan, R., Roy, B. Khandelwal, G. & Rahman, A., (1984) "Changes in Organizational Climate and Management Education, 1968 to 1981: Some Warning Signals", Economic and Political Weekly, Vol. 19, No. 8, pp. M15-M21.
4. Bowonder, B. and Rao, S.L. (2004) "Management Education in India its evolution and some contemporary issues, "available at: http://www.aima-ind.org /pdf/ Director_ Conclave_ 9_Paper.pdf (accessed 25 October 2010).
5. Cornuel, E. (2005) "The role of business schools in society", Journal of Management Development, Vol. 24, No. 9, pp. 819–829.
6. Crowther, D. and Carter, C. (2002) "Legitimating Irrelevance: management education in higher education in institutions", The International Journal of Educational Management, Vol. 16, No. 6, pp. 268–278.
7. D'Mello, B. (1999) "Management Education: A Critical Appraisal", Economic and Political Weekly, Vol. 15, No. 22 (May 31, 1980), pp. Published, Vol. 34, No. 48, pp. M169-M176.
8. Dr. Priya, A. (2007) "Global World & Quality of Management Education in India", available at: http://www.indianmba.com/faculty_column/fc631/fc631.html(accessed 25 October 2010).
9. Engwall, L. (2007) "The anatomy of management education", Scandinavian Journal of Management, Vol. 23, pp. 4–35.
10. Ganesh, S. R. (1980) "Performance of Management Education Institutions: An Indian Sampler", Higher Education, Vol. 9, No. 3, pp. 239–253.

11. Gill, A. & Lashine, S. (2003) "Business education: A Strategic market-oriented focus",The International Journal of Educational Management, Vol. 17, No. 5, pp. 188–194.
12. MacNamara, M., Meyler, M. & Arnold, A. (1990) "Management Education and the Challenge of Action Learning", Higher Education, Vol. 19, No. 4, pp. 419–433.
13. Matthai, R. J. (1980) "The Organisation and the Institution: Management Education in India", Economic and Political Weekly, Vol. 15, No. 22, pp. M69-M72.
14. McNulty, N. G., Katkov, A. & McNulty, N. C., (1992) "Management Education in Eastern Europe: "Fore and After", The Executive, Vol. 6, No. 4, pp. 78–87.
15. Pai Panandiker, V. A. (1991) "Management Education: A Long-Term View", Economic and Political Weekly, Vol. 26, No. 48, pp. M131-M132.
16. Patel, I. (1996) "India", International Review of Education, Vol. 42, No. 1/3 (1996), pp. 75–96. © Research Journal of Internatıonal Studıes - Issue 18 (January, 2011) 25.
17. Patry, M. (2010) "Business Education and the Current Economic Crisis: An Institutional Perspective", available at: http://www.gfme.org/business_schools/ business_education.htm (accessed 20 October 2010).
18. Powell, N. K. and Westwood, J. B. (1978) "Buyer-Behaviour in Management Education", Journal of the Royal Statistical Society. Series C (Applied Statistics), Vol. 27, No. 1, pp. 69–72.
19. Pylee, M. V. (1967) "Management Education in India", Management Science, Series C, Vol. 13, No. 10, pp. C209-C217.
20. Ravichandran, N. (2009) "A perspective on management education in India", available at: http://www.financialexpress.com/printer/news/527793 (accessed 24 October 2010)
21. Roy, S. K. (1970) "Management Education: A Perspective for Its Evaluation", Economic and Political Weekly, Vol. 5, No. 9, pp. M19-M22.
22. Sahu, K. C. (1991) "Reorienting Management Education", Economic and Political Weekly, Vol. 26, No. 48, pp. M133-M136.
23. Saxena, N. (2009) "How to improve management education in India?", available at: http://timesascent.in/article/83/2009091020090910145228171479914ef/How-to-improvemanagement-education-in-India.html, (accessed 20 October 2010).
24. Sharma, B. and Roy, J. A. (1996) "Aspects of the internationalization of management education", Journal of Management Development, Vol. 15, No. 1, pp. 5–13.
25. Sheth, N. R. (1991) "What Is Wrong with Management Education", Economic and Political Weekly, Vol. 26, No. 48, pp. M123-M128.

26. Thorat, S. (2005) "Higher Education in India Emerging Issues Related to Access, Inclusiveness and Quality", paper presented at the Nehru Memorial Lecture, 26 November, University of Mumbai, Mumbai, available at: http// www.ugc.ac.in/chairman _nehru_lecture.pdf (Accessed 29 October 2010).
27. "Management Education in India.", available at http: //www .sooperarticles. com/educationarticles/international-studies-articles/management-education-india-30505.html (accessed on 24 October 2010).
28. http://www.education.nic.in/stats/statpub.asp (accessed on 8 December 2010).
29. http://www.aicte-india.org/misappgrowth.htm (accessed on 8 December 2010).

34

Impact of Incorporating Transactional and Transformational Leadership on Managerial Effectiveness: An OD Intervention

Tulika Saxena
Associate Professor, Dept. of Management, STEP-HBTI, Kanpur
E-mail: tulika_28@yahoo.com

ABSTRACT

Leadership is the factor that makes all the difference in today's competitive and dynamic world. This paper evaluates how at times declining transformational leadership functions causes poor corporate leadership. This paper makes an attempt to identify how far India faces true leadership crisis. It deals with the issues and challenges of effective leaders working as managers. This research is based on the study of managerial leadership from a sample of 45 senior managers, out of which 20 respondents on the first day and 25 managers on the second day participated in the HRD workshop belonging to public sector, Indian organization of repute. The study emphatically distinguishes between transactional (management) and transformational (leadership) functions of corporate leaders serving as managers in organizations and argues that quest for managerial leadership is essentially a transformational journey towards new identity. Data was generated through standard questionnaire method and various phases of observation to yield qualitative and quantitative information, treated by rank-orders, in order to explore the priorities assigned to transactional and transformational components of corporate leadership. The paper also attempts to identify dominant deficient and backup dimensions of leadership among senior managers as a part of their managerial efficacy.

INTRODUCTION

The corporate manager has to function, both as a leader and as a manager, i.e., he has to perform transformational as well as transactional functions. Transactional functions are primarily concerned with achievement of tasks and work is done based on agreed plans, and a contract to reward people for good work is the key component. Leaders have an obligation to get things done, ensure achievement of targets and maximize efficiency and effectiveness of the organization as a whole. Transformational functions, on the other hand are primarily concerned with getting performance from people beyond expectations, by going beyond the contractual relationship by inspiring them, stimulating them and paying attention to them.

No matter what leaders set out to do—whether it's creating strategy or mobilizing teams to action—their success depends on how they do it." (Goleman, 2002, p. 3)

Leadership has been defined in so many ways and by different authors and experts. Noel Tichy and Cohen (1997) the authors of "Leadership Engine" point out:

The scarcest resource in the world today is the leadership talent capable of continuously transforming organizations to win in tomorrow's world. The individuals and organizations that build Leadership Engines and invest in leaders developing other leaders have a sustainable competitive advantage. (p. 8)

According to Tichy and Cohen: Winning leaders with a proven record take direct responsibility for developing other leaders .Winning leaders can articulate and teach others about how to make the organization successful. They tell stories about their past and explain their learning experiences and beliefs .They have well-developed methodologies for teaching others.

Leadership talent can be nurtured and it is never too late or early to develop one own leadership abilities and talent of others. Leaders are normally viewed as those people who motivate one or more people to do a specific thing. Warren Bennis says that the basis of the leadership is the capacity to change the mindset or framework of the other person. (Tichy and Cohen, 1997) Briane Lee (1997) of Franklin Covey after reviewing a number of studies on leadership states after a review of modern definitions of leadership that leadership is: "An intensely human enterprise, and does not fit neatly into definitions and boxes. Leaders have all the spontaneity, unpredictability, frailty, vulnerability and potential that is possible in the human race. If we are to lead with honor, we must start with the premise that flexibility, adaptability, and wisdom are possible, that we have seeds of greatness in us, and if we care deeply about the lives of others, we can work together to accomplish worthwhile things."(p. 265).

The ability to spend more time framing contexts and less time defining the content more through coaching and supporting rather than directing and controlling becomes the model for middle managers (Ghosal and Bartlet, 1997).

LITERATURE REVIEW

Although the Oxford English Dictionary (1933) noted the appearance of the word "leader" in the English language as early as the year 1300, the word "leadership" did not appear until the first half of the nineteenth century. Surveys of job satisfaction from the 1920s onward illustrated the importance of leadership.

Many researches have studied (Bennis & Nanus, 1985; Conger & Kanungo, 1978; House, 1977, Kuhnert & Lewis, 1987; Sashkin, 1988; Tichy & Devanna, 1986) behavior and traits of transformational leaders which includes empathy, need for power, good rhetorical followers to gain their commitment, and make them feel that they are being traded with due respect and dignity. Thus, they reflect the behavior and traits required for initiating change such as strong analytical and diagnostic skills, a high energy level, a business strategist and risk taker, crisis management skill, and good negotiation skill.

According to the accepted view (Bass, 1985) transactional and transformational leadership should not be viewed as opposing approaches to getting things done. Transformational leadership is built on top of transactional leadership; it produces levels of follower effort and performance that go beyond what would occur with a transactional approach alone. Moreover, transformational leadership is more than charisma. "The purely charismatic leader may want followers to adopt the charismatic world view and go on further. The transformational leader will attempt to instill in followers the ability to question not only established views but also eventually those established by the leader."

Burns conceived leaders to be either transformational or transactional, but the paradigm was modified by Bass (1985a, 1985b), who proposed that transformational leadership augments the effects of transactional leadership on the efforts, satisfaction, and effectiveness of subordinates. The transformational-transactional differentiation has formed the basis of sundry and other books since Burns's seminal work (Bass, 1985a; Bennis & Nanus, 1985; Tichy & Devanna, 1986). Burns identified two types of political leadership transactional and transformational. The more traditional transactional leadership involves an exchange relationship between leaders and followers, but transformational leadership is based more on leaders shifting the values, beliefs and needs of their followers. An example of the later was the interviews with top executives of major companies conducted by Tichy and Devanna. They found that effective transformational leaders share the following characteristics. They identify themselves as change agents. They are courageous, they believe in people, they are value-driven, they are lifelong learners, they have the ability to deal with complexity, ambiguity and uncertainty, and they are visionaries.

The characteristics and approaches of transactional and transformational leaders based on research findings of Bass (1990).

Transactional Leaders

Contingent Reward: Contracts exchange of rewards for effort, promises rewards for good performance, recognizes accomplishments.

Management by Exception (active): Watches and searches for deviations from rules and standards, takes corrective action.

Management by Exception (passive): Intervenes only if standards are not met.

Laissez-faire: Abdicates responsibilities, avoids making decisions.

Transformational Leaders

Charisma: Provides vision and sense of mission, instills pride, gains respect and trust.

Inspiration: Communicates high expectations, uses symbols to focus efforts, expresses important purposes in simple ways.

Intellectual Stimulation: Promotes intelligence, rationality, and careful problem solving.

Individualized Consideration: Gives personal attention, treats each employee individually, coaches, and advises.

Transformational leadership brings about change, innovation and entrepreneurship. They describe the process of corporate transformation that recognize the need for revitalization, created a new vision and institutionalize change (Seltzer & Bass, 1990).

Transformational leadership style emphasizes the importance of vision building and the ability to communicate this vision, and simultaneously, enthuse subordinates to make their vision a reality: "to innovate, to change, and indeed to conquer new frontiers in the marketplace or on the shop floor" (Guest, 1990).

Shamir and Howell (1999) proposed transformational organization impose fewer constraints on members activities, and offer fewer cues as to the appropriate behaviors, appeal to shared values and identities and linking members self-concepts to the organizational members to exercise discretion and suppress the expression of individual differences by both leaders and followers. Effective leadership entails the factors and dominions of vision trust, listening, authenticity, integrity, hope, addressing the true needs of the followers.

Research on transformational leadership (Bass, 1985, 1990; Trichy and Devanna, 1986; Teppar, 1993; Keller, 1992; Chatterjee, 1997; Zohar, 2001) has identified several characteristics of leadership. These become relevant to the degree to which organizations are transformational or transactional. Transactional leadership is reported (Bass, 1990) to be a prescription for mediocrity and transformational leadership is supposed to lead to superior performance in organizations facing demands for renewal and change.

Till date, effective leadership eludes many people and organizations, more so because, no quantitative research has been able to demonstrate which precise leadership behavior would yield most positive result. Most of the leadership experts proffer advice based on inference, experience and instinct, which only at times is correct. Different scholars have attempted to categorize the leadership styles, but in practice, never any leader can be singled as adopting just one of the style. Thus, optimizing the mix of the different style to attain the highest level of effectiveness for a leader has been the main contention among the researchers (Goleman 2000). Here the research work of relevance (Goleman, 2000) suggested that it is the power and emotions that can help to decide upon the right style at right time and in the right measure.

STATEMENT OF THE PROBLEM

This study attempts to identify the impact of two different leadership styles on the managerial effectiveness in the organization as perceived by 45 top and middle level managers in an Indian organization. Senior managers are highly sensitive to the cultural nuances, unique to India and sought to incorporate culture-specific modes in bringing about transformation and change. A priority between transactional and transformational functions of leadership is emerging as a crucial challenge for managerial leadership for ensuring the sustained success to an organization in the highly competitive business environment. Leaders must be supported by organizational culture and corporate management to have autonomy to serve in their own style as per need of the situation and environment.

MAIN OBJECTIVES OF THE STUDY

- To study the priorities for transactional and transformational functions of corporate leadership assigned by the senior managers and its impact on their managerial effectiveness.
- To perform a macro-analysis of corporate leadership profile of the senior managers.
- To find out the dominant, dormant and backup dimensions/functions of corporate leadership of senior managers.

LEADERSHIP FUNCTIONS

Leaders need to perform both transactional and transformational functions: (leaders include senior manager), a list of the main functions were prepared and classified into two groups: transactional and transformational.

Transactional Functions

Leaders have an obligation to get things done, ensure achievement of targets and maximize efficiency and effectiveness of various groups. Transactional function includes following dimensions:

Policy Making: The leader arranges to set priorities and directions for organizational work, and create linkages among several aspects of the organization.

Planning: The next logical step is to plan various activities in order to translate policies into action.

Developing Systems: Organizational leaders work towards institutionalization of practices and change. This can be done by developing systems on various aspects of the organization.

Monitoring Performance: Managerial control of workforce requires effective monitoring. Monitoring is done against the accepted standards and agreed plans.

Coordinating: When individuals and groups work in synergy, duplication is avoided and mutual support is ensured.

Rewarding: Senior managers reward good performance of exemplary behavior of individuals and teams. This reinforces their behavior, and also the behavior of others.

Coaching: This includes helping them to know their own strengths and weaknesses, and improve their performance in future.

Transformational Functions

While transactional functions are primarily concerned with achievement of tasks, transformational functions go beyond the immediate task and build individuals and groups and enable them to achieve targets that the organization or individual would never have expected. The following functions fall in this category:

Visioning: The management cadre creates vision for the organization. Vision is the dream, which inspires people and makes them proud of working in the organization.

Modeling: A way to inspire people is to set a personal example of a desirable style and behavior.

Setting Standards: High standards and norms inspire individual employees to follow them in their own work.

Building Culture and Climate: Senior managers pay major attention to building climate of excellence, commitment, mutual support, etc.

Boundary Management: The important function of top leaders is to create conditions conducive to better performance by various groups.

Synergising: The strength of an organization depends on the strength of its teams. Team building is one of the very important roles of management.

Searching and Nurturing Talent: Competent, committed individuals with a larger vision are the ultimate strength of an organization. Senior managers pay attention to serve as mentor for the organizational employees.

RESEARCH METHODOLOGY

The interactive HRD workshop was conducted on 45 participants. On the first day, numbers of participants were twenty and on the second day, it was twenty-five.

The timings of the workshop were from 10 a.m. to 1 p.m. and 2 p.m. to 5 p.m. with a lunch break of an hour.

Design of the Study

The first session comprised administration of the questionnaire to the managers while they were on the job and collection of filled in questionnaires and personal meeting programs with the subjects. To determine the functional factors of effective leadership, it was felt appropriate to address the questionnaire to managerial cadre alone.

Respondents were requested to go through the instructions given on the questionnaire and put their queries before filling out, during the workshop. The respondents were assured that this was an academic exercise and their responses would be kept confidential and will be used for research purpose only.

In the second phase, the subjects gave their reactions about the relevance of the items in the tools with their day-to-day functions.

The third phase comprised action/brainstorming phase. In this session the results of the responses to the questionnaire were correlated and discussed with the participants to arrive at conclusions and suggestions.

Sample

The study has covered 45 senior managers serving a public sector organization as respondents; composed of a comparatively small group of executives, i.e., top and the middle management and are responsible for the overall management of the organization.

Tool

Senior Managerial Functions Schedule Senior Managerial Function Schedule (SMFS) developed by Udai Pareek was used for the study. SMFS consists of a list of fourteen functions (seven are transactional and seven are transformational) is as follows:

Policy making
Visioning
Planning
Modeling/inspiring
Setting standards
Developing systems
Monitoring performance
Boundary management
Coordinating
Synergising

Rewarding
Developing Talent/mentoring
Coaching
Building culture and climate

The Instrument and Its Administration: Senior Management Functions Schedule is designed to find out which transactional and transformational functions are being given priority by senior managers in an organization. The instrument is meant for the top leaders/senior managers.

SMFS consists of a list of fourteen functions (seven are transactional and seven are transformational.) The respondent is required to indicate the priority of his attention/time to different functions by distributing hundred points among the fourteen listed functions.

Scoring: Scores given to each function gauge the priority of the function. The responses of senior managers are added to give a profile of the group. The various functions can also be rated on a scale from 1 to 10, although forced distribution of hundred points gives a more authentic profile. The total of transactional functions (items number 1, 3, 6, 7, 9, 11 and 13) and transformational functions (2, 4, 5, 8, 10, 12 and 14) may also be calculated.

Reliability: Cronbach Alpha for a group of 19 was found to be 94.

Validity: Responses from a group of eighteen senior insurance managers were factor analyzed (principal components analysis with varimax rotation). Factor analysis produced six factors, explaining 85% variance. The factor analysis provides construct validity of the instrument.

Factors, 1, 3 and 5 contain seven transformational functions. These factors have been named HRD-institution building function, norm building function, synergising and boundary management function respectively. Three transactional factors are 2, 4 and 6. They are, respectively, policy-system development, promoting excellence and coordinating.

DATA ANALYSIS AND RESULTS

Macro-Analysis of Corporate Leadership Profile

In order to project an empirical picture of the profile of Transactional and Transformational Functions of Leadership among senior managers of the organizations, Rank orders on 14 functions were calculated and are presented in the table.

Profile Analysis of Corporate Leadership (Transactional Functions and Transformational Functions) (*N* = 45)

A. Transactional Functions

S.No.	*Functions*	*Rank*
1.	Policy making	3
2.	Planning	1
3.	Developing systems	7
4.	Monitoring performance	5
5.	Coordinating	6
6.	Rewarding	4
7.	Coaching	13

B. Transformational Functions

S.No.	*Functions*	*Rank*
8.	Visioning	2
9.	Modeling	12
10.	Setting standards	10
11.	Boundary management	11
12.	Synergizing	14
13.	Developing talent	9
14.	Building culture and climate	8

Profile Analysis of Corporate Leadership (Transactional Functions and Transformational Functions)

The above tables presents the picture of the feeling of 45 senior managers on various dimensions of Transactional and Transformational Leadership. It can be noticed that this group of senior managers had accorded the highest rank to the planning. The II and III highest rank were accorded by the respondents to the component of Visioning and Policy Making respectively. IV rank was accorded to the dimension of Rewarding by this group. V rank was accorded to the dimension of Monitoring Performance .VI rank was accorded to the dimension of Co-ordinating. VII rank was accorded to the dimension of Developing Systems. VIII rank was assigned to Building culture and climate. IX rank was assigned to Developing talent. X rank was assigned to Setting standards. XI rank was assigned to Boundary management. Lowest rank was accorded to Synergising, II lowest rank was assigned to Coaching and III lowest rank was accorded to Modeling.

CONCLUSION AND SUGGESTIONS

- The dominant dimensions for the select group of participants were planning, visioning, policy making and rewarding.

- The dormant dimensions for the select group of participants were—Synergising, Coaching, Modeling and Boundary management.
- The backup dimension for the select group of participants were—Monitoring performance, Coordinating, Developing systems, Building culture and climate & Developing talent.

Transactional vs Transformational Functions Scores: The present study reveals a significant homogeneity in the profiles of senior managers in giving priority to transactional functions, over transformational functions. The analysis of the data throws up some pertinent issues for managers. The responses of senior managers were analyzed and deficiency areas were identified to suggest action plans for attaining corporate leadership.

The study has clearly demonstrated that transformational style is the most desirable style and it is associated with creation of empowerment, growth, learning, morale and satisfaction on the part of the employees. Leadership programs in future therefore should focus on the transformational style as a desirable style along with routine transactional style. The results also indicated the potential of all the 14 dimensions chosen in predicting the leadership style. Leadership style based feedback should perhaps focus on this in future.

An insight into our cultural milieu and norms will help us evolve leadership styles and management systems, which are best suited to corporate functioning. Enough attention should be paid to the process of managerial autonomy in the organization, taking steps to make work a source of development and growth for managers rather than being treated merely as an activity for which they are paid. If India has to catch up with the rest of the world, we need more and more transformational leadership together with transactional one.

LIMITATIONS OF THE STUDY

Scarcity of resources limits thc horizon of any study, as researches have to restrict the size of the sample due to practical limitations. Corporate leadership is multidimensional and each dimension of these variables are full unit in it sclf. Future studies dealing with the single dimensions are desirous. To furthcr validate the findings a large number and varied organizations needed to be included into the sample. Other most obvious limitation of the research is that, the results will depend on how truly subjects respond to the questionnaires.

References

1. Goleman Daniel (1998), Working *with Emotional Intelligence*, Bantam Books, New York.
2. Allio J, Robert (2002) *Leadership Myths and Reality,* Tata McGraw-Hill Publishing Company Limited, New Delhi.

3. Pareek Udai (2002) *Instruments for OD*, Tata McGraw-Hill Publishing Company Limited, New Delhi.
4. Singh, Pritam (2002). *Leaders of Tomorrow*. Sixteenth Convocation, Indian Institute of Management, Lucknow.

35

Leadership Skills: Need of the Contemporary Era

Vijeta Gautam
Research Scholar, Department of Humanities & Social Sciences, MNIT, Allahabad
E-mail: vijetagautam81@gmail.com

Jyotsna Sinha
Lecturer, Department of Humanities & Social Sciences, MNIT, Allahabad

ABSTRACT

There are leaders and there are followers, as the saying goes, and developing good leadership skills can create the distinction between the two. Many people believe a strong leader is born and not made. This is not necessarily the case. As with anything, educating yourself to encourage become a great leader or a person with superb leadership skills takes time, energy and commitment. A leader is a person who has strong principles, courage and dedication to a clear vision. In business, possessing high-quality leadership skills are a must for any interested individual to succeed on an executive level. Developing a powerful vision, building a strong team and bringing out the best in those you lead are key facets to experiencing success as a leader in your field or industry. Leader is often a well-principled individual who is focused on a common goal and eliminates excess fear and doubt to recognize and reward the team for the greater cause. The chapter focuses on leadership skills as need of the hour.

INTRODUCTION

Soft skills are very essential to any individual. These are needful and also helpful for development in different kinds of institutions. Soft skills are communication skills, problem solving skills, decision-making skills free from stress and frustrations, ability to work in a team, personality development, leadership, etc. Leadership qualities are very essential for soft skills. The chapter deals only with need and importance of qualities of a leader. A leader is person who influences the attitude and behavior of others in group activity. Leaders exist in both formal and informal groups. Formal leadership is institutional while informal leadership is personal. Formal leaders are those appointed or elected to manage an organization. Informal leaders are not appointed or elected but emerge in informal groups. They do not possess formal authority but they influence the members of the group because followers believe that the leader can provide them satisfaction.

Bartky considers that "an educational leader always tries to get others to accept his decisions or his objectives or encouraging them to join him in some common purpose". He has identified three types of educational leaders, namely: (i) educational statesman, (ii) teacher, (iii) educational administrator. Educational statesman is concerned with presenting the facts /objective and persuading others to present his point of view with the clear expression of his opinion. The teacher adopts the method of persuasion. The educational administrator has to run the organization. The means of influence which he has to adopt will depend upon the group factors that operate and other situational factors. The leadership of a teacher depends upon his character, energy, knowledge, information, impressiveness and his consideration for good of others and so the capacity for giving guidance, working with a team and stimulating the community to progress towards the objectives to be achieved.

CHARACTERISTICS OF LEADERSHIP

The characteristics of leadership are mentioned as below:

- Leadership is basically a personal quality. Leadership is the ability to form a group of followers voluntarily.
- Leadership is the willingness of people to follow that makes a person a leader. People accept a person as their leader when they feel that he can satisfy their needs and goals.
- Leadership is a process of interpersonal influence by which one person (leader) influences others (followers) in a situation strive willingly towards the realization of common goals.
- Leadership is a continuous process of influencing behavior.
- Leadership is exercised in a particular situation at a given point of time and under a specific set of circumstances. The effectiveness of leadership depends upon the situational variables. Different leadership styles will be appropriate under different circumstances.
- Leadership is a reciprocal relationship. A leader not only influences his group but is at the same time influenced by it.

QUALITIES OF A GOOD LEADER

The qualities of a good leader are mentioned as below:

• ***Sound Physique:*** Sound physical and mental health is essential to bear the burdens of leadership. Physical stamina, nervous energy, mental vigor are important leadership qualities.

• ***Intelligence:*** A successful leader must have above average knowledge and intelligence. Mental ability to think preciously, analyse accurately, interpret clearly.

• ***Empathy:*** The leader must have the ability to see things from others' point of view. He must respect the viewpoints and feelings of others.

• ***Maturity:*** A leader should possess a high level of emotional stability and cool temperament. He needs a high degree tolerance. He must have an open mind and flexible attitude so as to observe new ideas as and when necessary.

• ***Self-confidence:*** A successful leader has confidence in him and a strong will power. He is fully aware of himself and has a strong self-motivation to take initiative and accomplish results.

• ***Foresight and vision:*** A leader can look forward and anticipate events. He has a high degree of imagination, moral courage, breadth and determination.

• ***Objectivity:*** A good leader must be fair and objective in dealing with sub-ordinates. He must be free from bias and prejudice while becoming emotionally involved with the followers. Honest, fair plan, justice and integrity of character are important traits of good leader.

• ***Decisiveness:*** To be an effective leader, one must have sound judgment and ability to take quick decision.

• ***Responsibility:*** A leader needs to have a sense of responsibility and willingness to assume responsibility for the consequences.

• ***Human Relation Attitude:*** A successful leader must have the capacity to understand people, work with them and to gain their confidence, loyalty and voluntary cooperation. He must have ability to communicate effectively with tact. The head of the institution has to face a number of problematic situations. Support from the staff. Parents and the public and the availability of essential resources are relevant on problem solving.

ROLE OF THE LEADER OF AN INSTITUTION

The head of an educational institution should be aware of his role and responsibilities. He should be prompt and punctual in playing his roles as an organizer, as a supervisor, as a teacher, as a leader, as an administrator, as a coordinator, as a motivator, as a moral builder, as confidence builder, as a philosopher, as a scholar, as a professional person and as a human relationship person which are discussed below.

(i) As an Organizer

The head of the institution must systematically organize the routine work of the institution. He should know how to plan work intelligently, execute that effectively and evaluate the results critically. His organizing ability is essential to run the school free from any sort of confusion, wastage, duplication, indecision and discrimination.

(ii) As an Administrator

Administration is a very complex process, which involves planning, programming, organizing, staffing, training, controlling, implementing, monitoring, evaluating, etc.

(iii) As Supervisor

Supervision should be comprehensive. Its scope covers all the activities of the institution. It includes supervision of the work, supervision of the moral development of the staff, supervision of the maintenance of registers and accounts of the office and supervision of co-curricular activities, etc.

(iv) As a Motivator

Sound leadership creates an urge accomplishment and transforms potential into performance. A good head of the institution improves the loyalty and commitment of staff towards the institution. He creates and maintains an environment conducive to high performance. Good leadership is itself a motivating force for individual which inspires people to work hard.

(v) As Moral Builder

Good leadership is indispensable to high employee morale. The leader lifts a man's vision to higher sites, raises his performances and builds up his personality. He shapes the thinking and attitudes of the group and maintains discipline. He develops good human relations and facilities interactions between the members of the group. He maintains voluntary co-operation and discipline among followers.

(vi) As a Coordinator

The head of the institution should co-ordinate the abilities and work competencies of all the staff for the common good of the institution. He has to provide positive support to staff that are lagging behind with a view to raise their level of performance. There may be wide range of inborn qualities, aptitudes and acquired skills of staff due to individual difference. The individuality of each staff should be recognized.

(vii) As a Confidence Builder

An effective leader creates and sustains self-confidence and enthusiasm among his employees. He sets an example for others. He provides advice and guidance by which subordinates can recognize their qualities and capacity. The head of the institution acts as a coach and counselor to his employees.

Thus, it serves as an aid to formal authority and determines the effectiveness of an institution.

(viii) As a Philosopher

The head of the institution must possess and cultivate as sound philosophy of life as well as a sound philosophy of education. He must adopt his own ideas in education to the national goals and objectives of education. He must be clear about his own ideas and the national policy about education.

(ix) As a Scholar

The head of the institution must be a man of extraordinary scholastic and academic achievement. His extraordinary academic stature is essential to maintain leadership in the academic sphere. To enjoy desired reputation he should be in a position to make valuable suggestions on practically all matters of life.

(x) As a Professional Person

In order to be able to provide leadership, the head of the institution must have undergone professional training apart from his academic qualifications. He will have to ensure professional growth in order to be in tough with the latest developments in the concerned field. His professional training and updating will enable him to hold progressive views in work related matters, apply new methods and techniques in experiments with new products and techniques of education, carry out action research in his situation to solve some of the immediate problem and to inspire the staff to emulate his example.

(xi) As a Human Relationship Person

The head of the institution will have to be expert in human psychology and human relations. He should maintain cordial, pleasant and affectionate relationship with his staff. He must organize staff meetings when the situation so demands for planning the work, organize various activity and distribution of work.

References

1. Cribbin, James J. (1972) Effective Managcrial Leadership, AMACOM, New York.
2. Gupta, C.B. (2001). Principles and Pracitce of Management, Mayur Paperbacks, New Delhi.
3. Jones et al. (1969) Secondary School Administration, McGraw Hill, New York.

4. Likert, Rensis. (1951). New Parterns of Management, McGraw Hill, New York.
5. Madon and McDowell (1986). Administrative Management, Vikas Publishing House, New Delhi.
6. Morphet et al. (1974). Educational Organisation and Administration, Prentice Hall Inc, New Jersey.
7. Sidhu, K S. (1982) School Organization and Administration, Sterling Publishers Pvt. Ltd., New Delhi.

Index